Byzantium and its Image

Professor Cyril Mango

Cyril Mango

Byzantium and its Image

History and Culture
of the Byzantine Empire
and its Heritage

VARIORUM REPRINTS
London 1984

British Library CIP data   Mango, Cyril
     Byzantium and its image — (Collected studies series;
     CS191)
     1. Byzantine Empire — History
     I. Title
     949.5 DF552

     ISBN 0-86078-139-9

Published in Great Britain by   Variorum Reprints
     20 Pembridge Mews London W11 3EQ

Printed in Great Britain by   Galliard (Printers) Ltd
     Great Yarmouth Norfolk

     VARIORUM REPRINT CS191

CONTENTS

This volume contains a total of 360 pages

PREFACE

The eighteen studies reprinted here are devoted to various aspects of the history and culture of the Byzantine Empire with an occasional glance at the Byzantine heritage of modern Greece. In selecting them I have excluded my writings on archaeological topics as well as those that are concerned with the monuments and topography of Constantinople.

The arrangement is as follows: the first five studies, all originally delivered as lectures, are of a general nature; the rest are placed, more or less, in chronological order with regard to the events discussed, starting in the seventh/eighth centuries and ending in the early nineteenth, but with particular emphasis on the Middle Byzantine period. A number of errors and omissions are made good in the Addenda, which also contain a few references to subsequent publications that appeared pertinent or important.* Minor corrections have been made in the text.

One of the attractions of Byzantine studies is that they still offer many opportunities of discovery. That is true of the most basic level, that of facts out of which the plot of history must be constructed. Unlike his colleagues in better explored fields, the Byzantine historian cannot assume that the facts are 'given'; on the contrary, he has to keep re-examining the evidence and will often find important facts that have been overlooked or new solutions to old puzzles. Several articles reprinted here are concerned with establishing what happened where and when or who wrote what and why. All I can say of them is that they are either right or wrong; and even if they are wrong, they may help others to find the correct answer.

The process of discovery does not, however, stop at this rather obvious stage. Byzantine civilization is, in my view, profoundly elusive, not only because it is insufficiently documented, but also because it was, consciously or unconsciously, camouflaged by the Byzantines themselves, whose mental attitudes were very different from ours and whose literature conceals more than it reveals (see papers II and III). There is an old cliché that Racine depicted men as they were and Corneille as they ought to have been. In this respect the Byzantines were like Corneille: if indeed they were capable of seeing themselves as they were, they very seldom chose to put it into words. The task of the Byzantine historian is, therefore, to identify the layers of distortion — some of them clear and palpable, others barely perceptible, yet all the more insidious — and to peel them away in order to uncover the reality underneath. I hope I shall not be charged with excessive positivism in assuming that such a reality exists and that it can be apprehended to some extent, even if our understanding of it is inevitably conditioned by the gradual shift in our own viewpoint.

CYRIL MANGO

Oxford
July 1983

---

* References to the Addenda are indicated by daggers (†) in the margin by the passages concerned.

I

BYZANTINISM AND ROMANTIC HELLENISM

The Chair which I have the honour of occupying was founded at a critical moment of modern Greek history: on 15 May 1919 the Greek army landed at Smyrna on a mission that seemed to foreshadow the restoration of the Byzantine Empire; and on 7 October of the same year the first holder of this Chair, Professor Arnold J. Toynbee, delivered his inaugural address in the presence of no less a person than Venizelos, the militant Prime Minister of Greece.[1] The leader of the Greek community of London made an introductory statement in which he laid a twofold duty on the newly appointed professor: first, to refute the calumnies that had been uttered against the medieval Greek Empire by Edward Gibbon and second, to see to it that the modern Greek language was taught at King's College in its archaic or puristic form, alone fit for gentlemen, and not in demotic which was the idiom of socialist youths.

Toynbee's occupancy of this Chair was rather brief, but it was made memorable by the publication of a perceptive and fair-minded book on the Greco-Turkish conflict,[2] a book which, in those feverish days, could scarcely endear its author to the people whose civilization he was supposed to be interpreting.

Professor Toynbee's successors—and there have been only two of them— had the prudence not to involve themselves too deeply in current affairs. F. H. Marshall devoted himself to the study of Greek letters in the sixteenth and seventeenth centuries, while Romilly Jenkins ranged over the entire field of Greek civilization, from classical archaeology to the poetry of the nineteenth century, his most fundamental work being devoted to Byzantine history and philology. His extraordinary breadth as a hellenist made Jenkins the ideal occupant of this Chair, and his migration across the Atlantic constitutes a loss to this University which I cannot hope to make good.

Since the Koraës Professor is expected to study both Byzantine and modern Greek civilization, the first question he has to decide in his own mind is what these two civilizations have in common. It is not a new question, nor, alas, is it a safe one. Much of the claim of modern Greece upon the sympathy of western Europe has been based on the assumption of a direct historical continuity reaching back three thousand years: from modern Greece to Byzantium, from Byzantium to the Hellenistic world and thence to ancient Greece. Whoever asserts this continuity is classed as a philhellene; whoever denies it runs the risk of being labelled a mishellene or hater of the Greeks. Yet this question, to which no simple answer can be given, deserves to be re-examined from time to time. In attempting to do so tonight, I shall not conjure up the old

* Inaugural lecture in the Koraës Chair of Modern Greek and Byzantine History, Language and Literature, delivered at King's College, London, on 27 October 1964. Except for the addition of a few references, the text is printed here in the form in which it was delivered.

[1] *The Place of Mediaeval and Modern Greece in History*, Inaugural Lecture, London, 1919.
[2] *The Western Question in Greece and Turkey*, London, 1922.

ghost of racial continuity. All that could be said on this topic has already been said, most recently and eloquently by Professor Jenkins himself.[3] Instead, I shall speak of intellectual continuity. First, I shall endeavour to describe that compact body of accepted beliefs and ideals that made up the self-image of the Byzantine Empire; secondly, I shall discuss the dominant ideology of modern Greece as it emerged in the last century. In this way we may be able to judge what resemblance, if any, there is between the two cultures.

In summarizing the essential traits of Byzantinism I can only repeat what others have said at much greater length and with much greater learning.[4] Above all, Byzantinism was the belief in a single Christian, Roman Empire. This Empire embraced, ideally speaking, the entire Christian community, in other words, the civilized world. Its government was the reflection of the heavenly autocracy—or should we say that the heavenly government was patterned after the one on earth? It matters little. For just as the Deity reigned above, surrounded by its court of the nine angelic choirs and the innumerable host of saints, both civil and military, so the Christ-loving emperor ruled in his Sacred Palace amidst his immense *comitatus* of eunuchs, generals and civil servants. The elaborate ceremonial of the palace, on the one hand, the iconography of religious art, on the other, served to underline this basic parallelism.

The fortunes of the Empire were the particular concern of divine Providence. In the old dispensation this privileged position had been enjoyed by the Israelites; now it had passed to the new Israel, the Christian people. To be sure, there were unbelievers and barbarians, but these did not exist in their own right. Their purpose was punitive: just as in the days of the Old Testament the Egyptians and Assyrians had acted as instruments of chastisement, so now the Persians, the Slavs or the Arabs fulfilled the same function of recalling the Christians to the path of piety. If the barbarians were victorious, this was not because of their own virtue, but because of the sins of the Christian Romans.[5] As long as the Byzantines maintained the true faith and followed the commandments they were bound to win on all fronts.

The course of human history, which was essentially the history of the Chosen People, showed clearly the position of the Roman, i.e. the Byzantine, Empire in the general scheme of things. There were to be four world empires, as indicated by the prophets Daniel and Zechariah—that of the Assyrians, that of the Persians, that of the Macedonians and that of the Romans.[6] The

[3] *Byzantium and Byzantinism*, Lectures in Memory of Louise Taft Semple, Cincinnati, 1963, pp. 21ff.

[4] Among many excellent discussions of this topic, see F. Dölger, *Byzanz und die europäische Staatenwelt*, Ettal, 1953, pp. 10ff.; O. Treitinger, *Die oströmische Kaiser- und Reichsidee*, 2nd ed., Darmstadt, 1956; L. Bréhier, *Les institutions de l'empire byzantin*, Paris, 1949, pp. 53ff.; N. H. Baynes, *The Thought World of East Rome*, London, 1947. The important subject of Byzantine eschatological thinking, on which I have tried to lay stress in this lecture, still awaits its investigator.

[5] 'While then God's people [i.e. the Byzantines] waxes strong and triumphs over its enemies by His alliance, the rest of the nations, whose religion is at fault, are not increased in strength on account of their own good works, but on account of our bad ones, through which they are made powerful and exalted to our detriment.' So spoke Photius after the Russian attack on Constantinople in 860: *The Homilies of Photius, Patriarch of Constantinople*, Cambridge, Mass., 1958, p. 107.

[6] See, e.g., Georgii Monachi *Chronicon*, ed. de Boor, Leipzig, 1904, ii, pp. 432f.

Roman Empire was the final one, in token of which the reign of Augustus coincided with the incarnation of Christ. But contrary to pagan belief, the Roman Empire, too, was to be finite and was destined to be overthrown by the Antichrist: *et cum cessaverit imperium Romanum, tunc revelabitur manifeste Antichristus*, as the Sibylline books already proclaimed in the fourth century.[7] The last Byzantine emperor, John by name, would defeat the Ishmaelites and then proceed to Jerusalem to lay down his crown on the rock of Golgotha, thus bringing the historical process to a full circle. This would be followed by great convulsions, by the irruption of Gog and Magog whom Alexander had confined behind the Caspian Gates, by slaughter and every kind of abomination; finally, by the appearance of Antichrist himself. But his reign was to last no longer than three and a half years; after which, Christ would come to judge the quick and the dead.[8]

Within this general context of past and future the city of Constantinople held a central position. By virtue of the *translatio imperii* ordained by Constantine the Great, it had become the New Rome—this indeed was the basis for the Byzantine conviction that theirs was the only Roman Empire. But in addition to being the New Rome, Constantinople was also the New Jerusalem.[9] Entrusted by its founder to the protection of the Virgin Mary, it was further fortified by the possession of practically all the major relics of Christendom— the True Cross, the Crown of Thorns, the nails, the sponge, the reed, the Virgin Mary's robe which acted as the palladium of the City, and thousands of other relics, from Noah's axe and Moses' staff to the teeth of St. Christopher and the eyebrows of St. John the Baptist.[10] The Holy Land had yielded all its treasures to Constantinople. Today, we may be tempted to regard this as the result of human pilfering, but to the Byzantines it was yet further proof of divine approbation: for surely, the Lord places His most prized possessions in the care of those He trusts.[11] Consequently, God's protection would not forsake the City until the hour of the final consummation; and when the City fell, the world, too, would come to an end.

Such, in brief outline, was the Byzantine conception of their own Empire at the time when this empire was at its height, say in the ninth and tenth centuries—a conception that combined with such clear logic the data of history with those of divine revelation as to exclude any other alternative. Byzantinism on this definition—and it is, I think, a fair one—was much more Biblical than Greek. A classical scholar can hardly ever regard it with

---

[7] E. Sackur, *Sibyllinische Texte und Forschungen*, Halle, 1898, p. 186.

[8] These events are variously described in the great mass of Byzantine eschatological literature. See, e.g., V. Istrin, *Otkrovenie Mefodija Patarskago i apokrifičeskija videnija Daniila*, Moscow, 1897, Texts, pp. 40ff., 62ff., 72ff. (pseudo-Methodius), 135ff. (pseudo-Daniel); *Vita S. Andreae Sali*, PG, cxi, col. 852ff.

[9] See P. J. Alexander, 'The Strength of Empire and Capital as seen through Byzantine Eyes', *Speculum*, xxxvii, 1962, pp. 346f.

[10] Cf. N. H. Baynes, 'The Supernatural Defenders of Constantinople', *Analecta Bollandiana*, lxvii, 1949, pp. 165ff.; A. Frolow, *Recherches sur la déviation de la IVe Croisade vers Constantinople*, Paris, 1955, pp. 49ff. A convenient, though incomplete, list of relics in P. Riant, *Des dépouilles religieuses enlevées à Constantinople au XIIIe siècle par les Latins*, Paris, 1875, pp. 177ff.

[11] Joseph Bryennios, ed. Eugenios Boulgaris, 'Ιωσήφ . . . Βρυεννίου τὰ εὑρεθέντα, ii, Leipzig, 1768, p. 28.

sympathy, witness the case of J. B. Bury, one of our greatest Byzantinists, whose heart, however, was elsewhere. Indeed, to our way of thinking, Byzantinism was a gloomy philosophy: it was static and backward-looking since it did not anticipate any progress other than reclaiming what had been lost. But then, what was the golden age that the Byzantines strove to perpetuate? Clearly, it was the age of the early Christian Empire, the age of Constantine, Theodosius and Justinian, in other words, the *Spätantike*. This was only logical since the period of Late Antiquity had coincided with the greatest extension of the Christian Empire: to reconquer the patrimony of Constantine the Great was the objective of every ambitious Byzantine emperor down to the twelfth century. But in addition to the political motive, there was also an unbroken intellectual continuity between the period of Late Antiquity and the Byzantine Middle Ages. This may sound like a truism, and yet it is an observation of fundamental importance for every branch of Byzantine civilization, for education, theology, law, literature and the visual arts. I do not have the time now to enlarge on this topic, but may I remind you of the fact that as late as the fourteenth and fifteenth centuries Byzantine schoolboys learnt their grammar, their rhetoric and their logic from textbooks of the fourth century? That Byzantine literature, both highbrow and lowbrow, merely continued the forms that had been fully elaborated by the sixth century? That Church homiletics never departed from the exemplars that had been set by the Fathers of the fourth century, except in the direction of greater obscurity, and that hymnography never rose above the level that had been set by Romanus in the sixth? That even when the Byzantine intellectual went a-whoring after pagan philosophy, it was not Plato, but the Neoplatonists and especially Proclus that fascinated him most?

Conversely, the Byzantines in general did not evince the slightest interest in what we understand by classical Greece. This is a truth that has been blurred by much loose talk about 'Byzantine humanism' and 'Byzantine hellenism'. If you open a Byzantine compendium of universal history you will be surprised to note that Pericles, Themistocles, Leonidas are not even mentioned; that Xerxes and the Persian Wars are dismissed in one sentence, and this in connection with Daniel's prophecy of the Four Beasts.[12] True, a few classical authors were read in school because the same authors had been read in school in the good old days of Justinian. But that there was anything in the Greek poets other than rules of scansion and a supply of ready-made quotations; that Herodotus and Thucydides were not merely specimens of the Ionic and Attic dialects, respectively—these were thoughts that hardly ever entered the Byzantine's mind.[13]

Down to the eleventh century the Byzantine philosophy of Empire tallied reasonably well with the facts. This philosophy, as we have seen, had one

---

[12] See, e.g., Zonaras, *Epit. hist.*, III, vi, ed. Dindorf, i, p. 192.

[13] See, e.g., the appreciation of Herodotus in Photius' *Bibliotheca*, cod. 60: Herodotus is a model of the Ionic dialect; he indulges in many fables and digressions which are inappropriate to the genre of historiography; his narrative starts with Cyrus and finishes with Xerxes. This analysis occupies one-seventieth of the space that Photius devotes to a certain monk Job who wrote a treatise on the Incarnation (cod. 222); yet modern scholars see fit to call Photius a humanist.

invaluable escape clause: the Empire could be humbled and defeated for the purpose of correction and for that purpose alone. Indeed, the Empire had been repeatedly and deservedly chastised, but each time it had succeeded in restoring itself. The geographical myopia of the Middle Ages as well as the linguistic barrier between East and West tended to obscure the existence of other Christian states which did not regard themselves as vassals of the Byzantine emperor. In the eleventh century, however, Asia Minor, which was the basis of Byzantine power, was irrevocably lost to the Turks, and the Empire started on that course of slow distintegration which was to terminate, four centuries later, in the fall of Constantinople. Could the imperial myth be maintained? Could it be maintained in the face of the all too obvious fact that the leadership of the Christian world had passed to the heretical West? I know that a few Byzantine intellectuals, especially in the fourteenth and fifteenth centuries, when the extinction of their state was clearly imminent, were forced to doubt the traditional views.[14] But these were isolated cases.

The opinion has often been expressed that as the Byzantine world fell apart, so hellenism was reborn. The proportion of truth contained in this view seems to be rather slight. It is a fact that starting in the twelfth century, but more particularly after the occupation of Constantinople by the Crusaders in 1204, certain Byzantine authors took pleasure in calling themselves Hellenes;[15] it is also true that there was, especially in the fourteenth century, an upsurge—not a renascence, if you please—of classical scholarship and even of scholastic science. Finally, just as the Byzantine world was ready to collapse there arose that enigmatic figure, George Gemistos Pletho, the Platonist of Mistra, who advocated the regeneration of ancient Sparta and pressed his utopian advice on two Byzantine rulers who, naturally, did not pay the slightest attention to him. Much careful investigation is yet needed before we can appraise the meaning of these phenomena;[16] even so, it is clear that expressions of hellenism during these two or three centuries were largely rhetorical; that they were confined to a very small circle of intellectuals and had no impact on the people. The handful of Byzantine neo-hellenists was eventually absorbed into the broad stream of the Italian Renaissance, a stream that they did not generate but to which they contributed in a minor capacity as language-teachers, copyists of manuscripts, editors of texts and proof-readers.

If we wish to hear the true voice of Byzantium during the critical period preceding the fall, we should turn not to the misty speculations and pseudo-Olympian theology of Pletho, but to that pillar of the establishment, the good monk and popular preacher Joseph Bryennios. We are now in the early fourteen hundreds, and our man is aware that the Orthodox Empire had shrunk to one city. 'You,' he addresses his Byzantine audience, 'you alone are the flower of the Romans, the descendants of the Elder Rome and the children of this, the New Rome. Do not be vexed at your faith, since it is the only one under the sun that is pious, true, pure and correct; and do not

---

[14] See I. Ševčenko, 'The Decline of Byzantium seen through the Eyes of its Intellectuals', *Dumbarton Oaks Papers*, xv, 1961, pp. 169ff.

[15] See K. Lechner, *Hellenen und Barbaren*, diss., Munich, 1954.

[16] The latest book on Pletho, by F. Masai, *Pléthon et le platonisme de Mistra*, Paris, 1956, is rather disappointing in this respect.

murmur against God: He permits you to fall into these tribulations not because He is turning away from you in hatred, but because He is cleansing you thereby and making you worthy of His kingdom.'[17] It is the old philosophy with only a slight shift of emphasis from the real to the supernatural. True, the emperor no longer rules the world; but no matter how far you go, nay to the very end of the universe—our preacher went as far as Cyprus[18]— you will not hear another emperor being commemorated except the emperor of the Romans, nor another patriarch, except the Ecumenical one. Could *this* be the result of human effort? No indeed, it was a miracle and clear proof that God was supporting 'our' cause.[19]

The cornerstone of this philosophy was the approaching end of the world. The exact date of the Last Judgment was a great secret, not known even to the highest angels; even so, it was something of an open secret, since it would take place at Jerusalem, seven thousand years after the Creation, i.e. in A.D. 1492, on a Sunday, in the seventh hour of the night.[20] The truth of this belief was established not only by the magic of the number 7, a number that ran like a repeating pattern through the whole tapestry of the universe (even the figures of rhetoric listed in the *Progymnasmata* of Aphthonius were twice seven), but also by evident and unmistakable signs of the approaching end. For just as the death of a body is foreshadowed by sickness and gradual disintegration, as the collapse of a house by cracking walls and falling plaster, so indeed is the end of the world indicated in advance by the disappearance of all goodness and virtue, the growth of wickedness and superstition, and by the fact that the Roman Empire had contracted as never before.[21]

The man who bridged the transition from Byzantium to the Turcocracy, the first patriarch of Constantinople under Turkish rule, Gennadios Scholarios, traced the lines that Greekdom was to follow for centuries to come. He has been called 'the last Byzantine and the first Hellene':[22] in fact, he was neither. Like the other intellectual leaders of dying Byzantium, Gennadios had been faced with a terrible choice: on the one hand, to admit the bankruptcy of a way of thinking that had been held axiomatic for a thousand years, to bow before the Pope and pray for whatever military aid the West might be willing to contribute; on the other, to uphold traditional beliefs and trust in Providence. Some Byzantines chose the first alternative and ended up in Italy; Gennadios consciously and, we hope, honestly chose the second—and he had the people behind him. His philosophy, in spite of his deep study of Aristotle and a journey to Italy, was precisely that of the monk Joseph. Need we be surprised? Everything was happening as predicted: Constantinople had fallen, its sanctuaries had been profaned, Antichrist was now ruling and the world had precisely forty years to go.[23] Was one to sell one's faith when the

---

[17] Bryennios (see *supra*, note 11), ii, p. 109.
[18] On his career, see N. B. Tomadakis, Ὁ Ἰωσὴφ Βρυέννιος καὶ ἡ Κρήτη κατὰ τὸ 1400, Athens, 1947.
[19] Bryennios, ii, pp. 34f.
[20] *Id.*, ii, pp. 370f.
[21] *Id.*, ii, p. 191.
[22] C. N. Sathas, *Documents inédits relatifs à*

l'histoire de la Grèce au moyen âge, iv, Paris, 1883, p. vii.
[23] According to Scholarius' computation, the world was to end in 1493/4. He was quite convinced of this: see A. Vasiliev, 'Medieval Ideas of the End of the World', *Byzantion*, xvi, 1942/3, pp. 497ff.

race was almost over and the Christian athletes were about to receive the crowns of victory?

This way of thinking I should like to call 'messianic Byzantinism'. It was Byzantinism without the Empire, but otherwise little changed. At any moment the awaited liberator-king—was it John or Constantine?—the mythical king who had been turned to marble and slept a mysterious sleep in a cave near the Golden Gate, would wake up and cast out the infidel; after which it would be the end of the world.[24] In the meantime, the only thing that mattered was to keep the faith uncontaminated, and this is what the Ecumenical Patriarchate, now the head of the Greek nation, strove to do. It defended the faith of the Seven Councils against the inroads of the Roman Catholics; later against Lutherans and Calvinists; finally, against science, freemasonry, French philosophy and the Greek classics. As late as 1797 the head of the Patriarchal Academy took it upon himself to refute the Copernican system in four dialogues;[25] while a patriarchal encyclical bade the faithful 'not to cultivate Hellenic letters and the foolish wisdom of the Europeans as being contrary to the Christian life, but only grammar, founded on the exposition of the Church Fathers; as for those Platos and Aristotles, Newtons and Descartes, triangles and logarithms, they only cause indifference to things holy.'[26]

Alas, the world showed no sign of ending. The year 1492 may have marked the beginning of a new era in the West, but it made no difference whatever to the Greeks. The date of the Second Coming had to be accordingly adjusted. In the sixteenth century it was believed that only five sultans were destined to rule over Constantinople.[27] When this was proved false, the downfall of the Ottoman Empire was postponed until the reign of the third Mehmed (1595–1603) because he bore the same name as Mehmed the Conqueror.[28] In the seventeenth century it was predicted that Constantinople would be liberated two hundred years after its fall, i.e. in 1653, when another Mehmed, this time the Fourth, happened to be Sultan.[29] In the eighteenth century it was rumoured that the devastation of Constantinople would happen in 1766,

[24] On King John and the emperor turned into marble see N. Polites, Παραδόσεις, Athens, 1904, i, p. 22; ii, pp. 658ff.; Eulogios Kourilas, 'Τὰ χρυσόβουλλα τῶν ἡγεμόνων τῆςΜολδοβλαχίας καὶ τὸ σύμβολον 'Ἰῶ ἢ 'Ἰωάννης,' Εἰς μνήμην Σπ. Λάμπρου, Athens, 1935, pp. 245ff.; N. A. Bees, 'Περὶ τοῦ ἱστορημένου χρησμολογίου τῆς Κρατικῆς Βιβλ. τοῦ Βερολίνου,' Byz.-neugr. Jahrb., xiii, 1937, pp. 244 γ'ff.

[25] Sergios Makraios, Τρόπαιον ἐκ τῆς ἑλλαδικῆς πανοπλίας κατὰ τῶν ὀπαδῶν τοῦ Κοπερνίκου ἐν τρισὶ διαλόγοις, Vienna, 1797. Contrary to the title, this work contains four dialogues. In the dedication to the Patriarch Anthimos of Jerusalem, the author proudly claims to have routed the Copernicans like a flock of sheep and to have razed the bastion of their System to the ground.

[26] Quoted by D. Thereianos, 'Ἀδαμάντιος Κοραῆς, i, Trieste, 1889, p. 42. Cf. the encyclical of the Patriarch Neophytos (1793)

which condemns the new heresiarchs, τοὺς Βολταίρους λέγομεν, καὶ Φρανκμαζόνας, καὶ 'Ροσούς [i.e. Rousseau], καὶ Σπινόζας. These are bracketed together not only with the ancient heresiarchs like Basilides, but also with the 'Hellenes' Anaximander, Thales and Orpheus: M. I. Gedeon, Κανονικαὶ διατάξεις, Constantinople, 1888, pp. 281f.

[27] Istrin, op. cit., (supra, note 8), p. 324; Bees, op. cit. (supra, note 24), pp. 242 ff.

[28] See, e.g., Acta Mechmeti I. Sacracenorum principis . . . Vaticinia Severi et Leonis in Oriente Impp . . . interitum regni Turcici sub Mechmete hoc III praedicentia. Iconibus . . . exornata . . . per Io. Theod. & Io. Israelem de Bry, 1597, esp. pp. 86f.

[29] Paisios Ligarides, Χρησμολόγιον, Cod. Hieros. Taphou 160, fols. 1v–2r. Cf. my study 'The Legend of Leo the Wise', Zbornik radova Vizantološkog Inst., vi, 1960, p. 87.

followed by the inundation of England in 1767 and the Second Coming in 1773.[30] Beguiled by such fancies which were fed by a vast oracular literature, and effectively cushioned against the march of ideas in western Europe, the bulk of the Greek people retained their Byzantine mentality right up to 1800, and even later.[31]

Now we move into another world. A new myth, this time a myth manufactured in western Europe, was about to usurp the place of Byzantinism as the guiding ideal of the Greek people: it was the myth of romantic hellenism. Formed largely in the second half of the eighteenth century, this hellenism had its serious side: academic classicism, antiquarianism spurred on by Winckelmann and the excavations of Herculaneum, Philosophy with a capital P. More influential in terms of popular appeal was the escape to a golden never-never land, to a simple rusticity which ancient Greece seemed to offer: everyone wanted to be a shepherd in Arcady. The fashion for all things Grecian knew no bounds: Grecian odes, Grecian plays, Grecian costumes, Grecian wigs, Grecian pictures, Grecian furniture. For the sub-literary public a stream of insipid Grecian romances poured from the presses: *The Adventures of Periphas, The Loves of Lais, The Loves of Poliris and Driphe, The Adventures of Neocles, Son of Themistocles*, and scores more.[32] But the work that reflected most fully what the eighteenth century imagined about ancient Greece is that laborious masterpiece, *The Travels of the Younger Anacharsis* by the not very religious abbé Jean-Jacques Barthélemy.[33] The fictional Anacharsis was a Scythian youth (hence a noble savage) who toured Greece between 363 and 338 B.C. He had a genius for meeting famous people: Plato, Aristotle, Isocrates, Xenophon, Demosthenes, Euclid—everybody who was anybody—vied with one another to talk to the Younger Anacharsis. And what splendid conversationalists they all were! What sublime, coruscating ideas they all expressed, how delicate were their manners, how simply and frugally they all lived! For twenty-five years Anacharsis went on interviewing famous Grecians, taking copious notes on history, religion, art and manners. After the battle

[30] D. Sarros, 'Παλαιογραφικὸς ἔρανος', 'Ο ἐν Κων-πόλει Ἑλληνικὸς Φιλολογικὸς Σύλλογος, xxxiii, 1914, p. 83. Further dates for the downfall of the Ottoman Empire continued to be advanced throughout the nineteenth century. They were based on the enormously popular Vision of Agathangelos and the prophecies of Leo the Wise and the Patriarch Tarasius. A reprint of these texts for the benefit of the semi-literate public appeared as late as *ca.* 1940 at Nicosia under the title 'Οπτασία τοῦ μακαρίου Ἱερωνύμου Ἀγαθαγγέλου, etc.

[31] See N. Iorga, *Byzance après Byzance*, Bucharest, 1935. A revealing illustration of the survival of Byzantinism vis-à-vis the Greek classics is provided by the following incident. In the early years of the nineteenth century the Patriarch of Constantinople Kyrillos VI remarked to a learned gymnasiarch that he could not understand why Thucydides and Demosthenes were thought to be superior to that model of eloquence, Gregory Nazianzen; and that in his opinion the verses of Ptochoprodromos (the twelfth-century poetaster) were much more harmonious than those of Euripides (Thereianos, *op. cit.*, i, p. 41). The Patriarch was showing as much discernment as the 'humanists' of eleventh-century Byzantium who found it difficult to decide whether Euripides or George of Pisidia was the better poet (cf. R. J. H. Jenkins, 'The Hellenistic Origins of Byzantine Literature', *Dumbarton Oaks Papers*, xvii, 1963, p. 41).

[32] See M. Badolle, *L'abbé Jean-Jacques Barthélemy et l'hellénisme en France*, Paris, 1926, pp. 181ff.

[33] *Voyage du jeune Anacharsis en Grèce*, 5 vols., Paris, 1788.

of Chaeronea, which destroyed the liberty of Greece, he returned to his native Scythia. In his youth, he concludes, he had sought happiness from an enlightened nation; in his old age he found peace amidst a people who knew no other goods than those of nature.

It is hard for us to believe that this tedious work which fills five quarto volumes, a work stuffed with an immense erudition, with endless notes and chronological tables, should have gone through forty editions and thirteen abridgments, that it should have been translated into English, German, Spanish, Italian, Danish, Dutch, Modern Greek and even Armenian. Such, however, was the passion for all things Greek; and when, one year after the publication of *Anacharsis*, the French Revolution broke out, it was as if Greece and Rome had come back to life. No speech at the National Assembly was complete without a reference to Sparta and Lycurgus; the Supreme Being was honoured with tripods and libations; Mme Vigée-Lebrun gave Grecian parties; and if the citizens of Paris had only had the money to buy some new clothes, they would surely have arrayed themselves in tunics and sandals.

In the midst of this excitement it dawned on the public that there existed actual, live Greeks, genuine descendants of Themistocles, who were waiting breathlessly to regain their liberty with the help of their western brethren.[34] What better cause than liberty, especially when it was the Greeks, the inventors, so to speak, of liberty who were seeking it? Greeks, it is true, had been seen before, mostly by gentlemen-travellers and consular officials attached to the emporia of the Levant, and these informants often reported that the Greeks were the most degraded race on earth. But if they were degraded, this was surely because of tyranny and superstition. If they could be freed from the Turk and from their own deplorable clergy, if perchance they could be persuaded to abandon trade and take up the ennobling pursuit of agriculture, then the Greeks would immediately regain all of their ancestral purity and virtue.[35]

Among the citizens of revolutionary Paris lived Adamantios Koraes, the refugee scholar and self-appointed mentor of emergent Greece, after whom this Chair has been whimsically named. I say 'whimsically' because, if there was one thing that Koraes loathed—next, of course, to the Ottoman Turks —it was Byzantium. To this expatriate who acquired his classics in Holland and his philosophy in France, Byzantium stood for obscurantism, monkishness, oppression, inertia. He often derided those accursed 'Graeco-Roman' emperors who dissipated their resources on the enrichment of monasteries, who convoked councils and disputed profoundly about the procession of the Holy

---

[34] For an amusing commentary on this see Gobineau, 'Le royaume des Hellènes' in *Deux études sur la Grèce moderne*, Paris, 1905, pp. 93ff.

[35] C. F. de Volney, *Considérations sur la guerre actuelle des Turcs*, London, 1788, p. 106: 'Enfin, pour ressusciter les Grecs anciens, il faudra rendre des moeurs aux Grecs modernes, devenus la race la plus vile et la plus corrompue de l'univers: et la vie agricole seule opérera ce prodige; elle les corrigera de leur inertie par l'esprit de propriété, des vices de leur oisivité par des occupations attachantes; de leur bigoterie par l'éloignement de leurs prêtres; de leur lâcheté par la cessation de la tyrannie; enfin de leur improbité par l'abandon de la vie mercantile et la retraite des villes.'

I

38

Ghost while the Turks, sword in hand, were capturing town after town.[36] The message of Koraes to his compatriots was this: Break with Byzantium, cast out the monks, cast out the Byzantine aristocracy of the Phanar. Remember your ancient ancestors. It was they who invented Philosophy, that Philosophy which was scorned by the Byzantines but now, borne on the wings of typography, scatters her blessings all over enlightened Europe (Koraes was constantly speaking of 'enlightened Europe'). Greece should have no king. Form instead an egalitarian democracy and invite some visiting Lycurgus, preferably an American, to draw up your code of laws. Thereafter imitate the virtue of Hercules, the sagacity of Odysseus, and all of those other countless examples of excellence which the Greek classics have set before you.[37]

Such advice was so typical of its age that it could have come from any literate Frenchman. And yet, Koraes was by birth and early education a Byzantine. His maternal grandfather whose library Koraes inherited and whose memory he cherished had published a book in many thousands of iambic verses entitled *Thirty-six Refutations of the Latin Religion*, a book that in substance, if not in style, could have come from the pen of a thirteenth-century Byzantine polemicist.[38] Koraes himself started his literary career in the field of church homiletics and was well acquainted with ecclesiastical circles. But once in Europe, he cast his Byzantinism overboard and became a European liberal pure and simple. He now realized that the French were, of all modern nations, most similar to the ancient Greeks; hence, the modern Greeks, in order to reach the level of their own ancestors, could do no better than imitate the French.[39]

The Greek Revolution, which Koraes applauded from a distance, was fought, as everyone knows, with the enthusiastic support of all liberal-minded Europeans. Even Pushkin who, like Anacharsis, came from Scythia, composed in 1821 an ode in which he pledged lifelong allegiance to the goddess Elleferia [sic]; adding sadly that her beauty was not made for the cold climate of Russia.[40] The European governments were somewhat less enthusiastic, but then they had to reckon with prosaic things like the balance of power and the fate of the Ottoman Empire. In any case, after much unnecessary bloodshed and devastation, the Kingdom of the Hellenes was set up and, under Bavarian supervision, it moulded itself as best it could into a semblance of ancient Greece. Casting out all reminders of the Turkish occupation, it equipped itself with an Areopagus, a Boule, nomarchs, demarchs, prytanes

[36] For his indictment of Byzantium, see, e.g., Άτακτα, i, Paris, 1828, p. ζ' ff. The perusal of three or four pages of a Byzantine author was sufficient to exacerbate Koraes' gout: 'Απάνθισμα ἐπιστολῶν, ed. Iakovos Rotas, i, Athens, 1839, p. 133.

[37] Koraes often repeated this advice. See, e.g., his introduction to the 2nd ed. of his trans. of Beccaria, Περὶ ἀδικημάτων καὶ ποινῶν, Paris, 1823; the *Letter on Democracy*, ed. P. Kontogiannis, Ἑλληνικά, viii, 1935, pp. 181ff.

[38] Diamantes Rysios, Λατίνων θρησκείας ἔλεγχοι 36, Amsterdam–Venice, 1748. Refu-

tation 31 (pp. 180 ff.) which condemns in upward of 400 verses the Latin custom of shaving the beard deserves particular notice.

[39] Τί πρέπει νὰ κάμωσιν οἱ Γραικοὶ εἰς τὰς παρούσας περιστάσεις, Venice, 1805, pp. 44, 52.

[40] *Polnoe sobranie sočinenij*, ed. Akad. Nauk SSSR, ii/1, 1947, p. 197. His enthusiasm vanished, however, by 1824 when he had met the Greek shopkeepers of Odessa and Kishinev. 'That all the enlightened peoples of Europe,' he wrote to his friend Vjazemskij, 'should be raving about Greece is unforgivable childishness' (same ed., xiii, 1937, p. 99).

and all the other trappings of its golden past. Following the lead given by Koraes, the language was purged of impurities and barbarisms to the point where hardly anyone could write it correctly, much less speak it. Infants were baptized with names such as Anaximander, Aristotle, Pelopidas, Olympias, even Aspasia.[41] At the same time the Byzantine tradition was discarded, at least in its outward manifestations: the Greek Church made itself independent of the Ecumenical Patriarch, and even the teaching of theology was transferred from the monasteries to a faculty of divinity patterned after German models. And yet, the spontaneous flowering which everyone expected did not take place. Enlightened Europe lost interest. The Europeans blamed it on the Greeks, the Greeks on the Europeans. Something, in any case, went amiss.

As one reads the accounts of European travellers to Greece in the forties and fifties of the last century, one senses their disappointment. For one thing, Greece had become rather too easy of access to remain exotic: a regular steamship service now connected the Peiraeus to Marseille, and, as a French novelist observes, it took him less time to visit King Otto at Athens than it had taken Mme de Sévigné to visit her daughter at Grignan.[42] When the romantic traveller disembarked, he saw nothing but arid, dusty, sun-baked clay. Athens was a dirty village. The country was full of brigands. Malaria was endemic. The descendants of Themistocles looked like any other Balkan population and dressed in Balkan costume, unless they donned the European redingote, which was even worse. A sensitive French lady who was very shocked by the ungainly proportions of Greek women was assured that 'C'est la nature'. But, she cried out, this is not the nature of Venus de Milo![43] And as for the flowering of letters, Athenian booksellers at that time offered nothing but bad translations of the worst Parisian novels.[44] The visitor concluded that Greece had not fulfilled her role; that the hopes of Europe had been betrayed.

The Greek, on his side, pointed out that his tiny country was not viable economically; that the great majority of the Greek nation remained subjects of the Sultan; that most of the brigands came across the Turkish border; and that the great powers were now concerned to safeguard the integrity of the Ottoman Empire rather than to champion Greece, that Greece to which they owed their civilization.

Behind this misunderstanding there lurked a deeper cause which neither side understood at the time. A symptom of it is that the *Travels of Anacharsis* fell into oblivion around 1850. Travellers now confessed that the Acropolis, in all its perfection, left them cold, that Greek sculpture appealed to their intellect and not to their emotions.[45] By 1850 a well-known French poet had to excuse his admiration for the Parthenon which, he explained, was rather better than the Madeleine; but he feared lest his solitary voice was drowned by the noisy

[41] 'On commence à risquer Aspasie. On en arrivera à Phryné, quand les parrains grecs auront vidé tout le sac de l'histoire et de la mythologie': A. Grenier, *La Grèce en 1863*, Paris, 1863, p. 67.

[42] Edmond About, *La Grèce contemporaine*, Paris, 1854, p. 1. On the steamship connection see Marchebeus, *Voyage de Paris à Con-* stantinople par bateau à vapeur, Paris, 1839.

[43] [Valérie de Gasparin,] *Journal d'un voyage au Levant*, i, Paris, 1848, p. 157.

[44] A. Grenier, *op. cit.*, p. 60: 'On fait passer en grec (Dieux immortels, quel grec!) les fantaisies les plus intraduisibles, les plus directement émanées de l'asphalte parisienne.'

[45] Valérie de Gasparin, *op. cit.*, i, p. 110.

hosannah that was pealing out amidst the turrets, the ogees, the gargoyles, the flying buttresses of Notre-Dame.[46] The Gothic myth had replaced the mirage of Greece.

This new preoccupation with the Middle Ages and feudal gloom had an important side-effect, for it led, via the Crusades, to the rediscovery of Byzantium. Châteaubriand set the fashion by going to the East 'en pèlerin et en chevalier, la Bible, l'Evangile et les Croisades à la main'.[47] Starting in the thirties, i.e. simultaneously with the appearance of Victor Hugo's *Notre-Dame de Paris*, Byzantine studies picked up again in Europe, having lain dormant since the seventeenth century. We may note the works of Fallmerayer, Buchon, Finlay, Hopf in history, of Didron,[48] Texier, Labarte in archaeology. It was a slow start, and these pioneer scholars were far from appreciating Byzantium on its own merits. Nevertheless, Byzantium had been put back on the map, and this, too, was done by enlightened Europe. Greece was faced with a new intellectual challenge.

Clearly, the rejection *en bloc* of the Byzantine heritage could not persist for long. There was, first of all, the Great Idea, that is the dream of incorporating within the Greek Kingdom both Constantinople and those Turkish provinces that had substantial Greek settlements. We must remember that in the middle of the last century Greece had a population of less than a million and a half, whereas three to four million Greeks lived in the Ottoman Empire; that the Greek population of Constantinople was about five times as big as the total population of Athens. All Greeks were enthusiastically committed to the Great Idea; a newspaper that neglected to advocate it two days running was apt to lose its circulation.[49] Now, the Great Idea was, of course, nothing else than messianic Byzantinism in new dress. The change of costume—and, if I may say so, the Great Idea wore the *redingote*—was of crucial importance: for whereas Byzantinism had had a religious foundation and made little distinction between nationalities provided they were Orthodox, the Great Idea was nationalistic. But the objectives were the same, and furthermore the Great Idea, too, was deeply messianic: no one bothered to think clearly how it could be achieved, what would happen after its realization, by what means the Greater Greece could stretch as far as Trebizond without including most of Turkey, or what would be done to the Turkish population which was in a majority in those parts. Here, too, we perceive the heritage of Byzantinism: for the Turks were not part of the divine dispensation. Perhaps they could be locked up, like Gog and Magog, behind the Caspian Gates.

Even in new dress, the Great Idea had rather more to do with Constantinople, St. Sophia and the Ecumenical Patriarchate than with Periclean Athens. Other factors were also at work in the same direction: Bulgaria was

---

[46] Victor de Laprade, 'Considérations sur le génie de la Grèce', being the introduction to E. Yemeniz, *Voyage dans le Royaume de Grèce*, Paris, 1854, pp. xxxiif.

[47] This description is due to Lamartine in the Preface to his *Voyage en Orient*.

[48] *Manuel d'iconographie chrétienne*, Paris, 1845. This work, the result of a journey to Greece and Mt. Athos in 1839, is dedicated, appropriately enough, to Victor Hugo. 'Mon illustre ami,' writes the author, 'en quelques semaines vous avez construit, dans Notre-Dame de Paris, la cathédrale du moyen âge; moi, je voudrais passer ma vie à la sculpter et à la peindre.'

[49] Grenier, *op. cit.*, p. 231.

awakening under Russian prodding and claiming her substantial share of the Byzantine heritage, including all of Macedonia. To counteract such pretensions, it was necessary to show that Byzantium had been thoroughly Greek, not only in language but also in spirit, in the essentials of its civilization.

The task of reconciling Hellas to Byzantium was undertaken by Constantine Paparrigopoulos, the father of modern Greek historiography. His monumental *History of the Greek Nation* had the avowed purpose of re-establishing the unity of hellenic civilization which, so he believed, formed an unbroken continuum from Homer to King Otto.[50] In the Middle Ages, he admitted, this hellenism underwent a certain adulteration owing to Oriental influence and the influx of barbarians which resulted in the introduction of various regrettable institutions. Yet hellenism never lost its primitive character and gave birth, in the eighth century, to a most remarkable reform. This reform, oddly enough, was Iconoclasm. The modern historian who has been taught to regard Iconoclasm as an Oriental movement, rather akin to Islam and championed by Syrians, Anatolians and Armenians, feels rather puzzled at this point. Paparrigopoulos, too, was aware that the Iconoclast leaders were orientals, but this only confirmed his theory, since obviously hellenism must have retained more of its original purity in the oriental Greek centres whereas it had become sadly altered at Constantinople. As seen by Paparrigopoulos, the Iconoclasts were liberal and humane; they suppressed slavery and monkishness while championing secular education and rational economic reform. In other words, they sought to establish the kind of sensible society that prevailed only in the nineteenth century. True, the Iconoclasts were in the end defeated, but the effects of their movement lived on. By repulsing the Arabs and hellenizing the Slavs the Empire showed all too clearly what could be accomplished by hellenism united in a single state. There is no need to pursue any further this emended outline of medieval history, for its principles are sufficiently obvious: everything that was good in Byzantium, that is good by the standards of enlightened Victorian Europe, was hellenic, everything that was bad was due to the dilution or adulteration of hellenism.

The *History* of Paparrigopoulos became one of the sacred texts of modern Greece and generations of Greeks have grown up on it. Whatever minor corrections subsequent scholarship might bring, this *History* was to remain 'a possession for ever'; so wrote Pavlos Karolidis, the leading Greek historian in succession to Paparrigopoulos.[51] Indeed, it would be fair to say that the overall picture of hellenism through the ages, as drawn by Paparrigopoulos, has prevailed in Greece until now, and that most subsequent investigations, whether in pure history, folklore, literature or language, have taken it for granted. This overall picture has been conveyed by another eminent Greek man of letters of the last century by means of the following metaphor: medieval hellenism was like a cup of wine that had been poured into an amphora of water. The liquid thus obtained kept something of the colour and savour of wine, but its colour was pale and its savour insipid. A distillation lasting several centuries was needed for this liquid to regain its original

---

[50] His views are conveniently summarized in his *Histoire de la civilisation hellénique*, Paris, 1878.

[51] Preface to 4th ed. of Paparrigopoulos' Ἱστορία τοῦ ἑλληνικοῦ ἔθνους, i, Athens, 1902, pp. 5f.

consistency, in other words, for hellenism to reappear in its true form in modern Greece.[52]

In this way Byzantinism and hellenism were fused into one. The mystic marriage of Pericles and Theodora was consummated. The Parthenon and St. Sophia were seen as complementary expressions of the same national genius.

Until the latter part of the nineteenth century, Greece, in her intellectual life, had merely reacted to external stimuli. Now she began taking stock of herself. It was a veritable *crise de conscience* which took the form of an epic controversy over language: the purists on one side, the demoticists on the other. The more lively and creative spirits were naturally in the ranks of the demoticists. They rebelled against the alien burden of classicism, against the unbelievably tedious form of education then in use, against that archaic language which hindered literary writing and made poetry impossible; above all, they rebelled against the tyranny of western Europe. To create a genuine Greek civilization, they wished to return to the popular tradition; and this tradition led them back, inevitably to Byzantium. A programme of this future civilization was drawn up in 1913 by a leading demoticist, author and diplomat, Ion Dragoumis. He foresaw a Greece that was rather more oriental than western. The arts would return to the point where the Byzantines left off: the architect would seek his models among the churches and houses of Mistra, the painter would turn to Byzantine frescoes and mosaics, the composer to the chants of the Orthodox Church. European clothing would be banished and replaced by that of the Greek village. As for religion, it would be that of nationality.[53] On this point, at least, demoticists and purists seemed to be agreed.

It is amusing to observe the reversal that had taken place in the course of one century. In 1800 it was the liberal, republican Koraes, the chief architect of the puristic *katharevousa*, who urged the return to ancient Greece and branded Byzantinism as the blackest reaction; in 1900 it was the entrenched oligarchy of professors, high-school teachers and royalists who manned the Acropolis of ancient Athens, while the demoticists, those 'socialist youths' whose possible influence on this Chair was so feared in 1919, looked back for inspiration to the days of Byzantium.

We have now come dangerously close to the present time, and it may be prudent to stop and draw some conclusions from our rapid survey. Have we found continuity or discontinuity? I think we have found both though not in equal proportions. We have followed one clear line of continuity from imperial Byzantinism to messianic Byzantinism and thence to the Great Idea, noting at the same time how this concept became perverted, robbed of its original significance and made to serve the ends of nationalism. In all other respects, however, we have found that Byzantinism, as a system of thought, had nothing in common with the hellenism of the nineteenth century; nor have we discovered a line of filiation leading from the one to the other. Hellenism, both romantic and national, was not of indigenous growth; it was implanted from abroad, and in being so implanted, out of its natural context,

[52] D. Bikelas, Περὶ Βυζαντινῶν, London, 1874, p. 74.

[53] Ἑλληνικὸς πολιτισμός in Ἴωνος Δραγούμη ἔργα, Ser. II, Athens, 1927, pp. 217 ff.

it produced a break in continuity. This, of course, was due to western inter-
ference. Emotionally, most of us regret this kind of thing. But could it have
been avoided and can the trend be now reversed? There is a fairly vocal
school today which bids Greece return to the Byzantine cloister where she
will find her soul again. Can we seriously believe that Greek youth will wish
to be brought up on the sermons of St. Basil and complete its education in
the monasteries of Mount Athos? Is not romantic Byzantinism just as utopian
as romantic hellenism? Greece has had a long and painful apprenticeship at
Europe's feet. In the last century she could do little more than imitate the
patterns that were thrust at her; but since about 1900 she has been making
her own distinctive contribution to European civilization. I, for one, do not
find in this any cause for regret, and I am sure that as enlightened Europe
surveys Greece today she can no longer claim that her hopes have been
deceived.

II

BYZANTINE LITERATURE AS A DISTORTING MIRROR

This is the second inaugural lecture I have had the privilege to deliver and I trust there will be no third. The previous one was given ten years ago in the Koraës Chair at King's College, London. On that occasion I chose a broad theme—I called it 'Byzantinism and Romantic Hellenism'—and I endeavoured to show the gulf that separated the Byzantine view of the world from the mirage of 'ancient Greece reborn' that was created in Western Europe towards the end of the eighteenth century, and how these two mutually exclusive ideologies were subsequently amalgamated to produce a kind of national myth. Alas, even as I spoke, I could notice the displeasure of some members of my audience; and when, at length, my lecture was published and translated into modern Greek[1]— it appeared before the glorious revolution of 21 April 1967— I was assailed in the Athenian press not only as an ignoramus, but, worse, as a traitor for having challenged the dogma of the unbroken continuity of Hellenic culture.[2] Thus chastened, I have selected this time a less controversial subject, yet one which, I hope, is not entirely devoid of general interest.

My distinguished predecessor in the Koraës Chair, the late Romilly Jenkins, delivered this memorable dictum: 'The Byzantine Empire remains almost the unique example of a highly civilized state, lasting for more than a millennium, which produced hardly any educated writing which can be read with pleasure for its literary merit alone.'[3] Jenkins wrote these lines in about 1939, before he had immersed himself thoroughly in the study of Byzantine texts; but he did not change his mind after this immersion had taken place. In 1962, when he surveyed the Hellenistic origins of Byzantine

---

[1] *Journal of the Warburg and Courtauld Institutes*, xxviii, 1965, pp. 29 ff. Greek version in 'Εποχές, 46, Feb. 1967, pp. 133 ff.

[2] And not only in the daily press. See the ponderous refutation by A. Vacalopoulos, 'Byzantinism and Hellenism', *Balkan Studies*, ix, 1968, pp. 101 ff.

[3] *Dionysius Solomós*, Cambridge, 1940, p. 57.

literature, he gave some praise to Byzantine scholars for their monumental compilations, and to Byzantine historians for their objectivity and knowledge of public affairs. But of literary and, especially, poetic merit, he had this to say: 'Byzantine civilization must be characterized from first to last, as wanting in that great gift which nature reserves for her favourites, poetic feeling and expression.'[1]

I do not wish to dispute this harsh verdict. There are some, it is true, who derive a *frisson* of mystical delight from the Hymns of Romanus the Melode, and they have been well served by my eminent predecessor here, Professor Trypanis. With this and a few other exceptions, Byzantine literature is not read for pleasure, but it is read all the same. In fact, I am sure that Michael Psellus and Anna Comnena have more readers today than they had in their own lifetime. The publication or re-publication of Byzantine texts that is being so actively pursued in our days is sufficient testimony of this. The new readers are historians in the broadest sense of the word, and they peruse Byzantine texts for the sake of information—be it purely historical, or economic, or intellectual and religious, or artistic—i.e. as a means to an end. And herein lies my subject. The historian tends to take Byzantine texts at face value. Do they offer him a true reflection of the past?

Lest I be misunderstood, I should like to make two preliminary observations. When I speak of Byzantine literature, I have in mind not only, and not even mainly belles-lettres, but the entire range of writing, exclusive of administrative and legal documents, practical manuals, and the like. Belletristic literature accounts for only a small part of this vast body of writing and is, perhaps, its least interesting part. My second observation is that Byzantine literature, thus broadly defined, falls, by and large, into two groups which, for the sake of convenience, we may designate as highbrow and lowbrow. The two groups are differentiated by language—ancient Greek in the former, contemporary or Biblical Greek in the latter. They are also normally distinguished by subject-matter and genre. These two groups of writing were addressed to different social classes. The highbrow group, at any rate after

---

[1] *Dumbarton Oaks Papers*, xvii, 1963, p. 43.

the seventh century, was confined to a small clique of educated civil servants and clergymen at Constantinople. It is important to realize how small this clique was: a recent estimate, made for the tenth century, puts at about 300 the total number of persons who at any given time were receiving secondary education.[1] Highbrow Byzantine literature had, therefore, almost no public; and once its topical interest was gone, it was usually relegated to obscurity in one or two manuscript copies. Lowbrow literature had a somewhat wider social basis, but, until the later Middle Ages, its content was entirely utilitarian and edifying. Books were scarce and fantastically expensive,[2] and the very process of reading too slow and laborious to be wasted on mere pleasure or even to be capable of yielding any pleasure. The eleventh-century provincial magnate Cecaumenos, who, in his intellectual outlook, is often regarded as the paradigm of the average Byzantine, gives some revealing advice on the subject of reading books, which he was rich enough to afford. It is a practice he strongly recommends; but, he says, one should not skip pages. One should start from the front cover and go to the very end, preferably two or three times, even if one does not understand the text, for often God grants understanding to the patient. Thus will reading be profitable; but to pick a few passages out of a book for the sake of idle gossip is a sign of frivolity.[3]

Both the highbrow and the lowbrow spheres of Byzantine literature present serious problems of interpretation, but they are not the same problems, and tonight I shall concern myself mainly with the highbrow. The most obvious feature of this literature is that it was written in a dead language and, as such, may be compared to the Latin and Greek compositions

[1] P. Lemerle, *Élèves et professeurs à Constantinople au Xᵉ siècle*, Acad. des Inscr. et Belles-Lettres, Lecture faite dans la séance ... du 28 nov. 1969, p. 11.

[2] The price of books in Byzantium is discussed in a forthcoming study by N. G. Wilson. For the connection between wealth and the owning of books see the characteristic passage in *Le Traité contre les Bogomiles de Cosmas le Prêtre*, ed. H.-Ch. Puech and A. Vaillant, Paris, 1945, p. 120: 'Car toi tu es riche, tu es comblé de tout, tu as l'Ancien et le Nouveau Testaments et les autres livres pleins de textes convaincants ...' Cf. also Nicetas Paphlago, *Vita Ignatii, Patrol. graeca*, cv, col. 509B.

[3] *Strategicon*, ed. B. Wassiliewsky and V. Jernstedt, St. Petersburg, 1896, pp. 47, 60.

that have been laboriously produced by countless generations of our schoolchildren and university students. This comparison has already been drawn by Jenkins, but for a different purpose. What I should like to point out is not that writing in a dead language can aspire to nothing higher than verbal dexterity, true though that may be; but that writing in a dead language about contemporary affairs inevitably results in the interposition of a certain distance. Of this I have practical experience, since my own professor of Greek, the late H. J. Rose, would occasionally prescribe for translation the leading article of *The Scotsman*. The resulting composition, which was intended to be comprehensible to an Athenian of the fifth century B.C., was not only riddled with qualifying clauses— 'as it were', 'as one might say', 'as they call it'—not only were specific modern terms and concepts converted into their nearest classical equivalents, thus robbing them of their specificity, but the effect as a whole was suggestive of those ethnographic excursuses that one finds in ancient historians. It was as if one were writing about the strange customs of some alien and distant tribe. Exactly the same phenomenon may be discerned in highbrow Byzantine literature as early as the fifth and sixth centuries.

It has long been observed that Procopius, in his *History of Justinian's wars*, uses the most extraordinary circumlocutions whenever he has to mention a Christian term or institution. He says, e.g., 'the most temperate among the Christians whom they usually call monks', or 'the priest whom they call presbyter', or 'the writings of the Christians which they commonly call Gospels', or 'the Easter festival which Christians hold in reverence more than any other', as if he had to explain to his readers the meaning of these everyday words. Ever since Gibbon, historians have concluded that Procopius was, if not a crypto-pagan, at any rate an out-and-out sceptic; and it is only in the past ten years that two gifted scholars, Professor and Mrs. Cameron of London University, have shown in detail that this was not the case. Procopius was writing secular history in the manner and phraseology of Herodotus and Thucydides: the rules of the genre did not allow him to use barbarisms without some apology. This affectation has been mistaken by modern scholars as a sign of religious detachment.[1]

The line between affectation and obfuscation is not easy to draw. I am sure that Procopius had no thought of misleading his readers by his neutral statements concerning the Christian faith. But consider this passage of his successor, the historian Agathias, which refers to the Persian king Chosroes Anushirvan for whose benefit certain works of Greek philosophy were allegedly translated into Pahlavi:

They say, indeed, that he has drunk in more of the Stagirite than the Paianian [Demosthenes] did of the son of Olorus [Thucydides] and that he is full of the doctrines of Plato the son of Ariston. The *Timaeus*, they say, is not beyond him, even though it is positively studded with geometrical theory, and inquires into the movements of nature, nor is the *Phaedo*, nor the *Gorgias*, nor any other of the more subtle and obscure dialogues—the *Parmenides*, for instance, I suppose.[2]

Did Agathias mean to imply that the above Platonic dialogues were translated for the Persian King? Some scholars have taken him at his word, but Mrs. Cameron believes—and she is surely right—that Agathias is here indulging in a rhetorical flourish: he wants to impress upon us that he is conversant with Plato and the names of the dialogues. As the centuries rolled on, the tendency to embroider, to show off one's erudition in a way that actually confuses the reader, becomes more and more pronounced. One example will have to suffice.

Nicetas Magistros, a fairly obscure author of the tenth century, wrote the Life of Saint Theoctista of Lesbos in which he inserted a description of the great church on the island of Paros—the Panagia Katapoliani that is still standing. The description is not particularly specific or accurate, but it looks

[1] Averil Cameron, 'The "Scepticism" of Procopius', *Historia*, xv, 1966, pp. 466 ff. Cf. Averil and Alan Cameron, 'Christianity and Tradition in the Historiography of the Late Empire', *Class. Quarterly*, lviii, 1964, pp. 416 ff.; Averil Cameron, *Agathias*, Oxford, 1970, pp. 75 ff.

[2] *Hist.* ii. 28. 2. I am quoting Mrs. Cameron's translation, 'Agathias on the Sassanians', *Dumbarton Oaks Papers*, xxiii/xxiv, 1969/70, p. 165; cf. her comment on p. 174.

genuine enough. Nicetas was especially impressed by a milky
white marble of which the ciborium of the church was made,
and he added what looks like a personal observation: 'I had
once seen a stone such as this in a statue of Selene driving
a chariot drawn by oxen.'[1] When I first encountered this
passage, I was struck by what appeared to be an altogether
unusual piece of visual awareness on the part of a Byzantine
author. Alas, the reference to the statue of Selene turned out
to be an almost literal quotation from Achilles Tatius, as
a learned colleague has recently pointed out.[2]

Procopius and Agathias are our main sources for the reign
of the emperor Justinian. They are reliable as far as they go,
i.e. as concerns the narration of public events; but, bound
as they are by the rules of secular historiography, they exclude
from their narrative just about everything that made up the
particular flavour of their period. If we did not possess a mass
of other material, such as ecclesiastical histories, Lives of
Saints, sermons, even Acts of Councils of the Church, imperial
laws, and business documents, our conception of the sixth
century would have been hopelessly schematic and one-
sided.

The age of Justinian was, of course, very different from
that of Pericles or even that of Augustus. Yet, Procopius and
Agathias still lived in a world that may be described as
antique. Urban life continued in the old Graeco-Roman
cities; there was still a pagan minority; schools of higher learning went on functioning in several provincial centres; above
all, there still existed a public of cultivated gentlemen, not
only in the capital, but also at Alexandria and Antioch, at
Caesarea and Gaza, not to mention many other cities. But then
came the cataclysm of the seventh century, the onslaughts of
Avars, Slavs, Arabs, and Bulgars, the loss of two-thirds of

---

[1] *Acta Sanctorum*, Nov. iv. 226B.

[2] L. G. Westerink, *Nicétas Magistros: Lettres d'un exilé*, Paris, 1973, p. 43 n. 1.
Much more telling, not to say monstrous, instances of obfuscation may be
quoted from the writings of Arethas of Caesarea, e.g. his Χοιροσφάκτης ἢ
Μισογόης (ed. L. G. Westerink, *Arethae scripta minora*, i, Leipzig, 1968, pp. 200 ff.)
which has confused modern scholars to no small extent; but it would take too
long to explain both what Arethas appears to be saying and how he has been
misunderstood.

the Empire's lands, the virtual disruption of urban life. The Byzantine state that emerged from this convulsion was barbarized and thoroughly medieval; yet, by some miracle, a small educated élite continued to exist at Constantinople and, from the ninth century to the fifteenth, they went on writing highbrow literature in ancient Greek. If we are disturbed by the discrepancy between reality and its literary reflection in Procopius and Agathias, how much more pronounced, not to say grotesque, had this discrepancy become by the time of Constantine Porphyrogenitus or Alexius Comnenus!

The continuation of erudite literature was made possible by the survival of secular education in its antique, i.e. rhetorical form. The curriculum, based on a combination of pagan and Early Christian authorities, remained unchanged and no textbook later than the sixth century was introduced. The privileged Byzantine boy learnt his grammar from Apollonius Dyscolus and the *Epimerismi in Psalmos* by George † Choeroboscus, his rhetoric from Hermogenes of Tarsus and Aphthonius, his logic from Porphyry's *Eisagoge*. The same blend of pagan and Early Christian is discernible in the literary models that were proffered for imitation: Saint Gregory Nazianzen had taken his place beside Demosthenes, and the Christian Synesius beside the pagan Libanius.[1] What applied to literary excellence applied equally to the sciences: medicine, astronomy, geography, philosophy, botany, even agricultural theory had all reached their definitive and canonical form in Late Antiquity. It is interesting to observe that the *Bibliotheca* of Photius, which consists of the notices or summaries of 279 works and represents, I believe, nearly the entire reading matter of a uniquely cultivated man, contains no more than four works later than about the year 600, i.e. pertaining to the 250 years prior to the composition of the *Bibliotheca*.[2] Likewise, the tenth-century *Souda* furnishes only a minimal amount of information on medieval Byzantine

[1] We still lack a comprehensive study of the curriculum of Byzantine schools. In the meantime, see P. Lemerle, *Le premier humanisme byzantin*, Paris, 1971, pp. 252 ff.
[2] Codd. 66, 67, 170, 233. I am not counting conciliar Acts and Lives of saints.

authors. The world of culture and useful knowledge lay in a distant past.

Among the literary genres bequeathed to Byzantium by Antiquity was the Dialogue in its Platonic and Lucianic forms. Down to the fifteenth century such dialogues continued to be written, and several of them—like the anonymous *Philopatris*, the *Phlorentios* by Nicephorus Gregoras, and the *Dialogue with a Persian* by the emperor Manuel II Palaeologus— were inspired by specific historical circumstances. Dialogue form has, of course, a certain built-in artificiality, but it does not preclude, in fact it even encourages, the introduction of realistic touches. A modern, yet sufficiently traditional example, like the *Soirées de Saint-Pétersbourg* by Joseph de Maistre, will make this plain. You will allow me to consider a Byzantine dialogue. It is by Michael Psellus, the famous polymath of the eleventh century, and is entitled $T\iota\mu\acute{o}\theta\epsilon os$ $\mathring{\eta}$ $\pi\epsilon\rho\grave{\iota}$ $\delta\alpha\iota\mu\acute{o}\nu\omega\nu$, usually referred to as *De operatione daemonum*.[1] This is a work of some notoriety. During the Renaissance it was considered as a serious treatise on demonology, and was first published, in a Latin version by Marsilio Ficino, in 1497;[2] a French version, intended as a weapon against the Protestants, then suspected of diabolical practices, followed in 1573.[3] Victor Hugo quotes it in his *Notre-Dame de Paris*,[4] though on the mistaken assumption that it had something to do with alchemy. More recently, the *De operatione* has been studied as a document of heresiology with particular reference to the Bogomils, and has been discussed by eminent scholars such as Bidez, Puech, Sir Steven Runciman, and Dimitri Obolensky.[5] Émile Renauld, the foremost modern exponent

---

[1] Ed. J. F. Boissonade, Nürnberg, 1838; *Patrol. graeca*, cxxii, cols. 817 ff. (reprinting the ed. by G. Gaulmin, Paris, 1615). I am quoting from the latter edition.

[2] Ficino's translation is based on a somewhat divergent Greek text which has been published by J. Bidez, *Michel Psellus: Épître sur la Chrysopée*, Catal. des manuscrits alchimiques grecs, vi, Brussels, 1928, pp. 119 ff.

[3] See É. Renauld, 'Une traduction française du $\Pi\epsilon\rho\grave{\iota}$ $\grave{\epsilon}\nu\epsilon\rho\gamma\epsilon\acute{\iota}\alpha s$ $\delta\alpha\iota\mu\acute{o}\nu\omega\nu$ de Michel Psellos', *Rev. ét. grecques*, xxxiii, 1920, pp. 56 ff.

[4] Bk. 7, ch. 5.

[5] Bidez, op. cit., pp. 97 ff.; Puech and Vaillant, op. cit., pp. 139 ff.; S. Runciman, *The Medieval Manichee*, Cambridge, 1960, pp. 90 ff.; D. Obolensky, *The Bogomils*, Cambridge, 1948, pp. 183 ff. Cf. also Ch. Zervos, *Un philosophe*

of Michael Psellus, has praised the *De operatione* as being, on the one hand, a precious historical source and, on the other, an exquisite specimen of the Byzantine literary language.[1]

We have before us a dialogue between two persons called Timotheus and Thrax who meet at Byzantium. Thrax has been absent for two years in the course of which he has come in contact with a group of heretics called Euchites or Enthusiasts. Pressed by Timotheus, he gives an account of their revolting practices, which included the eating of excrement, incest, the sacrifice of new-born infants, and devil-worship, and then launches into a detailed discussion of the nature and operation of demons. His informant on this score had been a Mesopotamian monk, called Mark, whom he encountered in northern Greece. Finally, the two friends part as it is about to rain.

The scholars who have studied this text have drawn from it a variety of conclusions. Some believe that the Euchites were simply Bogomils. Yet the doctrines and practices described by Psellus do not tally very well with those of the Bogomils as known to us from other sources; hence the conclusion that Psellus is indeed speaking of Euchites, i.e. Massalians; and this, in turn, is taken as proof of the existence of this ancient sect as late as the eleventh century. As to the doctrines themselves, some scholars accept them at face value, while others believe that they have been borrowed from much older, Neoplatonic sources, especially from Proclus. On only one point is everyone agreed, namely that Psellus's Euchites were living in Thrace, although the text places them squarely in Thessaly and the Chalcidic peninsula.[2]

---

néoplatonicien du XIe siècle: Michel Psellos, Paris, 1919, pp. 199 ff.; M. Wellnhofer, 'Die thrakischen Euchiten', *Byzant. Zeitschr.* xxx, 1929/30, pp. 477 ff.; P. Joannou, 'Les croyances démonologiques au xie siècle à Byzance', *Actes du VIe Congrès Intern. d'Études Byzantines*, i, Paris, 1950, pp. 245 ff.; id., *Démonologie populaire — démonologie critique au XIe siècle*, Wiesbaden, 1971.

[1] Loc. cit. In his *Étude de la langue et du style de Michel Psellos*, Paris, 1920, p. 438, Renauld goes so far as to say that the style of the *De operatione* is not unworthy of Plato.

[2] This mistake may be partly due to the fact that one of the interlocutors is called Thrax. The reason for this fictitious name is not immediately apparent. Thrax (who may conceal a real person) seems to have been sent from Constantinople on a mission to hunt out heretics, and was empowered to use torture

Imagine now that the *De operatione* had come down to us anonymously, like so many other works of Byzantine literature. Would anyone have dated it in the eleventh century? I think not. Indeed, on internal evidence one could build a strong case for a date no later than the sixth century, after which time the Euchites all but disappeared from view. Their original home is thought to have been in Mesopotamia and, in fact, the monk Mark is described by Psellus as a Mesopotamian. The abominations of the Euchites are said by him to be shared by the Gnostics,[1] which again points to an early period since there were no Gnostics in the eleventh century. At one point Timotheus exclaims: 'No one has heard of such evil, neither among the Celts, nor in the midst of whatever lawless and savage tribe inhabits Britain!'[2] Here, surely, is a remark that was made at a time when people at Constantinople had but a dim awareness of the extreme west of Europe and when the British Isles were still pagan. Timotheus then tells a little story. When he was a boy he was worried by the thought that liberal education and all other good things were declining. He consulted his grandfather who assured him that not only would there be no improvement, but that

in interrogating suspects. I see no reason to suppose that he was a military commander. The topographical indications furnished by the text are the following: 1. Thrax encountered his informant, the monk Mark, in the Chersonese which borders on Hellas, περὶ χερρόνησον τὴν ὅμορον Ἑλλάδος (col. 840) ; 2. He apprehended a possessed heretic at Elasson, ἐν Ἐλασῶνι. This man had prophesied that somebody would be sent out against his sect, would capture him, and try to take him prisoner to Byzantium. He had made this prediction, says Thrax, 'when I had not yet gone beyond the villages next to Byzantium' (col. 853). The Chersonese cannot be the peninsula forming the north shore of the Dardanelles, since it is described as being adjacent to Hellas—a name which, in the Byzantine as in the Classical period, normally denoted Greece proper, south of Thessaly. Hence Psellus is probably referring to the Chalcidic peninsula which, though not exactly bordering on Hellas, is, at any rate, sufficiently close. As for Elasson, it lies, of course, south of Mount Olympus. This topographical correction is of some significance. As long as the Euchites were supposed to be concentrated in Thrace, they could be connected, via the Armenian and Syrian settlements in that country, with the Paulicians and Massalians, as several scholars have connected them. Note, incidentally, that ἐν Ἐλασῶνι is the vulgate reading; some manuscripts have Ἐχασᾶνι or Χερσῶνι. I cannot take seriously the ingenious suggestion by P. Peeters that one ought to read Ἐλασᾶνι = el-Hassân, 'car une localité de ce nom, située près de Kaškar en Babylonie, a été l'un des foyers du Manichéisme' (in Bidez, op. cit., p. 117).

[1] Col. 829.   [2] Col. 836.

the end of the world was at hand and men would behave like wild beasts. One would see again all the horrors of the Dionysiac mysteries; the abominable deeds told in the Greek tragedies would be repeated: Cronus, Thyestes, and Tantalus would devour their children, Oedipus would lie with his mother, and Cinyras with his daughter.[1] Does this not point to a time when paganism was still a live issue? Was not the decline of liberal education expressed by the closing of the schools of Athens by Justinian? Was not the end of the world expected in the year 501 which marked the end of the sixth millennium after the Creation?[2] I could go even further. Demons, Psellus tells us, were heard at times to speak in Greek, at other times in Chaldaean, in Persian, or in Syriac.[3] We are, therefore, dealing with a period before the Arab conquest. Now observe the following detail. Timotheus is made to say that his sister-in-law was once possessed by a demon and was heard speaking in a barbarous and incomprehensible tongue. After much inquiry it was ascertained that the language in question was Armenian, which was all the stranger since the poor woman had never laid eyes on an Armenian.[4] The first migration of Armenians to Constantinople occurred in 571 and a few years later great numbers of them were settled in Thrace by the emperor Maurice.[5] From that time on the Armenian element became so widespread in the Byzantine Empire that the sound of their language could not have been found so utterly alien.

I have deliberately developed this fallacious argument. The *De operatione* is by Michael Psellus and so must date from about the middle of the eleventh century. Yet it does not contain a single element that might reveal the actual time of its composition. Psellus may well be speaking of the Bogomils. If he calls them Euchites, it is because he wants to give them an

[1] Col. 833.
[2] According to the era of Julius Africanus, or in 507/8 according to that of Panodorus. It was widely believed that the end of the world would fall within the reign of Anastasius I (491–518). See P. J. Alexander, *The Oracle of Baalbek*, Washington D.C., 1967, pp. 118 ff.
[3] Col. 860.
[4] Col. 857.
[5] See P. Charanis, *The Armenians in the Byzantine Empire*, Lisbon, c. 1963, pp. 13 ff.

old name and a Greek name at that. This is not evidence of
the survival of the Massalian sect. In the practices of the
Bogomils he probably had little interest; but he used them
as a peg upon which to hang his own bookish knowledge of
demonology. Students of heresies may take note. We are
accustomed to the fact that Byzantine authors called the
Russians Scythians, the Turks Persians, and the Bulgarians
Mysians (instead of the more appropriate Moesians). Could
Psellus have introduced the shocking term Πογόμιλοι into
a Platonic dialogue?

The example of the *De operatione* serves a double purpose.
On the one hand, it shows a close adherence to an antique
literary genre which determines its form and its language.
On the other hand, the time and setting that it evokes are
neither antique nor medieval, but those of the Early Christian
Empire. A very different example may help us to further
illustrate the latter point.

The emperor Constantine Porphyrogenitus is a figure of
central importance for every byzantinist. He was not so much
an original author as a compiler; yet it is from his compilations that we derive much of our knowledge of Byzantine
administration, court ceremonial, and foreign relations. The
purpose of his literary endeavours was, moreover, practical
and didactic, and to this end he even condescended at times
to using ordinary Greek.[1] Even so, we cannot say that his
works offer us a true reflection of the Empire in the tenth
century, so inextricably mixed is contemporary with antiquarian information. Take the treatise called *De thematibus*,
which is an account of the provinces, called 'themes', into
which the Empire was divided, their origin, their principal
cities, and their inhabitants.[2] It is not a work of literature, but
in so far as it is the only 'geopolitical' treatise that we have
of the Byzantine Empire, it is a document of primary impor-

---

[1] In the Preface to the *Book of Ceremonies* (ed. A. Vogt, i, Paris, 1935, p. 2)
Constantine makes this significant statement: 'With a view to making our work
clear and understandable, we have employed the simpler style of ordinary
speech, and those very words and terms which a long time ago were applied to
each object and are so used.' Had he written in a higher style, he would, of
course, have eschewed all such precise terms.

[2] Ed. A. Pertusi, Studi e Testi, 160, Vatican City, 1952.

tance; furthermore, had Constantine wished so, he could have gathered a mass of precise information from provincial governors, army commanders, and fiscal agents. But not at all: he preferred to consult Strabo, Dionysius Periegetes, Stephanus Byzantinus, and especially Hierocles, an author of the sixth century. The result is an extraordinary mosaic of snippets, most of which have no relevance to the tenth century. In speaking of the province of the Thrakesians, i.e. western Asia Minor, Constantine tells us, for example, that its population consists of 'Lydians, Maeonians, Carians, and Ionians; and the Ionians are those who inhabit Miletus and Ephesus, while those who live inland are the Sardians, Lydians, Maeonians, Carians, and the inhabitants of the Lesser Phrygia.'[1] The next province, that of Opsikion, i.e. north-west Asia Minor, is inhabited by 'Bithynians, Mysians, Phrygians, Dardanians, and Trojans.'[2] This information is given in the present tense. The fifteenth province in Constantine's enumeration is Cyprus, although it did not belong to the Empire at the time and had not, in fact, belonged to it for nearly 300 years. Yet he begins his account of the island by saying that Cyprus is governed by a *consularis*, i.e. a senator, and contains thirteen cities which he duly enumerates, starting with Constantia.[3] This information is borrowed directly from Hierocles who, as I have said, wrote in the sixth century. Of Sicily, which in Constantine's time was under the Arabs, he says: 'It is now held under the authority of Constantinople, for the Emperor of Constantinople rules the sea as far as the Pillars of Hercules.' This statement does not appear to be borrowed from any known source and may, therefore, represent what ought, ideally, to have been the case, even if Byzantine ships had not been in sight of Gibraltar since the early eighth century. The truth, of course, was well known to Constantine, who adds, without sensing the contradiction, that all the towns of Sicily are held by the godless Saracens, 'and only Calabria, which is opposite, is in Christian hands'.[4]

The difficulties which the historian has to overcome in dealing with a text like the *De thematibus* are all too obvious: he has to sift out all the antiquarian passages before he obtains

[1] Ibid., p. 68.　　[2] Ibid., p. 69.　　[3] Ibid., p. 80.　　[4] Ibid., pp. 94 ff.

a residue that may be applicable to the tenth century. In so doing he will discover that the documentation on which Constantine drew is, to a large extent, still available to us, and that his knowledge of the 'dark centuries'—the seventh and the eighth—was no less sketchy than ours. This is the historian's task. For my part, I should like to emphasize a different point: it is that Constantine, even in a work as factual as the *De thematibus*, conveys the impression that he is an unwilling participant in the affairs of the tenth century, while his real world, the one he is at home in, belongs to a bygone and happier age. The very institution of the themes is somehow distasteful to him: he sees them as inglorious little bits of territory into which the diminished Empire of the Romans was carved up, and this at a time when the emperors had forgotten 'their ancestral Latin tongue',[1] and so designated them by the vulgar Greek term *themata*. No decent historical author uses such a word; there were no themes in the days of Julius Caesar, of the admirable Augustus, of the famous Trajan, of Constantine the Great and Theodosius who embraced the true religion. Does Strabo, does Menippus, does Scylax of Caryanda, does Pausanias mention the Armeniac theme?[2] No, gentle reader, this is but a new-fangled barbarism.

The examples I have quoted are neither unrepresentative nor tendentious; and if they express a general truth about Byzantine letters, we should try, in conclusion, to define it.

We have found that Byzantine literary works tend to be divorced from the realities of their own time while remaining anchored in an ideal past. This judgement is reinforced by the lack of interest which the Byzantines themselves showed in their own authors: biographical details and dates are seldom supplied.[3] It is also a matter of common experience that an anonymous Byzantine text of a literary character is very difficult, sometimes impossible, to date: witness the case of the *Philopatris* which, after centuries of scholarly discussion, has come to rest in the last quarter of the tenth century—assuming this date to be right. To put it more simply, Byzantine literature was static, locked within the bounds of its inherited

---

[1] Studi e Testi, 160, p. 60.   [2] Ibid., p. 63.
[3] Cf. Westerink, *Nicétas Magistros*, pp. 11 f.

conventions. It was also, on the highbrow level, universal in the sense that it did not exhibit any local variations.

It is interesting to observe that a similar judgement has been expressed in a different context, that of medieval Russian literature, whose Byzantine character is very pronounced. One of the best connoisseurs of this literature, V. M. Istrin, has put it this way:

The literature of the eleventh to the thirteenth century is marked by a negative quality which consists in the absence of an idea content (*idejnost'*) . . . This absence should not be understood in the sense that the works of this period were mere literary exercises . . . Yet we cannot observe, first, that any specific idea was consistently put forward by Russian writers in a given century or, second, that an idea which arose at a given time was gradually altered and replaced by a new one . . . Such a development is unknown in the literature of the eleventh to the thirteenth centuries, and its works, no matter where and when they were produced, did not have that internal connection which would have obliged us to derive one work from a previous one, or one group of works from another.[1]

The dichotomy between literature and a changing reality is, I believe, one of the salient features of Byzantine culture. The business of everyday life was not considered a suitable subject for literary treatment. Many Byzantines travelled to strange lands, went on missions to Baghdad and Kiev, performed pilgrimages to Rome and Jerusalem, spent years in captivity among the Arabs, yet not one of them has recorded his experiences and observations. The only apparent exception —a personal account of a mission to the northern barbarians in the tenth century (I refer to the so-called *Toparcha Gothicus* fragments)—has recently been shown to be a nineteenth-century forgery.[2] I have no doubt that even Byzantine intellectuals exchanged stories of their adventures and did so in *dimotiki*, not in Attic Greek. But literature was something else. It resided on a higher level while, at the same time, serving the practical purpose of establishing a man's position within an exclusive professional caste. It was not meant to change

[1] *Očerk istorii drevnerusskoj literatury domoskovskogo perioda*, Petrograd, 1922, p. vi.

[2] See I. Ševčenko, 'The Date and Author of the So-called Fragments of Toparcha Gothicus', *Dumbarton Oaks Papers*, xxv, 1971, pp. 115 ff.

with the times, but rather to maintain a constant relation to its models. This is an attitude that survived in later Greek letters, certainly until the Revolution of 1821.[1]

Thus, Byzantine literature is both a dim and a distorting mirror. But, we may ask, is not some of the distortion of our own making? Is not the decoding of any past literature an interaction between text and reader? The texts, to use another metaphor, emit certain signals which, in our case, happen to be misleading. These signals are picked up by the readers, who often are, and indeed ought to be, classicists. They have been educated in those classics which we consider to be the best, while they have little familiarity with the authors of the Second Sophistic, the Cappadocian Fathers, and those late anthologies from which Byzantine authors drew most of their ancient tags. Always on the look-out for classical survivals or revivals, they inevitably fall into the very trap which Byzantine texts have set for them, and they see the chief significance of the Empire in its having transmitted to us the heritage of ancient Greek letters. Even the great historian Ernst Stein could say that Byzantium was 'l'Antiquité dans le moyen âge'.[2]

In reality Byzantium was something quite different and perhaps more interesting; and it is the discovery of its true self behind its antique mask that ought to occupy those of us who pursue this discipline.

[1] It would be instructive to trace the persistence of Byzantinism in Greek letters in the period 1453–1821. I am giving one example at random because it offers a perfect pendant to the attitude of Constantine Porphyrogenitus quoted in p. 14 n. 1 above. Martin Crusius, the Tübingen professor, wrote to Theodosios Zygomalas at Constantinople asking him for various items of historical information and for specimens of modern Greek (ἀνταιτούμενος δὲ χυδαίων λέξεων σαφήνειαν, ἐπιστολάς τε δημοτικὰς καὶ ἄλλα φιλομαθίας, ἀλλ' οὐ σπουδῆς). Zygomalas, who replied in 1581 in as elevated a style as he could manage, was clearly embarrassed by this request and referred contemptuously to the spoken tongue, 'which is a hodge-podge of many languages' (M. Crusius, *Turcograecia*, Basle, 1584, p. 75). Note, in particular, the contrast he makes between σπουδή (requiring classical Greek) and the inferior category of φιλομαθία, i.e. curiosity, which demanded the clarity of vulgar words. There are also some amusing instances of the same attitude in the Letters of Alexander Mavrokordato to which I drew attention in 'The Phanariots and the Byzantine Tradition', in *The Struggle for Greek Independence*, ed. R. Clogg, London, 1973, p. 52.

[2] 'Introduction à l'histoire et aux institutions byzantines', *Traditio*, vii, 1949/51, p. 96.

III

Discontinuity with the Classical Past in Byzantium

There exists a myth of Byzantium which also serves as a justification for the pursuit of Byzantine studies. This myth was largely created in the nineteenth century and still retains much of its potency. It represents Byzantium as a beacon of classical civilization shining in the barbarous gloom of the Middle Ages. The Byzantine Empire, we are assured, saw itself as the custodian of a priceless deposit of ancient culture, and more particularly of Greek culture, which it lovingly guarded century after century until forced by the advancing hordes of Asiatic Turks to convey it to Italy, thus causing the Renaissance in the West. This deposit, we are further told, was a perennial fount from which Byzantine authors and artists drew their inspiration. Thus, for examples, Charles Diehl: "Les chefs-d'oeuvre de la littérature grecque classique étaient la base de l'éducation publique; Homère était le livre de chevet de tous les écoliers et les femmes elles-mêmes prenaient à le lire un plaisir extrême. A l'Université de Constantinople les maîtres commentaient les écrivains grecs les plus illustres . . . Bien d'autres souvenirs évoquaient la gloire de l'antiquité grecque. Constantinople était pleine des chefs-d'oeuvre de l'art grec . . . et cet admirable musée rendait plus vivante encore aux yeux la grandeur de la tradi- tion hellénique".[1] Even the common folk of Byzantium, whether "de pure race hellénique" or Greek by adoption, allegedly retained in their consciousness a body of barely disguised lore and ritual that descended from the days of Greek paganism and which four centuries of Ottoman domination were powerless to obliterate. In short, Byzantium is portrayed both as conduit of the classical tradition to the West and as a bridge uniting ancient Greece to modern Greece.

Proponents of the myth do not deny the presence in the Byzantine amalgam of other elements, notably Christianity (itself happily penetrated by Hellenism) and the Roman tradition of governance and law. They are less ready to grant any creative role to the non-Greek peoples that undeniably dwelt in the Empire in considerable numbers, such as the Syrians, Egyptians, Jews, Armenians, Slavs and others, since the essence of Byzantium is seen to reside in its Greekness and its value as an object of study in the survival of that same Greekness, often threatened and obscured, yet always able to reassert itself.

This familiar and (to some) satisfying construction has not gone entirely un- challenged. I shall refrain from rehearsing here the various arguments that have been

---

1. *Les grands problèmes de l'histoire byzantine* (Paris, 1943), 8-9.

presented *pro* and *contra*, nor shall I attempt to summarize the present state of the controversy, much of which has ranged unprofitably over the same ground.[2] My purpose is merely to suggest some approaches that have not been sufficiently explored and to add a few random touches, but before doing so it will be necessary to set down certain distinctions.

The 'first concerns periodization. No one will deny that what we call the Early Byzantine or Late Roman world formed the direct continuation of antiquity. It was a world that was undergoing a profound transformation from within, yet remained attached to its own past for the simple reason that life went on pretty much as it had done before. This way of life came, however, to an abrupt and dramatic end in the course of the seventh century with the virtual disappearance of cities and a general shift to a rural or semi-rural existence. To the extent that antique civilization was based on the *polis*, Byzantium after the seventh century was necessarily something different. It was also different in the sense that there occurred simultaneously a widespread reshuffling of populations. Here we have the most striking and, perhaps, the most fundamental factors of discontinuity between antiquity and the Byzantine Middle Ages.

I do not wish to imply that the Byzantine Empire from the seventh century to the fifteenth remained bereft of towns. By slow degrees towns developed again and, if I am not mistaken, reached a peak in the eleventh and twelfth centuries. They were centres of economic activity with an artisanal and commercial class that was beginning to form a bourgeoisie. But they were quite unlike the cities of Late Antiquity with which they had no organic connection; furthermore, their ulterior progress was blocked by a concatenation of historical circumstances. This is not the place to evaluate the impact exerted by urban revival on the manifestations of Byzantine culture, but it is important to realize that the world of Michael Psellos differed in many respects from that of Photios, though not perhaps as markedly as the world of Photios stood apart from that of Procopius.

My second remark — I am now referring to medieval Byzantium — concerns a division of society into three cultural strata: a tiny intellectual élite, a larger public of relative literacy, and a huge mass of the illiterate amounting, at a rough guess, to over ninety-five per cent of the population. This division is not an arbitrary postulate invented for the convenience of historians. The few scores or hundreds of men who at any given time constituted the élite did form a closed caste. They had attended special schools where they had learnt ancient Greek grammar and rhetoric and, thus equipped, were qualified to serve in the *sekreta* of the imperial administration and the upper echelons of the Church. Their culture was impenetrable to a wider public because it was expressed in a dead language and presupposed a body of arcane

---

2. For a sampling of different opinions see R. Jenkins, *Byzantium and Byzantinism* (Lectures in Memory of Louise Taft Semple: Cincinnati, 1963); my own "Byzantinism and Romantic Hellenism", *JWarb*, 28 (1965), 24-43; R. Browning, *Greece — Ancient and Medieval* (Inaugural Lecture, University of London, Birkbeck College, 1966); D.M. Nicol, *Byzantium and Greece* (Inaugural Lecture, University of London, King's College, 1971).

knowledge. The humbler author, whether clerical or lay, who declared himself to be ἀμέτοχος τῆς θύραθεν σοφίας was, indeed, repeating a cliché but a true one none the less: he literally had no share of the ancient learning.

The almost unbroken, if at times rather tenuous, continuity of the intellectual élite, based on the survival of a particular kind of schooling, need not be doubted. Recent studies, in particular by P. Lemerle and L.G. Westerink, have also revealed many characteristics of this élite: its extremely small numbers, its essentially mandarin quality and the lack of any general interest aroused by its literary production. Grateful as we must always remain to the Byzantine intellectuals for having preserved the legacy of ancient Greek literature and philosophy, we must not forget that they have also done us a grave disservice. By expressing themselves in an artificial idiom and in a manner dictated by archaic conventions they have effectively obliterated the reality of Byzantine life. This is a topic I have discussed at greater length elsewhere;[3] a brief re-statement will suffice.

The reason why Byzantium so often appears to us in an antique guise is simply that it has been dressed in theatrical costume by its own learned authors. We are presented with a ritualized ballet in which the realm of the Romans (or, better still, of the Ausonians) is advancing or retreating amidst a troupe of Achaemenids, Babylonians, Scythians and Mysians. Historical personages are made to deliver gnomic utterances and rhetorical speeches of a kind that could never have been spoken. Of course, we all know that there were no Achaemenids in the Middle Ages and that, *pace* Constantine Porphyrogennetos, there were no Dardanians and Trojans living in the theme of Opsikion. We know, thanks to Romilly Jenkins, that Basil I, who was an illiterate Armenian, could not, upon mounting the throne, have quoted Demosthenes by saying, "We must have money: nothing that needs doing can be done without that".[4] But, no matter how alert we are, we are never quite sure where to draw the line: where affectation stops and truth begins.

There can be no doubt that behind the mock classical facade of Byzantium lay a reality that was very different. But why is this reality so elusive? Why does it require so much labour to recreate the manner in which the Byzantines went about their daily lives, and this in spite of the massive, but ill-digested and basically unhistorical compendium by Phaidon Koukoules?[5] I have already indicated one reason, namely that highbrow Byzantine authors (and these are the authors we most often read) have deliberately excluded all the detail and particularity of contemporary life. Another reason has to do with the nature of Byzantine representational art. Nearly all Byzantine painting that has come down to us is religious in content and is based on the faithful reproduction of iconographic formulas that can be traced back to the Early Christian period. It is worthy of note that in depicting such stereotyped

3. *Byzantine Literature as a Distorting Mirror* (Inaugural Lecture, University of Oxford, 1975).
4. "The Hellenistic Origins of Byzantine Literature", *DOP*, 17 (1963), 44.
5. *Byzantinon bios kai politismos* (6 vols., Athens, 1948-55).

DISCONTINUITY IN BYZANTIUM

compositions Byzantine artists carefully avoided any intrusion of contemporary costumes or settings: Christ, the apostles, the prophets always appear in antique garb and, whenever architectural backdrops are introduced, these, too, are drawn from the antique repertory. Only in the later Middle Ages do we find a few contemporary touches in religious iconography, but they are limited to subsidiary personages: Pontius Pilate and Cyrenius may occasionally appear in Byzantine court garb and the Roman soldiers who guard Christ's sepulchre may be arrayed in medieval helmets and coats of mail. By and large, however, it is erroneous to use Byzantine miniatures and frescoes as illustrations of Byzantine life: the Joshua Roll in the Vatican Library is a manuscript of the tenth century, but it does not portray Byzantine soldiers at that time. The same military costumes reappear on the so-called David plates of the seventh century and it is likely that their origin goes back to an even earlier period when the iconographic model was created.

The number of exceptions to the above rule is very·small indeed. The Madrid manuscript of Skylitzes, which is of Sicilian origin, is almost unique in showing, however summarily, little vignettes of Byzantine history whose originals, by definition, cannot antedate the events they portray.[6] For the rest, we have a series of imperial portraits and donor portraits that give us some idea of upper-class costume and are sufficient to dispel any notion that the Byzantines went about in himation, chlamys and sandals. It comes as a shock to see the humanist scholar Theodore Metochites decked out in caftan and huge turban like a Turkish pasha.

In order to reach, however sporadically, the level of everyday reality, we must address ourselves to lowbrow Byzantine literature and to texts that are documentary rather than literary, i.e. chronicles, saints' Lives that have not been retouched by 'metaphrasts', some legal and canonical enactments and a few, alas all too rare, down-to-earth writings like the *Strategikon* of Kekaumenos. The concrete detail that emerges from such an enquiry is often unexpected as a couple of examples will show. Since I have mentioned the turban of Theodore Metochites, I may be allowed a few more words on this oriental accoutrement. It is not perhaps remarkable that in the *Life* of St Theodore of Sykeon (the scene takes place on the gulf of Nicomedia) we should meet a cleric wearing a turban (*phakiolion*): the man was returning from the bath and probably wished to keep his head dry.[7] It is more interesting to note that in the so-called *Narratio de S. Sophia,* a popular text of the eighth or ninth century, we are told that when Justinian went out to inspect the construction of his cathedral, he wore a light turban (*soudarion amydron*) on his head.[8] I do not imagine that the historical Justinian ever covered his head in such fashion; yet a medieval Byzantine author evidently thought that this was suitable

6.   See now A. Grabar and M. Manoussacas, *L'illustration du manuscrit de Skylitzès de la Bibliothèque Nationale de Madrid* (Venice, 1979); and for the date, N.G. Wilson, "The Madrid Scylitzes", *Scrittura e Civiltà*, 2 (1978), 209-19.
7.   *Vie de Théodore de Sykéôn,* 157.54, ed. A.-J. Festugière, I (Brussels, 1970), 131.
8.   *Scriptores originum Constantinopolitanarum,* ed. Th. Preger, I (Leipzig, 1901), 85.

headgear for an emperor in casual attire. In the same text[9] there is a legendary story about the architect of St Sophia, mistakenly called Ignatius, who is left to starve on top of Justinian's monumental pillar. What then does he do? He cuts to ribbons his outer garment, his combination hose-cum-shirt (*hypokamisobrakion*), his cummerbund (*sphiktourion*) and his turban (*phakiolion*), ties them together, and hauls up a stout rope which his wife had brought in the night. A visual illustration of a turban worn by an official is provided by the portrait of the *proximos* John in the Adrianople Gospels of 1007, who, though an Armenian, is surely represented in Byzantine costume.[10]

My second example concerns the use of prayer rugs which are familiar to us in the Moslem world, but which we do not normally associate with Orthodox observance. Yet we read in the *Life* of Theophanes Confessor[11] that the future chronicler, when travelling in the country, slept on his prayer rug (τάπη τι ἐπευκτικῷ προσανεκλίθη) — this in about the year 780. In the *Life* of St Andrew the Fool, which I am inclined to date to ca. A.D. 700, we find that the saintly young man Epiphanios would get out of his bed and sleep on his prayer rug which was on the floor — the word is *epeuchion* which some manuscripts paraphrase by *tapes*.[12] The same term reappears in the Euchologion.[13] Furthermore, the rich Peloponnesian widow Danielis, when she visited the court of Basil I, took the interior measurements of the New Church in the palace and caused to be made big carpets, τοὺς παρ᾽ ἡμῖν ἀπὸ τῆς εὐχῆς τὸ ἐπώνυμον φέροντας — "called among us by the name of prayer", i.e., once again *epeuchia*, — whereby the entire floor of the church was to be covered.[14] In other words, the New Church and surely other churches, too, were carpeted like mosques. This is an indication that archaeologists, I believe, have not taken into account.

In quoting these examples I was not trying to prove that the Byzantines dressed and behaved like Arabs. My intention was merely to indicate the kind of detail that we can occasionally extract from our sources. We are still a long way from being able to visualize Byzantine life as it was actually lived and, in order to do so, we shall have to rely on both archaeological and written evidence. It is safe, however, to predict that this picture, as it is gradually built up, will differ very sharply from that of Graeco-Roman life which we know so much better.

If lowbrow Byzantine literature brings us into closer contact with reality than the stilted compositions of the educated élite, it also, I believe, gives us a much clearer conception of the average Byzantine's intellectual horizons. Chronicles, Lives of saints, stories about anchorites, various florilegia of useful sayings, oracles

9. *Ibid.*, II (1907), 285.
10. Reproduced, e.g., by N. Adontz, *Études arméno-byzantines* (Lisbon, 1965), facing p.162.
11. *Methodii Vita S. Theophanis Confessoris*, 17, ed. V.V. Latyšev, *Mém. de l'Acad. des Sciences de Russie*, VIIIe sér., Cl. hist. – philol., 13/4 (Petrograd, 1918), 12.
12. PG, 111, col. 705A.
13. J. Goar, *Euchologion sive rituale graecorum* (Paris, 1647), 832.
14. Theophanes Continuatus, *Chronographia*, ed. I. Bekker (Bonn, 1838), 319.

— that was the kind of literature that really circulated next, of course, to patristic, liturgical and devotional books. To dismiss this literature as monkish, as if its readership was confined to monks, while laymen read secular literature, shows a complete ignorance of the situation. Of course, monks read it, but everyone else who was capable of reading read it, too, and, for the most part, read nothing else — barring again the Bible and the Fathers. I should like, therefore, to insist on the view that the conceptual world of Byzantium can most fully be appreciated only on the basis of lowbrow literature.

This literature, too, was very traditional and one looks in vain for the propagation in it of any new ideas. People did not read books for ideas, but for edification and information. What interests us, however, in the present context is that lowbrow Byzantine literature stands at several removes from the classical tradition, and what classical lore it contains has been slanted in the Roman rather than in the Greek direction. Take the case of Kekaumenos who, for a military man, was exceptionally well read. In fact, he explicitly recommends the reading of books and was rich enough to own a few. We can tell at once that he knew best the Bible which he quotes more than a hundred times. He was also acquainted with Gregory of Nazianzus, John of Damascus and John Cassian (naturally in a Greek translation). Apart from works on military strategy and probably a number of florilegia, the only secular author he cites is Dio Cassius. He refers to Augustus, Hannibal, the younger Scipio and Trajan, but not to a single figure or event of Greek history, not even Alexander.

I do not wish to insist on this one example, nor is there need to do so, since we know very well what the average Byzantine thought about his place in history and the tradition to which he belonged.[15] To find this out, we have only to open a universal chronicle — Malalas or George Synkellos or George the Monk or Symeon the Logothete — it does not matter which, since they all tell substantially the same story. In this story, which I do not propose to summarize here, the hellenic tradition plays a very minor part. The Olympian gods are tacked on to Nimrod in chapter 10 of Genesis and — what is especially interesting — they lose all connection with Greece. Kronos is represented as king of Assyria and Persia, while his son Zeus, also called Pikos, is the ruler of Italy. Ares is an Assyrian, Perseus a Persian, while Hermes and Hephaistos are associated with Egypt. The Trojan War, if it appears at all, is seen not through the eyes of Homer, but through the romanticized version of Dictys Cretensis. Of classical Greece, the Persian and Peloponnesian Wars, not a word is said. Alexander is, of course, given some prominence, but he is represented as half-Egyptian, being the son of the magician Nectanebo, and his most significant deeds are his visit to Jerusalem, where he worshipped the true God, and his journey to India, where he discovered the virtuous Brahmans. The Hellenistic kings are dismissed in a few pages and shown in a very unfavourable light, since they were

15. I have discussed this at greater length in *Byzantium: The Empire of New Rome* (London, 1980), 189 ff; see now also E.M. Jeffreys, "The Attitudes of Byzantine Chroniclers towards Ancient History", *Byzantion*, 49 (1979), 199-238.

responsible for the second and third sack of Jerusalem, and for setting up in the Temple "the abomination of Desolation". This is as much as we are told of Greek history.

Not only has the hellenic tradition been limited in the chronicles; it has also been deliberately downgraded. We are repeatedly informed that the Hellenes were merely plagiarizers in the domain of arts and sciences. Geometry was invented by the Egyptians, astrology by the Chaldaeans and the Babylonians, magic and sorcery by the Persians, the art of writing by the Phoenicians. Moses, in particular, was the teacher of all wise men and, since he lived well before the Trojan War, indeed before the time of Zeus, his priority as a cosmologist could not be questioned. As for the Greek physicians, they cribbed their writings from Solomon's lost works on natural science. Even in the sphere of language and literature the Greeks are put in their place. Their loquacity, we are told, is surpassed by the conciseness of the Persians whose language is rich in proverbs and riddles. The Ishmaelites, who know nothing of Greek culture, are nevertheless very clever and can discern truth from falsehood. As for Latin, those who know that tongue affirm that it is more forceful than Greek and capable of profounder and more concise formulations. Besides, it was said on good authority that the Romans, too, had their poets, their prose writers and their orators. This downgrading of all things Greek had, of course, a long history behind it, and can be traced through Theodoret to the Jewish apologists, in particular Josephus who was much read in Byzantium. What interests us here is that it was retained and given considerable prominence in the chronicles.

The average Byzantine, then, did not feel any kinship with the ancient Greeks. He was more conscious of the history of Rome, especially from Augustus onwards, since that was the history of his own Empire. But, in a deeper sense, he was concerned not with this or that nation, but with the fate of the Chosen People, i.e. first the Jews and then the Christians. The nodal points of his historical scheme were the Creation, the Flood, Abraham, Moses, the Incarnation of Christ.

If it were true that in the later Middle Ages the Byzantine public at large became more conscious of its Greek origins — a view expressed in most textbooks —, it would be reasonable to look for some indication of this in the universal chronicles. I should like, therefore, to glance briefly at the *Biblion Historikon* ascribed to Dorotheos of Monemvasia. Compiled in the latter part of the sixteenth century, it went through a great number of printed editions until about 1800. Its importance in shaping the consciousness of the Greek people is not in doubt. It was also, to all intents and purposes, the only book of history that was read at the time by a sizeable proportion of the Greeks. It should be understood that the *Biblion Historikon* is not simply a carbon copy of a Byzantine chronicle: some material has been eliminated and a great deal has been added. The new elements, such as the detailed description of the pilgrimage sites of Palestine, the account of the marvels invented by the emperor Leo the Wise, the excursus on the origin of the Turks, on the conquest of the Morea by the Franks and the history of Venice — all of these were clearly of interest to the public. What, then, do we find about ancient Greece?

DISCONTINUITY IN BYZANTIUM

Surprisingly enough, the *Biblion Historikon* has even less to say on this topic than the ninth-century chronicle by George the Monk. The story of the Olympian gods has been excised and, in fact, nothing whatever is said about the Greeks until we reach the establishment of the Macedonian kingdom. At this point we are informed in passing that Philip was contemporary with the teachers and poets of the Hellenes, namely Sophocles, Heracleitus, Euripides, Herodotus, Socrates, the great Pythagoras, Isocrates and Demosthenes. Alexander remains, however, the son of the Egyptian Nectanebo. There are a few pages about the Ptolemies, largely concerned with the translation of the Septuagint, and then, unexpectedly, the Trojan War is introduced. It has been placed at this juncture because it explains the beginnings of Rome as represented by Aeneas. The early history of Rome is briefly told, but once we reach Augustus, the narrative becomes more leisurely and proceeds without break. If we look at the chronological tables contained in the book, we find that the kings of Rome are numbered consecutively from Romulus to Constantine, and the emperors of Constantinople from Constantine to the Sultan Murat (in the edition of 1631). The *Biblion Historikon* does reflect a definite scheme of history, but it is a scheme in which ancient Greece plays practically no part.

When we move to the lowest stratum of Byzantine culture, that of the illiterate folk, we find ourselves with little to say. The field has been pre-empted by folklorists whose methods are a puzzle to the historian. It is not, of course, inconceivable that certain remnants of pagan beliefs and practices should in places have survived the conversion of the common people to Christianity and lived on for centuries, transformed and misunderstood, but to be convinced of the existence of such continuity, we need a chain of evidence that is simply not there. The assumption that Christian saints have stepped into the shoes of pagan gods, that St Demetrios has somehow replaced Demeter, that Elijah is Helios in disguise, and St Tychon Bacchus, is no longer as widely held today as it was at the turn of the century. The Bollandist fathers, who take their hagiography seriously, have helped to dispel some of these fantasies. We no longer believe that the festival of the Virgin Mary on Tenos, commemorating a miracle that occurred in 1821, has anything to do with Apollo on Delos;[16] and we are frankly incredulous when Sir William Ramsay informs us that Helios with his chariot has been turned into St George at Konya, merely on the evidence of his Turkish name Araba Yorgi, i.e. George of the cart.[17] For the rest, we have been offered a rag-bag of miscellaneous oddments mixed with a good deal of wishful thinking, such as the alleged cult of Aristotle at Stagira as reported by Sir John Mandeville (who never went to the East), the equally dubious cult of Plato at

16. See H. Delehaye in *AnalBoll*, 29 (1910), 463.
17. *The Cities of St Paul* (London, 1907), 378.
18. Probably to be connected with the representation of the pagan "philosophers". The same may apply to St Plato at Konya, on whom our information is very defective. See N.A. Bees, "Darstellungen altheidnischer Denker und Autoren in der Kirchenmalerei der Griechen", *BNJ*, 4 (1923), 120-1, 125.

Konya, the painting of the "prophet Achilles", said to have been in a church of the Troad in the thirteenth century,[18] and the representation of the pagan "philosophers" who prophesy the advent of Christ. As we probe each of these items, the evidence of continuity melts away. Take the case of the "philosophers" who appear in a number of late church decorations, mostly post-Byzantine.[19] They are arrayed in regal vestments of medieval cut, wear crowns or even turbans, and hold scrolls on which their respective prophecies are inscribed. It does not greatly matter in the present context when and where this iconographic scheme was first devised, but it is worth noting that it forms the illustration or pictorial equivalent of a theme of early Byzantine religious propaganda that circulated in tracts entitled "Oracles of the Pagan Gods", "Prophecies of the Seven Sages" and the like. The intention was to show that just as the Hebrew prophets had foretold the Incarnation of Christ, so a similar, if dimmer revelation had been granted to certain pagan sages and sibyls. It was also alleged that ancient inscriptions had been found in the ruins of temples in which Apollo or some other god predicted the triumph of Christianity or the Immaculate Conception. The earliest collection of such spurious oracles appears to have been made in the reign of the Emperor Zeno (474-91) and, as time went on, they became progressively debased. Plato was made to prophesy, "Christ will be born of the Virgin Mary, and I believe in Him"; while the "philosopher" Aristophanes proclaimed, "He shall give unto the people the baptism of repentance, and blessed is he who shall hear Him". These crude fabrications became the fare of the lowbrow Byzantine public for whom the name of Aristophanes was interchangeable with that of Pythagoras or Plutarch or even that of some entirely fictitious figure like Odoneristos or Dialed. Were not all of them famous pagans? Far from showing a survival of classical antiquity in the consciousness of the popular masses, the representation of the "philosophers" reveals the persistence of an apocryphal
† Christian tradition and the extent to which antiquity had lost all content among the half-educated.

I shall not dwell here on the modern Greek folk song. Even if some *tragoudia* are hypothetically traceable to the Middle Ages, they have no relevance to the subject under discussion.[20] Those interested in Byzantine popular culture would be better advised to investigate the late medieval magical texts that have been published in the *Catalogus codicum astrologorum graecorum*, in A. Delatte's *Anecdota atheniensia* and elsewhere. Magic was part and parcel of Byzantine life; it was also

19. There is an extensive bibliography on this topic. To the basic references given by R. Browning, *Greece – Ancient and Medieval*, n.45, add: C. Mango, "A Forged Inscription of the year 781", *ZVI*, 8/1 (1963), 205-7; I. Dujčev, "Die Begleitinschriften der Abbildungen heidnischer Denker und Schriftsteller in Bačkovo und Arbanasi", *JÖBG*, 16 (1967), 203-9; G. Nandriş, *Christian Humanism in the Neo-Byzantine Mural-Painting of Eastern Europe* (Wiesbaden, 1970). The interpretations advanced by some scholars are entirely unwarranted.
20. Needless to say, popular songs have also been viewed in the light of classical survival. So e.g. S. Kyriakidis, *Hai historikai archai tes demodous neoellenikes poieseos* (Thessalonike, 1934).

inherently conservative. As has been pointed out by others there is a striking similarity between these grubby documents and magical papyri of a thousand years earlier. The lore they contain — the demonology and angelology, the prayers and invocations — seems, however, to owe much more to the Orient than to ancient Greece.

In attempting to make generalizations about a world as complex as that of Byzantium, we must use our historical judgment in regarding one strand more characteristic and influential than another. The enthusiasm of Psellos for Platonic speculation, the laudatory meaning of the word "Hellene" in the vocabulary of Anna Komnene, the admiration of ancient ruins by Theodore Doukas Laskaris — these and other oft-quoted examples are surely deserving of attention. They express attitudes that must have been shared by a number of people. But how great a number? When Plethon formulated his bizarre theories about regeneration through paganism, did he merely turn on the tap of perennial hellenism that was available to him because he was a Greek living in the Peloponnese? And what segment of public opinion did he represent?

Evidence that will help us to answer such questions is not entirely lacking. We can ascertain the number of manuscript copies in which various works are preserved. We can trace the influence of one author on another. We have some information about literary salons in the Comnene age. More importantly, we know what works were deemed worthy of translation — from Greek into Slavonic and, in the late Byzantine period, from highbrow Greek into demotic Greek. It is clear that the circulation of ideas was not the same in all periods of Byzantine history. Under the early Byzantine Empire education had not yet become the prerogative of a tiny clique: an author relatively as uncultivated as Cosmas Indicopleustes had access to the cosmological doctrines propounded by the academics of Alexandria. It is my impression that, after a long lull, ideas began to circulate once again, but not very widely, in the eleventh century when the literate public expanded somewhat as a result of urban revival. Many opuscules of Michael Psellos, like his *De omnifaria doctrina,* were *oeuvres de vulgarisation* addressed, in the first instance, to the court aristocracy. The philosophical teaching of Italos was publicly condemned in the *Synodikon,* whether his judges had any clear understanding of it or not.

Whatever allowance we make for such fluctuations, I persist in the belief that the true culture of Byzantium, i.e. the body of received doctrine and opinion that defined the outlook of a representative segment of the Byzantine public and filtered down to the ordinary folk was dominated, not by classical antiquity as we understand it, but by a construct of the Christian and Jewish apologists built up in the first five or six centuries A.D. This body of doctrine was very consistently worked out and its ingredients were mostly biblical with an admixture from other sources, both classical and oriental, but always subordinated to the teaching of the Bible. By giving a universal currency to this view of the world, Byzantium achieved a distinctive place in the history of thought.

IV

DAILY LIFE IN BYZANTIUM

Anyone who has read the historical novels of Robert Graves — *I Claudius* and *Claudius the God*, on the one hand, and *Count Belisarius*, on the other — may have observed that whereas the two Roman books create, a vivid illusion of contemporary life, the Byzantine one fails to do so: it tells an exciting story, but its atmosphere, its sense of 'being there' is decidedly thin. This disparity is not accidental. We know infinitely more about daily life in Imperial Rome in the 1st and 2nd centuries A. D. than in any period of Byzantine history. I may add that we know considerably more about Byzantine life from the 4th to the mid-7th century than about the four hundred years that followed; it is only in the mid-11th that the darkness begins to be somewhat dispelled.

It is useful to remember that our minute knowledge of Roman life is largely based on three categories of evidence: 1. A literature that, whatever its moralistic or satirical exaggerations, does provide a vivid reflection of contemporary usages; 2. Archaeology; and 3. Epigraphy. All three categories are sadly deficient for the Byzantine period; and while we may hope to fill out eventually our archaeological information, we have no prospect of either changing the character of Byzantine literature or of supplying an epigraphic documentation that largely peters out after the 6th century. To be sure, we do have many data at our disposal. Byzantine texts belonging to various genres — histories and chronicles, hagiography, epistolography, homiletics, civil and ecclesiastical law, etc. — provide nuggets of information that can be built up into a vast, if very incomplete mosaic. All scholars who have written on Byzantine civilization have, to a greater or lesser extent, collected such fragmentary evidence, and a large dossier of it exists in the six-volume work of Phaidon Koukoules[1]. I suppose we must be grateful for his life-long endeavours, but the faults of his method are so glaring that gratitude often gives way to irritation. Obsessed as he was by the notion of the continuity of hellenism, he jumbled together snippets of information covering fifteen centuries and more, without any regard for

---

[1] Βυζαντινῶν βίος καί πολιτισμός. Athens 1948—55.

historical development. Chariton of Aphrodisias, who lived before the Antonines, was in his eyes as much of a witness to the daily activities of οἱ βυζαντινοὶ ἡμῶν πρόγονοι as John Chrysostom or Leontios Machairas. The work of Koukoules is, unfortunately, *entièrement à reprendre*. The few probes I have made in some significant areas have convinced me that the history of Byzantine usages cannot be treated as an undifferentiated continuum and that, in particular, we must postulate a dramatic break between the life-style of Late Antiquity and that of the Byzantine Middle Ages.

In this paper I shall confine myself to two topics that are mutually related, namely public bathing and public entertainment. I have chosen them because in Antiquity they were considered as being perhaps the most distinctive characteristics of an urban, as distinct from a rural life. In speaking of baths, I shall be concerned not with personal hygiene as such, but with that peculiar institution of Graeco-Roman civilization, the *thermae* as centres of relaxation, social intercourse and even culture. This phenomenon has often been described in the past[2], and there is no need to do so again. It is enough to remember that while the institution was rooted in the Greek ideal of physical fitness, it was given a universal currency in the Early Empire. Attendance at the baths became a necessary part of everyday life, almost a ritual. People went there not merely to exercise and enjoy the comfort of warm water, but to meet their friends, to transact business, to picnic, to hear literary declamations, to display their finery as well as for other, less respectable purposes. Furthermore, the baths, with their elaborate architecture and lavish decoration, provided an elegant setting for social activity: some of them could be described as museums of art.

There is ample evidence, both literary and archaeological, that the public baths retained this function (except perhaps for their athletic use) in the cities of the Early Byzantine Empire down to about the 6th or 7th century. It is enough to recall here, amidst a mass of other material, the series of epigrams in the Palatine Anthology (IX. 606—40). Nor is there any reason to believe that the occasional denunciations on the part of Church Fathers and holy monks had the least effect on changing an institution that was so deeply rooted and universally enjoyed, the more so as members of the clergy attended the baths as regularly as any other

---

[2] E. g. by J. CARCOPINO, Daily Life in Ancient Rome, ed. H. T. ROWELL. London 1941, 254 ff.; J. P. V. D. BALSDON, Life and Leisure in Ancient Rome. London 1969, 27 ff.; R. GINOUVÈS, Balaneutikè. Paris 1962.

segment of urban society[3]. We have all heard about the bishop who bathed
twice a day because, he said, he could not do so three times a day[4]. It is
perhaps less well known that public baths began to be decorated with
subjects of Christian iconography, like the story of the miraculous punishment of the Arian Olympius[5]. And since the followers of St. John Chrysostom celebrated Easter service and performed baptisms in one of the
biggest baths of Constantinople (in 404)[6], it follows that they could not
have considered such a venue to be unsuitable by reason of immoral
associations.

The question I should now like to ask is whether the bath-centred life
of Late Antiquity survived into the Middle Ages, and the only place where
we can pursue such an enquiry is Constantinople. In spite of the paucity of
archaeological information, there can be no doubt that in the first three
centuries of its existence Constantinople had a considerable number of
public baths, a few of which should be visualized on a scale not much
inferior to those of Diocletian and Constantine in Rome. The *Notitia urbis
Constantinopolitanae* lists eight *thermae* (plus a ninth in the 14th Region),
most of which were built by imperial initiative. There is reason to believe
that the *Constantianae*, begun in 345 and not completed until 427[7], were
particularly spacious and splendid. They formed the subject of an *ekphrasis*
by the grammarian Helladius which, unfortunately, is lost[8]. The *Constanti-
nianae* appear to have been still in existence in the middle of the 8th
century, by which time, however, the many wonderful statues that had
once decorated them had disappeared (διέπεσαν)[9], except those of Perseus
and Andromeda[10] which, by the 10th century, had migrated to the Great
Palace[11]. I know of no reference to these baths after the 8th century.
Another important establishment, the baths of Dagistheus, begun by the
emperor Anastasius and completed by Justinian in 528[12], were certainly
abandoned by the early 9th century, when we find a monk living in their

---

[3] "Our fathers never washed their faces, ἡμεῖς δὲ καὶ τὰ λουτρὰ τὰ δημόσια ἀνοίγομεν" —
so complains a monk in Moschus, Pratum, ch. 168, *PG* 87/3, 3036 A.

[4] Socrates, Hist. eccl. VI 22, 4; Sozomen, Hist. eccl. VIII 1, 11.

[5] Theodoros Anagnostes, Kirchengeschichte, ed. G. C. HANSEN, Berlin 1971, 131—33.

[6] Palladius, Dialogus 9 (= 56 COLEMAN—NORTON); Socrates VI 18; Sozomen
VIII 21, 3.

[7] Chron. Pasch. 534. 580—81 Bonn.

[8] Suidas s. v. Ἑλλάδιος.

[9] Script. orig. Cp. I 67 PREGER.

[10] Ibid. 72.

[11] Ibid. II 195.

[12] Malalas 435 Bonn; Chron. Pasch. 618.

IV

340

cavernous hypocaust[13]. The 10th-century author of the *Patria* knows nothing of these baths, while preserving a vague tradition concerning a τρίκλινος παμμεγεθέστατος which was no longer in existence at the time of his writing[14]. We are much better informed concerning the famous baths of Zeuxippus, parts of which were excavated in 1927—8. This μέγιστον λουτρόν, decorated with close to a hundred statues[15], burnt down in 532 and rebuilt by Justinian, was still functioning in 713, when the emperor Philippicus bathed in it[16], but some time thereafter it was transformed into a barracks and a prison called Numera and remained as such until the 13th century[17]. To the author of the *Patria* the baths of Zeuxippus were no more than a memory: they had once been a marvellous structure, their water and air had been magically heated by a glass lamp, but certain senseless people came along and destroyed them. Who were these senseless people? One redactor suggested it was Julian the Apostate who begrudged to the Christians the enjoyment of such a splendid amenity[18].

Our evidence from Constantinople indicates, therefore, that the great public baths of the Early Byzantine period stopped functioning during the dark centuries. Some of them were put to different use, others probably stood as ruins, such as the enigmatic Kaminia which, it was said, was so vast that 2,000 people had once bathed there each day, and had been allegedly fired with naphtha[19]. What had been a normal component of everyday life became a memory fraught with magic. And when the emperors of the 9th century — in particular Basil I — undertook a programme of urban renewal, they did not, like their predecessors of the 4th, 5th and 6th centuries, build any baths or, for that matter, any other civic amenities, except churches, monasteries and hospices. To this trend there is one exception. While the tradition of luxurious bathing disappeared among the people at large, it was deliberately retained at the imperial court. The Great Palace had several baths, one of which, described as "the most beautiful, the biggest and the best lit", was built by Basil I.[20] I assume it was not the same as "the great bath of the Oikonomion", said to have been

---

[13] Pseudo-John Damascene, Epist. ad Theophilum, *PG* 95, 369 A. Cf. Genesius 14—15 Bonn.

[14] Script. orig. Cp. II 232.

[15] Anth. Pal. II.

[16] Theophanes 383 DE BOOR. Note that a painted portrait of Philippicus was set up in the bath: Script. orig. Cp. I 71.

[17] The relevant texts may be found in my "Brazen House", Copenhagen 1959, 37 ff.

[18] Script. orig. Cp. II 168 and apparatus.

[19] Ibid. II 136.

[20] Theoph. Cont. 336 Bonn.

constructed by Constantine the Great, which was decorated with statues
(ἔνζωδον δὲ ὑπῆρχεν), had seven ἐνθῆκαι (whatever that may mean), twelve
stoas and a big swimming pool. The latter, we are told on not very good
authority, continued to be heated until the reign of Nicephorus Phocas, but
was demolished by John I Tzimiskes[21]. Another "great bath", situated in
the palace of Marina and described as "the wonder of our State", was built
by Leo VI and restored by Constantine VII.[22]

I do not wish to imply by the above remarks that no public baths
remained in medieval Constantinople and that the people went unwashed.
Since few individuals had bathing facilities at home (including so aristocratic a personage as the father of Theophano, the future wife of Leo VI)[23],
they had, perforce, to make use of public establishments of one kind or
another. The frequency of ablutions may have declined since, in the 12th
century, a weekly visit to the baths was considered amply sufficient[24]. In
the capital, I am sure, it was possible to bathe in reasonable comfort; much
less so in the provinces[25]. The fact remains, however, that a peculiar
feature of antique urban life, that vie aux bains which was the focus of
civilized existence, had faded away[26].

Let us now consider public entertainment. I do not have to demonstrate here that, broadly speaking, three types of amusement were available in
the Early Byzantine period: the mime and the pantomime that took place
in theatres; wild animal fights that were given in amphitheatres (κυνήγια);
and chariot races that were held in hippodromes. I shall not concern myself
with wild animal fights which do not seem to have ever been popular in the
eastern part of the Empire (just as amphitheatres were uncommon there)
and which, in any case, were abandoned in the course of the 6th century[27].
The vitality of the theatre in Justinian's age (and somewhat later) is, on
the other hand, amply attested, even in hagiographic texts. John Moschus
has two stories about mimes, one about Babylas of Tarsus and his two girl-

---

[21] Script. orig. Cp. II 145.

[22] Theoph. Cont. 460—61.

[23] Vita Theophanous, ed. KURTZ (BHG 1794), 3.

[24] Poèmes prodromiques, ed. HESSELING and PERNOT, 52.

[25] See texts collected by KOUKOULES, Θεσσαλονίκης Εὐσταθίου τὰ λαογραφικά, I. Athens
1950, 157—65.

[26] It may be objected that in the Life of St. Andrew the Fool, PG 111, 764D, two
young men are represented as sitting in a public bath and watching an actress walk by. If
this text were of the 9th or 10th century, the objection would be valid. I hope to show
elsewhere, however, that it should be dated to the late 7th.

[27] See A. CAMERON, Porphyrius the Charioteer. Oxford 1973, 228—30.

342

friends (actresses ?), Komito and Nikosa, who embraced the monastic life[28], the other about Gaianos of Heliopolis who ridiculed the Virgin Mary on the stage, in the presence of a great crowd (ἐπὶ τοσούτου δήμου) and was suitably punished for so doing[29]. Mimes played in the theatre of Emesa in the mid-6th century[30], and, at about the same time, an aristocratic young couple from Antioch who 'went underground' for religious reasons, re-appeared at Amida, the husband disguised as a mime, the wife as an actress (πόρνη)[31]. The prohibition, addressed especially to actors and actresses, of donning monastic costume[32] must also refer to the mime. Pantomime dancers enjoyed at the time an even greater popularity that is extensively documented in the chronicles, the Anthology and other sources. The natural calamities that befell Edessa in the late 5th and early 6th centuries were attributed by the pious to the performances given there by the pantomime Trimerius[33].

The question has often been posed whether (or to what extent) the theatre survived in the Byzantine Middle Ages. Alas, the discussions of this topic have been marred by the wildest fantasies; and while we may easily forgive Constantine Sathas for his uncritical compilation, it is harder to feel indulgent towards Venetia Cottas and especially Albert Vogt. Much of the confusion has been caused by the word θέατρον itself, which in Byzantine texts has a wide range of meanings. It can denote the hippodrome, any kind of spectacle (often figuratively) or an audience[34], but it hardly ever and possibly never (except in the Early period) means a theatre. To take but one example, when Photius, in speaking of the split between Sergius and Baanes in the Paulician party, says ἡ στάσις αὐτοῦ δραματουργεῖται δημοσίῳ θεάτρῳ[35], he surely does not mean that "les théâtres s'empressèrent de mettre en scène la discorde des deux chefs"[36] — merely that they made a public spectacle of themselves. Elsewhere the precise meaning of θέατρον cannot be determined from the context. When, for example, we are told

---

[28] Pratum, ch. 32, *PG* 87/3, 2880—81.

[29] Ibid., ch. 47, 2901.

[30] Das Leben des hl. Narren Symeon von Leontios von Neapolis, ed. L. RYDÉN. Upsala 1963, 150.

[31] John of Ephesus, Lives of the Eastern Saints, ch. 52, *PO* 19, 164ff.

[32] Justinian, Nov. 123, 44 (A. D. 546).

[33] The Chronicle of Joshua the Stylite, transl. WRIGHT, 18ff.

[34] See H. HUNGER, Die hochsprachliche profane Literatur der Byzantiner I. Munich 1978, 210—11.

[35] Contra Manichaeos, I 22, *PG* 102, 73 B.

[36] Le théâtre à Byzance. *Rev. des quest. hist.* 115 (1931) 288. It is unfortunate that VOGT'S preposterous views were accepted by G. LA PIANA, The Byzantine Theater. *Speculum* 11 (1936) 189.

that St. Evaristus, who was born in 819 in Galatia, avoided in his youth
παιδιᾶς δὲ καὶ τῶν ἄλλων τῶν ἐν σκηνῇ καὶ θεάτροις ὅσα τοῖς νέοις ἀλογίστως
σπουδάζεται[37], we can scarcely guess whether this refers to rustic spectacles
or is simply a rhetorical flourish. And what exactly does Psellus have in
mind when he writes that, as a monk, he is obliged μή εἰς θέατρον παρακύψαι,
μὴ ἰδεῖν κυνηγέσιον[38]? Is he referring to the Hippodrome of Constantinople?
Still, the question remains: not that of the survival of the 'legitimate
theatre', since no such thing existed in the Early Byzantine period, but
that of the mime and the pantomime.

It may be instructive in this connection to consider what little we
know about the theatres of Constantinople. In the 5th century the capital
possessed at least four theatres: the *theatrum maius*, which marked the
limit of the First Region, the *theatrum minus* in the Second, and a theatre
each in the Thirteenth (Sycae) and Fourteenth Region. It also had an
amphitheatre in the Second Region, which has been identified (rightly or
wrongly) with the *theatrum maius*[39], as well as two *lusoria*, whatever
exactly that may mean. The amphitheatre and one of the first two theatres
were ascribed to Septimius Severus[40]. There can be no doubt that the
amphitheatre (Kynegion) survived as an empty shell until the end of the
8th century and possibly later: it was used as a place for the execution of
criminals. As for the theatres, the last we hear of any of them is in 528,
when Justinian restored that of Sycae (Galata) on the occasion of raising
that suburb to the status of a city[41]. Vogt's extraordinary assertion that 'le
Grand Théâtre' lasted down to the end of the Empire, that it was
patronized by the court and had a more elegant repertory than the other
theatres which played to the masses (possibly, he adds, in languages other
than Greek) is entirely groundless, since the texts he seems to have in mind
refer to the Hippodrome[42]. As far as I am aware, there is not a single

[37] *AnBoll* 41 (1923) 299.

[38] Scripta minora, ed. KURTZ and DREXL, II 292.

[39] R. JANIN, Constantinople byzantine. Paris ²1964, 50. 196—97. E. MAMBOURY, Les
fouilles byzantines à Istanbul. *Byz* 11 (1936) 236, had the odd idea that the 'Gothic column'
on the Seraglio Point marked the centre of the Kynegion. JANIN repeats the same about the
theatrum minus. Need one point out that neither an amphiteatre nor a theatre could have
been encumbered by such a monument?

[40] Malalas 292; Chron. Pasch. 495.

[41] Chron. Pasch. 618.

[42] Op. cit. 259. He quotes Psellus in SATHAS, Μεσ. βιβλ. V 214: οἶκον οὐ πάνυ λαμπρὸν
κατὰ τὸ Βύκινον ἱδρυμένον (τόπος δὲ οὗτος ἀγχοῦ που τοῦ μεγάλου θεάτρου πᾶσι κατάδηλος). This
certainly designates the Hippodrome, since the Boukinon was a stretch of the Sea Walls a
short distance to the south of it. When Constantine Rhodius, Descr. des œuvres d'art et de
l'église des Saints Apôtres, ed. LEGRAND et REINACH (1896), 13, vv. 257—58, speaks of
ἀγαλμάτων τε μηχανουργίᾳ τῶν εἰς θέατρον, he, too, refers to the Hippodrome.

reference to a theatre at Constantinople after the 6th century, and the same applies to provincial towns. On this score archaeological investigations may contribute some new evidence if it can be determined at what date antique theatres fell into disuse. At Aphrodisias, for example, paintings of Christian saints and angels were put up on the stage in about the 6th century, which suggests that secular performances ceased to be given.

The mime and the pantomime may have lingered on until the end of the 7th century when they were banned by Canon 51 of the Trullan Council. Does this mean that they were still widespread at the time? The answer is not clear, especially in view of the fact that the same canon also prohibits τὰ τῶν κυνηγίων θεώρια which were, almost certainly, extinct. I know, however, of no clear-cut evidence that would indicate the presence of a theatre in the Byzantine Empire at a later date, apart from the occasional performance given by mummers to which I shall return. Nothing can be deduced from the fact that old canonical prohibitions were occasionally repeated, e. g. in the Nomocanon of Photius[43]; for surely, if a secular theatre had continued to exist, it would have attracted explicit and repeated censure. Even so innocuous a performance as the parade of costumed boys on the feast of the Holy Notaries was regarded with disapproval[44] and eventually banned[45]. Why is it, then, that we find no condemnation of theatrical shows either in sermons or in the paraenetic literature of the Middle and Later Byzantine periods, e. g. in the *Strategicon* of Kekaumenos[46] or in the *Spaneas*? When, by contrast, we turn to a similar work of the Early period, such as the *Versus ad Seleucum* by Amphilochius of Iconium, we discover that the mime, the pantomime and the circus top the list of the evil pursuits that the proper young man ought to avoid at all cost.

But, it will be said, what of the hippodrome? Is it not true that the people of Byzantium (or, at any rate, of Constantinople) continued to be passionately attached to chariot racing until the end of the Comnenian era? Such, indeed, is the accepted view that has been propounded in numerous

---

[43] IX 27 in RALLES and POTLES, Σύνταγμα I 202. The regulation in question is clearly antiquarian.

[44] See Christophoros Mitylenaios, Gedichte, ed. KURTZ, 91ff., No. 136, who exclaims (vv. 169. 172) πόσην ἔχουσι τὴν ὕβριν τὰ παιδία, πόσην δὲ μᾶλλον οἱ γονεῖς τὴν αἰσχύνην.

[45] By the patriarch Luke Chrysoberges (1157—70). See Balsamon in RALLES and POTLES II 451—52.

[46] It is true that Kekaumenos refers on a number of occasions to μῖμοι (meaning, I think, buffoons) and παιγνιῶται (mummers or actors), whom he regards with contempt and associates with the genus πολιτικοί (vulgar folk): ed. LITAVRIN (1972), 132, 26; 156, 29; 216, 17; 276, 9. He does not, however, condemn their shows or attendance at them by respectable people.

studies[47]. I would suggest, however, that this view is in need of considerable modification.

Chariot racing, as it was practised in the Early Byzantine Empire, was, above all, a competitive sport that fulfilled much the same function and inflamed the same emotions as football does today. It required an elaborate and expensive apparatus both in terms of buildings and in terms of staff; it was run by professionals; it generated its enormously popular heroes (the successful charioteers), its clubs of supporters (the so-called demes) and its unavoidable hooliganism[48]. All of these features are perfectly familiar to us today. Now imagine that in the whole of the British Isles football were to be played only in London, not more than five or six times a year, and always as an extension of royal ceremonial. Would that still be football as we know it, or would it be something different, even if conducted according to the same rules?

Let us look first at the geographical distribution of the circuses themselves. In the Early Byzantine Empire they existed, not indeed in every city, but pretty much in every major city: not only at Constantinople, Antioch and Alexandria, but also at Thessalonica, Chalcedon, Nicomedia, Edessa, Laodicea, Apamea, Berytus, Tyre, Caesarea in Palestine, even at Gerasa, Bostra and Oxyrhynchus. The presence of a circus was considered to confer a special status on a city — which is why the emperor Anastasius built one in his native Dyrrhachium[49] — probably the last circus to have been constructed in the Empire. Yet it is an assured fact that in the Middle Byzantine period only the Hippodrome of Constantinople continued in use.

Next, we should consider the frequency of the games, a subject that is, unfortunately, shrouded in much obscurity. In 4th-century Rome 66 days per year were given over to the circus[50], and I imagine that roughly the same situation must have obtained in the Early Byzantine world. The well-known denunciations of St. John Chrysostom imply a high frequency, and the charioteer Porphyrius (c. 500 A. D.) is said to have won hundreds of victories[51]. But what of the medieval period? In posing this question I shall have to open a parenthesis concerning the Book of Ceremonies whose evidence has been somewhat uncritically applied to describe the games in the 10th century. First, it must be understood that, like most other

---

[47] E. g. by R. GUILLAND, La disparition des courses, in: Etudes byzantines. Paris 1959, 89ff.

[48] On all of this see A. CAMERON, Circus Factions. Oxford 1976.

[49] Malalas 417—18.

[50] BALSDON, Life and Leisure 248.

[51] Anth. Plan. 356 and CAMERON, Porphyrius 66.

compilations undertaken by Constantine Porphyrogenitus, the Book of Ceremonies is essentially an antiquarian work rather than a practical manual. It contains material of different dates, some of it going back to the 5th and 6th centuries, material that was included because the compiler happened to lay his hand on it and considered it interesting. Hence it is wrong to imagine that whatever is contained in this work, even in its First Book, applied to Constantine's age. Now, the block of chapters devoted to the conduct of the hippodrome games (I. 68—73 according to Reiske's numbering) is by no means homogeneous. It was already seen by Bury[52] that chapter 68, which introduces the Praetorian Prefect of the East, the Master of Offices and the Quaestor as being next in rank to the Master, is considerably more ancient than the 10th century; Bury tentatively dated it to the reign of Justinian II or to the first years of Leo III. Chapter 70, which assigns the same role to the Master of Offices and the Quaestor, must be of the same vintage; but both chapters were partly revised, almost certainly in the reign of Michael III, since they mention the Trikonchos and the Sigma that were built by Theophilus. Furthermore, chapter 70 assumes the existence of the fountains (*phialae*) of the Blues and the Greens; yet these were destroyed by Basil I[53]. We cannot pause here to enquire more thoroughly into the various strata embodied in the hippodrome chapters[54]; it is enough to realize that they cannot be regarded as providing a faithful description of the games in the 10th century.

The Book of Ceremonies lays down the protocol for three performances of chariot races: the so-called Golden Hippodrome in the second week after Easter, the λαχανικὸν ἱπποδρόμιον on 11 May, and the μακελλαρικὸν ἱπποδρόμιον during carnival week[55]. It refers rather vaguely to other, less solemn performances — the term is ἱππικὸν παγανόν (II, p. 137, Vogt) as opposed to ἱππικὸν προσκυνήσιμον (II, p. 154, Vogt) — as well as to the hippodrome season that terminated before Lent (II, p. 166, Vogt), but it is arguable whether these references pertain, say, to the 7th century rather than to the 9th or 10th. Now, if we set aside the Book of Ceremonies and consider the mentions of hippodrome games contained in other texts of the Middle period, we obtain the impression that the three solemn performances were

---

[52] The Ceremonial Book of Constantine Porphyrogennetos. *Engl. Hist. Rev.* 22 (1907) 433.

[53] Cf. J. EBERSOLT, Le Grand Palais de Constantinople. Paris 1910, 204—5.

[54] G. MILLET, Les noms des auriges dans les acclamations de l'hippodrome, in: Recueil d'études dédiées à ... N. P. Kondakov. Prague 1926, 279 ff., argues that some portions of the chapters in question go back to the 5th or 6th century.

[55] See V. GRUMEL, Le commencement et la fin de l'année des jeux à l'hippodrome de Constantinople. *EO* 35 (1936) 428ff.

maintained as a permanent fixture and that additional games were given on extraordinary occasions, e. g. to celebrate a military triumph, an imperial wedding, the birth of an imperial child or the visit of a foreign potentate[56], but there is nothing to suggest that they were held with any regularity, say once a week or once a fortnight. The races which the biographer of St. Basil the Younger attended with an uneasy conscience were those of the Golden Hippodrome[57]; so were those at which the incompetent charioteer Jephthah suffered a fall towards the middle of the 11th century[58]. The emperor Alexius I, we are told, attended the games on a windy day and caught a chill in his shoulder some six months before his death[59]. Since he died on 15 August, 1118, the games must have been some time in February, in other words they were those of the μακελλαρικὸν ἱπποδρόμιον. We can narrow the date down more accurately to 10—16 February, when carnival week fell in 1118. The same applies to the games described by Michael Hagiotheodorites, for he himself gives the date of 1 February, 1168[60]. Easter that year fell on 31 March, so that 1 February would have been Thursday of carnival week.

If the number of games was thus drastically reduced, the same applies to the number of races per day. In the Early period there could have been as many as fifty[61], whereas the Book of Ceremonies stipulates only eight (four in the morning and four in the afternoon). The latter must have provided a pretty meagre programme, unless it was supplemented by other attractions, such as acrobats, exotic animals, etc.

Norman Baynes has often been quoted for his dictum that the Byzantine populace had two idols — the saint and the champion charioteer. True enough for the Early period. We know many of the charioteers by name, the most famous being Porphyrius who was commemorated by seven statues in Constantinople. We also know several of his contemporaries — Faustinus, Constantine, Uranius, Julian[62]; Julianicus who was killed while competing in 563[63]; Calliopas Trimolaimes who took a prominent part in

---

[56] For a list of such occasions see R. GUILLAND, Etudes sur l'hippodrome de Byzance. *BSl* 26 (1965) 14 ff.

[57] Ed. A. N. VESELOVSKIJ, *Sbornik otdel. russk. jazyka i slov. Imp. Akad. Nauk* 53 (1891) 5—6.

[58] Christophoros Mitylenaios, ed. KURTZ, 3, No. 6. The longer description of hippodrome games ibid. 56 ff., No. 90, contains no indication of date, but clearly refers to a special occasion.

[59] Alexiad XV 11, 2 (= III 230 LEIB).

[60] Ed. K. HORNA, *WSt* 28 (1906) 193.

[61] See CAMERON, Porphyrius 209—10.

[62] Ibid. 136 ff.

[63] Malalas 495.

the events preceding the downfall of Phocas in 610[64]; Phileremos who was a celebrity at Apamea[65], and many more. But how many charioteers can we name for the entire Middle Byzantine period? Without claiming to have exhausted the evidence, I can think of only two — Uranicus who was honoured with a portrait by Constantine V[66], and the unfortunate Jephthah whom I have already mentioned. There is also Bambaloudes (reign of Michael III) who is cited in a gloss of the Ceremonial Book, but he was a δρομεύς, i. e. a foot runner[67]. The emperors Theophilus and Michael III do not count, of course; furthermore, it should be stressed that the latter raced in private, mostly in the suburban palace of St. Mamas, and his competitors were not professionals.

Then there is the matter of the 'factions'. We all know that the Blues and the Greens, who terrorized the entire Eastern Empire in the 6th and early 7th century, all but disappear from the record after 610; and were it not for the Book of Ceremonies, where their role is largely ceremonial, we would hear even less of them. A great deal of nonsense has been written about the 'suppression' of the factions, an event that is not mentioned in any Byzantine source. A more ingenious explanation has also been advanced, to wit that nearly all references to the factions are due to John of Antioch, whose Chronicle ended in 610, and that if Theophanes fails to mention factions after that date, it is merely because he is following another source, a source that was not interested in Blues and Greens[68]. Alan Cameron's brilliant enquiry into the true nature of the factions makes such theories entirely unnecessary. The factions were not suppressed; they simply faded away as the games became fossilized. Cameron has already traced the growth of their ceremonial function[69], and more could be said on this topic. In particular, our attention is attracted to the construction by Justinian II of the Fountain of the Blues (and possibly that of the Greens as well). These were not intended for sporting purposes[70], but provided the setting for ceremonial receptions and acclamations. Furthermore, they were within the Imperial Palace[71]. In view of the fact that Justinian II

---

[64] John of Antioch, frag. 110, Exc. de insid., ed. DE BOOR, 150.

[65] Moschus, Pratum, ch. 152, 3017 A.

[66] Vita S. Stephani iun., PG 100, 1172.

[67] De cer. II 158 VOGT.

[68] A. MARICQ, La durée du régime des partis populaires à Constantinople. Ac. R. de Belgique, Bull. de la Cl. des Lettres, 5ᵉ sér., 35 (1949) 74.

[69] Circus Factions 230ff.

[70] As imagined by F. DVORNIK, The Circus Parties in Byzantium. Byzantina-Metabyzantina 1 (1946) 130.

[71] EBERSOLT, Le Grand Palais 100ff.

went to considerable trouble to build the φιάλη of the Blues (he was obliged to demolish a church in the process)[72], we must assume that he attached some importance to this new arrangement.

Finally, we may remember that all Early Byzantine emperors favoured one or other of the factions. As Cameron has convincingly explained[73], this had nothing to do with the alleged political or religious orientation of the Blues and the Greens: it was merely a part of the emperor's 'public image', a way of showing that, like ordinary citizens, he, too, had a keen interest in the games he attended. Some time in the 7th or early 8th century, however, this long-standing tradition was abandoned[74], and in the Book of Ceremonies the Blues appear to enjoy a permanently preferred status — an unthinkable situation in a competitive context.

The conclusion is obvious. At a time that cannot (and need not) be too closely defined chariot racing ceased to be a competitive sport and became an imperial pageant. I do not know whether the iconoclastic emperors tried as a matter of policy to revive the defunct sport; if so, they failed in the long run. The hippodrome games were a product of the urban life of Late Antiquity; they could not survive the demise of that way of life without changing their essential character.

It may be opportune at this point to consider the commentaries of Balsamon and Zonaras on Canons 24, 51 and 62 of the Trullan Council[75]. Canon 24, we may remember, forbade all clerics and monks to attend hippodrome games and theatrical performances; Canon 51, to which we have already referred, was a general ban of the mime, the pantomime and wild animal shows; while Canon 62 sought to outlaw certain relics of pagan observance, namely the celebration of the Kalends, Vota, Brumalia and the feast of 1 March; the dancing of women in public; the wearing of female dress by men and vice versa, as well as that of comic, satyric and tragic masks; and the invocation of the name of Dionysus at vintage time.

With regard to the hippodrome, Balsamon is unable to justify the rigour of the conciliar regulation. He quotes with approval an opinion held

---

[72] Theophanes 367—68 DE BOOR.

[73] Circus Factions 175ff.

[74] It is not clear (nor particularly important) exactly when imperial support for one or other of the factions lapsed. An inscription from Ephesus suggests, but does not prove that Heraclius favoured the Greens: Y. JANSSENS, Les Bleus et les Verts. Byz 11 (1936) 534—35; and a lost inscription from Constantinople (CIG 8788) that Constantine III (or IV) favoured the Blues: H. GRÉGOIRE, Notules épigraphiques. Byz 13 (1938) 172. Leontius was proclaimed emperor by the Blues and Apsimar by the Greens, but it is doubtful what significance attaches to these manifestations: see CAMERON, Circus Factions 267—68.

[75] RALLES and POTLES II 357—60. 425—26. 449—52.

in his own time, namely that Canon 24 "forbids the hippodrome games such as they occurred once upon a time, not those that are held today by the emperor's leave and in the emperor's presence". He sees, quite correctly, that there was a profound difference between the games as he knows them and those that were given once upon a time. Of the latter he can say only what he has read in chronicles concerning the circus disturbances in the reigns of Anastasius, Justinian and Phocas; and he imagines (quite wrongly) that the trouble arose from the fact that formerly the demes were in full control of the hippodrome, organized the games at their own expense and simply invited the emperor to attend, "whereas today the races are held in the emperor's presence and there is no suspicion of any evil practice". He concludes that spectacles ought to be divided into two classes: those that are forbidden to everyone (both clerics and laymen) and those, τὰ καὶ σήμερον ἐνεργοῦντα, that are open to everyone. By way of confirmation, he adds that church lectors were numbered among the 'demes-men' (presumably to lead the acclamations) as a sign of ecclesiastical approval and to show that "the former disorder of the popular δημόται and all those unsuitable and indecorous practices have fallen into abeyance". We may remember that as far back as the middle of the 7th century the poet of the Blue faction was a deacon of St. Sophia[76].

The remarks of Zonaras concerning the theatre (with reference to Canon 51) are equally revealing. The canon, he says, is directed against those spectacles that cause a spiritual relaxation (διάχυσις) and incite uproarious laughter, e. g. those of the mimes "who at times imitate Arabs, at other times Armenians or slaves", and who, by hitting one another on the head and making loud noises, cause indecorous laughter among the simple-minded. Here we have a precious piece of information about the kind of mime that was practised in the 12th century: I would imagine a troupe of itinerant mummers enacting a simple farce. As for dancing on the stage (i. e. the pantomime), Zonaras has evidently no idea of what this referred to. He feels obliged to explain that σκηνή means simulation or acting, for which reason actors who pretend to be slaves or lords are called σκηνικοί. Note that loud laughter is acknowledged to be the only undesirable effect of acting[77]: indecency is not even mentioned. Balsamon echoes the same sentiments and adds that the 'imperial games', to wit the Kontopaiktes, the Maron, the Achilles and the Oktoechos, had been devised so as to conform to the spirit of the canons inasmuch as they did

---

[76] Miracula S. Artemii 21, ed. A. PAPADOPOULOS—KERAMEUS, Varia graeca sacra. St. Petersburg 1909, 25.

[77] Cf. Spaneas, v. 94, ed. LEGRAND, Bibl. gr. vulg. I 4: Ἄτακτα γέλοια καὶ σαλὰ βαροῦ καὶ ἀπόφευγέ τα.

not excite the audience to indecorous laughter. Of the games in question nothing, unfortunately, is known, except that the Kontopaiktes appears to have been an acrobatic performance[78]. The suggestion that they were theatrical plays[79] strikes me as extremely unlikely, as does also the statement that the Achilles was "a kind of pantomime dance, as in antiquity"[80].

We are not here concerned with the survival of pagan observances, except that Canon 62 gives Balsamon an opportunity to comment on the meaning of masks. After quoting Justinian's Novel 123, he remarks: "Actors assume different roles (παντοῖα προσωπεῖα ὑποδύονται) and fearlessly ridicule monks and clergymen". Here, if I am not mistaken, he is speaking of contemporary customs and, probably, of those same mummers who simulated Arabs and Armenians. He goes on to say that even clerics on certain feast days played different parts, some entering church in military costume, sword in hand, others processing as monks or as four-legged animals. Conductors of ecclesiastical choirs would snap their fingers like charioteers, cover their faces with seaweed (?) and imitate certain female occupations (ἔργα τινὰ γυναικεῖα), all to excite laughter. Balsamon had enquired why such abuses were tolerated, only to be told that they were sanctioned by long tradition. The same canon, he points out, should be used to abolish the unseemly rites performed by the clergy of St. Sophia on Christmas day and Epiphany, rites which, as he correctly observes, were first introduced by the patriarch Theophylact[81].

The testimony of Balsamon and Zonaras is of particular importance because the two canonists made a comprehensive survey of such contemporary practices as might have fallen under the conciliar condemnation of theatrical performances in the broadest sense. And what did they single out? The hippodrome pageants and the other 'imperial games' (which I would be inclined to regard as contests of physical prowess) were in their eyes entirely harmless. All they found to criticize were certain buffooneries performed by clergymen and some simple-minded farces. Need we look any further for that highly elusive entity, the 'Byzantine theatre'?

It hardly needs pointing out that the development I have tried to sketch in the realms of bathing and entertainment requires a much fuller treatment. Within the limits of this paper I have not been able to discuss all the relevant material, nor have I indicated the complex causes that brought about the changes in the Byzantine life-style. The great public

---

[78] See KOUKOULES, Βυζ. βίος III 258.

[79] So S. KYRIAKIDES, Λαογραφία 11 (1934—37) 284.

[80] KOUKOULES, op. cit. III 115.

[81] Scylitzes, ed. THURN, 243—44.

IV

baths fell into disuse not because the people tired of them, but, I suppose, because they proved too vast for a dwindling population, too expensive to heat and to keep in good repair. I do not know if the public financing of baths was discontinued, but it does seem that the smaller establishments that continued to function were privately operated[82]. Withdrawal of government financing was, almost certainly, an important factor in the demise of the theatre. Procopius is doubtless exaggerating when he accuses Justinian of causing the wholesale closure of theatres, hippodromes and amphitheatres, but he provides a valuable indication in identifying the motive for this policy, namely "so that the Treasury might not have to supply the usual sums to the numerous and almost countless persons who derived their living from that source"[83]. The βίος πᾶσιν ἀγέλαστος that ensued must have been particularly depressing for the unemployed theatrical workers. Deprived of central funding, the mime must have been left to private initiative and so passed into the hands of travelling troupes that performed, not in the abandoned theatres, but probably at fairs and in noblemen's houses. As for the pantomime, which drew the bulk of its subject-matter from pagan mythology, it was doomed in any case. What would a Byzantine pantomime have been about?

Sketchy as my survey has been, I should like to draw from it two inferences. The first concerns the role of imperial ceremonial in the Middle period. We have seen that the custom of luxurious bathing was maintained only in the palace when it had ceased to be generally available to the public; that chariot racing, when it was no longer a mass sport, remained the sport of emperors to be indulged in privately, except for the few occasions when the people were allowed to watch it. We may also remember that the ancient custom of reclining at table was kept up at imperial banquets in the Hall of the Nineteen Couches long after it had passed out of general use. These survivals suggest that the evocation of an extinct life-style, that of the Empire in its greatness, was a deliberate component of court ceremonial. Which is why, perhaps, the Book of Ceremonies is what it is — not a guide to existing procedure, but a collection of ancient precedents.

My second inference is of a broader kind. I have mentioned *en passant* the misrepresentation of the circus demes by modern commentators and, somewhat more fully, that the Byzantine theatre. Why is it that so much nonsense has been written on these topics by scholars who, in other

---

[82] See the standard contract for the lease of a public bath in SATHAS, Μεσ. βιβλ. VI 624—25.

[83] Anecdota 26, 8—10.

respects, were perfectly sensible? In the case of the circus, some of the confusion has been caused by the desire of endowing the factions with political and social relevance in terms that would be understandable to us today. But that was not the only cause: the other was the word δῆμος itself. Since, we are told, Byzantium was the heir of ancient Greece, does it not follow that the demes of Constantinople were descended from those of Attica? It has taken us nearly a hundred years to get rid of this fallacy, and I dare say there are still some scholars ready to defend it. Exactly the same applies to the theatre. We have been misled by words that meant one thing in antiquity and another thing in the Middle Ages; and we shall continue to be so misled as long as we regard Byzantium in terms of ancient 'survivals'. It is no easy matter to reconstruct the reality of Byzantine life, but we must endeavour to do so with a mind free from classical preconceptions if we are to understand this civilization as it was, not as we would like it to have been.

IVa

ADDENDUM TO THE REPORT ON EVERYDAY LIFE

The foregoing Report lays no claim to comprehensiveness
either in its bibliographic references or in the range of texts
discussed. My intention was to show as succinctly as possible
that certain typical manifestations of the urban life of the
Late Antique period, namely the public baths, the theatre and
the circus, did not and, in fact could not survive the collapse
of that particular way of life and all the 'structures' that
underpinned it during the dark centuries. Contrary to my
predecessors in this domain who looked for signs of continuity, I have tried to stress a discontinuity that is all
too evident.

With respect to bibliography, I regret having neglected to
cite an old but excellent work, namely A.P.Rudakov's
Očerki vizantijskoj kul'tury po dannym grečeskoj agiografii
(Moscow,1917; repr.London,1970) as well as G.G.Litavrin's
rather more popular Kak žili vizantijcj (Moscow, 1974); and,
in the case of the theatre, F.Tinnefeld's 'Zum profanen Mimos
in Byzanz nach dem Verdikt des Trullanums (691)', Βυζαντινά,
6 (1974), 321-43. The omission of certain other bibliographic
references is deliberate.

With regard to the public baths, I ought to have mentioned
their dependence on an adequate supply of water by aqueduct,
but even in the case of Constantinople that is a topic that
still requires a good deal of investigation. It is well known
that the aqueduct of Valens was cut during the Avar siege of
626 and remained out of commission until it was repaired by
Constantine V in 767,[1] yet some public baths continued to
operate in the meantime as I have shown. Perhaps they were
supplied by the aqueduct of Hadrian of which very little is

known[2]. The late F.Dirimtekin's researches[3] have revealed a
complex system of early aqueducts extending as far as the
Saray-Midye road,i.e. some 90km. northwest of Constantinople,
well beyond the Long Walls. Whether these fed the aqueduct of
Valens I am unable to say, but it is unlikely that they could
have remained in operation during the troubled years of the
7th century. It would seem, therefore, that the water supply
of the capital was seriously disrupted, but not entirely
cut off.

There are also a number of Byzantine texts that I might have
usefully quoted. For example, in the Miracula S.Demetrii
(I.14, §143 Lemerle) there is an interesting passage referring
to the Avaro-Slav siege of Thessalonica in 586, in the course
of which numerous barbarians deserted to the Byzantines and
entered the city with the result that disused public baths
were filled to the joy of the local inhabitants. This seems to
imply that the abandonment of public baths at Thessalonica
occurred already in the last quarter of the 6th century and
was due, at least in part, to the shrinkage of the population.
In the same chapter of the Miracula (§§132-34) there is an
intriguing reference to the theatre -- I have in mind the
dream of the archbishop Eusebius. Imagining that he was sitting
in the theatre and surprised to find himself in such an unsuitable place (ἐν οὕτως ἀναρμοδίῳ τόπῳ) he was about to
depart when a τραγῳδός   mounted the stage and bade him stay
because he was about to recite a lament over the bishop and
the latter's daughter. This implies that in 586 the theatre
still served as a place of public assembly at Thessalonica and
that the clergy, no doubt because of canonical prohibitions,
did not normally frequent it. At the same time it is clear that
the τραγῳδός was not a tragic actor or a member of a tragic
chorus: he was, as Lemerle correctly renders the term, a
'récitant', i.e.a professional declaimer of laments, I should
imagine mostly at funerals since the bishop was aware that such
persons announced great misfortunes, ὡς συμφορῶν μεγάλων
μηνύματα [μηνυταί?] οἱ τραγῳδοὶ καθεστήκασιν.   In the Life
of St.Andrew the Fool the verb τραγῳδεῖν means simply to sing[4]
as it still does in modern Greek.

Another curious passage occurs in the same Life of Andrew
the Fool (§43). It concerns an old woman -- in reality the

devil disguised as an old woman – who loudly complains about the Saint's scandalous behaviour. When questioned by passers by, she replies, "I am a stranger in these parts. I left my native land because I had a lawsuit here (i.e. at Constantinople) and, as everyone else does it, I parked myself with my belongings in the theatre (ὡς ἔθος μετὰ τῶν ἐπιφερομένων μοι ἐν τῷ θεάτρῳ περιπατοῦσα ἠπλήκευσα). When night had fallen, this madman appeared, snatched my possessions and fled." If the word θέατρον still means a theatre here rather than the hippodrome, one would be able to conclude that such buildings at Constantinople had fallen into disuse and served as a temporary refuge for impecunious visitors.

To continue with the theatre, I cannot attach any importance to the existence in the 9th century of a minor official called δομέστικος τῆς θυμέλης, subject to the chartulary of the Sakellion.5/ Bury described him as the successor to the old *tribunus voluptatum*, but what little we know about his functions links him, not with the stage or the public at large, but with entertainments given in the palace such as the famous Gothic dance (De cerimoniis, 382,1 Bonn). Besides, the obsolete term θυμέλη was used rather loosely by Byzantine authors: in Theoph.Cont. (142,5 Bonn) it refers once again to a palatine entertainment, but elsewhere it seems to denote the hippodrome. When George the Monk (768,7 Bonn) puns on the name of the iconoclast patriarch Theodotos Kassiteras (τῆς θυμέλης τὴν προσηγορίαν ἐπειλημμένον), he appears to be thinking of the term κασσίς, the helmet worn by charioteers.

As I have said, the baths, the theatre and the circus form but a small part of a vast subject that awaits its investigator. We still lack, e.g., a proper study of Byzantine costume and of Byzantine diet and cookery. In the case of the latter a body of material has lately been collected by Mme Patlagean6/, but it is confined to the poorer strata of society besides being limited in both time and geographical coverage. Among a variety of other topics I should like to mention briefly only one, that of domestic lighting. In this respect antiquity relied largely on oil lamps and we have before us many thousands of such objects dating from the early Byzantine period: ordinary clay

lamps with a handle and a spout, more or less elaborate
glass lamps, bronze lamps of elegant craftsmanship either for
hanging from chains or for placing on a stand, polycandela
that must have held glass lights and an assortment of bronze
and silver stands with a spoke at the top that have sometimes been
mistaken for candlesticks. The catalogue of Roman and Early
Byzantine lamps from the Athenian Agora lists about 3,000 items.
The series stops in the 7th century and only two items are
tentatively attributed to the 8th.7/For Corinth the catalogue
of Byzantine pottery, which describes about 1,800 items, does
not contain a single lamp.8

I admit that I have not examined in this respect all
available excavation reports. I am aware that the Great Palace
excavations have produced one small oil lamp with a pale green
glaze. "The ware", comments Talbot Rice, "is of a type found in
late Byzantine or early Turkish times, but the form is almost
Roman. The lamp is interesting in that similar ones from Byzantine sites are extremely uncommon."9/ I am also aware that
two fragments of glass lamps of 11th or 12th century date have
been found at Corinth among a mass of other glass objects that
were manufactured locally.10/ They are of a type that can still
be seen in mosques today, namely a bowl with a bulbous projection underneath.11/ Even so, I venture to suggest that the ordinary oil lamp in either clay or bronze ceased to be a part of
the Byzantine scene after the 7th or 8th century. How then did
the medieval Byzantines illuminate their houses after dark?

We have been told that in Western Europe, when imports of
oil from Africa and elsewhere were disrupted in the early Middle
Ages, there was a general shift to the candle, either of wax or
tallow: hence the appearance of the *cerarii* who were unknown before the end of the Merovingian period. Could the same have happened in Byzantium? It can hardly be coincidental that the profession of κηρουλάριος is first attested, as far as I can ascertain, in the 7th century. Its earliest mention seems to occur in
the Miracles of St.Artemius and is exactly dated to 643/4 (§21,
p.27 Papadopoulos Kerameus). The story is told by a deacon of
St.Sophia who, while returning home late in the evening, decided to buy some candles and light them in the Saint's

martyrium. He stopped at the stall of a κηρουλάριος to find that
the latter had only one pair left, reserved for another customer
who had paid for them. So the deacon was obliged to buy some candles without wicks, if that is the meaning of the expression
† πίνας οὐκ εἶχον. He went off with the imperfect candles, but
slipped in the muddy street and broke them to pieces. He collected the fragments, returned to the κηρουλάριος to whom he handed
the bits of wax and some extra money for the work of reshaping
them and received in return the pair that had already been sold.

It is true that the use of candles for liturgical and pro-
cessional purposes is attested well before the 7th century and
in this story, too, they are used in that capacity. I doubt,
however, that the κηρουλάριος who kept his shop open so late
in the evening limited his business to candles that were lit
in churches; or, for that matter, the κηρουλάριος who, in the
early 9th century, was forced to part with his personal fortune of 100 lbs. of gold by the avaricious emperor Nicephorus I
(Theophanes, 487-88 de Boor). The same goes for the κηρουλάριοι
whose activity is regulated in the Book of the Prefect and who
appear to nave dealt in oil as well as in wax, the oil being
used, however, in a subsidiary capacity to mix with the wax
(§ XI). The frequent mention of oil lamps as well as candles
in monastic typica, discussed at this Congress by Mrs Laskarina
Bouras, does not help solve the problem of ordinary domestic
lighting.

I am prepared to admit that candles may be more practical
to use than oil lamps, but they were also, if I am not mistaken, considerably more expensive as implied in the Miracles of
St.Artemius. That is why so respectable a person as the sacri-
stan of St.Demetrius at Thessalonica was in the habit of extingu-
uishing the larger candles that were lit in the Saint's ciborium and substituting them with smaller and thinner ones with
the intention of earning some extra money both for himself and
for the church (Mir.S.Demetrii, I 7). If candles were out of
reach of the poorer classes, it would follow that a great many
people in medieval Byzantium went to bed as soon as it got dark.

I have offered these tentative remarks in the hope of showing
both the importance of archaeological evidence and the far-reaching implications that may sometimes be drawn from the study of

daily life. Let us hope that a new Koukoules will emerge before the year 2000 and conduct his researches in a spirit
attuned to the present needs of our discipline.

NOTES

1 Theophanes, 440 de Boor.
2 Cod.Just.XI 43,6; Chron.Pasch.,619 Bonn.
3 Cahiers archéologiques,10(1959),217 ff.; Byz.Forschungen,
   3(1968),117 ff.
4 PG 111,709B.
5 N.Oikonomidès, Les listes de préséance byzantines, 121,14.
6 Pauvreté économique et pauvreté sociale à Byzance (Paris -
   the Hague, 1977), 36 ff.
7 The Athenian Agora, VII: Lamps of the Roman Period, by J.
   Perlzweig (Princeton,1961),198-9.
8 Corinth, XI: The Byzantine Pottery, by C.H.Morgan, II
   (Cambridge, Mass. 1942).
9 The Great Palace of the Byzantine Emperors. Second Report,
   ed. D.Talbot Rice (Edinburgh,1958),113.
10 Corinth, XII: The Minor Objects, by G.R.Davidson (Princeton,1952), 121.
11 On similar lamps see G.M.Crowfoot and D.B.Harden, Early Byzantine and Later Glass Lamps, Journal of Egypt.Archaeol.,
   17(1931), 196 ff.

V

ANTIQUE STATUARY AND THE BYZANTINE BEHOLDER

I

To adorn his new capital on the Bosphorus, Constantine the Great removed a multitude of antique statues from the principal cities of the Greek East.[1] These statues—those that were set up by Constantine as well as by others—continued to grace the streets and squares of Constantinople for the greater part of the Middle Ages. Their number gradually diminished as a result of fires, earthquakes, and vandalism; but an impressive collection of them was still in existence when the Crusaders captured Constantinople in 1204.

The fate of these statues has attracted some attention on the part of archaeologists interested in tracing the history of various masterpieces of ancient sculpture down to their ultimate disappearance.[2] Here, however, we shall be concerned not so much with the statues themselves as with the effect they produced upon the Byzantine spectator. How did he look upon these statues? Did he admire them and derive from them some inspiration for his own artistic creations? Was he, on the contrary, shocked by them, or, perhaps simply indifferent? The purpose of asking these questions is to set up a test case of the Byzantine attitudes towards antiquity. This inquiry offers a further advantage; for, whereas the common folk of Byzantium did not read Homer and Pindar, everyone—the butcher, the candlemaker, and the lower-class saint—could and did look at these statues. What is more, we have some inkling of what they thought of them.

By "antique statue" I mean any statue, whether Greek or Roman, manufactured before the fourth century A.D. Within this broad classification, which included statues of ancient rulers, philosophers, poets, mythological figures, as well as images of animals, I shall be concerned especially with statues of pagan divinities. The nature of the evidence will not, unfortunately, allow me, in most cases, to make a distinction between Hellenic, Hellenistic, and Roman statuary.

II

The deliberate assembling of ancient statues in Constantinople constitutes something of a paradox. We must not forget that paganism was very much of a live issue, not only in the fourth century, but until about the year 600. Statues of pagan divinities were, of course, an essential part in the celebration of pagan rites. The lives of the saints are full of references to the destruc-

---

[1] As St. Jerome so concisely put it, *Dedicatur Constantinopolis omnium paene urbium nuditate* (*Chronicon*, ed. Fotheringham [London, 1923]), p. 314₂₄.

[2] The only attempt at a full treatment of this subject is Christian Gottlob Heyne's "Priscae artis opera quae Constantinopoli extitisse memorantur," *Comment. Soc. Reg. Scient. Gotting., Class. hist. et philol.*, XI (1790–91), pp. 3–38. Most of the evidence is collected by J. Overbeck, *Die antiken Schriftquellen zur Geschichte der bildenden Künste bei den Griechen* (Leipzig, 1868).

56

tion of pagan statues. A few examples must suffice. At Gaza there stood in the center of town a nude statue of Aphrodite which was the object of great veneration, especially on the part of women. When, in 402, Bishop Porphyry, surrounded by Christians bearing crosses, approached this statue, "the demon who inhabited the statue, being unable to contemplate the terrible sign, departed from the marble with great tumult, and, as he did so, he threw the statue down and broke it into many pieces."[3] We may doubt that the collapse of the statue was altogether spontaneous. At the end of the fifth century a great number of idols, salvaged from the temple of Isis at Memphis, were concealed in a house behind a false wall. But their presence was detected by the Christians. The statues were loaded on twenty camels and taken to Alexandria where they were exposed to public ridicule and destroyed.[4] In the middle of the sixth century we hear of St. Abramius destroying pagan idols near Lampsacus on the Hellespont, in a village that was totally pagan.[5] At about the same time idols were subjected to popular derision by being hung in the streets of Antioch.[6]

These are a few examples chosen at random. We must also remember that, whereas some Christian thinkers rightly believed that the idols were inanimate, the general opinion prevalent at the time—as we have seen from the incident at Gaza—was that they were inhabited by maleficent demons.[7] Granted this attitude, how are we to explain the fact that the first Christian Emperor used statues of pagan divinities to decorate Constantinople? How was it also that these statues remained for the most part unmolested for so many centuries?

It would be a mistake, I think, to suggest—as some modern scholars have done—that these statues were used simply for decoration. The answer is rather to be sought in the ambiguity of the religious policy pursued by Constantine's government. Nor must we hold Constantine himself responsible: the task of decorating the capital must have been entrusted to subordinate officials—the *curatores*—who were probably pagan, and they simply did the kind of job that was expected at the time.[8] Besides, it has been proved that the foundation of Constantinople was accompanied by purely pagan rites.[9] To a Christian apologist all of this was highly embarrassing; consequently, Eusebius, or whoever wrote the *Vita Constantini*, tried to explain the erection of pagan statues as part of a subtle policy of making fun of the old gods: "The pompous (σεμνὰ) statues of brass," he writes, ". . . . were exposed to view in all the public places of the imperial city: so that here a Pythian, there a Sminthian Apollo excited the contempt of the beholder: while the Delphic tripods were deposited in the Hippodrome and the Muses of Helicon in the palace. In

---

[3] Marcus diaconus, *Vita Porphyrii*, chaps. 59–61, ed. Grégoire and Kugener (Paris, 1930), p. 47 ff.

[4] *Vie de Sévère*, *Patrol. Orient.*, II, p. 27 ff.

[5] *Acta SS. Abramii et Mariae*, *Acta Sanctorum*, March, vol. II, p. 933.

[6] *Vita S. Symeonis junioris*, *Acta Sanctorum*, May, vol. V, p. 371B.

[7] Conversely, in the eyes of fourth-century Neoplatonists, idols were animated with divine presence: see E. R. Dodds, "Theurgy and its Relationship to Neoplatonism," *Journal of Roman Studies*, XXXVII (1947), p. 63 f.

[8] So J. Maurice, *Numismatique constantinienne*, II (Paris, 1911), p. 488 f.

[9] A. Frolow, "La dédicace de Constantinople dans la tradition byzantine," *Rev. de l'hist. des religions*, CXXVII (1944), p. 61 ff.

V

short, the city which bore his name was everywhere filled with brazen statues of the most exquisite workmanship, which had been dedicated in every province, and which the deluded victims of superstition had long vainly honored as gods with numberless victims and burnt sacrifices, though now at length they learned to think rightly, when the emperor held up these very playthings to be the ridicule and the sport of all beholders."[10]

In addition to the Delphic tripods, Constantine also erected in the Hippodrome the statues of the Dioscuri, whose temple had stood on that spot. On the agora of ancient Byzantium he went so far as to build a temple to the Fortuna of Rome, and to restore another one, dedicated to Cybele, the Mother of the Gods. The statue of Cybele was of venerable antiquity: allegedly it had been made by Jason's companions.[11] In the Senate house Constantine erected statues of the Muses, taken from Mount Helicon, and in front of it he set up on stone pedestals the statues of Zeus of Dodona and Athene of Lindos. The Muses perished in the great conflagration of 404, caused by the followers of St. John Chrysostom, but the gods were unexpectedly preserved: a pagan miracle that gave comfort to the "more cultivated" (τοῖς χαριεστέροις) persons dwelling in the city, as Zosimus tells us.[12] Then, most important, there was the great bronze statue representing Apollo-Helios which Constantine set up in 328 as his own effigy on top of the porphyry column of the Forum; it wore a radiate crown, held a spear in its right hand and a globe in its left. † Tradition affirmed that it had been brought from Phrygia.[13]

A great collection of statues was also assembled in the baths of Zeuxippus; these are known to us through a tedious poem by the Egyptian Christodorus, which forms Book II of the Palatine Anthology. In all, eighty statues are described, all of them antique, and most, if not all, of bronze. The greater number represented mythological heroes, but there were also nine statues of gods, many of poets, orators, philosophers, historians, and statesmen. Very few were of Roman origin: a Julius Caesar, a Pompey, an Apuleius, a Virgil, as well as a group of the pugilists Dares and Entellus borrowed from Book V of

[10] *Vita Constantini*, III, 54, ed. Heikel, p. 101. Cf. Sozomen, *Hist. eccles.*, II, 5, PG, 67, col. 945, who adds to the list of statues one of Pan which had allegedly been dedicated by the Spartan regent Pausanias after the Second Persian War: cf. K. Wernicke, art. "Pan" in Roscher's *Lex. d. griech. u. röm. Mythol.*, III, col. 1408. For Constantine's prohibition of ἐγέρσεις ξοάνων, see *Vita Const.*, II, 45; IV, 25.
[11] Zosimus, II, 31, ed. Mendelssohn (1887), p. 88f.
[12] *Id.*, V, 24, p. 246f.
[13] *Chronicon Paschale*, Bonn ed., p. 528; from Ilion in Phrygia (sic): Malalas, Bonn ed., p. 320; from Ilion or Heliopolis in Phrygia: Zonaras, Bonn ed., III, p. 18. According to another tradition, the statue was a work of Phidias and was brought from Athens: Leo Grammaticus, Bonn ed., p. 87; Tzetzes, *Chiliades*, VIII, 333, ed. Kiessling (1826), p. 295. The statue was thrown down by a storm in 1106, but its head was salvaged and deposited in the imperial palace: Tzetzes, *op. cit.*, VIII, 339. See esp. Th. Preger, "Konstantinos-Helios," *Hermes*, XXXVI (1901), p. 457ff. The attempt on the part of I. Karayannopulos to cast doubt on the pagan origin of the statue ("Konstantin der Grosse und der Kaiserkult," *Historia*, V [1956], p. 341ff.) has been refuted by S. Kyriakides, "Ἱστορικὰ σημειώματα," Ἑλληνικά, XVII (1960), p. 219ff. The presence of a spear in addition to a globe in the hands of an Apollo-Helios need not be considered anomalous if the statue was of oriental origin; cf. the painting of the sun-god Jarhibol at Dura and, possibly, the representation of Apollo-Helios on a stele from Meonia, now at Leiden: both reproduced by E. H. Kantorowicz, "Gods in Uniform," *Proc. Amer. Philos. Soc.*, CV/4 (1961) p. 368ff., figs. 25, 36.

the Aeneid. The baths of Zeuxippus were burnt down in 532 and the statues must have perished at the same time. When, in 1928, part of the baths was excavated, two inscribed statue bases were found. They bore the names of Hecuba and Aeschines, both mentioned by Christodorus.[14]

The importation of statues into Constantinople greatly diminished, but did not entirely cease, after the reign of Constantine. Individual statues were apparently brought in under Constantius II,[15] Valentinian,[16] and Theodosius II.[17] A great collection was assembled in the palace of Lausus who was *praepositus sacri cubiculi* in the reign of Theodosius II (406–450) and was perhaps himself responsible for bringing it together. Its jewel was Phidias' chryselephantine statue of Zeus from Olympia. The removal of this masterpiece, which presumably occurred after the suppression of the Olympic festival in 394, is not to be regretted since the temple of Zeus at Olympia burnt down during the same reign. Besides the Zeus, the palace of Lausus also contained a Lindian
† Athene of emerald four cubits high, the work of Skyllis and Dipoinos; the Cnidian Aphrodite of Praxiteles, made of white marble; the Samian Hera, the work of Lysippus and Boupalos; a winged Eros holding a bow, from Myndos; the Kairos of Lysippus, long-haired in front, bald in back; and many other statues.[18] The palace of Lausus was burned down in 475 and all of these statues were destroyed.[19] The last instance of the importation of antique statues into Constantinople that I have been able to find is of two horses from the temple of Artemis at Ephesus, which were brought under Justinian.[20] It is, however, recorded that Constans II, during his infamous residence in Rome (663), despoiled that city of its ancient bronze ornaments, including even the copper roof tiles of the Pantheon, with a view to having them transferred to Constantinople. The loot was conveyed to Syracuse, but never reached its destination: it fell instead into the hands of the Arabs.[21]

The conflagrations that accompanied the frequent revolts of the fifth and sixth centuries took, as we have seen, a heavy toll of ancient statues. Even so, a great number of them remained. I would estimate their number during the "middle-Byzantine" period at probably over one hundred. We are told that

[14] *Second Report upon the Excavations Carried out in and near the Hippodrome of Constantinople in 1928 on Behalf of the British Academy* (London, 1929), p. 18 ff.

[15] Statues of Perseus and Andromeda: *Scriptores originum Constantinopolitanarum*, ed. Preger (Leipzig, 1901–07), II, p. 195, § 85.

[16] A statue called Perichytes as well as one of a donkey, both in the Hippodrome: *ibid.*, I, p. 64, § 64; II, p. 192 f., § 82. The Perichytes was nude except for a loincloth, and wore a helmet; it was stolen by western merchants some time between 935 and 959: *Vita S. Lucae Stylitae*, ed. A. Vogt, *Analecta Bollandiana*, XXXVIII (1909), p. 39 f.; ed. F. Vanderstuyf, *Patrol. Orient.*, XI (1915), p. 107 ff. For other instances of the theft of statues, see *Script. orig. CP*, I, p. 50 (under Theodosius II); II, p. 253, § 112 (under Caesar Bardas).

[17] Elephants at the Golden Gate (from Athens): *Script. orig. CP*, II, p. 182, § 58; four horses in the Hippodrome, the same as are now on the façade of San Marco (from Chios): *ibid.*, p. 190, § 75.

[18] Cedrenus, Bonn ed., I, p. 564.

[19] *Ibid.*, p. 616; Zonaras, III, p. 130. Not in A.D. 462 as stated by A. B. Cook, *Zeus*, III/1 (Cambridge, 1940), p. 970. Cf. A. M. Schneider, "Brände in Konstantinopel," *BZ*, XLI (1941), p. 384.

[20] *Script. orig. CP*, II, p. 165.

[21] Paulus diaconus, *Hist. Longob.*, V, 11, 13, PL, 95, cols. 602, 604. Cf. Hodgkin, *Italy and Her Invaders*, VI (Oxford, 1916), p. 278 f. We are not told specifically what the ancient ornaments of bronze were, but it is reasonable to assume that they included statues.

several were destroyed by the Emperor Maurice, apparently to counteract an outbreak of magical practices.[22] Some more were broken by order of Leo III.[23] But apart from these and a few other isolated cases,[24] there is no record of a deliberate suppression of ancient statues by the Byzantine government. Their presence was accepted, and the popular tales that were woven round them aided their preservation.

III

Byzantine attitudes toward ancient statuary should be considered on two levels: the popular and the intellectual. I shall start with the first.

The popular attitude was based on the assumption that statues were animated. I have mentioned the widely prevalent belief of the early Christians that pagan statues were inhabited by demons. This belief, as interpreted by strict churchmen, dictated immediate action: the statues had to be destroyed. But many statues survived even so, and the demons within them underwent, as it were, a gradual change of personality. From being actively maleficent, they became vaguely sinister; the best thing to do was to leave them alone. Some statues became talismans and fulfilled a useful role by averting various calamities and minor nuisances: palladia fall within this category. Others came to be considered as the magical doubles of prominent men or even of entire nations.[25] In short, as the original significance of the statues was forgotten, a new "folkloristic" significance arose in the popular imagination.

The demons, of course, did not immediately surrender their powers, as a couple of examples will show. On the very day when the Emperor Maurice was assassinated in Constantinople (in 602), a calligrapher in Alexandria, returning home late at night after a party, chanced to pass in front of the temple of Tyche. To his amazement, the statues that were erected there slid down from their pedestals and, addressing him in a loud voice, described the Emperor's downfall. This intelligence was conveyed to the prefect of Egypt, who enjoined secrecy on the calligrapher. Sure enough, nine days later messengers arrived in Alexandria bringing the tragic news.[26] As every Byzantine knew, demons had the faculty of swift locomotion and were thus able to apprehend events that took place at a great distance. This faculty they often passed off as foreknowledge, a gift they did not possess.[27]

Here is a somewhat different example taken from the *Life of St. Andrew the Fool*, a work of the ninth or tenth century. A woman in Constantinople, whose

---

[22] *Script. orig. CP*, II, p. 181, § 54 ("many statues" at Exakionion); p. 196, § 88 (statue of bull buried); p. 257, § 131 (statue of Tyche).

[23] *Ibid.*, p. 198, § 90.

[24] E.g. by the Caesar Bardas (864–66): *ibid.*, p. 184, § 61.

[25] See A. I. Kirpičnikov, "Čudesnyja statui v Konstantinopole," *Letopis' ist.-filol. obšč. pri Imp. Novoross. Univ.*, IV, *Vizant. otd.*, II (Odessa, 1894), p. 23 ff.; N. G. Polites, Τελέσματα in Λαογραφικὰ σύμμεικτα, I (Athens, 1920), p. 48 ff.

[26] Theophylactus Simocatta, ed. de Boor (Leipzig, 1887), p. 309 ff.

[27] See, e.g., Athanasius, *Vita S. Antonii*, chap. 31 f., PG, 26, col. 889 ff.; John Damascene, *De fide orthod.*, II, 4, PG, 94, col. 877A.

husband was given to dissipation, sought the help of a magician who performed over her certain demonic rites. The immediate objective was thereby achieved: the husband was brought to heel. But soon thereafter the woman began having disturbing dreams in which she saw herself pursued by Ethiopians and enormous black dogs. Then she saw herself standing in the Hippodrome, embracing the statues that were there, "urged by an impure desire of having intercourse with them." It took a saint to rid the poor woman of the demons.[28] We are not surprised that the nude statues of the Hippodrome should have been inhabited by demons of concupiscence; what is surprising is that practically no censure of them was expressed.

Our richest source of statue-lore is a confusing little book called Παραστάσεις σύντομοι χρονικαί, i.e. "Brief Historical Expositions," a kind of tourist's guidebook to the curiosities of Constantinople, compiled in the middle of the eighth century. At the end of the tenth century it was reworked and incorporated into a larger work, the Πάτρια Κωνσταντινουπόλεως, or "Traditions of Constantinople," which has, for a long time, been incorrectly ascribed to one Georgius Codinus.[29] In both of its versions this guidebook is on a very low intellectual level, and may thus be regarded as representing the attitudes of the common man. A few extracts will show what the common man thought about ancient statues.

There was an antique statue purporting to represent Phidaleia, the wife of Byzas, mythical founder of Byzantium. When the statue was removed, the spot where it had stood trembled for a long time, and it required the intervention of St. Sabas to stop the earthquake.[30] Moral: Do not move statues. Leo III destroyed many ancient monuments. Why did he do so? Because he was stupid (ἀλόγιστος).[31] Ardaburius, who was Master of Soldiers in the reign of Leo I, found a statue of Herodian (the grammarian?) and destroyed it in his anger; whereupon he discovered 133 talents of gold. He gave this treasure to the Emperor and, instead of being rewarded, was put to death.[32] Moral: Do not destroy statues. Incidentally, we know better why Ardaburius was put to death.[33] Here is a curious story told in the first person: it refers to the years 711–713. The narrator, one Theodore, and his friend Himerius went to the Kynegion, an ancient theatre on what is now the Seraglio Point. There they found a short and broad statue representing a certain Maximian who had built the Kynegion. As they were contemplating it curiously, the statue fell from its pedestal and killed Himerius. Theodore, afraid of a charge of murder, took refuge in St. Sophia. An inquiry was instituted and Theodore was acquitted. A text of Demosthenes (sic) was found stating that the statue in question was fated to kill a prominent man. The Emperor Philippicus had the statue buried because "it did not admit of destruction." The moral is added by our author:

---

[28] PG, iii, col. 776 ff.
[29] Both in *Script. orig. CP*, ed. Preger.
[30] *Ibid.*, I, p. 20 f., § 4 = II, p. 195, § 86.
[31] *Ibid.*, I, p. 22, § 5d = II, p. 198, § 90.
[32] *Ibid.*, I, p. 29, § 14 = II, p. 204, § 99.
[33] See J. B. Bury, *History of the Later Roman Empire* (London, 1923), I, p. 320.

"As thou investigatest these matters truthfully, pray not to fall into tempta-
tion, and be on thy guard when thou contemplatest ancient statues, especially
pagan ones."[34]

Other statues fulfilled useful purposes. A statue of Aphrodite served to
detect unchaste women until the sister of the Empress Sophia, wife of Justin
II, was exposed in this fashion, and had the statue destroyed.[35] A statue
having four horns on its head did the same service for deceived husbands.[36]
Bronze figures of mosquitoes, bugs, fleas, and mice kept these noxious animals
out of Constantinople, until Basil I broke the figures.[37] It was, in most cases,
Apollonius of Tyana, who in the Byzantine world enjoyed the same reputation as a great sorcerer as Virgil did in the West, who had endowed such statues
with their miraculous powers, both at Constantinople and at Antioch.[38] The
rite whereby a statue received talismanic powers was known as στοιχείωσις:
Psellus tells us how this was done, by the insertion into the statue's cavity of
certain mineral and vegetable substances, vessels filled with sympathetic
unguents, inscribed seals, incense, etc.[39]

Psellus, perhaps the most brilliant of all Byzantine intellectuals, himself
half-believed in this nonsense. It is not surprising, therefore, that emperors
and patriarchs should have shared the same belief in the sympathetic properties
of statues, especially ancient ones, although some of the stories I quote here
may be apocryphal. Thus, Michael I (811–813) is said to have amputated the
arms of a statue of Tyche with a view to making the populace powerless
against imperial authority.[40] In the second quarter of the ninth century, the
very learned Patriarch John the Grammarian averted a barbarian invasion by
mutilating a three-headed bronze statue in the Hippodrome. While the patriarch recited incantations, three men armed with hammers struck simultaneously at the three heads of the statue: two of them were cut off, while the
third did not fall to the ground. The same fate befell the three chiefs of the
barbarian tribe: two were killed, the third was wounded but escaped.[41] This
incident is illustrated in the Madrid manuscript of Skylitzes (fig. 1).

---

[34] *Script. orig. CP*, I, p. 35 f., § 28 = II, p. 163, § 24; Suidas, s.v. κυνήγιον, ed. Adler, III, p. 213.

[35] *Script. orig. CP*, II, p. 185 ff., § 65.

[36] *Ibid.*, II, p. 271, § 179.

[37] *Ibid.*, II, p. 221, § 24; p. 278, § 200.

[38] See J. Miller, "Zur Frage nach der Persönlichkeit des Apollonius von Tyana," *Philologus*, LI
(1892), p. 581 ff.; F. Nau in *Patrol. Syriaca*, II (1907), p. 1364 ff.; *Catal. codd. astrol. graec.*, VII (1908)
by F. Boll, p. 174 f.

[39] *Epist.* 187 in Sathas, *Biblioth. gr. med. aevi*, V (1876), p. 474. Cf. E. R. Dodds, *op. cit. (supra,*
note 7), p. 62, who suggests that Psellus drew these prescriptions from Proclus.

[40] *Script. orig. CP*, II, p. 205, § 101.

[41] Theophanes Continuatus, Bonn ed., p. 155 f.; Pseudo-Symeon, *ibid.*, p. 649 f.; Cedrenus, II, p.
145 f. The statue is described merely as ἀνδριὰς τρισὶ διαμορφούμενος κεφαλαῖς (Hecate?); it could not,
in any case, have been the Serpent Column as stated by L. Bréhier ("Un patriarche sorcier à Constantinople," *Rev. de l' Orient chrétien*, IX [1904], p. 267), since the Serpent Column, as we shall see (*infra*,
note 119), retained its three heads until 1700. The identity of the barbarian tribe has caused a great
deal of speculation: F. Uspenskij sees here an allusion to a Russian incursion into Byzantine territory
before 842 ("Patriarkh Ioann VII Grammatik i Rus'-Dromity u Simeona Magistra," *Žurnal Minist.
Narodn. Prosveščenija* (Jan. 1890), p. 24 f.), while Vasiliev, setting chronology aside, connects this
legend with the Russian attack of 860 (*The Russian Attack on Constantinople in 860* [Cambridge, Mass.,
1946], p. 240 f.).

62

Basil I removed a statue from the Basilica—it was of a seated man holding his chin, and therefore probably represented some ancient philosopher, although it was commonly believed to be that of Solomon—and buried it in the foundations of a church he was building, the Nea Ekklesia. The statue was changed to represent the Emperor who was thus figuratively offering himself in sacrifice (ὥστε θυσίαν ἑαυτὸν τῷ τοιούτῳ κτίσματι καὶ θεῷ προσάγων).[42] The motif of immuring a live person in the foundations of a building, to give it greater stability, is common in Greek folklore.[43]

The dissolute Emperor Alexander, upon becoming impotent, was persuaded by magicians to clothe the statues in the Hippodrome with rich vestments and burn incense before them. The statue of a wild boar was believed to be the Emperor's talisman, and he proceeded to provide it with teeth and genitals which had been missing. For these impious acts he was stricken down by the Lord as a second Herod.[44] A few years later, the decapitation of a statue in Constantinople brought about the death of King Symeon of Bulgaria (927).[45]

In the Forum of Constantine there stood two female statues of bronze. In the twelfth century one of them was known as the Roman, the other as the Hungarian. The Roman statue fell down, while the Hungarian remained upright. This was brought to the attention of Manuel Comnenus who was then fighting the Hungarians. He proceeded to set up the Roman statue, whereas he overturned the Hungarian one, hoping thereby to affect the fortunes of the war.[46]

The Empress Euphrosyne, wife of Alexius Angelus, was addicted to magic and divination. She cut off the snout of the Calydonian boar in the Hippodrome (the same one that had been reconditioned by Alexander) and caused the colossal Hercules of Lysippus to be flogged, a fate, adds our historian, that the hero had not suffered at the hands of either Eurystheus or Omphale. The same Empress had the limbs and heads of other statues broken. What purpose she hoped to achieve thereby, we are not told.[47]

The adventures of the wild boar were not yet over. In 1203 the Emperor Isaac Angelus had him removed from his base in the Hippodrome and taken to the palace, meaning in this way to check the wild fury of the mob. At the same time the populace broke to pieces the great Athena which stood outside the Senate House on the Forum of Constantine. She was 30 ft. high and had her right arm outstretched towards the south. By this gesture, it was thought, she was beckoning to the army of the Crusaders—the mob could not disting-

---

[42] Leo Grammaticus, Bonn ed., p. 257 f.; Pseudo-Symeon, p. 692. The statue is described in *Script. orig. CP*, II, p. 171, § 40.

[43] See, e.g., L. Sainéan, "Les rites de la construction d' après la poésie populaire de l'Europe orientale," *Rev. de l'hist. des religions*, XLV (1902), p. 359 ff.; N. G. Polites, Μελέται περὶ τοῦ βίου καὶ τῆς γλώσσης τοῦ ἑλληνικοῦ λαοῦ. Παραδόσεις, II (Athens, 1904), p. 1113.

[44] *Vita Euthymii*, ed. de Boor (Berlin, 1888), p. 69; Theoph. Cont., p. 379.

[45] Theoph. Cont., p. 411 f.

[46] Nicetas Choniates, Bonn ed., p. 196. Cf. L. Oeconomos, *La vie religieuse dans l'Empire byzantin au temps des Comnènes et des Anges* (Paris, 1918), p. 91.

[47] Nicetas Choniates, p. 687 f.; cf. Oeconomos, *op. cit.*, p. 96.

uish south from west—and for this act of treason she was destroyed.[48] But even the Crusaders were not immune to such fancies, for after capturing Constantinople, they took care to destroy the palladia of the city, "especially those which they learnt had been set up against their nation."[49]

The obvious conclusion to be drawn from the above evidence is that not only the ordinary Byzantine but even persons of high rank viewed ancient statuary through a mist of superstition. But this evidence also lends itself to a deeper interpretation, since it constitutes a chapter of a much-discussed topic, namely the transition from ancient Greek religion to modern Greek folklore. This transition is paralleled by the history of a word: στοιχεῖον, the Greek term for the astrological *elementum*, was, like the word ζώδιον, commonly used in Byzantine times to designate a statue, more precisely a bewitched statue. This in turn has given rise to the modern Greek στοιχειό, the usual word for a ghost and in particular for a spirit attached to a specific place.[50]

The superstitious re-interpretation of antique sculpture was paralleled by a Christian re-interpretation, although the latter cannot be documented quite as fully as the former. We have seen that a seated statue, probably that of a philosopher, was considered to represent Solomon. Another statue which held a staff with a serpent twined round it (Aesculapius?) was thought to be that of a bishop; Basil I playfully placed his finger in the serpent's mouth and was bitten by a live serpent that was coiled inside the hollow one of bronze.[51] An equestrian statue in the Forum Tauri which represented either Theodosius I or Bellerophon was regarded as that of Joshua.[52] The statues of Adam and Eve, as they are called in our sources,[53] were probably also antique.

It is perhaps to such a Christian re-interpretation that we owe, in some cases, the re-use of antique reliefs in Byzantine churches. The oldest church of Trebizond, that of St. Anne, has over the entrance door a much weathered relief representing a flying (?) figure and a warrior upon which was inscribed the dedicatory inscription of the year 884–885 (fig. 2).[54] Evidently this relief was considered to be of particular significance to have been used in so prominent a manner. The church of Merbaka in the Argolis has classical

---

[48] Nicetas Choniates, p. 738 ff. On this statue, see R. J. H. Jenkins, "The Bronze Athena at Byzantium," *Journal of Hellenic Studies*, LXVII (1947), p. 31 ff., who believes that it may have been the Promachos of Phidias.

[49] Nicetas Choniates, p. 848. Robert de Clari repeats, without a shade of disbelief, the popular tales concerning the statues of Constantinople: *La conquête de Constantinople*, ed. Philippe Lauer (Paris, 1924), p. 87 ff.

[50] The evolution of the word στοιχεῖον has been the subject of some controversy. In addition to the older studies by H. Diels and O. Lagercrantz, see esp. A. Delatte and Ch. Josserand, "Contribution à l' étude de la démonologie byzantine," *Mélanges Bidez* (= *Ann. de l'Inst. de phil. et d'hist. orient.*, II [1934]), p. 208 ff.; C. Blum, "The Meaning of στοιχεῖον and its Derivatives in the Byzantine Age," *Eranos*, XLIV (1946), p. 315 ff. On the modern Greek στοιχειό, see esp. Polites, Παραδόσεις (as in note 43 *supra*), I, p. 250 ff.; II, p. 1051 ff.

[51] Leo Grammaticus, p. 257; Pseudo-Symeon, p. 691 f.

[52] *Script. orig. CP*, II, p. 176; Nicetas Choniates, pp. 849, 857 f. The identification of this statue raises some difficulties: cf. my remarks in *Art Bulletin*, XLI (1959), p. 355, note 31.

[53] *Script. orig. CP*, I, p. 21, § 5 = II, p. 196, § 87.

[54] Cf. G. Millet, "Les monastères et les églises de Trébizonde," *Bull. de corr. hell.*, XIX (1895), p. 434; K. N. Papamichalopoulos, Περιήγησις εἰς τὸν Πόντον (Athens, 1903), p. 201.

reliefs conspicuously displayed on its north and south façades.[55] A more familiar example is provided by the relief of Hercules with the Erymanthian boar that decorates the west façade of San Marco; but it is difficult to say whether it was used as an allegory of Salvation,[56] or with an apotropaic intention.[57] However, there can be no doubt about the christianization of the sepulchral monument of the Barbii, fragments of which frame the entrance door to the cathedral of S. Giusto at Trieste; since one of the funerary busts has actually been provided with a halo.[58] What reason, other than convenience, dictated the ample re-use of classical carving in the church of Panagia Gorgoepekoos (Little Metropolis) at Athens,[59] I am unable to say; whether the old stones were regarded as being στοιχειωμένα or not, they were placed with no regard for their subject-matter except in such a manner as to form a symmetrical pattern (fig. 3).

IV

Next we should consider the attitude of the Byzantine intellectuals. Their statements on the topic of ancient statuary, unlike those of the common man, cannot be taken at face value; they can be evaluated only in the perspective of a long rhetorical tradition stretching back to antiquity. The ancients, we may remember, had not evolved anything that we would regard as a sophisticated form of artistic criticism. Their chief and practically only criterion of excellence was verisimilitude. The famous anecdotes concerning Myron's bronze cow which a live calf came to suck, the horse of Apelles at the sight of which live horses neighed, the grapes of Zeuxis that were pecked by live birds sufficiently illustrate this criterion. It is stated in the first sentence of the Elder Philostratus' *Imagines:* "Whosoever scorns painting is unjust to truth." As part of verisimilitude the ancients prized the ability to represent feelings or emotions (ἤθη), which was considered to have been an invention of the Hellenistic age.[60] Even when Philostratus (the other Philostratus who wrote the Life of Apollonius) speaks of the importance of imagination (*phantasia*), which is wiser than *mimesis*, he means no more than the ability to visualize exactly somebody or something that one has not seen, as in the case of the gods.[61] Typical of this attitude is the well-known epigram concerning the Cnidian Aphrodite: Aphrodite came to Cnidus to see her own statue, and having examined it, she exclaimed: "Where did Praxiteles see me naked?"[62] He had not: he had *phantasia*.

[55] A. Struck, "Vier byzant. Kirchen der Argolis," *Athen. Mitt.*, XXXIV (1909), p. 208, fig. 129. Cf. Polites, Παραδόσεις, I, p. 73; II, p. 755.

[56] So E. Panofsky and F. Saxl, "Classical Mythology in Mediaeval Art," *Metropolitan Museum Studies*, IV/2 (1933), p. 228.

[57] So O. Demus, *The Church of San Marco in Venice* (Washington, D. C., 1960), p. 134f.

[58] G. Caprin, *Trieste*, Italia artistica, No. 22 (Bergamo, 1923), fig. on p. 25.

[59] K. Michel and A. Struck, "Die mittelbyzantinischen Kirchen Athens," *Athen. Mitteilungen*, XXXI (1906), p. 281ff.; P. Steiner, "Antike Skulpturen an der Panagia Gorgoepikoos," *ibid.*, p. 325ff.

[60] This "invention" was ascribed to Aristides of Thebes, a contemporary of Apelles: Pliny, *Nat. hist.*, XXXV, 98.

[61] *Vita Apollonii*, VI, 19.

[62] *Anthol. Palat.*, XVI, 160, 162.

Countless students of rhetoric, laboring over their *ekphraseis*, reduced these artistic ideals to stale clichés. And when the *ekphrasis* came to be used to describe Christian subjects, its literary conventions, including the insistence on realism and the required comparison (*synkrisis*) with the famous artists of the past, were simply maintained. It is interesting to read the description of a painting representing the martyrdom of St. Euphemia by St. Asterius of Amaseia (*ca.* A.D. 400).[63] The picture was so good, "that you would think it was the work of Euphranor, or another one of the ancients who raised painting to such a high level, and made pictures that were almost animated." What Asterius admires in the scenes of martyrdom is their realism: the judge is certainly angry, "since art, when it so wishes, can indeed express anger even with inanimate matter"; the drops of blood seemed in truth to be trickling down from the martyr's mouth. Asterius adds that he used to admire, for its expression of conflicting emotions, a painting of Medea about to slaughter her children—he refers to the famous painting by Timomachus of Byzantium,[64] a replica of which, from Herculaneum, is at the Museo Nazionale of Naples. But now he has transferred his admiration to this painting of St. Euphemia, the author of which "has instilled feeling (ἦθος) into his colors, having mingled modesty with courage, two passions that are naturally contradictory."

This kind of appreciation was perhaps still appropriate to the relatively naturalistic art of the fourth century. It was, moreover, a standard ingredient of the *ekphrasis* genre, and as such, after passing through the hands of such practitioners as Libanius, Choricius, John of Gaza, etc., it was taken over by the Byzantines.

Now, the significant and, to us, astounding thing is that the Byzantines applied the same standard of criticism not only to ancient art, for which it had been invented, but also to their own art, *without any distinction.* Our own appreciation of Byzantine art stems largely from the fact that this art is not naturalistic; yet the Byzantines themselves, judging by their extant statements, regarded it as being highly naturalistic and as being directly in the tradition of Phidias, Apelles, and Zeuxis. When the Patriarch Photius described a mosaic of the Virgin in St. Sophia, he praised it as a "lifelike imitation" (ἡ ζωγράφος τέχνη οὕτως ἀκριβῶς εἰς φύσιν τὴν μίμησιν ἔστησε). The Virgin's lips "have been made flesh by the colors" and though still, they were not "incapable of speaking."[65] The same Patriarch, in describing a church pavement inlaid to represent various animals, says that it surpassed the art of Phidias, Parrhasius, Praxiteles, and Zeuxis who "are proved indeed to have been mere children in their art and makers of figments."[66] A certain painter Andrew, who flourished in the tenth century, is said to have been the equal of

[63] PG, 40, col. 333 ff.
[64] Overbeck, *Schriftquellen*, No. 2122 ff. Asterius merely repeats the standard appreciation of the Medea: cf. *ibid.*, Nos. 2128, 2129.
[65] Φωτίου ὁμιλίαι, ed. B. Laourdas, Ἑλληνικά, Suppl. 12 (Thessaloniki, 1959), p. 167₁₃; *The Homilies of Photius Patriarch of Constantinople*, trans. by C. Mango (Cambridge, Mass., 1958), p. 290.
[66] Ed. Laourdas, p. 102; Bonn ed. (along with Georgius Codinus), p. 198; Mango trans., p. 187. Cf. Nicephorus Gregoras, Bonn ed., II, p. 749: the carving in St. Sophia surpassed that of Phidias.

Apelles, Agatharchus of Samos, Heracleides, and Philoinos (Philinos?) of Byzantium[67]—this list of names is, of course, merely a display of learning and the last two appear to be unknown even to modern scholarship. The Emperor Leo VI, commenting on a mosaic of Christ in the dome of a church, says that it appeared to be not a work of art, but Christ himself, who had momentarily stilled his lips.[68] An image of the Virgin in the same church appeared to be opening her lips and speaking to her Child, so much it gave the illusion of "not being devoid of breath" (οὕτως ὥσπερ οὐκ ἄμοιρα πνοῆς ὑπάρχει τὰ εἰκονίσματα).[69] Countless epigrams on Byzantine icons labored the same point: the image was always so lifelike that it appeared to be on the point of speaking.[70] Consider another example: in his obscure polemic with Theodore Metochites, Nicephorus Chumnos argues that in literary composition one ought to take as models the best authors of antiquity, just as the artist is guided by the works of Lysippus and Apelles.[71] It would be naive to conclude from this that in the early fourteenth century Byzantine artists really had before them any of the antique masterpieces to which Chumnos alludes. Our learned author is merely using a literary *topos*.

To illustrate this fossilization of artistic criticism in the face of completely different artistic phenomena, I can do no better than to confront two epigrams, one ancient, the other Byzantine. The first, which is very short, concerns the Zeus of Olympia: "Either the god came down to earth from heaven to show his form to thee, O Phidias; or else it was thou who didst ascend to see the god."[72] The second epigram is by the fourteenth-century Byzantine author Nicephorus Callistus and it concerns the mosaic of Christ by the twelfth-century painter Eulalios in the church of the Holy Apostles: "Either Christ himself came down from heaven and showed the exact form of his features to him who had such expressive hands (τῷ τὰς χεῖρας ἔχοντι μᾶλλον εὐλάλους: a pun), or else the famous Eulalios ascended into the sky itself and with his

---

[67] Theoph. Cont., p. 382.

[68] Λέοντος τοῦ Σοφοῦ πανυγηρικοὶ (sic) λόγοι, ed. Akakios (Athens, 1868), p. 245.

[69] *Ibid.*, p. 246. Cf. p. 277 concerning an image of the Annunciation: εἴποις ἂν καὶ λογικῆς μὴ ἀμοιρεῖν τὰ εἰκονίσματα διαλέξεως, οὕτως ἐπὶ τῶν προσώπων φυσικὸν αὐτοῖς ὁ τεχνίτης χρῶμα καὶ ἦθος ἀνέθηκεν.

[70] See, e.g., John Mavropous, *Iohannis Euchaitorum metropolitae quae in cod. Vat. gr. 676 supersunt*, ed. Bollig and de Lagarde (Göttingen, 1882), p. 9, No. 14 (icon of St. John Chrysostom); No. 16 (icon of St. Basil): ἀλλ᾽ εἰ λαλήσει (ζῆν δοκεῖ γὰρ καὶ τύπος); p. 10, No. 17 (icon of Three Hierarchs): γραφέντες ζῆν δοκοῦσι καὶ λέγειν. *Die Gedichte des Christophoros Mitylenaios*, ed. Kurtz (Leipzig, 1903), p. 63, No. 101 (icon of prophet Elijah): ἰδοὺ γὰρ αὐτὸς ἐνθάδε ζῶν, ὡς βλέπεις; p. 75, No. 112 (icon of St. Michael being painted by the painter Myron): ἔμπνουν ἀναστήλωσον αὐτόν, εἰ δύνη. Manuel Philes, *Carmina*, ed. Miller, I (Paris, 1855), p. 3, No. III (Gabriel in the Annunciation): τί δὴ σιωπᾷς; τάχα γὰρ ζῶν ἐγράφης; p. 6, No. XII (Raising of Lazarus): ἅπαντα συνθεὶς εὐφυῶς ὁ ζωγράφος | μόνην παρῆκε τὴν βοὴν τοῦ δεσπότου; p. 21, No. XXXVII (icon of St. Mark): οὐ γὰρ ὡς ἄπνους τύπος, | ἀλλ᾽ ὡς ἔτι ζῶν καὶ κινεῖται καὶ πνέει; p. 33, No. LXIX (icon of St. John Chrysostom): γραφεὶς πάλιν ζῇς· τοῦτο τῆς εὐτεχνίας; p. 34, No. LXXVI (carving of St. George): ἔμπνους ὁ μάρτυς καὶ δοκῶν ζῆν ἐκ λίθου, etc.

[71] Boissonade, *Anecdota graeca*, III (Paris, 1831), p. 357: ἔστι γὰρ πάντως καὶ πρὸς τὰ ἐκείνων [the ancient authors] ἡμᾶς ὁρᾶν σπουδάσματα ... τρόπον γε τὸν ἴσον ὥσπερ οἱ τὰς εἰκόνας καὶ τὰς μορφὰς γράφοντες πρὸς πίνακας καὶ τύπους τοὺς πάλαι Λυσίππου τινὸς καὶ Ἀπελλοῦ, καὶ εἴ τις ἕτερος κατ᾽ ἐκείνους ζώσας εἰκόνας, καὶ πνοῆς μόνης καὶ κινήσεως ἀπολειπομένας, ἣν μορφῶν καὶ γράφων. This passage is analyzed by I. Ševčenko, *Études sur la polémique entre Théodore Métochite et Nicéphore Choumnos* (Brussels, 1962), p. 22.

[72] *Anthol. Palat.*, XVI, 81.

skilled hand accurately delineated the appearance of Christ."[73] The only difference lies in the prolixity of the Byzantine epigram.

Aesthetically, then, there appeared, to the Byzantines, to be no difference
whatever between ancient and their own art; the only difference was one of
subject matter. This distinction was important since an image was believed
to contain somehow the *eidos* of its archetype. Of the skill of the ancients there
could be no question; the pity of it was that they wasted it on such worthless
subjects.

It is interesting that between the reign of Justinian and the middle of the
twelfth century there does not appear to be a single *ekphrasis* devoted to a
work of ancient art.[74] The only pertinent text that is known to me is contained
in the "Description of the Statues and Tall Columns of Constantinople" by
Constantine Rhodius, who wrote under Constantine VII,[75] i.e. at the very height
of what modern scholars like to call the "Macedonian Renaissance." The poet
describes at some length the Seven Wonders of Constantinople, but these
wonders are not the works of ancient statuary. They are instead the equestrian statue of Justinian, Constantine's porphyry column, the Senate House
also built by Constantine, a column bearing a cross, a weather vane of the
time of Theodosius I, and the columns of Theodosius and Arcadius. It is in
describing the Senate House that the poet dwells on two ancient works: a
bronze door representing a Gigantomachy in relief that had originally belonged to the temple of Artemis at Ephesus, and the thirty-foot-high bronze
statue of Athena which we have already mentioned and which Constantine
Rhodius believed to have come from Lindos. Yet the poet's remarks about
these works of art are far from laudatory. He does admit that the reliefs on
the door were lifelike: the fire that darted from the Giants' eyes caused the
spectators to tremble. But he goes on to add: "It was with such errors that
the foolish race of Hellas was deceived as it accorded an evil worship to the
abomination of vain impiety. But the mighty and wise Constantine brought
it here to be a plaything for the city, a jest to children and a source of laughter
to men." This echoes the passage of Eusebius that we have quoted above. As
for the bronze Athena, it was a monument of "Lindian error." "For thus it
was that the madmen of olden times made in vain the idol of Pallas."[76] We
are reminded of similar remarks that Constantine's contemporary, Bishop
Arethas of Caesarea, penned in the margins of his copy of Lucian.[77]

---

[73] A. Papadopoulos-Kerameus, "Νικηφόρος Κάλλιστος Ξανθόπουλος," *BZ*, XI (1902), p. 46, No. 14; cf. N.
Bees, "Kunstgeschichtliche Untersuchungen über die Eulalios-Frage," *Rep. für Kunstwissenschaft*,
XXXIX (1916), p. 101.

[74] Note, however, a mutilated epigram by Christophoros Mitylenaios (first half of the eleventh
century) on a statue of Hercules in the suburban palace of Aretae: ed. Kurtz, p. 99, No. 143. As usual,
the statue is pronounced to be lifelike (... χεὶρ ἡ τεχνίτου | τοῦ παντελῶς ἔμψυχον Ἡρακλῆν ξέσαι).
On the palace of Aretae, see R. Janin, *Constantinople byzantine* (Paris, 1950), pp. 137, 406, who fails
to quote this text.

[75] Cf. G. Downey, "Constantine the Rhodian: His Life and Writings," *Late Classical and Mediaeval
Studies in Honor of A. M. Friend. Jr.* (Princeton, 1955), p. 212 ff.

[76] E. Legrand, "Description des oeuvres d'art et de l'église des Saints Apôtres de Constantinople,"
Rev. des ét. grecques, IX (1896), p. 40 f.

[77] *Scholia in Lucianum*, ed. H. Rabe (Leipzig, 1906), pp. 76, 78 ff., 218 ff.

In the middle of the twelfth century, Constantine Manasses, who died as a bishop, wrote an *ekphrasis*, unfortunately mutilated, which describes an antique relief of the story of Odysseus and Polyphemus. He starts by saying that this relief attracted his attention while he was visiting a friend, a nobleman addicted to the study of letters. It was made of reddish stone, and may have looked something like the fragment of an oval sarcophagus in the Museo Nazionale of Naples (fig. 4)[78] Manasses describes the scene: Odysseus offering a wineskin to the Cyclops, a hairy monster of savage appearance with an inflated belly; the companions of Odysseus lying slaughtered on the ground. Manasses dwells on the realism of the relief and compliments the artist for having used red stone to represent such a bloody scene.[79] There is nothing in this description that could not have been written a thousand years earlier; and if the author's name had not been preserved in the manuscript, scholars might well have attributed it to late antiquity.

It was not long thereafter that the antique statues of Constantinople met their doom. I have referred already to the destruction of the bronze Athena at the hands of a Byzantine mob in 1203. Once the city had fallen, most of the bronze statues were sent to the melting pot. Some were removed to the West: the four horses on the façade of San Marco and the colossus of Barletta survive as the only reminders of this spoliation. The historian Nicetas Choniates wrote a dirge on the statues that were then destroyed. He describes eighteen of them[80]—surely only a small fraction of the total: the colossal Hera, whose head alone required four pairs of oxen to drag it away, the Hercules of Lysippus, a Paris giving the apple to Aphrodite, a Bellerophon astride the Pegasus, and so forth. Nicetas' lamentations form a curious, a deeply mediaeval document. The continuum linking him with antiquity is not broken: Nicetas displays a wealth of mythological allusions, quotes freely from Homer. A statue of Helen, her body humid even in bronze, her lips parted as if about to speak, moves him to his most rhapsodic flourishes. Her charms did not avail against the insensitive barbarians; it was in revenge of the burning of Troy that the descendents of Aeneas, i.e. the Venetians, delivered her to the flames.[81] Although permeated with antique reminiscences, Nicetas' response to the statues is not antiquarian; it is rather allegorical, in places superstitious. With many of his Byzantine predecessors, he believes that a group representing an eagle killing a serpent had been set up with magical rites by Apollonius of Tyana to frighten snakes away from Constantinople; while another group representing an ox struggling with a crocodile suggests the desperate struggle between nations, in this case the Byzantines and the Latins.[82]

A violent jolt was needed to produce a different attitude towards pagan antiquity; to make it appear as a distinct epoch, one whose greatness shone

[78] C. Robert, *Die antiken Sarkophag-Reliefs*, II (Berlin, 1890), p. 159f., No. 148 and pl. LIII.

[79] L. Sternbach, "Beiträge zur Kunstgeschichte," *Jahreshefte d. Österr. Archäol. Inst.*, V (1902), Beiblatt, col. 83ff.

[80] P. 856ff. Cf. Edwin Pears, *The Fall of Constantinople, being the Story of the Fourth Crusade* (London 1885), p. 354f.

[81] Nicetas Choniates, p. 863f.

[82] *Ibid.*, pp. 861f., 866ff.

even through its ruins. This interposition of "distance" or of a "projection plane," as Panofsky calls it,[83] is indeed what separates the Renaissance in its attitude towards antiquity from the Middle Ages. In Byzantium such an interposition was never achieved, although there are some signs that it could have been. It was precisely in the thirteenth century that the Byzantines of Nicaea began calling themselves Hellenes in the national sense.[84] There exists one document of this period which, although it is not directly pertinent to the topic of statuary, is nevertheless so illuminating that it deserves quoting. It is a letter of the Emperor Theodore II Lascaris and describes a visit that he paid to the ruins of Pergamon.

"The city," he says, "is full of theatres, grown old and decrepit with age, showing as through a glass their former splendor and the nobility of those who built them. For these things are full of Hellenic elevation of thought (μεγαλονοίας) and constitute the image of that wisdom. Such things does the city show unto us, the descendents, reproaching us with the greatness of ancestral glory. Awesome are these compared to the buildings of today ...." He goes on to speak of the bridge spanning the river, the arches of which would have excited the admiration of Phidias. On either side of the big theatre stood round towers, "not the work of a modern hand, nor the invention of a modern mind, for their very sight fills one with astonishment." Among the ancient ruins were the hovels of the inhabitants which, by comparison, looked like mouse holes (μυῶν τρῶγλαι). "The works of the dead," he concludes, "are more beautiful than those of the living."[85]

One is reminded of Petrarch's similar experience when he visited Rome a hundred years later. But there is a difference: the significance of Theodore's attitude is that he contrasts the wretchedness of his age, not with the good old days of Justinian, but with the time of the Hellenes; he does not, however, condemn the intervening period. Petrarch took one further step, and a decisive one: he was the first to look upon the millennium separating himself from the decline of the Roman Empire as the Dark Ages.[86]

Interest in the material remains of antiquity was not, perhaps, entirely abandoned when the Greek Empire returned to Constantinople. In a romance of the early fourteenth century, a mythical king is represented visiting, for recreation, "the buildings of the Hellenes" (κτίσματα τῶν ἑλλήνων).[87] The

[83] Renaissance and Renascences in Western Art (Stockholm, 1960), p. 108.
[84] Cf. N. G. Polites, Ἕλληνες ἢ Ῥωμιοί; in Λαογραφικὰ σύμμεικτα, I (Athens, 1920), p. 126; M. A. Andreeva, Očerki po kul'ture vizantijskago dvora v XIII veke (Prague, 1927), p. 146; K. Lechner, Hellenen und Barbaren (diss. Munich, 1954), p. 64ff.
[85] Theodori Ducae Lascaris Epistulae CCXVII, ed. N. Festa (Florence, 1898), p. 107f. Cf. S. Antonia-dis, "Sur une lettre de Théodore II Lascaris," L'hellénisme contemporain, VIII (1954), p. 356ff.
[86] See T.E. Mommsen, "Petrarch's Conception of the 'Dark Ages'," Speculum, XVII (1942), p. 226ff.
[87] Le roman de Callimaque et de Chrysorrhoé, ed. M. Pichard (Paris, 1956), p. 31, v. 857. Byzantine romances of chivalry, all of which appear to fall between the thirteenth and fifteenth centuries, show a marked interest in mythological representations. Callimachus and Chrysorrhoe, v. 419ff. describes an astral ceiling containing pictures of Cronos, Zeus in the guise of a "great emperor," Ares caressing Aphrodite, Athena seated on a throne, and the Graces. Carvings of love scenes with erotes decorated the Castle of Love in Belthandros and Chrysantza, v. 339ff. (ed. E. Kriaras, Βυζαντινὰ ἱπποτικὰ μυθιστο-ρήματα [Athens, 1955], p. 107f.). The Palace of Love in Libistros and Rhodamne contained an eros in green marble; the birth of Eros; the Judgment of Paris, and figures of erotes in stucco. The Silver

tireless poetaster Manuel Philes wrote an epigram on a representation of Kairos,[88] and another on a "painting by Apelles" which was said to represent Alexander's table.[89] Actually, there were very few antique remains in Constantinople at this time. A catalogue of surviving statuary, which seems to be fairly complete, is given in the early fifteenth century by Manuel Chrysoloras in a letter in which he compares the Old and the New Rome. This letter was written from the Old Rome, and Chrysoloras, who spent many years in Western Europe, had absorbed much of contemporary humanism. He looks at his country from the outside, and his remarks are therefore of particular interest. That there used to be many statues in Constantinople, he says, is shown by the remaining pedestals and the inscriptions upon them. Most of these were in the Hippodrome. Some statues he had seen himself which later disappeared. Of surviving antique statuary only two specimens are quoted: one, a reclining figure of marble, the other a set of reliefs at the Golden Gate, representing the Labors of Hercules and the Punishment of Prometheus. Why were there no more statues? Because Constantinople was built at a time when such things were neglected on account of religion, and men avoided the representation of idols. How indeed were they to make them, when in Rome, where statues existed from an earlier period, they were being at that very time destroyed? Statuary started in Greece and reached a wonderful development in Italy. The Byzantines, for their part, cultivated other arts, such as painting and mosaic.[90]

To round off this sketchy survey of the attitude of Byzantine intellectuals, I should add that I know of no Byzantine collector of antiquities after the fifth century A.D. It has been stated that Theodore Metochites, the prime minister of Andronicus II, had such a collection in his palace, but this assertion is based on a misunderstood text.[91] Contrast this with the West, where in the middle of the twelfth century a bishop of Winchester purchased pagan statues in Rome and despatched them home,[92] not to mention the collection of classical sculpture made by Frederick II.[93]

Castle in the same poem had statues of the twelve virtues, the twelve months, and the twelve forms of love: *Le roman de Libistros et Rhodamné*, ed. J. A. Lambert (née Van der Kolf) (Amsterdam, 1935), p. 70, v. 261ff.; p. 110, v. 938ff.; p. 116, v. 1017; p. 122, v. 1108ff. It has been assumed that these descriptions reflect the decoration of actual Byzantine palaces: so, e.g. Bury, *Romances of Chivalry on Greek Soil* (Oxford, 1911), p. 15; Koukoules, Βυζαντινῶν βίος καὶ πολιτισμός, IV (Athens, 1951), p. 303; but the problem ought to be re-examined with reference to western romances. The present state of research on these poems is summarized by M. I. Manoussacas, "Les romans byzantins de chevalerie," *Rev. des ét. byz.*, X (1953), p. 70ff.

[88] Ed. Miller, I, p. 32, No. LXVII. Cf. A. Muñoz, *Studi d'arte medioevale* (Rome, 1909), p. 8f.

[89] Ed. Miller, II, p. 267f. This was actually a mosaic of the *asarotos* type which decorated a bedroom in the Great Palace: a fuller description of it is given by Constantine Manasses, ed. Sternbach (as in note 79 *supra*), col. 74ff.

[90] PG, 156, col. 45ff.; German trans. by F. Grabler in *Byzantinische Geschichtsschreiber*, II (1954), p. 132ff.

[91] R. Guilland, "Le palais de Théodore Métochite," *Rev. des ét. grecques*, XXXV (1922), pp. 85f., 93. The word παλαιά (in v. 214 of Metochites' poem), which Guilland translates as "antiquités," refers in reality to *old houses* which Metochites had purchased: I owe this correction to Prof. Ihor Ševčenko.

[92] See J. B. Ross, "A Study of Twelfth-Century Interest in the Antiquities of Rome" in *Medieval and Historiographical Essays in Honor of J. W. Thompson* (Chicago, 1938), p. 308f.

[93] See E. Kantorowicz, *Kaiser Friedrich der Zweite*, 2nd ed. (Berlin, 1928), p. 482f.; Ergänzungsband (Berlin, 1931), p. 210.

V

The last question I should like to ask is whether the classical statuary collected in Constantinople or surviving in other towns exerted any influence on
Byzantine art. It is important to state this question in a precise manner. No
one doubts that the amalgam which is usually termed Early Christian or
Early Byzantine art had Graeco-Roman art as its chief ingredient. It is equally
undeniable that Byzantine art proper went through certain periods, in particular
those that are often called the Macedonian and Palaeologan Renaissances,
when a classicizing style and classicizing motifs, such as personifications,
were more in evidence than during other periods. The specific question we are
asking is whether Byzantine artists, especially during those times of revival,
sought their inspiration *directly* from antique statues and reliefs or whether
the antique influence reached them through other, more indirect and contam-
inated channels.

A hundred years ago, Jules Labarte based his entire theory of the evolution
of Byzantine art on the existence of antique statues. Ever since the foundation of Constantinople, he says, eastern artists had before them, as an unfailing
guide, the masterpieces of ancient sculpture. The artistic revival under Justinian resulted from their study. The new school that arose after Iconoclasm
attempted likewise to imitate the models of ancient art that still abounded
in Constantinople. In the eleventh century decadence set in, but the presence
of ancient masterpieces did not allow Byzantine artists to stray altogether
from the right path. But then came the Latin occupation and the destruction
of ancient statues. When the Greeks returned to Constantinople, they found
themselves deprived of antique models. Is it surprising therefore that, from
this time on, Byzantine art went from bad to worse?[94] Today no-one holds
such extreme views. Yet the supposition—so natural to us today—that on
occasion a Byzantine artist would copy a statue here or there, has not been
entirely abandoned.[95] Can such a supposition be substantiated?

It is naturally in the realm of the plastic arts that one would begin to look
for the possible influence of ancient statuary. But it is a matter of common
knowledge that the Byzantines, as a rule, did not cultivate sculpture in the
round or even high relief in stone.[96] If then ancient statues were not imitated

[94] *Histoire des arts industriels au moyen âge et à l'époque de la Renaissance,* I (Paris, 1864), pp. 31,
52, 96; III (1865), pp. 14, 33 f.

[95] Thus, J. Ebersolt, *Les arts somptuaires de Byzance* (Paris, 1923), p. 130, says that Byzantine
artists "pouvaient puiser à pleines mains dans les chefs-d'oeuvre de l'art antique." J. Beckwith, *The
Art of Constantinople* (London, 1961), p. 7, speaks more cautiously of the antique statues "at more
than one time providing a source of form from which sprang the streams of perennial hellenism to
feed the Byzantine style."

[96] Sculpture in the round, after the sixth century, was used only for statues of emperors and occasionally members of the imperial family, but even that is confined to a few periods. The tradition
continued down to the reign of Philippicus (711–13). Then, naturally enough, there was a break
corresponding to the Iconoclastic period. At the very end of the eighth century statues were set up of
Constantine VI and his mother, the Empress Irene. For several centuries thereafter no statues appear
to have been made; our next example is of Andronicus I (1183–85), which was apparently planned
but never set up. Eighty years later a group of sculpture commemorating the deliverance of Constantinople from the Latins was set up by Michael VIII. Cf. Ebersolt, *Les arts somptuaires,* p. 131. This

by Byzantine artists in the same medium, we must extend our search to painting and the minor arts. Here we can make at once a preliminary observation. We are all familiar with late-mediaeval western representations of mythological subjects in which the Olympian gods and goddesses, the heroes of the Trojan war, etc., appear in the guise of Gothic knights and ladies. This phenomenon is not, on the whole, observable in Byzantium. There are, it is true, a few examples of ancient subjects in Byzantine garb, but they are widely scattered in time and do not appear to be characteristic of any given period: we may quote for the ninth century the Gregory manuscript in Milan, *Ambros. E. 49–50* (fig. 5),[97] for the eleventh the Gregory in Jerusalem, *Taphou 14* (fig. 6),[98] and another in the Panteleimon monastery of Mount Athos, *cod. 6*,[99] for the fifteenth the gross sketches in the margin of the famous codex A of the Iliad, *Marc. gr. 454* (fig. 7).[100] Generally, however, when a Byzantine artist was called upon to depict a mythological subject, which happened rather seldom, or a pagan statue, which happened more often, especially in illustrations appended to the lives of saints, he was able to give such representations a more or less authentic look. The "antiquité romanesque" of the West was predicated upon an estrangement from antiquity such as happened, for example, in France in the thirteenth and fourteenth centuries,[101] but which did not happen in Byzantium.

Once this has been said, however, it should also be admitted that Byzantine art does not exhibit a single instance of such intimate contact with specific antique models as we find, though transposed in subject matter, in the portal of Reims cathedral or in the work of Nicolo Pisano. Modern scholars have nevertheless suggested that some Byzantine representations were modelled after ancient statues. Thus, Ainalov asserted that the personification of the city of Gibeon in the Joshua Roll (fig. 8) reproduced the Tyche of Antioch by the Hellenistic sculptor Eutychides, one replica of which exists in the Vatican (fig. 9).[102] On inspection, the resemblance turns out to be rather slight; Ainalov could have found closer parallels. But now Prof. Weitzmann tells us that the city of Gibeon does not reproduce a Tyche type at all, but was adapted from the type of Io watched by Argus.[103]

---

curve is quite suggestive: it is particularly interesting that no statues whatever were made during the so-called Macedonian Renaissance. As for the revival of sculpture in the twelfth century, we may also quote a text by Theodore Balsamon: commenting on canon 100 of the Quinisext Council, which forbade the representation of erotic subjects, he notes that in the houses of the rich there were not only pictures of this kind, but even human figures carved out of stucco: Rhalles and Potles, Σύνταγμα τῶν θείων καὶ ἱερῶν κανόνων, II (Athens, 1852), p. 546.

[97] A. Grabar, *Les miniatures du Grégoire de Nazianze de l'Ambrosienne* (Paris, 1943), pls. LXX, 1–2, LXXI, 2, LXXII, 1.

[98] K. Weitzmann, *Greek Mythology in Byzantine Art* (Princeton, 1951), figs. 2, 17, 20, 29, 33, 52, 59, 70, 74, 76–78, 89, 92.

[99] Diehl, *Manuel d'art byzantin*, II (Paris, 1926), p. 628 and figs. 304, 305; Weitzmann, *op. cit.*, figs. 22, 38, 39, 58, 68, 87.

[100] D. Comparetti, *Homeri Ilias cum scholiis. Cod. Venet. A, Marc. 454*, Codices graeci et latini, VI (Leiden, 1901), fols, 1ʳ–ᵛ, 4ʳ–ᵛ, 6ʳ–ᵛ, 8ᵛ, 9ʳ–ᵛ.

[101] Cf. J. Adhémar, *Influences antiques dans l'art du moyen âge français* (London, 1939), p. 292 ff.

[102] *The Hellenistic Origins of Byzantine Art*, trans. by E. and S. Sobolevitch (New Brunswick, N. J., 1961), p. 134.

[103] *The Joshua Roll* (Princeton, 1948), p. 65.

Much has been made of the seated Hercules on an ivory casket at Xanten (fig. 10).[104] The pose of the hero, who is resting on a basket after having cleaned the Augean stables, corresponds exactly to that of the Lysippan colossus which, as we have seen, was in the Hippodrome of Constantinople until 1204. It cannot be denied that the ultimate model of the ivory was the statue of Lysippus, of which, unfortunately, no ancient replica has survived; yet it is equally clear that the carving was not copied directly from the statue. It is difficult to imagine that in the original, Hercules would have been represented beardless;[105] besides, the summary style of the carving suggests that it was copied from a small model, possibly a manuscript.[106] Similar observations could be made on other Byzantine representations that have been quoted in this connection, such as the group of Oedipus and the Sphinx on a glass bowl in the Treasury of San Marco (where the Sphinx has been turned into an angel and Oedipus made to sit on a throne);[107] the Olympian gods on a ninth- or tenth-century inkwell in the cathedral treasury of Padua;[108] or the nude figure of Life which the exemplary monk renounces in a manuscript of St. John Climacus, *Vatic. gr. 394* (fig. 11).[109] Each time we find a Byzantine representation of a classical subject, it appears, upon inspection, to be separated from its ultimate classical model by a long chain of transmission, usually in the minor arts.[110]

Since space does not allow me to substantiate this conclusion with the help of several other examples, I shall confine myself to one monument, the famous Menologium of Basil II in the Vatican Library, *cod. gr. 1613*. Out of the 430 miniatures contained in this manuscript, twenty include classical figures, either statues or reliefs, of which six are required by the text and fourteen have no obvious *raison d'être*.[111] The Vatican Menologium is not necessarily an original, but the corpus of illustrations it contains could not have been compiled before the beginning of the tenth century.[112] This brings us, therefore, once more to the Macedonian Renaissance: if Byzantine artists ever copied ancient sculpture, then this is surely the time when they might have done it.

When we examine the twenty representations of ancient sculpture in the Menologium, we realize that, with a few exceptions, they are all variants of

[104] H. Graeven, "Mittelalterliche Nachbildungen des Lysippischen Herakleskolosses," *Bonner Jahrb.*, CVIII/CIX (1902), p. 258ff.; A. Furtwängler, *Der Herakles des Lysipp in Konstantinopel*, Sitzungsb. Bayr. Akad., Philos.-philol. Klasse (1902), p. 435ff.

[105] Cf. F. P. Johnson, *Lysippos* (Durham, N. C., 1927), p. 195.

[106] So Weitzmann, *Greek Mythology*, p. 161.

[107] *Id.*, "The Survival of Mythological Representations in Early Christian and Byzantine Art," *DOP*, 14 (1960), p. 50f.

[108] P. Toesca, "Cimeli bizantini," *L'Arte*, IX (1906), p. 35f. The inkwell was made for a certain calligrapher Leo; the attempt to identify him with the ninth-century scholar Leo the Philosopher does not appear to be convincing (B. Hemmerdinger, *Essai sur l'histoire du texte de Thucydide* [Paris, 1955], p. 39).

[109] A. B. Cook, *Zeus*, II/2 (Cambridge, 1925), p. 867; J. R. Martin, *The Illustration of the Heavenly Ladder of John Climacus* (Princeton, 1954), p. 50ff. and fig. 72.

[110] The small group of Byzantine reliefs with mythological subjects, such as the Hercules in the Byzantine Museum of Athens (A. Xyngopoulos, "Βυζαντινὸν ἀνάγλυφον τοῦ Ἡρακλέους," Ἀρχαιολ. Ἐφημερίς [1927–28], p. 1ff.) or the Pan in Berlin (K. Museen zu Berlin, O. Wulff, *Altchristliche und mittelalterliche ... Bildwerke*, II [Berlin, 1911], p. 125, No. 2216), are so mediaeval in style that the nature of their immediate models can hardly be determined.

[111] See I. Ševčenko, "The Illuminators of the Menologium of Basil II," *DOP*, 16 (1962), p. 268.

[112] *Ibid.*, p. 261f.

two basic types. The first, which is used to decorate sarcophagi or troughs, consists of a row of nude standing figures, some holding hands, others grasping spears.[113] They are skilfully rendered in grisaille, but there is no attempt at composition: the figures are simply strung together (figs. 12, 13, 14). A row of standing figures is, of course, a common type of sarcophagus decoration, but one would be hard put to indicate a specific classical model that the Byzantine miniaturists might have used here. The second type, used both for statues and to decorate sarcophagi, is a nude, standing figure holding a spear in one hand; the other hand may be free, but usually it holds an orb with a piece of drapery hanging below it (figs. 15, 16, 17).[114] The ultimate model may have been an imperial statue, perhaps even that of Constantine-Helios on the porphyry column. But the model has been misunderstood: the hanging bit of drapery under the orb is derived from a fully or partially draped figure; and when we turn to a manuscript of St. Gregory in Paris (*Coislin 239*), we find that some of the pagan gods depicted therein, e.g. Isis (fig. 18), do hold orbs over one end of the garment that is thrown over the left forearm.[115] The type used in the Vatican Menologium is therefore related to a type that was current in manuscript illumination.

Yet, the appearance of classical motifs in the Menologium is not due simply to servile copying. The miniatures were executed by eight painters. Now, if we take the fourteen instances of classical figures that are not required by the text, we discover that eight of them are the work of the same painter, Pantoleon by name, while the other painters account for only six. Obviously, then, Pantoleon had antiquarian interests. Let us compare two miniatures showing essentially the same composition: one, on p. 371, by Pantoleon, represents St. Isidore of Pelusium (fig. 19); the other, on p. 145, by the painter Symeon, represents St. John Chozebites (fig. 20). It would be rather farfetched to suggest that the picture of St. Isidore is accompanied by a statue because Isidore wrote some works, now lost, directed against the pagans. The inclusion of a classical motif into this and other miniatures is, in my opinion, equivalent to quotations from classical authors. We may push this analogy one step further: just as Byzantine writers usually derived their classical quotations not from complete texts of the classics but from some mediaeval Bartlett, so the painter Pantoleon took his "quotations" not directly from antique works of art, but from another mediaeval manuscript.

One may, I think, sum up the relation of the Byzantine renaissances to classical art in the same words that have been used to describe the Carolingian Renaissance: "... its artistic activities did not include major sculpture in stone; the models selected for imitation were as a rule productions of the minor arts and normally did not antedate the fourth and fifth centuries A.D.; and the classical values ... were salvaged but not 'reactivated.'"[116]

[113] *Il Menologio di Basilio II (cod. Vat. gr. 1613), Codices e Vaticanis selecti VIII*, II (Turin, 1907), pp. 3, 146, 154.
[114] *Ibid.*, pp. 13, 46 (nude figures with spear and shield), 59, 83, 105, 125, 202, 283, 371, 391, 406.
[115] Weitzmann, *Greek Mythology*, fig. 88; cf. figs. 46, 72.
[116] Panofsky, *Renaissance and Renascences*, p. 106.

VI

When Constantinople fell to the Turks only two specimens of ancient sculpture appear to have been left in it. The first was a set of twelve reliefs at the Golden Gate representing the Labors of Hercules and other subjects—the same that had been mentioned by Chrysoloras. An unsuccessful attempt to acquire these reliefs was made by an English ambassador, Sir Thomas Roe (1621–1628). They gradually fell to pieces and disappeared completely at the end of the eighteenth century.[117] Some small fragments of them were excavated in 1927, the best being a head of Selene.[118] The other specimen was the famous Serpent Column in the Hippodrome, made by the victorious Greeks after the battle of Plataea. Its preservation in Turkish times was due to the fact that it was considered a talisman against snakes. Its heads were broken off in 1700, perhaps by members of the German embassy.[119] The mutilated trunk is thus † the only survivor, still standing *in situ*, of one of the greatest collections of ancient sculpture ever assembled. Here ends our sad story—sad, because the Byzantines derived so little benefit from the statues that they took care to preserve. Byzantium fulfilled its historic role by transmitting to the more receptive West the Greek heritage on parchment and paper; it was unable to transmit in the same fashion and at the right time the heritage in bronze and marble.

---

[117] J. Ebersolt, *Constantinople byzantine et les voyageurs du Levant* (Paris, 1918), pp. 82, 103, 132, 150, 156f., 186, 200.

[118] Th. Macridy and S. Casson, "Excavations at the Golden Gate, Constantinople," *Archaeologia*, LXXXI (1931), p. 63 ff. and pl. XLI, fig. 2.

[119] The lower jaw of one of the serpent's heads was apparently broken off by Mehmed II: see *Second Report upon the Excavations*, etc. (as in note 14 *supra*), p. 1 ff. The exact date when all three heads disappeared has been in doubt: Ebersolt, *Constantinople byzantine et les voyageurs du Levant*, p. 176, note 1, infers that this must have happened some time in the eighteenth century. See, however, *Voyages du Sr. A. de la Motraye*, I (The Hague, 1727), p. 278: "Au mois de Juin [1700] la colonne *Serpentine*, à laquelle il restoit encore deux têtes de ses Serpens cordelez ou entrelacez, les ayant perdues pendant une nuit obscure, les *Turcs* ne firent non plus aucune perquisition pour découvrir ceux qui pouvoient les avoir abatues ... Cependant les *Francs* soupçonnerent quelques-uns des gens de l'Ambassadeur d'*Allemagne* de les avoir rompues & emportées." Cf. also J. Pitton de Tournefort (who visited Constantinople in 1701), *Relation d'un voyage du Levant*, II (Lyon, 1727), p. 228f.: "On dit que le Sultan Mourat avoit cassé la tête à un de ces serpens: la colonne fut renversée & les têtes des deux autres furent cassées en 1700, après la paix de Carlovitz. On ne sçait ce qu'elles sont devenues, mais le reste a été relevé, & se trouve entre les obelisques," etc.

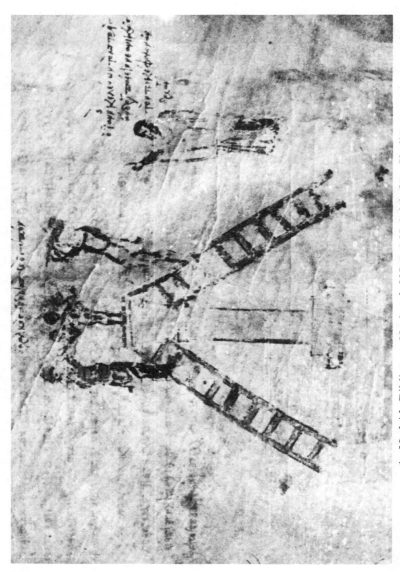

1. Madrid, Biblioteca Nacional. MS 5–3 N–2 fol. 65r, Skylitzes

2. Trebizond, Church of St. Anne, South Façade. Relief over Entrance Door

3. Athens, Panagia Gorgoepekoos, from east

5. Milan, Biblioteca Ambrosiana.
Cod. E. 49–50, p. 755

6. Jerusalem, Greek Patriarchate.
Cod. Taphou 14, fol. 313r

4. Naples, Museo Nazionale.
Sarcophagus

8. Rome, Biblioteca Vaticana.
Cod. Palat. gr. 431, sheet XII

7. Venice, Biblioteca Marciana.
Cod. Marc. gr. 454, fol. 1v

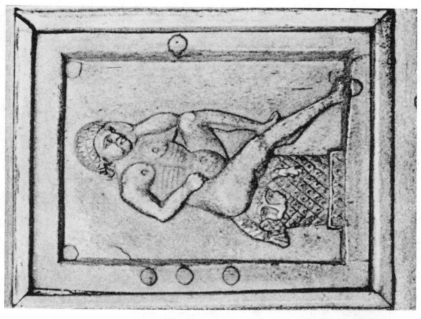

10. Xanten, St. Victor. Ivory Casket, detail

9. Rome, Vatican Museum, Tyche of Antioch

11. Rome, Biblioteca Vaticana. Cod. Vat. gr. 394, fol. 12, detail

13. Rome, Biblioteca Vaticana.
Cod. Vat. gr. 1613, p. 146, detail (enlarged)

12. Rome, Biblioteca Vaticana.
Cod. Vat. gr. 1613, p. 3, detail (enlarged)

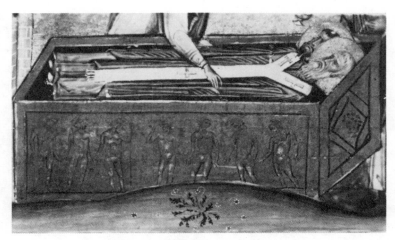

14. Rome, Biblioteca Vaticana.
Cod. Vat. gr. 1613, p. 154, detail (enlarged)

V

16. Rome, Biblioteca Vaticana. Cod. Vat. gr. 1613, p. 371, detail (enlarged)

15. Rome, Biblioteca Vaticana. Cod. Vat. gr. 1613, p. 13, detail (enlarged)

18. Paris, Bibliothèque Nationale.
Cod. Coislin 239, fol. 122v, detail

17. Rome, Biblioteca Vaticana. Cod.
Vat. gr. 1613, p. 406, detail (enlarged)

19. Rome, Biblioteca Vaticana. Cod. Vat. gr. 1613, p. 371

20. Rome, Biblioteca Vaticana. Cod. Vat. gr. 1613, p. 145

VI

LA CULTURE GRECQUE ET L'OCCIDENT
AU VIIIᵉ SIÈCLE

Il y a neuf ans le Professeur Agostino Pertusi a présenté ici-même une leçon intitulée « Bisanzio e l'irradiazione della sua civiltà in Occidente nell'alto medioevo »[1], dans laquelle il a tenté de préciser les voies de transmission – j'entends les routes géographiques – et les centres de rayonnement des influences byzantines en Occident pendant le Haut Moyen Age – excellente leçon qui provoqua une vive discussion. Il ne s'agit donc pas de reprendre le même aspect du problème. D'une part, notre tâche est plus limitée puisqu'elle ne concerne que le VIIIᵉ siècle; de l'autre, elle dépasse l'aspect géographique pour embrasser la valeur et le contenu de ces influences qui furent, nous le verrons, réciproques.

Pour commencer, essayons de résumer quelques faits qui paraissent établis. L'effondrement de la culture grecque en Italie se place au VIᵉ siècle. Ici un premier paradoxe qui ressort de l'admirable étude de Pierre Courcelle:[2] la floraison des lettres grecques associée au nom de Boèce eut

---

(1) *Settimane di studio*, XI, 1963 (Spoleto 1964), 75-133 et la discussion, 159-226. Pour une vue d'ensemble sur les relations culturelles entre Byzance et l'Occident je renvoie à l'article récent de W. BERSCHIN, « Abendland und Byzanz. Literatur und Sprache », *Reallexikon der Byzantinistik*, Reihe A, I (1969-70), 227 sq.

(2) *Les lettres grecques en Occident de Macrobe à Cassiodore*, 2ᵉ éd. (Paris 1948), 257 sq.

684

lieu sous la domination ostrogothique. La reconquête de Justinien, au lieu d'encourager cette floraison, contribua à la détruire. La dernière période de l'activité de Cassiodore, la période vivarienne, qui se déroule sous le régime byzantin (c. 550-575), manifeste une tentative de sauver quelques épaves de la culture grecque dans un milieu qui devient de plus en plus indifférent à ces études. Comme le dit Courcelle, « ...il n'attend pas de la conquête byzantine un renouveau de la culture grecque et se rend compte qu'il est urgent de préserver pour la chrétienté occidentale la lumière de l'Orient, qui bientôt ne luira plus jusqu'à elle »[3]. D'ailleurs le Vivarium n'a pas survécu à la mort de son fondateur. Donc, pas de correspondance entre conquête byzantine et hellénisation. Il serait intéressant de rechercher les causes de ce phénomène.

Deuxième paradoxe: Ravenne, siège de l'administration byzantine, malgré les colonies grecques et levantines qui y sont installées, malgré ses nombreux monastères grecs, n'a produit à ma connaissance aucune œuvre de littérature grecque, même la plus banale. Jusqu'à sa chûte en 751, Ravenne est démeurée une ville de langue et de culture latines[4].

Si nous jetons un coup d'œil au-delà des Alpes – car l'Afrique se sépare pour toujours du domaine byzantin vers l'an 700 – nous constatons qu'en Gaule la culture grecque disparaît vers la fin du Ve siècle[5], en Angleterre même plus tôt, tandis qu'en Espagne quelques vestiges en survivent jusqu'au début du VIIe[6]. Quant à l'Irlande, on est

(3) *Ibid.*, 341.

(4) Voir A. GUILLOU, *Régionalisme et indépendance dans l'Empire byzantin au VIIe siècle : l'exemple de l'Exarchat et de la Pentapole d'Italie* (Rome 1969), 112 sq.

(5) COURCELLE, *Lettres grecques*, 246 sq.; P. RICHÉ, *Education et culture dans l'Occident barbare* (Paris 1962), 83 sq.

(6) Parmi les membres du clergé espagnol, Martin de Bracara († 580) et Jean de Biclar († après 614) savaient le grec, mais tous les deux ont séjourné

à peu près d'accord aujourd'hui que la connaissance du grec n'était pas très poussée dans ses monastères. Je cite Dom Cappuyns: « ... sur un point nous devons être fermes: l'Irlande du haut moyen âge n'a pas connu véritablement le grec. Quelques expressions d'origine liturgique ou patristique; quelques éléments, – l'alphabet, l'étymologie de certains mots usuels –, puisés dans les ouvrages encyclopédiques d'Isidore, de Cassiodore et de Bède; peut-être quelques glossaires gréco-latins: voilà tout ce qu'elle peut réclamer en matière d'hellénisme » [7].

Quand nous nous approchons de la période qui nous concerne, le seul cas concret que nous puissions relever d'une influence grecque directe au-delà des Alpes est celui de Théodore de Tarse. Ceci a été discuté tant de fois, qu'il suffirait de faire quelques observations. D'abord, notons le fait que Théodore, né en 602, était originaire de Tarse en Cilicie, c'est-à-dire d'une ville qui fut brièvement occupée par les Perses en 613 et qui passa sous le contrôle arabe vers 645 [8]. Nous ne savons pas à quelle date Théodore quitta sa patrie, mais nous ne nous tromperions pas en supposant qu'il le fit à cause des invasions étrangères. Voici donc un exemple concret de cette émigration levantine vers l'Italie que nous allons examiner plus tard. La tradition d'après laquelle Théodore étudia à Athènes me paraît suspecte [9]: je ne crois pas qu'on pût apprendre

en Orient. C'étaient cependant des cas exceptionnels: Licinien de Carthagène, Léandre et Isidore de Séville ignoraient cette langue. Voir RICHÉ, *Education*, 349.

(7) M. CAPPUYNS, *Jean Scot Erigène* (Louvain – Paris 1933), 28. Malgré une bibliographie très étendue, on ne peut rien dire de très précis à ce propos. Pour l'essentiel voir M. ROGER, *L'enseignement des lettres classiques d'Ausone à Alcuin* (Paris 1905), 268 sq.; B. BISCHOFF, «Das griechische Element in der abendländischen Bildung des Mittelalters », *Byz. Zeitschr.*, XLIV (1951), 28 sq.

(8) Ibn al-Athir cité par E. W. BROOKS, « The Arabs in Asia Minor (641-750), from Arabic Sources », *J. of Hell. Studies*, XVIII (1898), 183.

(9) Elle remonte au témoignage du pape Zacharie qui écrivait à peu près un siècle plus tard, *Ep.* XI, *PL* LXXXIX, 943C: *et novissime tuis temporibus*

686

grand' chose à Athènes au VIIe siècle [10]. En tout cas, il semble avoir habité Rome assez longtemps, peut-être au monastère de S. Anastase [11], où il acquit sa connaissance du latin.

Seconde observation: l'élection de Théodore au siège de Cantorbéry était entièrement fortuite, ayant été provoquée par la mort soudaine de Wigheard, le candidat des rois de ᴋent et de Northumbrie. Le choix du Pape se porta alors sur l'abbé Hadrien qui refusa le poste; puis sur un certain moine André qui s'excusa lui aussi à cause de sa santé, et ce n'est qu'alors que Théodore fut nommé. Pourtant le Pape n'était pas très sûr de Théodore, et il insista pour qu'Hadrien l'accompagnât afin que le nouvel évêque n'introduisît pas dans son église quelque coutume contraire à la vraie foi : *ne quid ille contrarium veritati fidei Graecorum more in ecclesiam cui praeesset introduceret* [12]. En d'autres termes, notre principal exemple du rayonnement de la culture grecque en Europe septentrionale n'est qu'un accident. Les circonstances que je viens de raconter projettent aussi une lumière intéressante sur l'absence de clercs qualifiés à Rome dans la seconde moitié du VIIe siècle.

Troisième observation: Théodore avait 68 ans quand il débarqua en Angleterre. Quoi qu'il vécût encore vingt ans – il est mort en 690 – il est peu probable qu'un homme d'un âge si vénérable ait eu assez d'énergie pour enseigner

---

Theodorus ex Graeco Latinus ante philosophus, et Athenis eruditus, Romae ordinatus... Riché, *Education*, 420 n. 57, observe avec raison: « Ne veut-il pas dire simplement que Théodore a une culture grecque? ».

(10) A. Frantz, « From Paganism to Christianity in Athens », *Dumbarton Oaks Papers*, XIX (1965), 199, se montre assez réaliste à cet égard.

(11) Cette supposition est due à A. Michel, « Die griechischen Klostersiedlungen zu Rom bis zur Mitte des 11. Jahrhunderts », *Ostkirchliche Studien*, I (1952), 41.

(12) Bède, *Eccl. hist.*, iv. 1, éd. B. Colgrave et R. A. B. Mynors (Oxford 1969), 330.

la langue grecque, sans mentionner les graves difficultés
administratives qu'il devait affronter. Il paraît que la
propagation du grec fut l'œuvre surtout d'Hadrien, homme
plus jeune, qui est décrit comme étant *Grecae pariter et
Latinae linguae peritissimus* [13]. Puisqu'il était africain, le
grec n'était pas probablement sa langue maternelle; pourtant, on peut supposer qu'il connût le grec parlé soit
en Afrique, soit dans son monastère d'Hiridanum près
de Naples. Or, tout ce qu'on apprit de grec en Angle-
terre à la fin du VIIe et au début du VIIIe siècle était
dû entièrement aux efforts de Théodore et d'Hadrien dont
l'importance dans le domaine de l'éducation est soulignée
dans la lettre bien connue d'Aldelm à Eahfrith [14], Aldelm
ayant lui aussi étudié à Cantorbéry vers 670. On peut
supposer que le vénérable Bède qui poursuivit assidûment
l'étude du grec jusqu'à ce qu'il pût, vers la fin de sa vie,
entreprendre un travail sérieux sur le texte du Nouveau
Testament, puisa ses connaissances à la même source [15].

N'imaginons pas toutefois qu'un grand nombre d'hellénistes sortit de l'école de Cantorbéry. L'assertion de
Bède, *usque hodie supersunt de eorum* [c.-à.-d. de Théodore
et d'Hadrien] *discipulis, qui Latinam Graecamque linguam
aeque ut propriam in qua nati sunt norunt* [16], a été souvent
citée. Pourtant, Bède ne mentionne que deux clercs qui
connaissaient le grec, à savoir Tobie, évêque de Rochester
mort en 726 [17], et Albin qui succéda à Hadrien comme
abbé des Saints-Pierre et Paul près de Cantorbéry, ce

---

(13) *Ibid.*, p. 328. Cf. M. COENS, « Utriusque linguae peritus », *Anal. Bolland.*, LXXVI (1958), 133.
(14) *Ep.* V, éd. R. Ehwald, *MGH, Auct. ant.*, XV, 492 sq. Cf. M. L. W.
LAISTNER, *Thought and Letters in Western Europe, A. D. 500 to 900*, 2ᵉ éd.
(Ithaca, N. Y., 1966), 154.
(15) LAISTNER, *Thought and Letters*, 161; RICHÉ, *Education*, 437.
(16) *Hist. eccles.*, iv. 2, p. 334.
(17) *Ibid.*, v. 8, p. 474.

688

dernier étant plus familier avec le latin qu'avec le grec [18]. En outre, l'existence d'hellénistes présuppose l'existence de livres grecs. Malheureusement, aucun catalogue de bibliothèque du VIIe ou VIIIe siècle ne nous est parvenu d'Angleterre, mais la liste des ouvrages utilisés par Bède a été dressée [19]: elle comporte au moins 142 titres, nombre très élevé pour cette époque. Tous les livres en question n'appartenaient pas nécessairement aux monastères de Wearmouth et Jarrow; quelques uns d'entre eux furent probablement empruntés à Cantorbéry ou ailleurs. Pourtant le seul texte grec que Bède a certainement eu sous la main est une copie bilingue des Actes des Apôtres, copie qui existe toujours (*Laud. gr.* 35). Il a pu aussi avoir accès au texte intégral du Nouveau Testament, aux Septante et à Josèphe, mais ceci n'est pas sûr [20]. Et pourtant, Bède était le plus grand savant de son époque, et l'une des trois ou quatre personnes de sa génération en Angleterre capables de lire le grec. S'il avait pu avoir accès à d'autres ouvrages grecs, il les aurait sans doute mentionnés.

Le *cod. Laudianus* mérite une brève parenthèse. On le date généralement de la fin du VIe ou du VIIe siècle, et il provient certainement de l'Italie puisque sur ses deux dernières pages (fol. 277[r.-v]) se lisent l'incipit d'un édit d'un certain Flavios Pankratios, duc de Sardaigne,

---

(18) *Ibid.*, v. 20, p. 530: *in tantum studiis scripturarum institutus est, ut Grecam quidem linguam non parva ex parte, Latinam vero non minus quam Anglorum, quae sibi naturalis est, noverit.*

(19) M. L. W. LAISTNER, « The Library of the Venerable Bede » dans *Bede, his Life, Times, and Writings*, éd. A. Hamilton Thompson (Oxford 1935), 237 sq.

(20) *Ibid.*, 257 sq. Laistner ne mentionne pas à ce propos la Vie de S. Anastase le Perse († 628) au sujet de laquelle Bède écrit (*Hist. eccles.*, v. 24, p. 568): *librum vitae et passionis sancti Anastasii male de Greco translatum et peius a quodam imperito emendatum, prout potui, ad sensum correxi.* Ceci semble indiquer que Bède a simplement corrigé le texte latin sans avoir eu recours à l'original grec.

LA CULTURE GRECQUE ET L'OCCIDENT AU VIIIᵉ SIÈCLE 689

ainsi que diverses commémorations qui indiquent que le manuscrit a appartenu à une maison religieuse grecque (fig. 2-3) [21]. Au bas de la page précédente (fol. 226ᵛ) est inscrit un prétendu oracle d'Apollon (fig. 1) qui fait partie de l'ouvrage intitulé *Théosophia* [22]. Il n'importe pas pour

(21) Voir P. BATIFFOL, « Librairies byzantines à Rome », *MEFR*, VIII (1888), 306 sq. Je remercie mon ami André Guillou d'avoir mis à ma disposition les trois photographies du *Laudianus* que je reproduis ici, et de m'avoir signalé l'étude de B. R. MOTZO, « Barlumi dell'età bizantina », *Studi cagliaritani di storia e filologia*, I (1927), 65 sq. qui se rapporte à ce sujet. Les notations grecques qui nous intéressent sont les suivantes:

Fol. 227ʳ:

> † θεωτωκε βοηθη του δουλου σου
> Γληγωριου διακονου κ(αι) Επιφανο[υς ?]
> υπατησης διαπαντος αμην †

Puis, en une cursive qui ressemble déjà à la minuscule byzantine:

> † θεοτοκε βοηθει της δουλης σου Ευπ[ρ-]
> αξιας διακονισις αμην †
> † θεοτοκε βοηθει του δουλου σου Ιωαννου
> το επικλιν Καραμαλλος μετα τον δι[α-]
> φεροντον αυτον αμμιν †

Fol. 227ᵛ:

> ταυτας ορουντες οι εταασται του λογου
> φερουσας ημιν γνωστικας ευεξιας
> απλουμεν τον νουν προσλαβιν τας ικμαδας †
> οπλιζαι κ(αι) νυν την σοφιν σου βαλβιδα

(Je n'ai pas pu retrouver la source de ces quatre vers mal transcrits)

> † Φλ. Πανκρατιος συν θ(εω) απο επαρχ(ων) δουξ Σαρδινιας
> δηλα ποιω τα υποτεταγμενα. Επιπερ θεοστυγεις κ(αι)
> κρ . . . .
> Καραμαλος (répété de la page précédante)
> Θεώδορος
> Μηνας
> [Λ]ουκια

(22) Il s'agit d'une inscription qui a été soi-disant trouvée sous Léon Iᵉʳ (457-74) dans un temple payen de Cyzique qu'on était en train de convertir en église sous le vocable de la Sainte Vierge. Texte édité par K. BURESCH, *Klaros* (Leipzig 1889), 111-12; H. ERBSE, *Fragmente griechischer Theosophien* (Hamburg 1941), 180 et 117 sq. (commentaire). Le même oracle se retrouve avec des variantes assez considérables chez Malalas, éd. Dindorf, 77-8, et dans le *Vatic. gr.* 2200 du VIIIᵉ-IXᵉ siècle que nous aurons l'occasion de mentionner plus tard: PITRA, *Anal. sacra spic. Solesm. parata*, V/2 (1888), 307. Voici le

690

notre enquête si le manuscrit provenait de la Sardaigne, peut-être d'un des monastères de Cagliari [23], ou de Rome [24]. Il n'est pas connu non plus par quelle voie il parvint en Angleterre. Quelques savants supposent qu'il y fut apporté par Théodore, ce qui est bien possible quoique nous n'ayons aucune preuve que Théodore importât des livres en Angleterre; d'autres pensent avec plus de raison qu'il avait été acquis un peu plus tôt par Benoît Biscop et Céolfrid [25]. En tout cas, il était en Angleterre dès le début du VIIIe siècle, et passa un peu plus tard en Allemagne [26].

Une dernière remarque concernant l'Angleterre. La connaissance du grec engendrée par Théodore et Hadrien semble s'être évanouie avec la génération de Bède [27]. A notre connaissance, il n'y a aucun lien entre ce phénomène et le renouveau du grec à la cour carolingienne. Alcuin ignorait la langue de Byzance.

texte du *Laudianus* qui en est sans doute le témoin le plus ancien, mais que n'a pas attiré l'attention des spécialistes:

Επιγεγραπται εις το μαντιον του Απολλονος· Προφιτευσον ημιν Φυβε Απολλον τινος εσται δομος ουτος κ(αι) εδοθη χρισμος· οσα μεν προς αροριν [lire ἀρετὴν] οροραν ποιηται εγω δε εφετμευω τριςενα μουνον υψιμεδοντα θεον ου λογος αφητος [lire ἄφθιτος] εν αδαϊ κορη ενκυ[μ]ος εσται, οστις οσπερ τοξον πυρφωρον μεσον διαδραμο(ν) [κόσμο]ν απαντα ζωγρισας πατρι προσαξι δωρον· αυτης [ἔσται δόμος]ουτος Μα[ρία] δε [τὸ ὄνο]μα αυτης.

En dessus de l'oracle se trouve un *credo* latin d'une écriture continentale du VIIIe siècle, ainsi que quelques notations importantes. Sur ces dernières voir E. A. LOWE, « An Eighth-Century List of Books... », *Speculum*, III (1928), 13 sq.

(23) Cf. P. GOUBERT, *Byzance avant l'Islam*, II/2 (Paris 1965), 195.

(24) C'est la thèse de BATIFFOL, *loc. cit.*

(25) Ainsi J. H. ROPES, *The Text of Acts = The Beginnings of Christianity*, éd. F. J. Foakes Jackson et K. Lake, I/3 (Londres 1926), lxxxv.

(26) LOWE, « An Eighth-Century List of Books », 3 sq.

(27) Il n'y resta qu'un faible résidu. Voir, par. ex., le texte grec barbare des leçons et cantiques liturgiques contenu dans le manuscrit Oxford, *MS Auct. F. 4. 32*, fol. 24-28, écrit au pays de Galles au début du IXe s.: *Saint Dunstan's Classbook from Glastonbury*, introd. de R. W. Hunt = Umbrae codicum occidentalium, IV (Amsterdam 1961), pp. X-XII; *Greek Manuscripts in the Bodleian Library. An Exhibition Held in connection with the XIIIth Intern. Congress of Byz. Studies* (Oxford 1966), No. 35 et pl. XIII.

Regardons maintenant la Gaule et le Royaume franc.
Nous y constatons une pénurie décourageante d'informa-
tions: en effet, pour la première moitié du VIIIe siècle
nous n'en avons aucune [28]. Et pourtant, dès que le Royaume des Francs apparut en tant que grande puissance
européenne, il se trouva en relations diplomatiques avec
Byzance, ce qui n'était pas le cas de l'Angleterre. Un
coup d'œil à travers les *Regesten* de Dölger est instructif
à cet égard. Dans la première moitié du siècle, la seule
personne en Occident autre que les fonctionnaires impé-
riaux qui se trouvait en relations formelles avec le basi-
leus était le Pape de Rome, lui aussi, en principe, un
sujet de l'Empire (11 numéros dans les Regestes) [29]. Dans
la seconde moitié du siècle jusqu'a la chûte d'Irène en
802, la situation change brusquement: j'ai compté quatre
communications diplomatiques adressées au Pape [30], trois
aux rois lombards [31], et onze à la cour franque [32]. La
création des échanges diplomatiques comportait l'emploi
et la formation d'interprètes qualifiés puisqu'il y avait
un grave danger de malentendus et de fraude. L'ambassade
impériale à Pépin le Bref vers 765 nous en fournit un

(28) D'après l'opinion généralement admise, c'est en Gaule qu'un certain
Petrus monachus traduisit vers la fin du VIIe s. ou au début du VIIIe les Révélations du pseudo-Méthode à partir d'une version grecque faite sur l'original
syriaque. Voir E. SACKUR, *Sibyllinische Texte und Forschungen* (Halle 1898),
55 sq.; F. NAU, « Révélations et légendes », *Journal asiatique*, XIe sér., IX
(1917), 417; M. KMOSKO, « Das Rätsel des Pseudomethodius », *Byzantion*,
VI (1931), 275 qui croit que la traduction a été faite à Lérins; A. SIEGMUND,
*Die Überlieferung der griechischen christlichen Literatur in der lateinischen
Kirche* (Munich 1949), 172-3; P. J. ALEXANDER, « Byzantium and the Migration of Literary Works and Motifs », *Medievalia et humanistica*, n.s., II (1971),
61.
(29) F. DÖLGER, *Regesten der Kaiserurkunden des oströmischen Reiches*,
I (Munich – Berlin 1924), Nos. 264, 266, 267, 268, 269, 271, 273, 279, 291,
298, 310.
(30) *Ibid.*, Nos. 314, 341, 343, 349.
(31) *Ibid.*, Nos. 312, 319, 348.
(32) *Ibid.*, Nos. 318, 320, 322, 325, 326, 339, 345, 350, 353, 354, 357.

692

exemple intéressant. A cette occasion l'empereur Constantin V se plaignit que ses lettres à Pépin et au Pape Paul avaient été falsifiées à dessein par les interprètes royaux et pontificaux [33]. Vraie ou fausse, cette accusation correspond à une situation bien réelle.

Quelques années auparavant, entre 758 et 763, Pépin avait demandé des livres grecs au Pape. Sa lettre est malheureusement perdue, mais nous avons la réponse du Pape: *Direximus itaque excellentissimae praecellentiae vestrae et libros, quantos reperire potuimus*: *id est antiphonale et responsale, insimul artem gramaticam, Aristo[te]lis, Dionisii Ariopagitis, geometricam, orthografiam, grammaticam, omnes Greco eloquio scriptas, nec non et horologium nocturnum* [34]. Quelles circonstances provoquèrent cette requête ? Pépin avait-il soumis une liste de *desiderata*, comme le suppose le Père Loenertz [35]? Ces livres étaient-ils destinés à la bibliothèque de Saint-Denis [36]? Etaient-ils, au contraire, rassemblés pour l'éducation de la jeune Gisèle, fille de Pépin, fiancée à l'empereur byzantin Léon IV [37]? Le choix des titres, qui se composent de quelques livres liturgiques, quelques manuels scolaires, un ouvrage théo-

---

(33) *Ibid.*, No. 325. Texte dans *MGH*, *Epist.* III, 546 = *Cod. Carol.*, 36.

(34) *MGH*, *Epist.*, III, 529 = *Cod. Carol.*, 24.

(35) « La légende parisienne de S. Denys l'Aréopagite », *Anal. Bolland.*, LXIX (1951), 235-6.

(36) C'est l'opinion de RICHÉ, *Education*, 495, qui se fonde sur la présence parmi les livres énumérés d'un ouvrage de l'Aréopagite. Mais à cette époque S. Denys de Paris et l'Aréopagite étaient-ils déjà identifiés? D'après LOENERTZ, *op. cit.*, 232, ceci ne s'est produit qu'à l'occasion de l'ambassade byzantine à Louis le Pieux en 824. D'autre part, RICHÉ, *op. cit.*, 468-9, émet la supposition gratuite que les livres en question furent apportés à Rome par des moines « chassés de Constantinople » que le pape accueillit au monastère de S. Etienne. Le passage du *Lib. Pont.* (éd. Duchesne, I, 465) qu'il cite à ce propos ne dit cependant que: *ubi* [à S. Etienne] *et monachorum congregationem constituens grece modulationis psalmodie cynovium esse decrevit*.

(37) C'est la théorie de W. OHNSORGE, « Der Patricius-Titel Karls des Grossen », *Byz. Zeitschr.*, LIII (1960), 309 n. 67 = *Konstantinopel und der Okzident* (Darmstadt 1966), 13.

logique bien difficile et peut-être un ouvrage de philosophie profane, ne nous laisse pas deviner une intention
bien définie [38]. Au moins peut-on dire que Pépin avait
en vue un enseignement quelconque, soit dans un monastère soit à la cour, et il est significatif qu'il devait s'adres-
ser à Rome pour se procurer une grammaire grecque.

Vingt ans plus tard nous trouvons Paul le Diacre
à la cour de Charlemagne (782-6), en train d'enseigner le
grec à des clercs en vue d'un autre projet de mariage,
celui de Rothrude avec Constantin VI:

Hac pro causa Graecam doces clericos grammaticam
nostros, [ut] in eius pergant manentes obsequio
et Graiorum videantur eruditi regulis [39].

Mais Paul le Diacre savait-il bien le grec ? On ne peut
pas attacher beaucoup d'importance aux louanges exces-
sives que lui décerne Pierre de Pise: *Graeca cerneris Home-*
rus, Latina Vergilius, in Hebraea quoque Philo [40]. Paul
lui-même est probablement plus près de la vérité quand
il répond modestement:

Graiam nescio loquellam, ignoro Hebraicam.
Tres aut quattuor in scolis quas didici syllabas,
ex his mihi est ferendus maniplus ad aream.

Et il ajoute que si ses élèves ne faisaient voir à Constantinople que les rudiments de grec qu'ils avaient appris
de lui, ils feraient une mine bien ridicule [41]. Pourquoi
donc a-t-on chargé Paul de cette tâche, quand un vrai
Byzantin, l'eunuque Elissaios avait été envoyé à la cour

---

(38) En supposant que les livres ont atteint leur destination, il est digne
de remarque que l'ouvrage de l'Aréopagite n'ait suscité aucun intérêt, tandis
qu'en 827 une réception triomphale lui a été accordée.
(39) *Die Gedichte des Paulus Diaconus*, éd. K. Neff (Munich 1908), **62**.
(40) *Ibid.*, 61.
(41) *Ibid.*, 66-7. Neff croit que Paul a appris le grec à Pavie, tandis que
RICHÉ, *Education*, 465, opte pour Cividale.

694

de Charlemagne afin de donner une instruction grecque
à Rothrude? [42]. Nous n'en savons rien. Peut-être se méfiait-
on d'Elissaios, ou était-il incapable de communiquer avec
les clercs occidentaux. Le fait demeure que l'instruction
de futurs diplomates fut confiée à un Lombard dont la
connaissance du grec était insuffisante, et dont même la
loyauté devait être suspecte.

Telles sont nos données principales pour la diffusion
du grec en Europe transalpine au VIIIe siècle. Le sujet,
quoique souvent traité, n'a pas été complètement épuisé.
Je songe surtout aux glossaires bilingues et aux exercices
d'école, dont l'étude pourrait donner quelques éléments
nouveaux [43]. Toutefois, je n'en attends pas de grandes
surprises.

Toutes les indications que nous avons recueillies nous
mènent à l'Italie et surtout à Rome. C'est à Rome que
Benoît Biscop acquit des livres et des peintures pour
ses monastères de Northumbrie; c'est de Rome que Théodore et Hadrien furent envoyés à Cantorbéry; c'est à
Rome que Pépin écrivit pour se procurer des livres grecs.
L'étude des monuments artistiques conduit à la même
conclusion [44]. Je suis persuadé que la clef de notre problème doit être cherchée à Rome.

Nous avons déjà signalé le naufrage des études grecques
en Italie au VIe siècle. Il se peut que la théorie de Courcelle d'une renaissance ostrogothique soit un peu exagérée.
Denis le Petit n'eut pas de successeur; et quand, au début

(42) Théophane, *Chronographie*, éd. de Boor, 455.

(43) Sur les glossaires voir surtout l'article de Bischoff cité à la note 7;
sur les exercices scolaires M. L. W. LAISTNER, « Notes on Greek from the Lectures of a Ninth Century Monastery Teacher », *Bull. of the John Rylands Library*, VII (1922-3), 421 ff.

(44) Voir, par ex., D. H. WRIGHT, « The Italian Stimulus on English Art
around 700 », *Stil und Überlieferung in der Kunst des Abendlandes = Akten
des 21. intern. Kongr. für Kunstgesch. in Bonn*, 1964, I (Berlin 1967), 84 sq.

du siècle, Eugippe compila ses *Excerpta* de S. Augustin, il ne jugea pas nécessaire de réproduire le passage de la *De doctrina christiana* (II.16) qui insiste sur la valeur pour un exégète de connaître le grec et l'hébreu [45]. Quoi qu'il en soit, le grec était presqu' inconnu à Rome vers la fin du VIe siècle. Grégoire le Grand en était ignorant, et il se plaint de la difficulté d'obtenir des traductions convenables. La même situation existait à Constantinople en sens inverse [46]. Pourtant, au siècle suivant, un important élément grec fut réintroduit à Rome grâce à l'immigration de levantins qui fuyaient devant les invasions, perse et arabe.

Le problème de cette immigration a été discuté à plusieurs reprises. Afin d'éviter tout malentendu, je dois préciser que je ne soulève pas la question apparentée de l'hellénisation de la Sicile et de l'Italie méridionale, phénomène qui présuppose un mouvement massif de populations [47]. Il ne s'agit que de la colonie de lettrés grecs porteurs d'influences byzantines que nous rencontrons à Rome dès le VIIe siècle. Sans qu'on puisse préciser le nombre de ces refugiés, il est hors de doute qu'il ne fut pas négligeable.

Nous disposons maintenant d'un répertoire statistique † des monastères romains du haut moyen âge [48]. Tout compte fait du caractère souvent équivoque de notre documentation, nous obtenons néanmoins les résultates suivants. Au Ve et VIe siècles il n'y avait à Rome aucun monastère

(45) RICHÉ, *Education*, 172-3.

(46) *Ibid.*, 189-90.

(47) Voir les remarques judicieuses de A. GUILLOU, « Grecs d'Italie du sud et de la Sicile au moyen âge: les moines », *MEFR*, LXXV (1963), 79 sq., et de A. PERTUSI, « Bisanzio e l'irradiazione della sua civiltà » (cité à la note 1), 98-9. On y trouvera la bibliographie antérieure.

(48) G. FERRARI, *Early Roman Monasteries*, Studi di antichità cristiana, XXIII (Cité du Vatican 1957).

696

grec; au VIIe nous en comptons 6 sur 24 (nombre total); au VIIIe 8 à 10 [49] sur 38; au IXe 11 sur 57. Ces chiffres sont, bien entendu, approximatifs. Ce qui nous importe c'est que pour quelques uns de ces monastères on peut établir leur dépendance de l'immigration levantine.

C'est dans les Actes du Concile du Latran de 649 que nous rencontrons pour la première fois les moines grecs établis à Rome. Trente sept d'entre eux se présentèrent à la seconde session du Concile, et ils y sont décrits comme *abbates, presbyteri et monachi Graeci, jam per annos habitantes in hac Romana civitate, nec non in praesenti adventantes* [50]. A leur tête se trouvaient Jean, abbé de S. Sabbas près de Jérusalem, Théodore, abbé de S. Sabbas en Afrique (tous les deux peut-être récemment arrivés) ainsi que deux abbés déjà établis à Rome, Thalassius du monastère des Arméniens appelé Renati [51], et Georges

---

(49) Dans ses tables statistiques, FERRARI, *op. cit.*, 411 sq., compte dix monastères grecs au VIIIe siècle, mais il admet lui-même que deux d'entre eux, à savoir S. Césaire *in palatio* et S. Cassien, ne sont pas documentés avant le IXe.

(50) MANSI, X, 903A.

(51) Il n'est pas facile de décider si Thalassius « le romain » était le même personnage que l'abbé africain Thalassius, l'auteur de quatre *Centuries* sur la vie ascétique, l'ami et le correspondant de S. Maxime. Ils sont identifiés par Wagenmann et Seeberg, art. « Maximus Confessor », *Realenzyklopädie für protest. Theol. und Kirche*, 3e éd., XII (1903), 463, et, tacitement, par R. DEVREESSE, « L'église d'Afrique durant l'occupation byzantine », *MEFR*, XLVII (1940), 157, qui le prend pour un Arménien. Leur identité est cependant niée par J. Gouillard, art. « Thalassius », *Dict. de théol. cath.*, XV (1946), 202-3. Un Thalassius qui « avait illustré toute l'Afrique » (τὸν πᾶσαν τὴν 'Aφρικὴν κοσμήσαντα) figure dans un récit de miracle qui se situe à Carthage sous l'administration du patrice Nicétas, c'est-à-dire entre 619 et 629. Sur ces dates voir Ch. DIEHL, *L'Afrique byzantine* (Paris 1896), 525. Le récit fait partie d'un recueil consacré aux Pères du Sinaï, recueil composé par le moine Anastase vers 650. Ceci signifie-t-il que Thalassius aussi était un moine sinaïte? Voir F. NAU, « Le texte grec des récits du moine Anastase... », *Oriens christ.*, II (1902), 83 sq.; traduction française du même auteur, *Les récits inédits du moine Anastase* (Paris, 1902), 40 sq.; même texte isolé chez F. COMBEFIS, *Bibl. graec. patrum auct. novissimum*, I (Paris 1672), 324 sq. Le récit concernant Thalassius passa dans la chronographie byzantine, par ex. celle de Georges le moine, *Chronicon*, ed. C. de Boor, II (Leipzig 1904), 678 sq. (où

monasterii de Cilicia, qui ponitur in aquas Salvias. Quant au monastère dit Renati, je constate dans le texte imprimé une imprécision: la version latine donne *monasterium Armenissarum*, la version grecque μονὴ τῶν 'Ἀρμενίων[52], ce qui paraît préférable puisqu'il s'agissait certainement d'un monastère d'hommes régi par un abbé[53]. L'existence d'un monastère arménien n'est nullement exclu[54]; je me demande toutefois si la vraie leçon ne serait pas *monasterium Armeniacorum*, c'est-à-dire monastère composé de moines du thème des Arméniaques en Asie Mineure, thème qui avait été organisé avant 627[55]. On se rappellera que le Pape Conon (686-7) est décrit comme étant *oriundus patre Thraceseo*[56], c'est-à-dire que son père n'était pas Thrace, mais un ressortissant du thème des Thracésiens en Asie Mineure occidentale. Quant au monastère cilicien, je crois que son établissement doit être lié non pas à l'invasion arabe, mais à celle, antérieure, des Perses. Comme nous l'avons déjà indiqué, la Cilicie passa sous la domination arabe vers 645, ce qui ne laisse pas assez de temps pour l'organisation d'un monastère à Rome dès 649.

Cette hypothèse est confirmée par deux cas concrets et bien connus. Sophrone de Damas et son ami Jean

---

Thalassius est transformé en évêque), et fut traduit en slave. Cf. C. DE BOOR, « Zur Vision des Taxaotes », *Byzant. Zeitschr.*, V (1896), 306 sq. Les relations entre l'africain Thalassius et S. Maxime se placent vers 628-34. Il aurait donc pu avoir émigré à Rome quelques années avant 649. Si l'on admettait ceci, on pourrait ajouter un intellectuel de plus à la colonie grecque de Rome.

(52) MANSI, X, 903C.

(53) Thalassius mis à part, nous connaissons aussi Georges, prêtre et moine du monastère Renati, qui prit part au VIe concile œcuménique en 680/1: MANSI, XI, 231C.

(54) Des Arméniens se rendaient en groupes très nombreux au Sinaï: F. NAU, « Le texte grec des récits du moine Anastase », 81-2. Ils auraient donc pu être rejetés vers l'Italie par la grande vague d'émigration que nous étudions ici.

(55) G. OSTROGORSKY, *Gesch. des byzant. Staates*, 3e éd. (Munich 1963), 84 n. 4.

(56) *Lib. Pont.*, I, 368.

698

Moschos, syrien lui aussi, quittèrent la Palestine à la première annonce de l'offensive perse. Ayant traversé la Syrie et la Cilicie, ils firent voile vers l'Egypte où ils séjournèrent jusqu'à 614. Mais ayant reçu la nouvelle de la chûte de Jérusalem et de la déroute des armées romaines, ils s'embarquèrent pour Rome, où Jean Moschos mourut en 619 ou 634. Sophrone revint plus tard en Palestine. Il ne faut pas oublier que le *Pré Spirituel* fut composé ou, au moins, terminé à Rome, premier produit littéraire de la colonie grecque [57].

† Plus intéressant encore est le cas de S. Maxime le Confesseur. Ayant embrassé la vie religieuse à Chrysopolis, en face de Constantinople (vers 614), il prit la fuite vraisemblablement en 626, au temps de l'invasion perse. Quatre lettres qu'il adressa à un évêque, peut-être Jean de Cyzique, se rapportent à cette période. Il y prie l'évêque de rassembler de nouveau ses ouailles dispersées, si en effet le danger ennemi s'est dissipé. Certains avaient trouvé un refuge proche, d'autres se sont enfuis loin et ont traversé la mer: c'était un « terrible exil ». Une communauté de nonnes dirigée par la dame Eudocie est revenue. Maxime prie son pasteur de le recevoir lui aussi [58]. Nous ne savons pas d'où ces lettres ont été écrites, ni si Maxime est jamais revenu à son monastère. Nous le retrouvons en Afrique du nord dès 632, où il demeure jusqu'à 645-6, lorsqu'il se rend à Rome. Il y aurait sans doute passé

(57) Voir S. VAILHÉ, « Jean Mosch », *Échos d'Orient*, V (1901-2), 107 sq.; ID., « Sophrone le sophiste et Sophrone le patriarche », *Rev. de l'Orient chrétien*, VII (1902), 360 sq.; G. Bardy, art. « Sophrone de Jérusalem », *Dict. de théol. cath.*, XIV/2 (1941), 2379 sq.

(58) Sur la chronologie de ces événements voir surtout V. GRUMEL, « Notes d'histoire et de chronologie sur la vie de S. Maxime le Confesseur », *Échos d'Orient*, XXVI (1927), 24 sq.; P. SHERWOOD, « Notes on Maximus the Confessor », *Amer. Benedictine Review*, I (1950), 347 sq.; ID., *An Annotated Date-List of the Works of Maximus the Confessor*, « Studia Anselmiana », XXX (Rome 1952). Les lettres en question sont les Nos. 28-31, PG XCI, 620 sq.

le reste de sa vie, si la police impériale ne l'avait emmené de force à Constantinople pour le faire mourir en exil à Cherson (662) [59]. Voici donc le trajet habituel du réfugié: de l'Asie Mineure ou de la Syrie en Afrique du Nord, avec une escale en Crète [60]; puis à Rome, s'arrêtant en Sicile ou en Sardaigne [61].

C'est aussi dans les Lettres de S. Maxime que nous apprenons l'arrivée en Afrique Proconsulaire, vers l'an 640, des moines et des nonnes de la Syrie et d'Egypte, fuyant cette fois-ci devant les Arabes. Parmi eux il y avait des hérétiques monophysites qui causèrent un grand scandale [62]. L'incident est bien connu: il n'est pas besoin de le raconter ici [63]. De l'Afrique une partie de ces moines se rendit à Rome. Le *libellus* présenté par les moines grecs au Concile du Latran le dit expressement: *et prius quidem communiter, dum Afrorum habitaremus provinciam, hanc apostolicam summam expetivimus sedem* [64]. C'est sans doute aussi en traversant l'Afrique qu'est arrivée à Rome cette communauté de Syriens nestoriens qui s'établit au monastère dit Boetiana et qui fut ensuite dispersée par le pape Donus (676-8) [65]. Pour les autres monastères grecs de Rome il est difficile d'indiquer leurs attaches géographiques. Je suppose que la fameuse maison de S. Saba avait des liens avec la Palestine. Quant à la Domus Arsicia, je constate qu'un de ses moines, qui prit part au

---

(59) Sur la partie finale de la carrière de Maxime voir surtout R. Devresse, « La Vie de S. Maxime le Confesseur et ses recensions », *Anal. Bolland.*, XLVI (1928), 23 sq.

(60) *PG* XCI, 49C. Il s'est peut-être aussi arrêté à Chypre. Cf. Grumel, « Notes d'histoire... », 32.

(61) Grumel, *loc. cit.*

(62) *PG* XCI, 460 sq., 584 sq.

(63) Diehl, *L'Afrique byzantine*, 543 sq.; Grumel, « Notes d'histoire... », 28-9.

(64) Mansi, X, 906B.

(65) *Lib. Pont.*, I, 348.

700

Concile de Constantinople en 680, s'appelait Conon [66], un nom typique de la Cilicie et de l'Isaurie.

Tandis que le nombre de monastères grecs de Rome s'est accru aux VIIIe et IXe siècles, je ne trouve aucune preuve que ceci doit être mis en rapport avec l'iconoclasme, sauf une tradition tardive d'après laquelle S. Maria in Campo Martis fut concédée par le pape Zacharie à des moniales expulsées de leur couvent de Ste Anastasie à Constantinople [67]. Cette tradition me paraît fausse, car je ne connais à Constantinople aucun couvent de nonnes sous le vocable de Ste Anastasie [68]. D'ailleurs, l'hypothèse iconoclaste n'est pas nécessaire pour expliquer l'accroissement des monastères grecs de Rome, car l'émigration des chrétiens levantins ne cessa pas au VIIIe siècle. L'évêque de Messine qui assista au VIIe Concile Oecuménique en 787 declara que quand il était enfant en Syrie il avait vu de ses propres yeux les mesures iconoclastes du caliphe Yezid en 721 [69].

Une génération après le Concile du Latran commence la série des papes levantins et grecs qui, à l'exception de Grégoire II (715-31), un Romain, occupa le siège de S. Pierre entre 685 et 752. Certes, ce n'est pas une coïncidence si cette série se termine avec la chûte de l'Exarchat; pourtant, Jules Gay avait certainement raison en observant que l'élection de papes orientaux n'était nullement dictée par les exarques, et que, une fois élus, ces papes ne poursuivirent pas une politique servile envers le gou-

---

(66) MANSI, XI, 232C. Sur S. Saba voir F. ANTONELLI, « I primi monasteri di monaci orientali in Roma », Riv. archeol. crist., V (1928), 114 sq.

(67) Les éléments de cette tradition sont donnés par FERRARI, Early Roman Monasteries, 207 sq., qui la considère mal fondée.

(68) Sur les sanctuaires de Ste Anastasie à Constantinople voir R. JANIN, La géographie ecclésiastique de l'Empire byzantin, I/3 (Paris 1953), 26 sq.

(69) MANSI, XIII, 200B. Il portait pourtant le nom purement latin de Gaudiosus: ibid., 140B, 365E, etc.

vernement impérial [70]. L'explication qu'il fournit, à savoir qu'à cette époque les papes devaient encore être au courant des affaires de leurs diocèses hellénophones et capables de tenir tête aux hérésies, est cependant trop abstraite et vague pour rendre compte d'un phénomène concret, tel que l'élection de candidats appartenant à un groupe déterminé. Une étude plus poussée du duché byzantin de Rome, des tensions et des intérêts matériels qui s'y manifestaient, de ce qu'on appelle aujourd'hui les « groupes de pression », nous apportera peut-être un jour une solution plus satisfaisante de ce problème. En attendant, on pourrait observer que la charge du pape exigeait quand même un minimum d'instruction qui était probablement assez difficile à trouver en dehors de la colonie levantine. Les circonstances accompagnant la convocation du VIe Concile Oecuménique rendent quelque vraisemblance à cette observation. On se rappellera que dans sa lettre d'invitation (12 août, 678) l'empereur Constantin IV sollicita le pape Donus d'envoyer une délégation composée de théologiens instruits (*viros utiles... notitiam habentes totius a Deo inspiratae doctrinae, et peritiam irreprehensibilem habentes dogmatum*) munis des livres nécessaires. Il y suggéra même la composition de cette délégation, à savoir trois membres du clergé romain, douze métropolites ou évêques, et quatre moines de chacun des quatre monastères « byzantins » [71]. La lettre fut reçue par le pape Agathon qu'elle plongea dans l'embarras. Après avoir convoqué un concile préliminaire à Rome (Pâques

---

(70) « Quelques remarques sur les papes grecs et syriens avant la Querelle des iconoclastes (678-715) », *Mélanges G. Schlumberger*, I (Paris 1924), 40 sq.

(71) MANSI, XI, 198D-200B. Je me sens quelque peu gêné par l'expression ἐκ τῶν τεσσάρων βυζαντίων μοναστηρίων. Les commentateurs ont cru qu'il s'agissait de quatre monastères grecs de Rome, par. ex., HEFELE-LECLERCQ, *Histoire des Conciles*, III/1, 474; ANTONELLI, « I primi monasteri di monaci orientali », 118. Un tel usage du terme βυζάντιος me paraît toutefois insolite.

702

680), il désigna enfin ses représentants, mais il n'a pu trouver que trois évêques « convenables » au lieu de douze. Dans sa première lettre à l'empereur il s'empresse de dire que ces prélats n'étaient pas très versés dans l'étude de l'Ecriture Sainte, mais qu'ils suivaient en toute simplicité de cœur les doctrines des Pères et des conciles œcuméniques précédents (*nam apud homines in medio gentium positos, et de labore corporis quotidianum victum cum summa haesitatione conquirentes, quomodo ad plenum poterit inveniri scripturarum scientia...*) [72]. Dans la seconde lettre, adressée à l'empereur par le Concile romain, le pape mentionne nommément Théodore de Cantorbéry, *magnae insulae Britanniae archiepiscopum et philosophum,* qu'il tenait surtout à consulter [73]. Ceci donne à croire que Théodore était le seul prélat en Occident capable de comprendre les subtilités du problème monothélite. L'expérience de ce Concile a-t-elle poussé les électeurs romains à nommer des papes plus instruits qu'on ne pouvait trouver que parmi la colonie levantine?

Quoiqu'il en soit, les papes orientaux appartenaient au même milieu des réfugiés qui fondèrent les monastères grecs de Rome. Chaque fois que le *Liber Pontificalis* nous donne quelques renseignements sur l'origine de ces papes, nous pouvons suivre le même itinéraire allant de la Syrie ou de l'Asie Mineure en Sicile et, de là, à Rome. Ainsi, Jean V (685-6) était *natione Syrus, de provincia Antiochia* [74] ; Conon (686-7), comme nous l'avons déjà dit, *oriundus patre Thraceseo, edocatus apud Siciliam* [75] ; Serge (687-701), *natione Syrus, Antiochiae regionis, ortus ex patre Tiberio in Panormo Siciliae* [76].

(72) Mansi, XI, 235C.
(73) *Ibid.*, 294B.
(74) *Lib. Pont.*, I, 366.
(75) *Ibid.*, I, 368.
(76) *Ibid.*, I, 371.

La colonie grecque de Rome a fait œuvre littéraire †
dont les limites exactes n'ont pas encore été déterminées.
Cette production se compose d'œuvres originales écrites
en grec, et de traductions tant du grec en latin que du
latin en grec. Quel est le niveau culturel de cette littérature?

Sous la rubrique d'œuvres originales on peut classer
quelques Vies de saints qui datent à peu près de l'époque
qui nous concerne: ce sont les Vies du pape Martin Ier,
de Grégoire évêque d'Agrigente, et de Grégentios, évêque
des Homérites en Arabie, ainsi que la Passion incolore
de Ste Tatiana. Il est vrai que parmi ces ouvrages le
second seulement est attesté en tant qu'œuvre romaine;
mais la Vie de Grégentios est clairement apparentée à
celle de Grégoire [77], tandis que des indices internes suggè-
rent une origine romaine pour la Vie du pape Martin
et la Passion de Ste Tatiana [78].

De ces quatre documents la Vie du pape Martin est
la plus sincère [79]. En effet, cette Vie est basée entièrement
sur un dossier concernant l'exil de Martin, dossier qui
semble être parvenu à Rome, sans doute en copie unique,
et qui fut traduit plus tard en latin par Anastase le Bibliothécaire [80]. L'auteur n'a eu aucun accès aux sources latines, pas même au *Liber Pontificalis*, et n'a fait aucun
effort pour suppléer à sa source: rien n'y est dit de la
carrière du pape avant le Concile du Latran. Quelques
passages méritent d'être relevés. L'auteur dit, par exemple,
que tandis que tout l'Orient était envahi par l'hérésie,

---

(77) Voir E. PATLAGEAN, « Les moines grecs d'Italie... », *Studi medievali*
3e sér., V (1964), 583 sq.

(78) Cette dernière a été éditée par F. HALKIN, « Sainte Tatiana. Légende
grecque d'une ' martyre romaine ' », *Anal. Bolland.*, LXXXIX (1971), 265 sq.

(79) Ed. P. PEETERS, « Une Vie grecque du pape S. Martin I », *Anal. Bolland.*, LI (1933), 225 sq.

(80) *Ibid.*, 231 sq.

704

Martin a fait briller de Rome les rayons de l'Orthodoxie [81]; il appelle la basilique du Latran « la première qui fut bâtie et établie au monde entier par Constantin de pieuse mémoire » [82]; et il commet une curieuse erreur au sujet du fameux canon 82 du Concile in Trullo, erreur bien naturelle pour un auteur qui était habitué à l'art religieux de l'Occident: car, au lieu de dire que ce Concile a voulu abolir la figuration du Christ sous la forme de l'Agneau, il dit exactement le contraire [83]. La connaissance qu'il montre de la topographie de Constantinople est peut-être tirée de sa source, tandis que ses sympathies grecques se manifestent quand il attribue le Concile du Latran à l'initiative de Maxime le Confesseur et des autres évêques et abbés qui avaient été chassés par les hérétiques. La langue du document est d'une remarquable incorrection, mais je n'oserais pas affirmer que les latinismes qu'elle renferme (par exemple, le curieux terme λούππακες) [84] sont nécessairement dûs au séjour de l'auteur en Occident.

La Vie de S. Grégoire d'Agrigente, écrite par Léonce, abbé de S. Sabas à Rome, est un document beaucoup plus complexe. Le but dans lequel il a été composé ne m'est pas clair, car je ne peux pas suivre Mme Patlagean en y voyant une apologie du primat romain [85]. Il

(81) *Ibid.*, 254.
(82) *Ibid.*, 255.
(83) *Ibid.*, 262.
(84) *Ibid.*, 258.
(85) « Les moines grecs d'Italie », 590 sq. Texte de la Vie dans PG XCVIII, 549 sq. Il est digne d'attention que le pape y est présenté sous une lumière défavorable. Voir col. 660: ὦ τῆς ἀνοίας, ὦ τῆς ἀσπλαγχνίας, ὦ τῆς κακίας, ἧς πεπλήρωται ὁ τὸν πρῶτον ἐπέχων τῶν ἀποστόλων θρόνον. Quant à la chronologie de la Vie, les études de A. P. CHRISTOPHILOPOULOS, « Πότε ἔζησεν ὁ Γρηγόριος Ἀκράγαντος »; Ἐπετ. Ἑταιρ. Βυζαντ. Σπουδῶν, XIX (1949), 158-61, et de I.C., « Per la cronologia della vita di S. Gregorio Agrigentino », *Boll. della Badia greca di Grottaferrata*, n.s., IV (1950), 189-207; V (1951), 77-91, n'ont abouti à aucun résultat utile.

se peut que l'auteur ait simplement voulu célébrer la mémoire d'un saint local. Ce qui est, d'autre part, digne d'attention, c'est le contraste entre le cadre historique, qui est tout à fait vague et contradictoire, et le cadre géographique qui est très précis, au moins en ce qui regarde l'Italie. L'action se place à une époque indéterminée entre le IVe siècle et le VIIe. Parmi les protagonistes figure un hérétique, Leucius, qui a été condamné par le Concile de Laodicée, donc au IVe siècle (l'auteur sait qu'il s'agit d'un concile local); l'empereur est tantôt Justin, tantôt Justinien; le pape qui joue un rôle important dans le récit n'est jamais nommé; l'évêque de Jérusalem est Macaire, peut-être Macaire II (552; 563-4-vers 575); mais S. Grégoire assiste aussi à Constantinople au concile qui condamne les Monothélites, donc le VIe Concile de 680-1, etc. [86]. La question se pose donc de savoir si cette confusion est voulue ou si elle est simplement due a l'ignorance de l'auteur. Je penche pour la seconde solution. L'abbé Léonce avait entendu parler d'un hérétique Leucius condamné au temps de pape Gélase, du concile de Laodicée, de Serge, Cyrus et Paul (sans, toutefois, connaître la nature de leur impieté), de l'empereur Justinien, du patriarche Macaire de Jérusalem, mais il ne savait pas comment tous ces personnages s'entreliaient chronologiquement. Ecrivant probablement après le transfert de la Sicile à la juridiction de Constantinople tout en essayant de se placer à une époque antérieure, il tombe dans une contradiction évidente: Grégoire est nommé au siège d'Agrigente par le pape, et quand il est accusé d'immoralité, c'est au pape qu'il fait appel; et pourtant, quand le pape se décide enfin à examiner son cas, il ne peut pas le faire

(86) *PG* XCVIII, 572-3, 576 (Macaire de Jérusalem), 608 (Concile de Constantinople), 612 (empereur Justin), 613, 665, 700 (empereur Justinien), 641 sq. (Leucius).

706

sans le consentement de l'empereur et du patriarche de Constantinople.

Quand, d'autre part, nous examinons les indications géographiques, tout devient clair et précis. L'auteur, qui était sans doute originaire d'Agrigente, est très au courant de la topographie sicilienne. Il nous informe que le Saint est né à un village appelé Praetorion, sa mère étant du village de Thyris [87]. Il connaît un lieu nommé Passararia près de Phintias, et la rivière qui rejoint la mer près d'Agrigente, c'est-a-dire l'Hypsas [88], ainsi que la région au sud de la ville qu'il appelle *peripolis* et le port (*emporion*) qui était sans doute a l'embouchure de la rivière [89]. Dans la même ville il nomme une localité appelée Modiolus [90]. A Palerme, il connaît la maison de Libertinus appartenant à l'évêché d'Agrigente [91]. A Rome, il nomme les monastères de S. Sabas, S. Erasme [92], et Ste Cécile, ce dernier étant à cette époque un couvent de nonnes [93]. Ses horizons englobent aussi une bonne partie de la Méditerranée. Il cite le martyrium de S. Julien à Carthage et l'église de S. Léonce à Tripoli en Phénicie [94]. Naturellement, il a aussi quelques notions des lieux saints de la Palestine [95]. A Constantinople il connaît le monastère des SS. Serge et Bacchus [96], ce qui s'explique puisque ce monastère avait des attaches avec le Saint Siège [97], et l'église de Ste Irène [98]. Tous ces lieux – Constantinople,

(87) *Ibid.*, 553.
(88) *Ibid.*, 581.
(89) *Ibid.*, 581, 629, 632.
(90) *Ibid.*, 644.
(91) *Ibid.*, 629.
(92) *Ibid.*, 616, 620-1.
(93) *Ibid.*, 689.
(94) *Ibid.*, 564-5.
(95) *Ibid.*, 569, 593.
(96) *Ibid.*, 600.
(97) JANIN, *Géographie ecclésiastique*, 468.
(98) *PG* XCVIII, 609.

Jérusalem, Tripoli, Carthage – se trouvaient sur le parcours de l'émigration levantine, et même si notre auteur ne les avait pas visités lui même, il aurait pu facilement s'en informer parmi ses confrères.

Le niveau culturel envisagé dans la Vie de S. Grégoire est assez primitif. A l'âge de huit ans notre saint est placé par ses parents dans un *didaskaleion* pour apprendre les lettres sacrées; en fait, il est présenté à l'évêque qui le place sous la charge d'un instituteur. Étant particulièrement doué, il complète son éducation en deux ans, ayant appris le calcul, la succession des fêtes et le Psautier [99]. Ceci est considéré comme une préparation suffisante pour une carrière cléricale. Le penchant de Grégoire pour les livres attire des mentions répétées: il lit la Vie de S. Basile [100], les ouvrages de S. Jean Chrysostome, et il est à même d'expliquer un traité difficile de S. Grégoire de Nazianze [101]. C'est cependant dans le désert palestinien que notre Saint apprend d'un vieil ermite « toute la rhétorique, la grammaire, la philosophie et l'astronomie », au point de devenir « un second Chrysostome » [102]. Evidemment l'auteur n'avait qu'une notion bien vague de la signification de ces disciplines; ce n'étaient plus les arts libéraux enseignés dans un établissement d'éducation supérieure, mais une science secrète dont la clef est détenue par un vieillard du désert.

Nous retrouvons les mêmes horizons dans la Vie de S. Grégentius de Tephar. Une fois de plus le cadre historique est assez embrouillé. Une fois de plus l'auteur connaît bien Rome et Agrigente [103]. Il a aussi quelques notions

(99) *Ibid.*, 553-6.
(100) *Ibid.*, 557.
(101) *Ibid.*, 600-1, 645.
(102) *Ibid.*, 597.
(103) Ed. partielle de la Vie par A. A. Vasiliev, « Žitie sv. Grigentija, episkopa Omiritskago », *Vizant. Vremennik*, XIV (1907; paru en 1909), 23 sq.

708

d'Alexandrie, peut-être de seconde main. Mais quand il dépasse ces frontières, tout devient flou. Le village de Bliarès, situé au pays des Avares à deux jours de voyage de la Mer du Nord, où notre Saint est né et a été élevé, appartient évidemment au domaine de la fantaisie [104]. Et pourtant, même dans ce lieu bizarre, Grégentios fut placé à l'âge de sept ans dans un *didaskaleion* pour apprendre les lettres sacrées, tout comme Grégoire l'a été à Agrigente. Cependant, il passa presque tout son temps à l'église ou « il montra tant d'amour pour les croix et les saintes icones, qu'il les contemplait et les embrassait toute la journée » [105]. De Bliarès le Saint se dirigea vers la ville de Morynè, ou il y avait une résidence épiscopale, une Grande Eglise, et d'autres églises dédiées à la Théotokos et à S. Nicolas [106]. Hélas, cette ville est inconnue, de même que la ville suivante que le Saint visita, Anténora, elle aussi un évêché [107]. A Agrigente nous quittons enfin les ténèbres. Mais quand le Saint se rend à Milan pour prier au tombeau de S. Ambroise, il y va en bateau [108]. Ses pérégrinations ultérieures en Arabie et en Ethiopie sont puisées dans la Passion de St. Aréthas; tout ce que notre auteur ajoute de son cru appartient à la fantaisie [109].

Laissant de côté quelques œuvres de faussaire qui pourraient être attribuées à la colonie grecque de Rome – je songe au *Constitutum Constantini* si on se fie à la théorie

---

Cf. les remarques critiques de P. Peeters, *Anal. Bolland.*, XXXI (1912), 108-9. Pour Agrigente et Rome, Vasiliev, 49-50, 52 sq.

(104) Peeters, *loc. cit.*

(105) Vasiliev, *op. cit.*, 41-2. La Vie a été donc composée, selon toute vraisemblance, pendant l'époque iconoclaste.

(106) *Ibid.*, 47-8.

(107) E. Patlagean, « Les moines grecs d'Italie », 586, croit qu'il s'agit de Murano et de la nouvelle Padoue.

(108) Vasiliev, *op. cit.*, 51.

(109) Peeters, *loc. cit*

d'Ohnsorge [110], et aux deux lettres du pape Grégoire II à Leon l'Isaurien [111] – nous arrivons aux traductions. Là aussi peu de surprises nous attendent: ce sont surtout des écrits hagiographiques, des actes officiels [112], quelques extraits de chroniques [113]. En somme, rien qui dépasse les horizons d'un moine ordinaire [114]. Sans pouvoir en fournir une démonstration rigoureuse, car la datation de ces textes est souvent très difficile, j'ai l'impression qu'au VIIIe siècle on a fait plus de traductions du latin en grec qu'inversement. Parmi ces traductions on peut citer les Vies de S. Ambroise [115] et de S. Martin de Tours [116], et surtout les *Dialogues* de Grégoire le Grand, dont la version grecque est due au pape Zacharie [117]. Destinées d'abord

(110) « Das Constitutum Constantini und seine Entstehung ». *Konstantinopel und der Okzident* (Darmstadt 1966), 93 sq. Voir cependant, ici-même, le mémoire de H. FUHRMANN, pp. 257 sq.

(111) Dans son importante étude « Aux origines de l'iconoclasme: Le témoignage de Grégoire II? », Centre de Recherche d'Hist. et Civil. Byzant., *Travaux et mémoires*, III (1968), 275-6, J. Gouillard attribue ce texte à un moine de Constantinople qui était « au fait de certaines sources occidentales ». Pour ma part, je songerais plutôt à une origine romaine.

(112) Tels les actes du Concile de 787 traduits à la demande du pape Adrien Ier. Voir SIEGMUND, *Die Überlieferung der griech. christlichen Literatur*, 175-6.

(113) Tel le *Laterculus Malalianus*, *MGH, Auct. ant.*, XIII, 424 sq. L. TRAUBE, « Chronicon Palatinum », *Byzant. Zeitschr.*, IV (1895), 489 ff., reproduit dans *Vorlesungen und Abhandlungen*, III (1920), 201 sq., a démontré que cette sèche énumération d'empereurs a été composée à Rome au VIIIe siècle.

(114) Il est intéressant de constater que les traductions faites au siècle suivant par Anastase le Bibliothécaire se limitaient aux mêmes catégories d'ouvrages. Cf. G. ARNALDI, art. « Anastasio Bibliotecario », *Dizionario biografico degli Italiani*, III (1961), 37.

(115) Voir E. DEKKERS, « Les traductions grecques des écrits patristiques latins », *Sacris erudiri*, V (1953), 202.

(116) Voir H. DELEHAYE, « Quatre miracles de S. Martin de Tours », *Anal. Bolland.*, LV (1937), 31-2; ID., « La Vie grecque de S. Martin de Tours », *Studi bizant. e neoellenici*, V (1939), 428 sq.

(117) S. G. MERCATI, « Sull'epigramma acrostico... », *Bessarione*, XXXV (1919), 67 sq., a démontré, en se fondant sur une épigramme conservée dans le *cod. Ambros. gr.* 246, que Zacharie lui-même était soucieux d'expédier sa traduction en Orient (p. 75, v. 36: ἀποστεῖλαι σπεύδοντα τοῖς τῆς ἑῴας), et qu'il chargea un certain moine Jean d'en faire une copie.

710

à la colonie grecque de Rome, ces traductions, ainsi que
d'autres faites au début du siècle suivant, telle la Passion
de S. Denys [118], telle la Passion de Ste Anastasie [119], pri-
rent rapidement le chemin de l'Orient. Photius lisait déjà
les *Dialogues* de Grégoire et il renvoie à d'autres ouvrages
du même auteur traduits par le pape Zacharie [120].

L'activité littéraire que je viens de retracer présuppose
l'existence de scriptoria et de bibliothèques, même si ces
dernières n'étaient pas bien garnies. En effet, il est établi
qu'au moins un scriptorium grec fonctionnait à Rome au
VIIIe siècle. Le *Vatic. gr.* 1666 de l'an 800 en provient [121].
Ecrit en une onciale arrondie de type franchement occi-
dental, décoré avec des initiales de style « lombard », ce
manuscrit contient justement les *Dialogues* de Grégoire
le Grand. Un second manuscrit, le *Paris, gr.* 1115, pose
un problème plus délicat. Il s'agit d'un recueil écrit en
1276 pour la bibliothèque impériale de Constantinople et

(118) *BHG* 554, qui est une mauvaise traduction de la Passion latine,
BHL 2178, *Post beatam et gloriosam.* Voir R. Loenertz, « Le panégyrique
de S. Denys l'Aréopagite par S. Michel le Syncelle », *Anal. Bolland.*, LXVIII
(1950), 94 sq.; Id., « La légende parisienne de S. Denys l'Aréopagite », *ibid.*,
LXIX (1951), 225 sq.
(119) Voir H. Delehaye, *Etude sur le légendier romain*, Subsidia hagio-
graphica 23 (Bruxelles 1936), 155; Loenertz, « La légende parisienne », 233.
(120) *Bibliotheca*, cod. 252; cf. *De S. Spiritus mystagogia*, PG CII, 393C.
H. Delehaye, « S. Grégoire le Grand dans l'hagiographie grecque », *Anal.
Bolland.*, XXIII (1904), 452, croit que Photius s'est trompé en attribuant
à Zacharie d'autres traductions de S. Grégoire que celle des Dialogues.
(121) P. Batiffol, « Librairies byzantines à Rome », *MEFR*, VIII (1888),
301 sq.; S. G. Mercati, « Sull'epigramma acrostico »; *Codices Vaticani graeci*,
Codd. 1485-1683 par C. Giannelli (Cité du Vatican 1950), 408-9. Sur les initiales voir C. Nordenfalk, *Die spätantiken Zierbuchstaben* (Stockholm 1970),
152, 167, 210 et pl. 69. Un autre manuscrit du VIIIe/IXe siècle qui a été attribué
à Rome est le *Crypt. B. a. LV.* C'était à l'origine un grand homiliaire en deux
tomes, mais il n'en subsiste que quelques folios palimpsestes qui font partie
actuellement de quatre manuscrits. L'écriture du *Cryptensis* ressemble à celle
de trois folios, appartenant eux aussi à un homiliaire, qui servent de feuilles
de garde du *Paris. lat.* 4403B. Voir Ch. Martin, « Fragments palimpsestes
d'un discours sur la Pâque », *Ann. de l'Inst. de Phil. et d'Hist. Orient. et Slaves*,
IV = *Mélanges F. Cumont* (1936), 321 sq.

copié, d'après le colophon, d'un codex « trouvé dans la vieille bibliothèque de la Sainte Eglise de l'ancienne Rome » portant la date de 6267 de la Création, ce qui donnerait 759 d'après le calcul byzantin [122]. Le manuscrit de Paris est une somme ecclésiastique: il contient deux florilèges, l'un consacré aux Natures du Christ, l'autre aux images, divers textes patristiques, même quelques fragments de chroniques: bref, c'est un receuil qui n'a pu être constitué que dans une bonne bibliothèque. Ce qui fait, cependant, difficulté c'est que le manuscrit contient au fol. 239 une lettre synodale de Jean patriarche de Jérusalem (inconnu par ailleurs) dirigée contre le concile iconoclaste d'Hiéria (754), lettre qui fait allusion à l'exécution du patriarche Constantin II de Constantinople en 766 [123]. Ceci signifie-t-il que le colophon est une fabrication? Je ne le crois pas, car non seulement il est très précis, mais la date de 1276 qui suit de si près l'Union de Lyon (1274) fournit un contexte logique pour la migration à Constantinople d'un manuscrit appartenant à l'Eglise de Rome. Evidemment, on peut se tirer d'affaire si on corrige 6267 en 6367 (ce qui donnerait 859 de notre ère), comme le proposait déjà Montfaucon [124]; mais c'est un expédient arbitraire et qui

---

(122) Le manuscrit est décrit par TH. SCHERMANN, *Die Geschichte der dogmatischen Florilegien vom V.-VIII. Jahrhundert*, Texte und Untersuchungen, N.F., XIII/1 (1905), 6 sq. La partie du colophon qui nous intéresse est la suivante: μετεγράφη δὲ ἀπὸ βιβλίου εὑρεθέντος ἐν τῇ παλαιᾷ βιβλιοθήκῃ τῆς ἁγίας ἐκκλησίας τῆς πρεσβυτέρας Ῥώμης, ὅπερ βιβλίον ἐγράφη καὶ αὐτὸ ἐν ἔτει Ϛσξζ', ὡς ἀριθμεῖσθαι τοὺς χρόνους τοῦ τοιούτου βιβλίου ἄχρι τοῦ παρόντος ιζ' πρὸς τοὺς πεντακοσίους.

Voir aussi BATIFFOL, « Librairies byzantines », 298; P. J. ALEXANDER, « Hypatius of Ephesus », *Harvard Theol. Rev.*, XLV (1952), 177 n. 2; R. DEVREESSE, *Introduction à l'étude des manuscrits grecs* (Paris 1954), 54 n. 8, 91, 185 n. 9, 187-8, qui promet une analyse plus détaillée de ce manuscrit, analyse qui, à ma connaissance, n'a pas paru.

(123) Il s'agit d'une version de l'*Adversus Constantinum Cabalinum* faussement attribué à S. Jean Damascène: *PG* XCV, 309 sq.

(124) *Palaeographia graeca* (Paris 1708), 66. DEVREESSE, *Introduction* 54 n. 8, opte pour la même solution.

712

n'explique pas d'ailleurs l'absence dans le manuscrit de Paris de toute allusion au VIIe Concile Oecuménique. Pour ma part, je crois que la bonne solution est celle qui a été indiquée naguère par B. M. Melioranskij [125], mais qui est restée presqu' inaperçue: le prototype était daté non pas d'après l'ère byzantine, encore peu répandue au VIIIe siècle, mais d'après l'ère alexandrine. Il a été donc écrit en 774-5, mais pas nécessairement à Rome. Il s'agit plutôt d'un florilège syro-palestinien expédié à Rome à une époque indéterminée, peut-être déjà à la fin du VIIIe siècle.

Ceci nous amène au problème des bibliothèques de Rome. Les études de plusieurs érudits, notamment De Rossi, Marrou et Courcelle, ont abouti à peu près à l'hypothèse suivante [126]. Une bibliothèque composée surtout d'ouvrages ecclésiastiques fut organisée au *clivus Scauri* par le pape Agapit I (535-6) en relation avec le projet d'une académie chrétienne à Rome. Les livres, nous dit-on, furent plus tard transférés par Grégoire le Grand au *scrinium* du Latran. A ce fonds s'ajouta vers la même époque la collection provenant du Vivarium de sorte que le *scrinium* devint une véritable bibliothèque. Les textes allégués devant le Concile du Latran en 649 nous en indiquent en partie le contenu. Cependant, cette bibliothèque s'est appauvrie petit à petit à cause de la coutume d'en aliéner les livres, jusqu'à ce qu'elle ne disparut définitivement vers le XIe siècle.

Il ne convient pas d'insister sur la fragilité de cette construction. En ce qui concerne cependant les livres grecs,

---

(125) *Georgij Kiprjanin i Ioann Ierusalimljanin* (St. Pétersbourg 1901), 83.

(126) G. B. ROSSI, « De origine, historia, indicibus scrinii et bibliothecae sedis apostolicae », préface aux *Codices Palatini Latini*, I (1886), pp. LV sq.; H. I. MARROU, « Autour de la bibliothèque du pape Agapit », *MEFR*, XLVIII (1931), 124 sq.; COURCELLE, *Lettres grecques*, 342 sq. Cf. RICHÉ, *Education*, 174-5; R. DEVREESSE, *Le fonds grec de la Bibliothèque Vaticane des origines à Paul V*, Studi e testi 244 (1965), 1-2.

je dois faire l'observation suivante: les passages patristiques et hérétiques présentés à la 5e session du Concile du Latran furent lus à partir d'un florilège préalablement établi [127]. Il n'y a donc pas de raison valable, sauf dans le cas où les Actes nous le disent expressément [128], que les ouvrages d'où ces extraits ont été tirés, aient pu se trouver effectivement dans le *scrinium* du Latran. En plus, il a été démontré que le même florilège se retrouve en partie dans le *Tomus spiritualis* de Maxime le Confesseur [129]. Ceci renforce l'opinion que Maxime a été l'auteur de la documentation présentée au Concile, et nous mène en même temps à une autre supposition. Ce florilège, composé de passages assez courts, n'a-t'il pu être préparé par Maxime avant son arrivée à Rome, disons à Carthage, pour être complété plus tard par des citations des Pères latins? D'autre part, nous savons qu'il existait sur la même question un florilège très étendu, et qui est aujourd'hui perdu, œuvre du patriarche Sophrone de Jérusalem [130]. En tout cas, les extraits lus devant le Concile de 649 ne nous permettent nullement de reconstituer le contenu de la bibliothèque du Latran. Quant aux livres grecs du Vivarium, même en admettant qu'ils vinrent au Latran, ils étaient au plus une quinzaine [131].

(127) MANSI, X, 1070E: *deflorata a nobis sanctorum patrum testimonia.*
(128) Un *codex beati Dionysii* a été pris à la bibliothèque apostolique: *ibid.*, 975E. Les autres cas se rapportent à des documents: *ibid.*, 914A, 944B, 1037E.
(129) R. DEVREESSE, « La Vie de S. Maxime » (cité à la note 59), 46-7; J. PIERRES, *S. Maximus Confessor, princeps apologetarum synodi Lateranensis,* Diss. Pont. Univ. Greg. (Rome 1940), 27* sq.
(130) MANSI, X, 896A; Photius, *Bibl.*, cod. 231, en donne le contenu. Cf. VAILHÉ, « Sophrone le sophiste » (cité à la note 57), 378 sq.; F. DIEKAMP, *Doctrina patrum de incarnatione Verbi* (Münster in Westf. 1907), pp. LX sq.
(131) COURCELLE, *Lettres grecques*, 319 et n. 6; ID., « Nouvelles recherches sur le monastère de Cassiodore », *Actes du Ve Congrès Intern. d'Archéol. Chrét.*, 1954 (1957), 517-8.

714

On pourrait supposer que les monastères grecs de Rome possédaient eux aussi quelques livres, mais je n'en sais rien.

* * *

Avant d'exprimer à notre tour quelques hypothèses, il convient de résumer les résultats de notre enquête. Nous avons constaté à la fin du viie et au viiie siècle un faible rayonnement des lettres grecques en Europe transalpine, rayonnement qui n'a pas laissé de résultats permanents à cause de son caractère intermittent et fortuit. Le centre de cette diffusion fut Rome où une importante communauté de moines byzantins s'établit avant 649 à cause des invasions perse et arabe et des dislocations économiques que ces invasions provoquèrent [132]. Le niveau intellectuel de cette communauté semble avoir baissé petit à petit. La première génération d'immigrants comprenait de grandes figures, tel Sophrone de Damas, tel Jean Moschos, tel Maxime le Confesseur; il n'eurent pas de dignes successeurs. Séparés de leur patrie avec laquelle ils entretenaient pourtant de relations assez suivies, leur loyauté se porta vers l'Eglise de Rome qu'ils parvinrent à dominer pendant 70 ans. Dans mon exposé je me suis gardé de souligner le rôle de l'iconoclasme, car je ne crois pas qu'il ait exercé en soi une influence importante sur la migration vers l'Occident de clercs byzantins [133]. L'importance de l'iconoclasme pour notre enquête doit être cherchée ailleurs.

(132) On doit se garder en effet d'attribuer cette migration uniquement à l'action militaire. Sur la dépopulation volontaire d'une grande région de la Syrie du Nord, privée de ses anciens débouchés commerciaux vers l'Occident, voir G. TCHALENKO, *Villages antiques de la Syrie du Nord*, I (Paris 1953), 430 sq.

(133) C'est aussi l'avis de J. GAY, « Quelques remarques » (cité à la note 70), 47.

L'adoption par le gouvernement impérial d'une doctrine hérétique obligea le parti orthodoxe à faire appel à la plus haute autorité ecclésiastique, c'est-à-dire au Saint Siège. Ce fut déjà le cas dans l'affaire monothélite qui ne dura pas très longtemps; le même procédé fut adopté pendant le siècle iconoclaste. Les patriarcats orientaux, tombés sous le joug arabe, ne comptant plus, le recours à Rome devint pour l'opposition orthodoxe une arme indispensable. Or, ce recours se faisait précisément par l'entremise de la colonie grecque de Rome. Envisagé de cette façon, l'action de l'iconoclasme fut cause d'union plutôt que de division: elle encouragea les contacts entre les intellectuels orthodoxes de Constantinople et leurs confrères grecs de Rome ainsi qu'avec l'Eglise romaine.

C'est surtout par la Correspondance de S. Théodore Studite que nous connaissons le mécanisme de ces contacts. Théodore lui-même n'a jamais quitté les confins de l'Empire byzantin, mais il envoya des communications nombreuses à Rome pendant son second exil (808-11) provoqué par « l'affaire mœchienne », ainsi que pendant son troisième exil (816-20) occasionné par la résomption de l'iconoclasme. Pendant toute cette période Théodore avait son homme de confiance à Rome, à savoir Basile, abbé de S. Sabas, qu'il semble avoir connu personnellement [134]; il y avait aussi d'autres amis, par exemple, un *chartophylax* dont le nom n'est pas donné [135]. Malgré les dangers du voyage et la vigilance de la police, Théodore a pu expédier ses disciples à Rome à plusieurs reprises. Il mentionne souvent ces émissaires qui portaient ses lettres en Occident: le moine Epiphane qui fit plusieurs

---

(134) Il le qualifie de γνώριμος καὶ φίλος: *Ep.* 192, ed. J. Cozza-Luzi dans MAI, *Nova patrum bibliotheca*, VIII/1 (1871), 165. Basile est aussi le destinataire des lettres I. 35 et II. 221 de Théodore, *PG* XCIX, 1028 sq., 1669.

(135) *Ep.* 35, *PG* XCIX, 1212A.

716

traversées jusqu'à ce qu'il fût arrêté [136]; le moine Euphé-
mien qui y alla deux fois, la première en compagnie de
Denis, lui aussi membre de la communauté studite [137];
enfin Lètoius et Syméon, les disciples favoris de Théodore [138]. Lorsque l'Iconoclasme revint au pouvoir en 814,
deux membres importants du clergé byzantin se rendirent
à Rome: c'étaient l'évêque de Monembasie et l'abbé Méthode, le futur patriarche de Constantinople. Théodore
comptait beaucoup sur leur intercession auprès du pape [139].
Ces contacts n'étaient possibles que grâce à l'existence de
la colonie grecque de Rome. Ce qui est, en outre, significatif c'est que les personnages mêlés à ces affaires, tel
Théodore, tel son oncle Platon, tel l'abbé Méthode, appartenaient à l'élite de la société byzantine.

Ici nous devons envisager un problème qui a une portée
beaucoup plus générale. Le mouvement que nous appe-
lons la renaissance Carolingienne commença au dernier
quart du VIIIe siècle, et fut précédé par l'introduction
de la minuscule caroline peu après l'an 750 [140]. A Byzance
nous observons un phénomène semblable: une renaissance
qui se manifeste vers les années 830, précédée elle aussi
† par une réforme de l'écriture. Le plus ancien manuscrit
daté en minuscule grecque est l'Evangile Ouspensky (Lé-
ningrad, Bibl. de l'Etat, 219), écrit en 835 par l'abbé
studite Nicolas; on s'accorde, cependant, à admettre que

---

(136) *Ep.* I. 35 (Epiphane est envoyé à Rome pour la seconde fois); II.
35 (Théodore lui confie des lettres au pape et à Méthode parce qu'il est ἀρχαι-
ογνώριστος à Rome); Cozza-Luzi, *epp.* 276-7 (Epiphane en prison à Constantinople).

(137) Cozza-Luzi, *epp.* 192-3. Mort de Denis: *Ep.* II. 112, PG XCIX,
1373 sq.

(138) *Ep.* II. 221, *PG* XCIX, 1669.

(139) Cozza-Luzi, *epp.*, 192-3; *Ep.* II. 35, PG XCIX, 1209 sq.

(140) Je ne méconnais pas la différence qui sépare la translittération grecque
de la « suite de translittérations » que connurent les textes latins. On se rap-
portera à A. Dain, *Les manuscrits*, 2e éd. (Paris 1964), 126 sq.

la minuscule fut introduite quelques décénnies plus tôt, disons vers 800.

Le parallélisme entre ces phénomènes ainsi que la priorité de l'Occident ne sont pas restés inaperçus. Pourtant, les historiens se sont refusés à admettre une relation quelconque entre les renaissances Carolingienne et byzantine [141]. En ce qui concerne la renaissance à proprement parler, c'est-à-dire la réforme de l'enseignement et la récuperation de l'héritage littéraire antique on doit avouer que les promoteurs de ce mouvement à Byzance – je songe à Léon le Mathématicien et Photius – n'avaient pas de relations connues avec l'Occident. Mais quant à l'ecriture de libraire, même si nous manquons de preuve décisive, je crois qu'un rapport ne doit pas être exclu d'emblée. Il ne s'agit pas, bien entendu, de l'origine graphique de la minuscule grecque qui se développe à partir de la cursive notariale telle que nous la retrouvons dans les papyrus du VIIIe siècle [142]. Ce qui est beaucoup plus important pour l'histoire culturelle c'est l'utilisation de la minuscule ou de la cursive dans la production des livres: or, il semble certain, que les συρμαιόγραφα (quel que soit le sens exact de ce terme) [143] constituaient une

(141) Voir en dernier lieu le bel ouvrage de P. LEMERLE, *Le premier humanisme byzantin* (Paris 1971), ch. I.

(142) Voir, par ex., T. W. ALLEN, « The Origin of the Greek Minuscule Hand », *J. of Hell. Studies*, XL (1920), 1 sq.; G. ZERETELI, « Beispiele griechischer Kursive kurz von der Ausbildung der Minuskel », *Aegyptus*, XIII (1933), 84 sq.; A. BATAILLE, *Les papyrus*, Traité d'études byzantines, II (Paris 1955), 13. A noter, cependant, que la chaîne de transmission n'est pas complète: il y a un « missing link ».

(143) On a beaucoup discuté sur la signification du verbe συρμαιογραφεῖν qui est employé pour décrire l'activité de copiste de Théodore Studite et de son oncle Platon mort en 814. Voir en dernier lieu J. LEROY, « Un témoin ancien des Petites Catéchèses de Théodore Studite », *Scriptorium*, XV (1961), 55 sq.; LEMERLE, *Le premier humanisme*, 116-8, 309; O. KRESTEN, « Litterae longariae, quae graece syrmata dicuntur », *Scriptorium*, XXIV (1970), 305 sq.; ID., « Einige zusätzliche Überlegungen zu συρμαιογραφεῖν », *Byzant. Zeitschrift*, LXIII (1970), 278. Un élément important du problème a été relevé par A.

718

nouveauté à Byzance vers l'an 800. Nous devons donc choisir entre deux possibilités: ou bien ce développement s'est produit à Byzance en vase clos, ce qui revient à dire qu'il répondait à des bésoins particuliers qui sont nés précisément à cette époque [144]; ou bien les libraires byzantins étaient conscients des innovations de métier qui avaient été appliqués ailleurs, en Occident ou, peut être même en Orient chrétien [145]. C'est pour la seconde possibilité que je penche.

Je n'ignore pas, certes, les objections qu'on pourrait élever. Les manuscrits grecs de cette époque qu'on peut attribuer à l'Italie sont, comme nous l'avons indiqué, en onciales [146]. En outre, la minuscule latine n'était pas

DILLER, « A Companion to the Uspenski Gospels », *Byzant. Zeitschr.*, XLIX (1956), 335, et repris par Kresten: c'est que Platon a reçu pendant sa jeunesse une instruction de notaire, τὴν παίδευσιν τῆς νοταρικῆς μεθόδου (*PG* XCIX, 808B). Il employait donc, vraisemblablement, la cursive notariale. D'autre part, on n'a pas le droit d'affirmer, comme on l'a fait à maintes reprises, que Platon s'adonna à la transcription de livres en cursive dès le milieu du VIIIᵉ siècle. Il n'entra au couvent qu'en 759 à l'âge de 24 ans.

(144) Mais alors lesquels? On ne peut pas songer, comme le fait ALLEN, *op. cit.*, 11-12, à la conquête arabe de l'Egypte qui mit fin à l'exportation du papyrus sans faire remonter l'origine de la minuscule grecque vers l'an 650. D'autre part, il serait bien difficile de prouver que la production de livres à Byzance s'est sensiblement accrue à la fin du VIIIᵉ siècle. Théodore Studite lui-même nous assure que l'« abondance de livres » dans les monastères (il écrit en 814) était due uniquement au travail personnel de Platon, donc d'un seul scribe: *PG* XCIX, 820A.

(145) Le problème de l'Orient reste ouvert. Il existe un petit groupe de manuscrits en cursive dont le plus fameux est le *Vatic. gr.* 2200 sur papier. On l'attribue à l'Egypte ou à la Syrie et on le date du VIIIᵉ-IXᵉ siècle d'après l'écriture. Malheureusement, on ne sait rien de l'histoire de ce manuscrit avant son entrée à la bibliothèque Colonna. Pour la description voir DIEKAMP, *Doctrina patrum*, IX-XIV.

(146) Bien entendu, la cursive grecque était pratiquée en Italie. Outre le *Laudianus*, on peut indiquer les notes marginales du *codex Bezae* à partir du fol. 114ᵛ. Voir l'édition phototypique, *Codex Bezae Cantabrigiensis* (Cambridge 1899). Les différentes thèses se rapportant à l'origine de ce manuscrit sont discutées par ROPES, *The Text of Acts* (cité à la note 25), LVI-LXXXIV. Les notes en grec sont toutes antérieures à l'an 800: E. A. LOWE dans *J. of Theol. Studies*, XIV (1912-3), 385-8. Voir aussi du même auteur, « The Codex Bezae and Lyons », *ibid.*, XXV (1924), 270-4. Ces notes nous révèlent un milieu illettré qui parlait un dialecte grec populaire caracterisé par la rédu-

encore très répandue en Italie au VIIIe siècle, quoiqu'elle
y fût certainement pratiquée [147]. Une série d'indices nous
porte à croire, cependant, que les relations entre les scriptoria d'Italie, de Byzance et du Proche Orient étaient
plus étroites qu'on ne l'aurait supposé à première vue.
Il est en effet à peu près certain que l'initiale décora-
tive et surtout zoomorphe se répand justement à l'époque
qui nous occupe de l'Occident vers Byzance – le *Vatic.
gr.* 1666 étant un des chaînons de cette transmission [148].
La difficulté que nous éprouvons a distinguer les manuscrits grecs de ces diverses contrées est admirablement
illustrée par le cas du *Paris. gr.* 923 du IXe siècle: ce célèbre
volume a été attribué à l'Italie par André Grabar [149], à la
Palestine par Kurt Weitzmann [150], et à Constantinople par
Werner Jaeger [151]. D'autre part, des manuscrits latins en
minuscules étaient écrits dès le IXe siècle quelque part en
Orient, peut-être au Mont Sinaï où ils sont conservés [152].

plication des consonnes, par ex. αναγνοσμα, l'instrusion du γ entre voyelles,
par ex. παρασκευγη au lieu de παρασκευή, et l'addition d'une voyelle initiale
devant le *s impurum* (ισκηνοποιια au lieu de σκηνοπηγία). Cette dernière
particularité pourrait trahir une influence sémitique. Cf. J. RENDEL HARRIS,
The Annotators of the Codex Bezae (Londres 1901), 13 sq.

(147) E. A. LOWE, *The Beneventan Script* (Oxford, 1914), 41.

(148) NORDENFALK, *Die spätantiken Zierbuchstaben*, 210.

(149) « Les manuscrits grecs enluminés provenant d'Italie », Acad. des
Inscr. et Belles-Lettres, *Comptes rendus*, Juillet-Oct. 1970, 404 sq. K. WEITZ-
MANN, *Die byzant. Buchmalerei des 9. und 10. Jahrhunderts* (Berlin 1935), 80-
81, a exprimé la même opinion qu'il a ensuite changée.

(150) « Die Illustration der Septuaginta », *Münchener Jahrbuch der bildenden Kunst*, III/IV (1952/3), 105; *Ancient Book Illumination* (Cambridge,
Mass. 1959), 155 n. 67.

(151) « Greek Uncial Fragments in the Library of Congress in Washington », *Traditio*, V (1947), 101, qui indique que ce manuscrit a été acquis à
Constantinople en 1729/30 par l'abbé Sevin. Antérieurement, il appartenait
à Nicolas Maurocordato, prince de Valachie. Cette circonstance rend une origine italienne assez invraisemblable. D'autre part, les princes phanariotes
entretenaient de relations étroites avec le Patriarcat de Jérusalem.

(152) E. A. LOWE, « An Unknown Latin Psalter on Mount Sinai », *Scrip
torium*, IX (1955), 177-99; ID., « Two Other Unknown Latin Liturgical Fragments on Mount Sinai », *ibid.*, XIX (1965), 3-29; J. GRIBOMONT, « Le mysté-
rieux calendrier latin du Sinaï », *Anal. Bolland.*, LXXV (1957), 105-34.

720

Est-il donc un pur hasard que la minuscule grecque apparaît pour la première fois dans le milieu studite, c'est-à-dire un milieu qui, comme nous l'avons vu, entretenait des relations étroites avec Rome (mais aussi avec la Palestine) ? Considérons aussi le cas de S. Méthode qui appartenait au même monde du monachisme bithynien que Théodore. Né en Sicile, Méthode y étudia, d'après son biographe, l'écriture rapide (ὀξυγραφίαν κατωρθωκὼς ἐκ παιδός)[153]. Même si ceci se rapporte à la sténographie plutôt qu'à la cursive, on doit noter que Méthode ne délaissa pas l'intérêt qu'il portait à l'écriture rapide: à un âge plus avancé il copiait, nous dit-on, sept Psautiers pendant le carême, c'est-à-dire un Psautier par semaine[154]. Ici il ne s'agit sûrement pas de sténographie: je crois que ces Psautiers étaient écrits en minuscule qui exigeait moins de temps que l'onciale. Nous savons d'autre part que pendant son séjour à Rome, vers 815, Méthode s'adonna au travail littéraire[155].

Il peut paraître surprenant que notre enquête sur les relations culturelles entre l'Orient grec et l'Occident latin au VIIIe siècle nous a indiqué des échanges assez complexes dans lequels l'Occident avaient parfois le pas sur l'Orient plutôt que le contraire. Car, depuis ce qu'on peut appeler la « contre-offensive byzantine », menée il y a déjà cent ans par des savants comme Paparrigopoulo, Schlumberger et Charles Diehl, on s'est mis d'accord que Byzance, héritière de la Grèce antique, a été de tout temps plus cultivée que le rustre Occident. Que ceci soit vrai pour cer-

(153) *Vita Methodii*, *PG* C, 1245B.
(154) *Ibid.*, 1253B.
(155) H. USENER, « Acta S. Marinae et S. Christophori », *Festschrift zur fünften Säcularfeier der Carl-Ruprechts-Universität zu Heidelberg* (Bonn 1886), 48: Τοῦ ἁγίου Μεθοδίου ἀρχιεπισκόπου Κωνσταντινουπόλεως σχόλια, ἅπερ ἐποίησεν εἰς τὸ μαρτύριον τῆς ἁγίας Μαρίνης ἐν τῷ μαρτυρολογείῳ ὅπερ ἔγραψεν ἰδιοχείρως καθεζόμενος ἐν ῾Ρώμῃ εἰς τὸν ἅγιον Πέτρον.

taines périodes, je ne le nie pas; mais est-il vrai pour le VIIIe siècle? Je vous rappelle qu'il n'existe actuellement aucun manuscrit grec daté entre le Dioscoride de Vienne du début du VIe siècle et le *Vatic. gr.* 1666, que nous avons mentionné et qui fut copié justement à Rome en l'an 800 [156]. Un coup d'œil sur la littérature byzantine nous apporte un résultat également négatif. Le seul écrivain grec de quelqu' envergure de cette époque, S. Jean Damascène, vivait en marge du monde byzantin, et représente, ainsi que S. André de Crète, la survivance de la grande tradition chrétienne de la Syrie. A Constantinople la production littéraire fut très mince. Le patriarche Germain, né vers 649, appartient réellement au VIIe siècle quoiqu'il eut vécu jusqu' a un âge très avancé. La génération suivante d'intellectuels surgit un siècle plus tard: le patriarche Nicéphore né vers 750, Théophane vers 752, Théodore Studite en 759. Il s'agit certes de gens instruits; mais peut-on dire qu'ils représentaient un niveau plus élevé que Bède, Paul le Diacre ou Alcuin? Même les historiens de profession comme Georges le Syncelle et Théophane se contentèrent d'une documentation bien médiocre. L'assemblage des livres, le sauvetage de la littérature antique ne furent entrepris à Byzance qu'au IXe siècle: si donc, au courant du VIIIe, Byzance a peu apporté à l'Occident, ce n'est pas parce que l'Occident était incapable d'assimiler davantage; c'est aussi et surtout parce que Byzance n'avait pas grand' chose à donner.

---

(156) DEVREESSE, *Introduction à l'étude des manuscrits grecs*, 288.

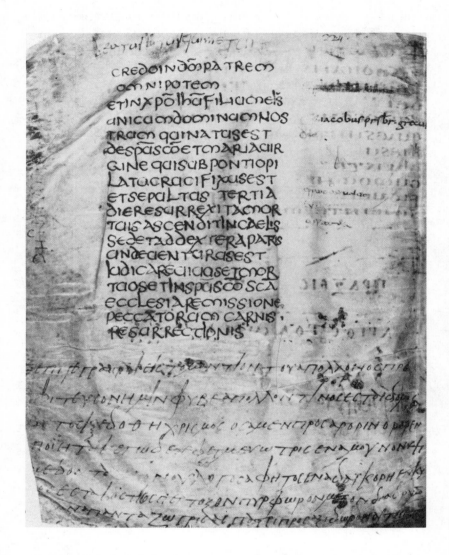

F<small>IG</small>. 1 – Oxford, Cod. Laudianus gr. 35, fol. 226ᵛ. *Photo Bodleian Library.*

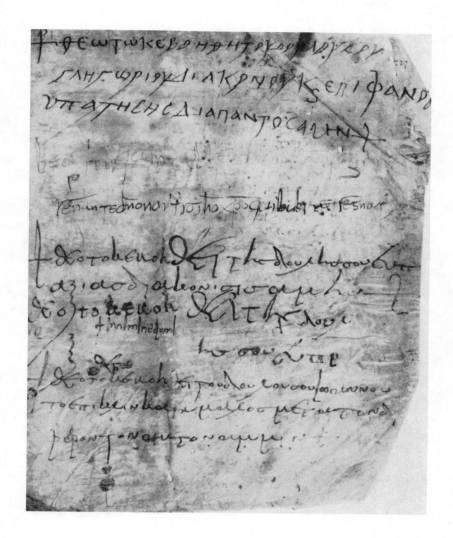

FIG. 2 – Oxford, Cod. Laudianus gr. 35, fol. 227ʳ. *Photo Bodleian Library.*

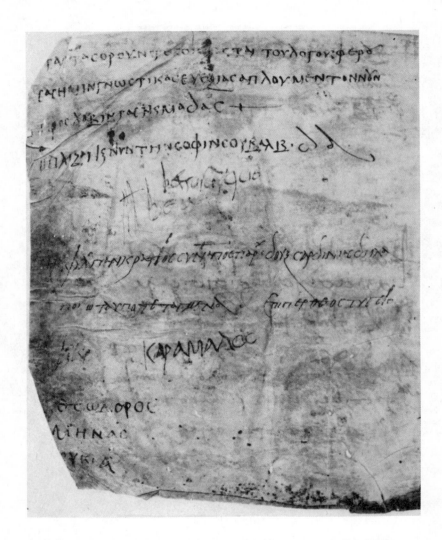

Fig. 3 – Oxford, Cod. Laudianus gr. 35, fol. 227ᵛ. *Photo Bodleian Library.*

VII

THE AVAILABILITY OF BOOKS IN THE
BYZANTINE EMPIRE, A.D. 750–850

THE period I have chosen to discuss in this paper is one of crucial importance in the history of Greek letters, since it witnessed the introduction of the minuscule script and the beginning of that movement which is often called the Middle Byzantine (or Macedonian) Renaissance and to which we owe the *codices vetustissimi* of the ancient Greek authors. This period was also dominated by Iconoclasm. We may recall that the Iconoclastic Council of Hiereia took place in 754, the Seventh Ecumenical Council in 787, the second Iconoclastic Council in 815, and the final liquidation of Iconoclasm in 843. The synchronism of these phenomena has, of course, been noticed by many scholars, and various conclusions have been drawn from it. Some scholars attribute the classical revival to the Iconoclasts who are alleged to have promoted secular learning, while others maintain that this revival did not start until after 843; some see a direct connection between the transliteration of manuscripts and the classical revival, while others deny any such connection.[1] The view I should like to offer is based on a different set of considerations, which will appear in the course of this paper.

An exhaustive treatment of our subject would have required a detailed examination of all the authors who were active during this period, beginning with St. John Damascene, who died *ca.* A.D. 750, followed by the Patriarch Nicephorus, George Syncellus, Theodore the Studite, Theophanes Confessor, Ignatius the Deacon, and ending with Photius, whose literary activity may have started before 850. After perusing the works of these authors, it would be necessary to extract from them all the quotations and literary references they contain, and then decide whether these quotations were taken directly from original texts or at second hand, as was so often the case in Byzantium. Such a Herculean task cannot, however, be attempted here. Instead, I shall present a few vignettes in the hope that they will throw some light on the subject under discussion.

The first text will be the Acts of the Seventh Ecumenical Council, but before examining this highly instructive document, I should call to mind certain considerations. From the fifth to the seventh century, ecclesiastical councils had manifested a growing reliance on Patristic testimony, presented in the form of florilegia. This trend is particularly apparent at the Lateran Council

---

[1] For a recent survey of the problem, see P. Lemerle, *Le premier humanisme byzantin* (Paris, 1971), 109 ff.

of 649,[2] and, even more markedly, at the Sixth Ecumenical Council (680–81) which devoted so much attention to the identification and control of Patristic texts that it has been called a council of antiquaries and paleographers.[3] Thus, there was an established tradition in this respect prior to the outbreak of Iconoclasm. In the iconoclastic controversy, too, great reliance was placed on Patristic authority. This led to a concerted bibliographic effort, an effort that was sponsored by the State and must have been, therefore, as exhaustive as conditions permitted. Since, furthermore, the Fathers of the Church have, by and large, very little to say on the subject of images, the enquiry had to be carried out rather attentively. It also entailed problems of authenticity and attribution, not to mention the orthodoxy or heterodoxy of the authors adduced. Of course, the preliminary work had, to some extent, been done earlier, perhaps even before the official promulgation of Iconoclasm in 730; but there is evidence to show that the Council of 754 was preceded by careful bibliographic preparation. In the *Admonition of the Old Man concerning the Holy Images*, which dates from between 750 and 754 and describes a disputation that took place in Cilicia between the iconophile monk George of Cyprus and an iconoclastic bishop called Cosmas, the latter uses the testimony of three Early Christian writers, namely Epiphanius of Salamis, George of Alexandria, and Severus of Antioch, and he adds, "Wherefore, their writings are being perused in the palace every hour of the day."[4] This was not a particularly happy choice of authorities since George of Alexandria was an Arian and Severus a Monophysite. The bishops of 754 did considerably better, as we can tell from the florilegium appended to their Definition. Nor were the Iconophiles idle in this respect, already starting with St. John Damascene. In brief, we may state that the Council of 787 had been preceded by half a century of bibliographic enquiry on both sides; it is also clear that the proceedings of the Council had been very carefully prepared.

According to my count, the Acts of 787 contain quotations from seventy Patristic, conciliar, hagiographic, historical, and other sources in addition to those embedded in the iconoclastic florilegium which was read out and refuted. A list of them has been drawn up by P. van den Ven,[5] so there is no need to repeat it here. There are, however, two points that ought to be made.

First, we cannot help noticing the extreme bibliographic accuracy that was observed during the proceedings. In each case the actual codex was produced before the assembly; the lector usually started with the *incipit* and then went on to read the relevant passage. The reason for this scrupulousness is made

[2] The Patristic extracts presented at the Lateran Council have been used to reconstruct in part the contents of the Pontifical Library, but cf. my remarks in "La culture grecque et l'Occident au VIIIe siècle," *I problemi del Occidente nel secolo VIII*, II, Settimane di studio, XX (Spoleto, 1973), 712 f.
[3] G. Bardy, "Faux et fraudes littéraires dans l'antiquité chrétienne," *RHE*, 32 (1936), 290 ff.; cf. J. de Ghellinck, *Patristique et moyen âge*, II (Brussels–Paris, 1947), 353.
[4] B. M. Melioranskij, *Georgij Kiprjanin i Ioann Ierusalimljanin* (St. Petersburg, 1901), xxvii.
[5] "La patristique et l'hagiographie au concile de Nicée de 787," *Byzantion*, 25–27 (1957), 325 ff., listing 77 works. My count is slightly different in that I have, on the one hand, excluded the citations contained in the iconoclastic florilegium (12), and, on the other, have added the Acts of earlier councils (5) that were adduced in 787.

clear: it is alleged that at the Council of 754 the Iconoclasts did not produce the actual books, but circulated extracts on loose sheets which are referred to as πιττάκια, and these extracts were sometimes falsified or taken out of context.[6] The two bishops, Gregory of Neocaesarea and Theodosius of Amorium, who had taken part in the Iconoclastic Council and had the mortification of re-canting in 787, were repeatedly questioned about these πιττάκια. Why was it that they, who were bishops and therefore able to know better, had not de-manded to see the actual passages in the books? To which they could only reply, "We did not trouble to do so. Our minds were darkened."[7] The insis-tence on accuracy in 787 led to some rather comical situations. On one occasion the famous 82nd canon of the Quinisext Council was read out from a sheet of papyrus (ἀπὸ χάρτου), whereupon the abbot of the Studius monastery jumped up to ask why this passage had been read from a sheet and not from a book. The Patriarch Tarasius reassured him by explaining that that was the original document which bore the signatures of the Fathers; and the matter was clinched by Bishop Peter of Nicomedia who produced a codex containing the same canons.[8]

The second point I wish to make concerns the spontaneous interventions. The majority of the books produced at the Council came from the Patriarchal Library of Constantinople. This is, in fact, explicitly stated by the Patriarchal notary, "We have come bearing the holy books which we have brought from among those deposited in the library of the holy Patriarchate of Constantinople, namely the canons of the Holy Apostles and of the holy Synods, and the books of our holy Father Basil and of the other holy Fathers."[9] In one case it is stated that a book, the *Miracula SS. Cosmae et Damiani*, had been provided by the church of these Saints at Constantinople;[10] in another, that a book con-taining various *martyria* and the story of the Camuliana image had come "from the *skevophylakion* of the holy chapels of the Patriarchate"[11]—presum-ably a collection separate from the main Patriarchal Library. Of the total of seventy books used at the Council, fifty appear to have been provided by what we may call the Organizing Committee; the remaining twenty were produced on the spot and, as it were, spontaneously by various bishops and abbots.[12]

---

[6] Mansi, XIII, 36 E, 37 B–C, 173 D.
[7] *Ibid.*, 37 B.
[8] *Ibid.*, 40–41.
[9] *Ibid.*, XII, 1019 D.
[10] *Ibid.*, XIII, 67 E.
[11] *Ibid.*, 189 B.
[12] The latter may be tabulated as follows:
BISHOPS
  1. Vicars of the Pope: a. Leontius of Neapolis, *Contra Iudaeos*, bk. 5 (Mansi, XIII, 44 A); b. St. Basil, Spurious Letter to Emperor Julian (*ibid.*, 72 D).
  2. Vicars of Oriental Patriarchs: a. St. Nilus, Letter to Olympiodorus (*ibid.*, 32 C; also produced by Organizing Committee: 37 C); b. Anastasius of Antioch, Letter to a scholasticus (53 D); c. St. Basil, Homily against Sabellians (69 D).
  3. Bishop of Catania: St. Basil, Panegyric of Barlaam (80 B).
  4. Bishop of Constantia in Cyprus: Anastasius of Antioch, On the Sabbath (56 E).
  5. Bishop of Cyzicus: John of Thessalonica, Dialogue with a pagan (164 B).
  6. Bishop of Nicomedia: a. Ps.-Athanasius, Legend of Berytus image (24 E); b. Canons of Quini-sext Council in a codex (41 B).

These interventions assumed a standard form. For example, John, the vicar of the Oriental Patriarchs, showed a book by Anastasius of Antioch and said, "This book, O reverend Fathers, I found in the Imperial City in the possession of Procopius the silentiary. And when I found it, I was very pleased because we have exactly the same copy in the East."[13] Whereupon the relevant passage was read out. Or again, bishop Euthymius of Sardis got up and said, "I have in my hands a book by the holy Confessor Maximus and I offer it to be read." The passage was read out. Then bishop Peter of Nicomedia said, "I, too, have the same book of St. Maximus, and if you so desire, let the aforesaid be read out." Whereupon the same passage was read once more to make doubly sure that it had not been falsified.[14]

Now, a number of questions come to mind. Were the books produced by individual participants not available in the Patriarchal Library? Or were they of an apocryphal or dubious nature so that Tarasius, even if he had them at his disposal, did not wish to have them cited by the Organizing Committee? Or was it a matter of negligence, or even pure chance in view of the wide range of pertinent literature that might have been tapped? Finally, were the spontaneous interventions really spontaneous, or had they been deliberately planned in advance to give some variety to the proceedings? To these questions we cannot give categorical answers, except perhaps to the second. Among the twenty books produced by individuals, there were two *spuria*, namely, the legend of the Berytus image attributed to St. Athanasius, and St. Basil's false Letter to the Emperor Julian, while the rest were perfectly respectable, even if some of them may not have been considered altogether authoritative; but then, the Organizing Committee, too, produced a good deal of hagiographic material that was not of the very best quality. As to our first question, I can cite only one example that may be meaningful. A book as common as the *Leimonarion* of John Moschus had to be produced by the abbot of the monastery of Maximinus. The next day the Patriarch Tarasius said, "Yesterday the abbot of Maximinus gave us the *Leimonarion*, and it was read; and we,

---

7. Bishop of Sardis: St. Maximus, *Acta* (37D). Same book produced by the bishop of Nicomedia (40C).

CHURCHES AND MONASTERIES

1. Church of the Anargyroi at Constantinople: *Miracula SS. Cosmae et Damiani* (67E).
2. Monastery of Chenolakkos in Bithynia: Asterius, Ekphrasis of martyrdom of St. Euphemia (16A).
3. Monastery of Chora at Constantinople: John Chrysostom, On the Washing of the Feet (67D).
4. Monastery τῆς Ἡρακλείας (probably τοῦ Ἡρακλείου in Bithynia): Life of St. Symeon Stylite the Younger (73B).
5. Monastery of Hormisdas at Constantinople: Sophronius, Encomium of Sts. Cyrus and John (57B).
6. Monastery of Hyakinthos at Nicaea: Evagrius, *Hist. eccles.* Also provided by Organizing Committee (189D).
7. Monastery τῶν Μαξιμίνου at Constantinople: Sophronius (*recte* John Moschus), *Pratum spirituale* (60C).
8. Monastery of St. Andrew τοῦ Νησίου: Ps.-John Chrysostom, *Quod veteris et novi testamenti unus sit legislator* (8E).
   A similar, though not altogether accurate, list has been drawn up by K. A. Manaphes, Αἱ ἐν Κωνσταντινουπόλει βιβλιοθῆκαι αὐτοκρατορικαὶ καὶ πατριαρχική (Athens, 1972), 96ff.

[13] Mansi, XIII, 53D.
[14] *Ibid.*, 37D.

too, have found in the library a copy of the same *Leimonarion* which had the folia dealing with icons cut out."[15] If he was, in fact, referring to the Patriarchal Library, we would have to conclude that it possessed only one copy of the *Leimonarion*, and that that copy was mutilated. As to the spontaneity of the interventions, I must confess to some skepticism; but even if they had been prearranged, they surely reflected a real situation.

Van den Ven states that the Council of 787 "n'a fait usage d'aucun florilège, fût-il de S. Jean Damascène."[16] To be sure, the texts that were adduced at Nicaea were read from the actual books, as we have seen; but does this mean that their selection was not dictated, at least in part, by a preexisting florilegium? Such a possibility ought to be entertained, and it brings us to the difficult problem of the Paris. gr. 1115, a manuscript that contains an extensive † florilegium on the subject of icons; more extensive, in fact, than that of the Council since it runs, at an approximate calculation, to 105 works as against 70.[17] Moreover, the two florilegia are certainly related—not so markedly with respect to the Patristic texts (there are about 18 items in common), as with respect to the hagiographic ones, where the selection is practically identical (19 out of the 23 hagiographic quotations found in the Acts of the Council reappear in the Paris manuscript, plus some additional ones).

According to its colophon (fol. 306[v]), the Paris manuscript was copied in 1276 (A.M. 6784) for the Imperial Library from an archetype dated A.M. 6267, "which was found in the old library of the holy Church of the Elder Rome ... so that the age of this book may be reckoned as 517 years before the present." By using the "Byzantine" era, we obtain A.D. 759 as the date of the archetype, but this poses a serious difficulty, as was observed long ago by B. de Montfaucon: for at fol. 239[r] the manuscript contains a "*Synodicon* of John, archbishop of Jerusalem" directed against the "falsely named Seventh Council" (i. e., the Council of 754), which *synodicon* alludes to the execution of the iconoclastic Patriarch Constantine II in 766.[18] Montfaucon's solution was to emend A.D. 759 to A.D. 859, which is rather arbitrary.[19] A more ingenious theory was advanced by Melioranskij who rightly observed that the "Byzantine" era was not widespread in the eighth century and that, by using instead the Alexandrian era, we obtain A.D. 774/75.[20] Yet, another difficulty remains; for at

[15] *Ibid.*, 192D. I assume Tarasius was referring to the Patriarchal Library, not to a library at Nicaea.
[16] *Op. cit.*, 336, 360.
[17] Described by T. Schermann, "Die Geschichte der dogmatischen Florilegien vom V.–VIII. Jahrhundert," *TU*, 28,1 (1905), 6 ff. Cf. *ibid.*, 74 ff.; P. Batiffol, "Librairies byzantines à Rome," *MélRome*, 8 (1888), 298; T. Schermann, "Propheten und Apostellegenden nebst Jüngerkatalogen," *TU*, 31,3 (1907), 2 ff., 143 ff., 141 f.; R. Devreesse, *Essai sur Théodore de Mopsueste*, ST, 141 (1948), 226 note 4, 240 note 8, 242 note 2; *idem, Introduction à l'étude des manuscrits grecs* (Paris, 1954), 54 note 8, 91, 185 note 9, 187 f. (promising a detailed study of this manuscript which, to my knowledge, has not appeared).
[18] It is difficult at present to express a definite opinion concerning this text (*BHG*³, App. V, 1387 f.) which has come down to us in several versions and is also contained in a very early (ninth-century?) palimpsest. See J. Noret, "Le palimpseste 'Parisinus gr. 443'," *AnalBoll*, 88 (1971), 149. No John, patriarch of Jerusalem, is recorded at the time that concerns us, but the episcopal list shows a gap at this very point.
[19] *Palaeographia graeca* (Paris, 1708), 66. Cf. also Devreesse, *Introduction*, 54 note 8.
[20] *Op. cit.* (note 4 *supra*), 83.

fol. 280ᵛ the manuscript contains the well-known account of the beginning of Iconoclasm in Syria, almost exactly as it was read at the Council of 787 (Mansi, XIII, 197), followed at fol. 283ᵛ by the anathema of Theodosius of Ephesus, Sisinnius Pastillas, and other Iconoclasts (Mansi, XIII, 400A–B, 416 C), i.e., items that appear to be derived from the Acts of the Council and not vice versa.

A solution of this problem can be provided only by a thorough study of the Paris. gr. 1115 which we cannot undertake here. In spite of the difficulty I have mentioned—a difficulty which is not insuperable[21]—the fact remains that the florilegium of the Paris manuscript was not drawn from that of the Council; the overlap is not sufficient and, furthermore, the texts that the two have in common often appear with considerable variations and with different *incipits* and *desinits*. Certain other considerations may also be significant: 1. the Paris manuscript makes no explicit reference to the Council of 787 (not to speak of the Feast of Orthodoxy in 843)—a strange omission had its archetype been written in, say, 859; 2. the date of the copy (1276), following closely as it does on the Council of Lyon (1274), fits into a period when a manuscript belonging to the Church of Rome could well have come to the notice of a Byzantine man of letters; 3. the archetype may have originated in the milieu of the Oriental colony in Rome whose prominence in the eighth century is well known; 4. the florilegium of the Paris manuscript contains a number of Western items (e.g., Ambrose and the *Life* of Pope Sylvester); and 5. it is also the only manuscript to have preserved the famous fragment of Hypatius of Ephesus, a text † which appears to have been unknown in Constantinople during the entire Iconoclastic period.[22] I have set down these considerations because, if the archetype of the Paris. gr. 1115 proves to have been written in 774/75 in the milieu of the Levantine colony of Rome, it would shed considerable light on the bibliographic resources that were available in Byzantine refugee circles.

To return to the Council of 787, the impression one gains from reading its Acts is that, whereas the Patriarchal Library was the chief repository of Christian literature at Constantinople, its holdings were not very extensive and showed many gaps which had to be supplemented by books belonging to churches, monasteries, and even private individuals.[23] This conclusion is

[21] It may be argued, e.g., that the archetype of Paris. gr. 1115 contained at the end a number of later additions which were incorporated into the copy. Furthermore, we cannot be sure that the account by John of Jerusalem, which was presented διὰ χάρτου in 787, had not been circulated earlier; it might even have been read at some earlier gathering in Palestine with the very same preamble containing the words ἐπὶ τῆς παρούσης ταύτης ἁγίας ὑμῶν καὶ ἱερᾶς συνόδου.
[22] See P. J. Alexander, "Hypatius of Ephesus," *HThR*, 45 (1952), 177 note 2.
[23] On this library, see Devreesse, *Introduction*, 94; J. Darrouzès, *Recherches sur les* ὀφφίκια *de l'Eglise byzantine* (Paris, 1970), 426 ff.; Lemerle, *op. cit.* (note 1 *supra*), 96 note 81; Manaphes, *op. cit.* (note 12 *supra*), 70 ff. In the ninth century this library was housed in a hall called Thomaites which had been burnt in December 790 (Theophanes, ed. de Boor, I, 467). It is difficult to ascertain how much damage the fire caused to the library. Zonaras (Bonn ed., III, 292–93) speaks of the destruction of τὰ σχεδιάσματα τῆς ἐξηγήσεως τῆς θείας γραφῆς, ἃ ὁ χρυσοῦς τὴν γλῶτταν συνεγράψατο Ἰωάννης, ἐκεῖσε που ἀποκείμενα. Leo Grammaticus (Bonn ed., 197) and Cedrenus (Bonn ed., II, 25) read τὰ σχέδη πάσης γραφῆς, which is less satisfactory. Was this perhaps an autograph by John Chrysostom? See also A. M. Schneider, "Brände in Konstantinopel," *BZ*, 41 (1941), 386; R. Guilland, "Recherches sur Constantinople byzantine: le Thomaïtès et le Patriarcat," *JÖBG*, 5 (1956), 27.

supported by a well-known passage which describes the preliminary work carried out in 814 in preparation for the second Iconoclastic Council. It may be recalled that a committee of six persons was appointed, its most prominent member being John the Grammarian, the future patriarch, and this committee conducted its researches for a number of months. Our contemporary source says the following: "[John] requested [from the Emperor] authority to examine old books everywhere, namely those that are deposited in monasteries and churches, and he was allowed to do so. ... And so they brought together a great multitude of books and searched through them, but they found nothing, fools that they were ... until they laid their hands on the *synodicon* of Constantine the Isaurian ... and, taking from it the *incipits* ((τὰς ἀρχάς)), they began finding the passages in the books, and these they stupidly brought forward, making marks in the places they had found. In this way they wished to persuade the senseless multitude that they had found it in old books that icons should not be worshipped."[24] Setting aside the gratuitous theory that the researches of John the Grammarian extended to classical authors as well,[25] there are two points worth making. First, the committee, which was given quarters in the imperial palace, had to conduct its search in churches and monasteries. This means that the resources of the Imperial Library were insufficient with respect to Patristic literature. An Imperial Library did exist at the time, but there is no reason to believe that it was particularly extensive.[26] Second, the *synodicon* of Constantine V, i.e., the Acts of the Council of 754, did give the *incipits* of the works quoted therein. We may suspect, therefore, in spite of the allegations made in 787, that the first Iconoclastic Council was not so slipshod in its bibliographic work.

Our second vignette concerns historiography. It is well to remember that the most ambitious work of Byzantine chronography dates from our period: the Chronicle of Georgius Syncellus, composed in the first decade of the ninth century. Georgius, as his title indicates, held a high rank at the Patriarchate and had, therefore, access to the Patriarchal Library. His friend Theophanes,

---

[24] *Scriptor incertus*, Bonn ed. (along with Leo Grammaticus), 350; similar details in the interpolated version of the Letter of the Oriental Patriarchs to Theophilus, PG, 95, col. 372 A. Cf. P. J. Alexander, "Church Councils and Patristic Authority," *HSCPh*, 63 (1958), 497 ff.; *idem*, *The Patriarch Nicephorus of Constantinople* (Oxford, 1958), 126 ff.

[25] Cf. B. Hemmerdinger, *Essai sur l'histoire du texte de Thucydide* (Paris, 1955), 34 f.; *idem*, "La culture grecque classique du VIIᵉ au IXᵉ siècle," *Byzantion*, 34 (1964), 131; *idem*, "Une mission scientifique arabe à l'origine de la renaissance iconoclaste," *BZ*, 55 (1962), 66 f. Cf. Lemerle, *op. cit.*, 140 note 127.

[26] Very little is known of this palace library which ought, of course, to be distinguished from the "public library" of the early Byzantine period. Among its holdings, during the reign of Leo V, was an illustrated book of prophecies (Theoph. Cont., Bonn ed., 35–36). For the reign of Theophilus there is a vague mention of books in the Emperor's possession, among them one of the Prophet Isaiah (Theoph. Cont., 104–5; Scylitzes, ed. H. Thurn, 62). The palace library reappears in the seventies of the ninth century in connection with the Arsacid genealogy of Basil I which was allegedly forged by Photius and deposited therein by a member of the palatine clergy (*Vita Ignatii*, PG, 105, col. 566 ff.; Ps.-Symeon, Bonn ed., 689 f.). There is every reason to believe that the library was expanded by Leo VI and Constantine VII; even so, it is interesting to note that it was housed in a μεσόπατον (intermediate floor?), beneath a fairly small pavilion or chamber (κουβούκλειον) called Kamilas: Theoph. Cont., 145; cf. Lemerle, *op. cit.*, 269 and note 9. This μεσόπατον, which was provided with a "look-out" (σκοπιά) having a marble grille (κλουβίου), appears to have been a single room of no great size.

36

who, after the death of Georgius in A.D. 810/11, completed the Chronicle, informs us that the latter had studied "many chronographers and historians," and had left to his continuator the references for bringing the work to a conclusion—the phrase used here is ἀφορμὰς παρέσχε,[27] which probably means "gave the *incipits*."[28] A cursory look at the Chronicle of Georgius, with its numerous references to ancient authors, and its lists of Egyptian, Chaldaean, Assyrian, Sicyonian, and other rulers, produces an impression of great learning; yet, it was shown long ago[29] that all the historical information of Georgius was derived from three sources, namely the Old Testament and the lost chronicles of Panodorus and Annianus, both dating from *ca.* A.D. 400. There are also occasional references to the Church Fathers, such as St. Gregory Nazianzen and St. John Chrysostom. There is no clear evidence that he used directly either Eusebius or Julius Africanus, both of whom he often quotes; and as for genuine classical literature, he had no recourse to it whatever.

† The case of Theophanes is particularly interesting because, as has recently been argued,[30] he composed his work not at Constantinople but at his Bithynian monastery of Megas Agros, west of the mouth of the Rhyndacus, and did so in the relatively short period of about three years, since he ceased writing before Leo V had revealed his iconoclastic inclinations in the latter part of 814. Does this mean that all the books used by Theophanes were in the library of Megas Agros? Probably not, because he says himself that he had to seek them out to the best of his ability (πολλὰς γὰρ βίβλους ἐκζητήσαντες κατὰ τὸ δυνατὸν ἡμῖν),[31] i.e., he must have borrowed them either from neighboring monasteries or even from Constantinople. The sources at his disposal were more numerous than those drawn upon by Syncellus, although he was not averse to taking shortcuts. For the early part of his work, down to the death of Theodosius II, he is mainly dependent on Socrates, Sozomenus, and Theodoret, There can be no doubt that these authors were available in ninth-century Constantinople; yet Theophanes appears to have used them not directly, but through the later compilation of Theodorus Lector. For the subsequent period, down to the reign of Heraclius, Theophanes is known to be dependent on Priscus, Procopius, Agathias, Malalas, Ioannes Epiphaneus, Theophylact Simocatta, and George of Pisidia, although it is not at all clear that he consulted all of these directly.[32]

---

[27] Theophanes, I, 3–4.

[28] Photius, *Bibliotheca*, cod. 40, ed. R. Henry (Paris, 1959–71), I, 25_{27}. uses the similar term ἀπαρχή in the sense of 'initial.'

[29] H. Gelzer, *Sextus Julius Africanus und die byzantinische Chronographie*, II, 1 (Leipzig, 1885), 176ff. Note the use by Syncellus of a manuscript from the library in Caesarea in Cappadocia: Devreesse, *Introduction*, 83f.

[30] C. Mango and I. Ševčenko, "Some Churches and Monasteries on the Southern Shore of the Sea of Marmara," *DOP*, 27 (1973), 265. In speaking of the "composition" of the Chronicle, we should bear in mind that it was, for the most part, a "scissors and paste job," as is apparent from the frequent changes of style and certain other telltale clues. Thus, on p. 355_{29} of de Boor's edition, a certain patrician John Pitzigaudis is described as ὁ πολλαχῶς λεχθεὶς πανεύφημος ἀνήρ, whereas he had been mentioned only once before, on the same page! One may suspect that Theophanes merely marked the passages to be excerpted in the originals and then handed them over to a copyist. This would account for the short time in which the Chronicle was put together.

[31] Theophanes, I, 4.

[32] G. Moravcsik, *Byzantinoturcica*², I (Berlin, 1958), 533f.

The value of Theophanes for us resides mainly in the post-Heraclian period for which he is our primary source, and even a cursory glance at this section of the Chronicle reveals at once how meager and sketchy his documentation was. This is not the place to reexamine the highly complex problem of the sources of Theophanes for the seventh and eighth centuries, one of which, apparently an iconophile chronicle written after 775, he shares with the *Breviarium* of the Patriarch Nicephorus.[33] It is important to point out, however, that we encounter here a situation quite unique in Byzantine annalistic literature, whose horizons did not normally extend far beyond Constantinople; for had Theophanes been able to lay his hands on an adequate Constantinopolitan chronicle for this period, he would have followed it consistently. Instead, he had to rely on an Oriental chronicle, probably composed in Palestine, a source he had in common with Michael the Syrian[34]—a clear indication of the interruption of historiography in the capital. Taking the Chronicle of Theophanes in its entirety, we may hazard the guess that it was based on not more than fifteen sources.

Our third vignette concerns the *Bibliotheca* of Photius. It is not, of course, † our intention to reexamine here, in all of their ramifications, the highly complex problems that are posed by this famous work or to discuss in full the many conflicting theories that have been put forward by modern scholars.[35] Our task is more restricted: it is to place the *Bibliotheca* within the context of our discussion, namely that of the availability of books at the time.

The basic facts concerning the *Bibliotheca* are these: it consists of notices of 279 works (codices) some of which are very short, being limited to the name of the author and the title of the work, and others very extensive (some contain lengthy extracts from the originals, others reproduce their tables of contents); the shorter notices are, by and large, grouped at the beginning of the *Bibliotheca*, whereas the longer ones gravitate toward its end; in some cases there are doublets, i.e., the same books are reviewed twice, without any explanation being offered of this anomaly; the works that are included were both Christian and pagan, the Christian ones being somewhat in the majority, and extended in time from the fifth century B.C. (Herodotus, Ctesias) to the ninth century A.D. (Sergius Confessor), the greatest concentration being in the period of the *Spätantike*—interestingly enough, we find very few Byzan-

---

[33] Cf. Alexander, *The Patriarch Nicephorus*, 158 ff.

[34] E. W. Brooks, "The Sources of Theophanes and the Syriac Chroniclers," *BZ*, 15 (1906), 578 ff. Brooks's supposition that the Oriental chronicle reached Constantinople after the destruction of the Palestinian monasteries in 813 appears, however, to be in need of modification. This must have happened somewhat earlier.

[35] Among recent contributions we may note J. Irigoin, "Survie et renouveau de la littérature antique à Constantinople (IXᵉ siècle)," *CahCM*, 5 (1962), 295 ff.; K. Tsantsanoglou, Τὸ Λεξικὸ τοῦ Φωτίου. Χρονολόγηση, χειρόγραφη παράδοση, in Ἑλληνικά, Suppl. 17 (Thessaloniki, 1967), 17 ff., and a review of same by K. Alpers, *BZ*, 64 (1971), 79 ff.; N. G. Wilson, "The Composition of Photius' *Bibliotheca*," *GRBS*, 9 (1968), 451 ff.; S. Impellizzeri, "L'umanesimo bizantino del IX secolo e la genesi della 'Biblioteca' di Fozio," *Studi storici in onore di Gabriele Pepe* (Bari, 1969), 211 ff.; Lemerle, *op. cit.*, 37 ff., 179 ff., 189 ff.

tine authors of the post-Heraclian period;[36] all the works were in prose save for cods. 183 and 184 which contained the paraphrase of certain books of the Old Testament into epic verse by the Empress Eudocia; the notices are not presented in any particular order, except that occasionally they form clusters having a common subject (e.g., acts of councils of the Church, ecclesiastical histories, lexica, etc.) or a common author; and all the books in question appear to have been read by Photius himself. In addition to the notices of books read, the *Bibliotheca* contains a dedicatory letter and a postscript, both addressed to the author's brother Tarasius. Photius speaks therein of having been chosen to go on an embassy to the Assyrians, i.e., the Arabs, and provides a few other details which we shall presently examine.

On the basis of the above data the most divergent theories have been expressed: according to most scholars, the preface and postscript should be accepted at face value, while according to others, they are merely a literary device;[37] some think that Photius had read all those books at Constantinople, others that he took them in his baggage and read them en route, and B. Hemmerdinger alone that he read them at Baghdad.[38] The same disagreement prevails concerning the date of the work: the one usually accepted is 855, but Mme H. Ahrweiler argues for 838[39] and Father Halkin for after 876.[40] The Baghdad theory is too absurd to merit further discussion; but serious scholars like E. Orth[41] and A. Severyns[42] believed that Photius did take along all 279 works on his embassy, while Mme Ahrweiler is a little more guarded: she thinks that Photius added his personal notes and books to the diplomatic papers he was carrying, but she does not specify how many.[43] If there is any truth in these interpretations, our view on the availability of books in the ninth century would have to be considerably modified.

First, we may ask a couple of common-sense questions: what would have been the cash value of those 279 works, and how long would it have taken a man to read them? The information we possess concerning the price of books in the ninth century is discussed elsewhere in this volume by Nigel Wilson,[44] and indicates that a manuscript of 300 to 400 folia would have cost about 15 to 20 nomismata for both parchment and transcription. This applies to manu-

---

[36] In addition to conciliar Acts and *Lives* of saints, the Byzantine works are limited to the *Breviarium* of Nicephorus (cod. 66), a lost History by Sergius Confessor (cod. 67), and the *Antapodotikos* of the Patriarch Germanus (cod. 233). One should perhaps add an anonymous anthology of Greek, Persian, Thracian, Babylonian, and other testimonia in favor of the Christian doctrine, whose author, according to Photius, lived after Heraclius (cod. 170). Cf. L. G. Westerink, *Nicétas Magistros: Lettres d'un exilé* (Paris, 1973), 11, who notes that "le nombre des articles de la Souda sur les auteurs postérieurs au VIᵉ siècle est négligeable."

[37] Cf. Krumbacher, 519; F. Halkin, "La date de la composition de la 'Bibliothèque' de Photius remise en question," *AnalBoll*, 81 (1963), 414 ff.

[38] "Les 'notices et extraits' des blibliothèques grecques de Bagdad par Photius," *REG*, 69 (1956), 101 ff.

[39] "Sur la carrière de Photius avant son patriarcat," *BZ*, 58 (1965), 348 ff.

[40] *Op. cit.*

[41] *Photiana* (Leipzig, 1928), 7 ff.

[42] *Recherches sur la Chrestomathie de Proclos*, I, 1 (Liége-Paris, 1938), 3 ff.

[43] *Op. cit.*, 360.

[44] *Supra*, p. 3 f.

scripts written to order, not secondhand ones, but I do not believe that the price difference would have been great given the scarcity of the commodity. It is, of course, almost impossible to translate medieval prices into modern equivalents since the entire structure of wages and prices was different from ours. We may, even so, arrive at a very rough approximation if we take into account the income—not of manual workers, who were seriously underpaid by our standards (6 to 10 nomismata a year)—but of civil servants and army officers, i.e., the social class that could afford to buy books. In the tenth century the average salary of a member of the *megale hetaireia*, who had to buy his commission for 16 lbs. of gold, was 40 nomismata,[45] while the notorious priest Ktenas who, in *ca.* A.D. 907/8, bought for himself the title of *protospatharios* (eighth from the top in the palatine hierarchy which consisted of eighteen ranks) received 72 nomismata a year.[46] If, in terms of modern American incomes, we translate 40 nomismata as $6,000, the cost of a manuscript—of the kind that Arethas ordered—would have been about $3,000, and the total value of the "library" of Photius well in excess of half a million. I doubt that he would have risked such an investment on his perilous embassy, not to mention the obvious fact that no Byzantine gentleman is known to have possessed as many as 279 books. As for the time required to read those works, I think that ten years would be a very modest estimate, unless either Photius did not read all of them from cover to cover or the *Bibliotheca* is the result not of individual effort but of teamwork. The first possibility is, I think, unlikely, not only because of the conscientiousness of the summaries, but also because of certain candid admissions on the part of the author: thus, in cod. 97, which contained an enumeration of Olympic victors by Phlegon of Tralleis, a list that extended to the 229th Olympiad, Photius confesses that he read only as far as the 177th because the book was so boring.[47] The second possibility would presumably have produced some variation in style, but none has been detected, except that from time to time Photius tends to slip into the diction of the authors he is reviewing—an understandable phenomenon.

We now come to the dedication and the postscript. In the latter, which, as Severyns has surmised,[48] was written first, Photius says roughly: "These 279 works are those I remember to have read myself in the course of my literary studies from the time I began having some critical understanding of literature until now. If I manage to come back alive from the embassy, I may send you, Tarasius, another collection no smaller than this one." Two points should be noted here. First, there is no mention of any literary circle; on the contrary, Photius claims to have read all the books himself, καθ' ἑαυτούς. Second, this is the sum total of his reading from the time of his youth until such time when he was dispatched on his embassy—the sum total exclusive of such books

---

[45] *De Cerimoniis*, Bonn ed., I, 692. Cf. G. Ostrogorsky, "Löhne und Preise in Byzanz," *BZ*, 32 (1932), 307.

[46] Constantine Porphyrogenitus, *De Administrando Imperio*, chap. 50, ed. Gy. Moravcsik and R. J. H. Jenkins, DOT, I (Washington, D.C., 1967), 244; *Commentary* (London, 1962), 194.

[47] Cod. 97, ed. Henry, II, 63, 65.

[48] *Op. cit.*, 7 ff.

40

ὧν ἡ σπουδὴ καὶ μελέτη τέχνας φιλεῖ καὶ ἐπιστήμας ἐργάζεσθαι, i.e., presumably, school textbooks.[49]

The dedicatory epistle, which is the document that most scholars take their stand on, says something a little different: Photius had been chosen to go on an embassy to the Arabs, and so he is sending Tarasius the summaries of those books which had been read in the latter's absence—the number 279 is quoted once more. Photius was able to accomplish this task rather rapidly because he succeeded in finding a secretary (ὑπογραφεύς). The summaries are presented in the order in which Photius remembers them; they may be insufficient because it is difficult to recall after a lapse of time the contents of so many books. Works of wide circulation such as Tarasius has surely studied are treated summarily.[50] Taking these indications at face value, scholars have conjectured that Tarasius was a regular member of his brother's "reading circle," and since he was presumably at Constantinople (but how do we know this?), it is Photius that must have been absent, i.e., on the embassy. The reference to finding a secretary is also considered to corroborate this view on the assumption that at Constantinople Photius would have found one without any trouble. The real problem, of course, is not whether the dedicatory epistle was penned at Constantinople or in Asia Minor, but rather how we can reconcile the information provided by the dedication and the postscript with the content of the *Bibliotheca*, some of which strongly suggests a date of composition after Photius had become patriarch, indeed a date in the latter part of his life.

Of the three dates that have been proposed for the *Bibliotheca*, namely 838, 855, and after 876, the only one, to my mind, that is supported by a solid argument is the last, put forward by Father Halkin who took his stand on cod. 252. This codex, it may be recalled, concerns a *Life* of Pope Gregory the Great whose Greek text, surviving in several manuscripts, is believed to have been adapted from a longer Latin *Life* composed in Rome by John Hymmonides not before 875. Even if we assume that the Greek version was made immediately after the publication of the Latin original, it could hardly have reached Photius at Constantinople before the following year at the earliest.[51] It is possible, of course, to parry this argument by assuming a lost common source,[52] but this is a somewhat arbitrary expedient. Furthermore, cod. 252 does not stand alone. I should like to draw attention here to cod. 52 which is concerned with the Acts of an obscure council held at Side in 383 to condemn the Messalian heresy. This leads Photius to a digression on Messalianism, in the course of which he says, "We, too, as far as we were able, in leading certain persons away from this error—for they have recently begun to sprout up again from that same root—have found that their souls were consumed with

---

[49] Ed. I. Bekker, 545. In fact, the *Bibliotheca* does contain notices of several textbooks.

[50] Ed. Henry, I, 1–2.

[51] Halkin, *op. cit.* It is only fair to point out that Halkin's discovery was anticipated by E. Dekkers, "Les traductions des écrits patristiques latins," *Sacris erudiri*, 5 (1953), 215.

[52] Cf. B. Hemmerdinger, "Le 'codex' 252 de la Bibliothèque de Photius," *BZ*, 58 (1965), 1–2; Ahrweiler, *op. cit.*, 358 note 63; Lemerle, *op. cit.*, 38 note 49.

much corruption of evil passions."[53] It seems to me that this attempt to convert a group of heretics would much better fit a time when Photius was in holy orders, i.e., after 858, rather than when he was a civil servant. In addition, certain codices reflect preoccupations which we know Photius to have had after he became patriarch. Thus, cod. 115 concerns a lost work directed against Jews and Quartodecimans. Why should Photius, as a layman, have been interested in the obscure sect of the Quartodecimans which had flourished in the fourth and fifth centuries? We learn, however, from his Homily XVII that in 867 he managed to convert a group of these very heretics whose survival comes to us as something of a surprise.[54] One should also consider in this connection Homilies XV and XVI, delivered either in 861 or in 867.[55] These formed part of a kind of "lecture course," probably delivered on five successive Sundays of Lent, which told in great detail the story of the Arian heresy, beginning with the career of Arius himself and his condemnation at the Council of Nicaea, and ending with the Second Ecumenical Council. For the most part, the sources that Photius used in composing these homilies can be identified, and include, in addition to the works of St. Athanasius and the ecclesiastical historians (Socrates, Sozomenus, Theodoret, and Philostorgius), a number of saints' *Lives*, namely those of Metrophanes and Alexander, Paul of Byzantium, and Athanasius.[56] It can hardly be coincidental that this entire documentation appears in the *Bibliotheca*, and it is surely more reasonable to assume that Photius studied these works when he was preparing his series of sermons rather than having done so some ten years before, when he was still a civil servant. One can even isolate some significant points of convergence. Thus, in Homily XV, Photius stresses the fact (or rather the fiction) that Constantine the Great received Orthodox baptism, and he adds parenthetically, "Let heretics who are anxious to ennoble their impiety with lies be allowed to weave their heretical stories."[57] On this topic he derived his information from Gelasius, and, in reviewing this author in the *Bibliotheca*, he does not fail to mention it: "He [Gelasius] says that Constantine received baptism by the mystical rites of an Orthodox minister, not, as some have supposed, at the hands of a heretic."[58] Photius' preoccupation with Constantine's baptism appears once again in his critical review (cod. 127) of the *Vita Constantini* by Eusebius, who specifies that the rite was performed at Nicomedia, but does not say by whom—an omission that Photius considers to have been deliberate and indicative of the author's lack of candor.[59]

Here and there in the *Bibliotheca*, one can pick up further indications pointing to the period when Photius was patriarch. In cod. 179 (a Manichaean treatise by Agapius) he stresses the utility of this "most godless and useless"

[53] Ed. Henry, I, 40.
[54] C. Mango, *The Homilies of Photius, Patriarch of Constantinople* (Cambridge, Mass., 1958), 279 ff.
[55] *Ibid.*, 20 ff.
[56] *Ibid.*, 237 f.
[57] *Ibid.*, 255.
[58] Cod. 88, ed. Henry, II, 14.
[59] *Ibid.*, II, 100.

work for confuting the Manichees themselves.[60] In cod. 197 (Cassian's *De institutis coenobiorum*) he commends the excellence of its teaching: any monastery that practices it will flourish, whereas a monastery that neglects it is doomed to failure. "Wherefore," he adds, "it is necessary not to disregard any of its precepts."[61] One can also feel the Patriarch's authority when, in cod. 228 (Ephraem), he comments: "As to whether the man has or has not given a proper discussion of the Trisagion, ... I cannot at the moment deliver an unhesitating judgment on either alternative."[62] I am sure that a careful study of the *Bibliotheca* in relation to other works of Photius, especially his Letters, will reveal further points of convergence that may be chronologically useful. It is a task that would be well worth undertaking.

How, then, are we to solve the riddle posed by the *Bibliotheca*? The most economical explanation would be, I think, the following. Photius did go on an embassy to the Arabs—we do not know exactly when, but most probably before he became patriarch.[63] On that occasion he composed for the benefit of his brother a work consisting of his *notes de lecture*—not, indeed, the *Bibliotheca* as we have it, but a much smaller collection of short notices which he may even have written from memory, as he himself claims.[64] The very supposition that, in dedicating the full *Bibliotheca* of 279 codices, a mammoth work that would fill over a thousand pages in a printed edition of standard format, he could have promised to overwhelm his brother with a second collection of equal size if he came back alive strikes me as absurd. The much smaller, original *Bibliotheca* that I envisage would have remained, so to speak, in the family. When he returned from the embassy, Photius went on adding to it and, indeed, continued to enlarge his dossier for the rest of his life: certainly during his first patriarchate (858–67), less actively during the period of his confinement in a monastery since he complained of the absence of books,[65] perhaps with renewed vigor when he returned to Constantinople and to learned pursuits *ca.* 875. Finally, the greatly enlarged dossier, with all of its repetitions, its unevenness of treatment, and its lack of organization, was "published."

[60] *Ibid.*, II, 187.

[61] *Ibid.*, III, 93.

[62] *Ibid.*, IV, 116: ἀλλ᾽ εἴτε εὖ εἴτε καὶ ἑτέρως περὶ τοῦ τρισαγίου διήτησεν ὁ ἀνήρ ... οὐκ ἔχω νῦν οὐδετέρᾳ γνώμῃ κρίσιν ἐπιθεῖναι ἀδίστακτον. One may also compare Photius' Letter to King Boris of Bulgaria in which he argues that the Christian religion is so perfect that the smallest blemish in it is immediately apparent (PG, 102, col. 657), with a similar sentiment expressed in cod. 229, ed. Henry, IV,141: ἡ μὲν γὰρ περὶ πίστεως ἔρευνα τῆς ἀληθείας παρατραπεῖσα ναυάγιον μέγα τῇ ψυχῇ προξενεῖ, διὸ δὴ καὶ βραχείας τῆς εἰς αὐτὴν τελούσης ἀντέχεσθαι δεῖ συλλαβῆς.

[63] Tsantsanoglou's suggestion, *op. cit.* (note 35 *supra*), 32f., that the embassy may have taken place in 876–77, appears to me unlikely. On the other hand, the 838 date is far too early and is excluded by other considerations, as I hope to show elsewhere.

[64] Preface, ed. Henry, I, 1–2. Wilson has recently argued that the *Bibliotheca* was, "for the most part," composed from memory: *op. cit.* (note 35 *supra*), 454. For a somewhat laborious refutation of this view, see T. Hägg, "Photius at Work: Evidence from the Text of the *Bibliotheca*," *GRBS*, 14 (1973), 213ff. It is quite evident that a great many codices (e.g., 167, listing the names of more than 450 authors excerpted by Stobaeus) could not have been written from memory. In fact, in cod. 186 (ed. Henry, III, 10), Photius openly admits that he is copying the manuscript he has before him instead of summarizing it: οὕτω μὲν καὶ ἡ τρίτη διήγησις. ἀλλὰ τί μοι δεῖ μικροῦ μεταγράφειν ταύτας, δέον πολλῷ κεφαλαιωδέστερον ἐπελθεῖν;

[65] *Ad Amphilochium*, quaestio CLXXX, PG, 101, col. 889B: τὴν συνέχουσαν ἡμᾶς τῶν ὑπογραφέων ἐρημίαν καὶ τῶν βιβλίων τὴν αἰχμαλωσίαν.

This may have happened when Photius was a very old man or even after his death. The editor, who may conceivably have been Arethas,[66] decided to retain the original dedication and postscript. The only alteration he had to make was in the number of codices as given in the title, the dedication, and the postscript—an easy task.[67] If this explanation proves acceptable, we may conclude that the 279 codices represent a lifetime of study on the part of an exceptionally voracious reader. I also suspect that they made up a substantial proportion of all the books that were available at Constantinople in the ninth century.

For all the bibliographic indications that the *Bibliotheca* contains—Photius often tells us that he had seen several manuscripts of the same work in some of which it was differently entitled or had a different number of chapters, etc.— it is completely silent on one point that would be of the greatest interest to us, namely the provenance of the books in question. For one category only can we make an informed guess, that is, the heretical books, several of which are analyzed in the *Bibliotheca*. To take but one example, Photius gives a critique of the apocryphal Acts of the Apostles, known as περίοδοι, i.e., *Peregrinations*, and comments that the Acts of John had been used by the Iconoclasts.[68] This is quite correct. The Council of 787 had condemned these very Acts and had decreed not only that they should no longer be copied, but that they should be burnt.[69] The same fate awaited, of course, the writings of the Iconoclasts,[70] but Canon IX proclaims that these "ought to be delivered to the *episcopium* of Constantinople to be deposited together with the other heretical books." Penalties were laid down against anyone concealing such literature.[71] In other words, the heretical works analyzed by Photius could have come only from the Patriarchal Library to which he must have had easy access. As for the secular books, we are reduced to conjectures. I find it hard to believe that all of them belonged to Photius himself—in fact, we know nothing of his personal library.[72] He probably borrowed them from various quarters.

In the preceding pages I have tried to show that in the Byzantine Empire between about A.D. 750 and 850 books were very scarce and, by ordinary standards, fantastically expensive; further, that there did not exist at the time a central library, except the one at the Patriarchate, which was naturally

---

[66] There is good reason to believe that Arethas owned and revised the archetype of our cod. M of the *Bibliotheca*. See A. Diller, "Photius' *Bibliotheca* in Byzantine Literature," *DOP*, 16 (1962), 390–91.

[67] The figure is expressed in a remarkably roundabout manner, namely as 300–21 in the title; $300-\left(\frac{300}{15}+1\right)$ in the preface; $300-\left(\frac{300}{300}+\frac{300}{15}\right)$ in the postscript. Might this be an indication of Arethas' pedantic hand?

[68] Cod. 144, ed. Henry, II, 85.

[69] Mansi, XIII, 173–76.

[70] *Ibid.*, 200 D.

[71] *Ibid.*, 430.

[72] Nicetas Paphlago merely tells us that Photius had a great many books *because* he was very rich: πάντα γὰρ συνέτρεχεν ἐπ' αὐτῷ, ἡ ἐπιτηδείοτης τῆς φύσεως, ἡ σπουδή, ὁ πλοῦτος, δι' ὃν καὶ βίβλος ἐπ' αὐτὸν ἔρρει πᾶσα (*Vita Ignatii*, PG, 105, col. 509 B). Cf. *ibid.*, col. 532 D (ὁ δυσαρίθμητος τῶν βιβλίων ἐσμός). The idea that the *Bibliotheca* represented Photius' personal library has, unfortunately, often been expressed; e.g., by J. B. Bury, *History of the Eastern Roman Empire* (London, 1912), 445 f.

limited to ecclesiastical material and not very complete at that. The bibliographic effort of the Orthodox monasteries, an effort that we associate in particular with St. Theodore the Studite, has to be seen in this context: for as long as the Patriarchate was in the hands of the Iconoclasts, the Orthodox opposition was denied access to the only repository of books that was reasonably comprehensive in its holdings. Hence the need to build up independent libraries. It appears (but this is a question that requires further investigation) that we have here a new departure in the function of the Byzantine monastery. The close contacts which the Orthodox monks maintained with their brethren in the Arab-dominated East as well as in the West may have facilitated this process; Palestine, it would seem, was still fairly well supplied with Greek manuscripts.

We should not, of course, exaggerate the extent of book copying that took place in the Orthodox monasteries. The beginning of this development is usually attributed to Theodore's uncle, St. Platon, who became a monk in 759 and died in 814. In his funeral laudation Theodore says that the "abundance of books" in the monasteries was due to Platon's personal activity, i.e., that of a single scribe.[73] We can calculate that a professional scribe required about four months to copy a manuscript of 300 folios,[74] and Platon did not devote all his time to this pursuit.[75] The number of manuscripts he copied should, therefore, be reckoned in the scores rather than in the hundreds. He did not, of course, stand alone; in addition to St. Theodore, we can name St. Macarius of Pelekete[76] and St. Theophanes Confessor[77], both of whom transcribed books in the latter part of the eighth century.

If the increased manufacture of books in the monasteries may be regarded as a by-product of the Iconoclastic controversy, this same controversy, as we have seen, also generated a wide-ranging and state-sponsored bibliographic search. The initial effort, prior to 754, was repeated with greater scrupulousness in the years before 787 and, once again, in 814. Traces of this endeavor are visible even in the *Bibliotheca* of Photius who often notes that a given work contained passages relevant to icons.[78] While in itself Iconoclasm had

---

[73] PG, 99, col. 820A: πῶς ἄν τις ἐξαριθμήσειεν τοὺς τὰ ἐκείνου πονήματα εἴτ' οὖν βιβλιδάρια ἔχοντας ἐκ διαφόρων θείων πατέρων ἀνθολογηθέντα ...; ταῖς καθ' ἡμᾶς δὲ μοναῖς πόθεν ἄλλοθεν ἡ τῶν δέλτων εὐπορία; ἢ οὐχὶ ἐκ τῶν ἐκείνου ἁγίων χειρῶν καὶ πόνων;

[74] This is based on the following calculation: St. Athanasius, a Bithynian monk of the first half of the tenth century, earned 900 nomismata in the course of 28 years' work as a copyist. He labored ceaselessly, except for Saturdays and Sundays: *Synax. eccles. Constant.*, ed. H. Delehaye, 727₄₀; cf. Lemerle, *op. cit.*, 128 note 72. This gives us an average of about 32 nom. per year. In about the same period Arethas paid 14 nom. for the transcription of the Bodleian Euclid (387 fols.): see *supra*, p. 3. A much shorter book, like the Psalter, could be copied in a week, but this constituted something of an achievement: *Vita Methodii*, PG, 100, col. 1253B.

[75] In his early days as a monk he gladly performed manual work (PG, 99, col. 813B). After he had become abbot, he naturally had to devote much time to administrative duties.

[76] "S. Macarii, monasterii Pelecetes hegumeni acta graeca," *AnalBoll*, 16 (1897), 145.

[77] C. Van de Vorst, "Un panégyrique de S. Théophane le Chronographe par S. Théodore Studite," *AnalBoll*, 31 (1912), 22, § 7: ἐργόχειρον ἐπίμονον, ἐξ οὖ τὰ πολλὰ δελτία καὶ τἄλλα ἐξ εὐφυοῦς χειρὸς ἀπεργάσματα. Cf. the *Vita* by Nicephorus the Skevophylax: ed. de Boor, II, 19: τῇ δὲ τῶν θείων βίβλων γραφῇ σχολάζων πανημέριον, ἣν οὐκ ἐκ παιδείας ἀνθρωπίνης, ἀλλὰ πόνῳ διηνεκῇ καὶ θείᾳ κτησάμενος χάριτι ἀκριβῶς μετήρχετο (while he was a monk on the island of Kalonymos).

[78] Cod. 29, ed. Henry, I, 17; cod. 52, *ibid.*, 39; cod. 110, *ibid.*, II, 81; cod. 114, *ibid.*, 85; cod. 119, *ibid.*, 93.

no connection with book production, let alone a classical revival, it certainly gave an impulse to a more systematic collection and study of Patristic literature. Once put in motion, this current eventually spilled over into secular letters.

When one surveys the literary production of Byzantium in the eighth century, one notices a gap of about fifty years, from the death of the Patriarch Germanus a few years after 730 until the Seventh Council. There did not occur, of course, a complete break in the educational process, such as is implied by the apocryphal story of the burning of the University with its books and professors. The Patriarch Tarasius, thought to have been born about 730, was certainly a cultivated man, even if he is not remembered as an author. It cannot, however, be a matter of coincidence that the literary figures who came to prominence at the end of the century belonged to the same generation: the Patriarch Nicephorus, born *ca.* 758; St. Theodore the Studite, born in 759; Theophanes Confessor, born in 760; Georgius Syncellus, born probably a few years earlier. These men, who reached their maturity at the time of the Seventh Council, formed a tightly knit group of civil servants: Tarasius held the post of *protoasecretis* before entering the Church; he was, furthermore, the great-uncle of Photius who, in turn, became *protoasecretis*. Nicephorus, son of an imperial secretary, held the same post as the subordinate of Tarasius. Theodore the Studite was the son of a Treasury official and was destined for a career in the civil service; his uncle, St. Platon, had also served in the Treasury. Theophanes, son of a governor of the Aegean Islands, held the palatine rank of *spatharios*. They were men of substance, and some of them claimed kinship with the imperial family. I would attribute the absence of such an intelligentsia in the immediately preceding period to the deliberate persecution of the aristocracy at the very beginning of the eighth century, under Justinian II, and again under Leo III. Of the latter Theophanes says that he punished "by mutilation, scourging, banishment, and fines especially those who were distinguished by their birth and education, so that the schools of learning were extinguished."[79]

Now, I take it that the minuscule script was introduced for the purpose of library books, i.e., for cabinet study as opposed to reading out loud, and was a means of both saving on parchment and speeding up transcription. Its introduction presupposed, therefore, the existence of a cultivated class, no matter how small, that could afford books, and such a class came into existence about 790. This was an iconophile intelligentsia, as opposed to the iconoclastic intelligentsia—men like John the Grammarian and Leo the Mathematician who belonged to the next generation. Is it a matter of chance that 790 is also the date that has been proposed on independent grounds for the introduction of the Greek minuscule?[80]

[79] Ed. de Boor, I, 405.
[80] Irigoin, *op. cit.* (note 35, *supra*), 288.

VIII

The Life of St. Andrew the Fool Reconsidered*

The Life of St. Andrew Salos, which enjoyed remarkable popularity both in Byzantium and in the Slavonic world, is one of the most puzzling products of Greek hagiography. A great deal has been written about it in recent years and a critical edition, by Dr. L. Rydén, is nearing completion[1]. If I have not waited for the appearance of this edition before offering some observations of my own, it is because Dr. Rydén has, so to speak, already laid his cards on the table[2].

There is no doubt that the Vita of Andrew Salos (henceforth VAS) is a *roman hagiographique*. It purports to be an eyewitness account of the exploits of a Scythian slave turned holy fool who roamed the streets of Constantinople in the reign of Leo I (457-74), but it is quite obvious that it was written at a considerably later time. Setting aside the question whether Andrew ever really existed (and there is no independent corroboration of his historicity), we can be reasonably certain that he did not have a cult or a liturgical commemoration until fairly late in the Middle Ages, since he first appears in synaxaria of the Palaeologan period. And herein lies the singularity of VAS — not in its being a fiction (Byzantine hagiography is full of fictions), nor in its reliance on an invented eyewitness (a device that was often used[3]), but in the absence of any apparent motive for the composition of so lengthy and elaborate a biography. The case of the Life of St. Theoctiste of Lesbos, which has been described as a hoax perpetrated by a man of letters[4], is not at all similar; nor is that of the Barlaam and Joasaph romance.

One way out of the difficulty would be to argue that the text, as printed by

---

* The possibility of a relatively early date of the Life of St. Andrew Salos was first suggested to me by my friend Professor Ihor Ševčenko. I very much regret that other commitments have prevented him from appearing as joint author of this article.

[1] Dr. Rydén has already published his text of the Andreas Salos apocalypse in *DOP* 28 (1974), 199 ff., and a short passage referring to St. Mary of Blachernae in *AnBoll* 94 (1976), 63 ff.

[2] *The Date of the Life of Andreas Salos*, DOP 32 (1978), 129-55 (henceforth RYDÉN, *Date*).

[3] E.g. in the Life of Symeon Salos by Leontius of Neapolis and probably in the Life of St. John the Almsgiver by the same author.

[4] L.G. WESTERINK, *Nicétas Magistros: Lettres d'un exilé*, Paris 1973, 27.

Migne[5], is not all of a piece. Indeed, it is very clumsily put together: while its core consists of a sequence of more or less disconnected episodes in the manner of a paterikon, the narrative is repeatedly interrupted by lengthy digressions. We are offered a vision of Paradise and Heaven (§§ 2c   ), a kind of natural and moral encyclopaedia (§§ 154-86) and the famous apocalypse (§§ 208-29) that is found in many manuscripts independently of the full Life. What is more, the Life has, not one protagonist, but two, namely Andrew and his protégé, the saintly young man Epiphanius, who is destined to become patriarch of Constantinople and a confessor. As Grosdidier de Matons has already calculated[6], 29 paragraphs of the text are devoted to the exploits of Epiphanius. It may be thought, therefore, that the Life, as we have it, represents a literary re-working of an older and more straightforward text or a conflation of several texts. I shall not, however, pursue this line of reasoning because of its inherently hypothetical nature.

The consensus of scholarly opinion places the composition of VAS in the 9th or 10th century. Some favour the end of the 9th century, others the beginning of the 10th, while Rydén opts for ca. 950-59[7]. But when we seek the evidence for such dating, we are confronted with a series of unprovable hypotheses, a vague sense of atmosphere and a few arguments *e silentio*. The only piece of concrete evidence that has been adduced concerns the church of the Virgin at the Forum of Constantinople: I shall consider it later. For the time being, however, it may be useful to set up *termini post* and *ante quem* that are reasonably assured: the Life was written after ca. 650 and before ca. 950. The earlier limit is established by the author's use of Moschus. This is probable in the case of §§ 4-6 (vision of wrestling in a theatre) which offer a close correspondence to *Pratum*, ch. 66[8], and quite certain for §§ 100-103 (the grave robber episode) which, as Grosdidier has already pointed out[9], represent a conflation of two consecutive chapters of the *Pratum*, namely 77 and 78. I shall not trouble the reader with a detailed demonstration, which he can make for himself, but should like to add one further remark: ch. 78 of the *Pratum*, which is prolix and full of pious platitudes, does not appear to me to be in the style of Moschus. It does, however, form part of the earliest known recension of that work, embodied in the Florence manuscript (Laurent., Plut. x, 3) and the Slavonic translation (the so-called *Sinajskij Paterik*)[10]. Now Moschus died, most probably, in 634[11], and it seems that his work, which proved extremely popular, began to attract accretions at an early date. If ch. 78 is one of these old accretions, a date of ca. 650 may be postu-

---

[5] *PG* 111, cc. 625-888. In the interests of brevity all subsequent citations of the Life are by the paragraph of Migne's ed., except for the Apocalypse which is cited by the pages of Rydén ed. in *DOP* 28.

[6] *Les thèmes d'édification dans la Vie d'André Salos*, *TM* 4 (1970), 314.

[7] See RYDÉN, *Date*, 129 n. 6 for a listing of previous opinions.

[8] *PG* 87/3, c. 2917.

[9] *Op. cit.*, 319.

[10] I owe this information to Dr. P. Pattenden who is preparing a critical edition of the *Pratum*.

[11] So H. CHADWICK, *John Moschus and his Friend Sophronius the Sophist*, «Journal of Theological Studies», n.s. 25 (1974), 50 ff. Cf. the remarks of I. ŠEVČENKO, in *La civiltà bizantina dal IV al IX secolo*, Bari 1977, 140 ff.

lated for the text which the author of VAS plagiarized. If he was also acquainted, as seems likely, with the Life of St. Symeon Salos by Leontius of Neapolis, we obtain roughly the same *terminus post quem*. A consideration of the apocalypse will lead us, quite certainly, to the same result.

The *terminus ante quem* is provided by the approximate date of the earliest known manuscript of the Life, namely the uncial fragment contained in cod. Monac. gr. 443.

In the hope of narrowing these broad limits, I shall consider a number of specific points arranged by categories. Before doing so, however, I should like to offer one observation that is central to my argument, namely that the author of VAS who calls himself Nicephorus (and whom, for the sake of convenience, I shall designate by the same name) was not a man of much education. His lowbrow Greek and rambling prolixity are sufficient indication of this. It is true that he was conversant with some hagiographical material and with a body of theological and pseudo-scientific lore of the kind that may be found in the Dialogues of pseudo-Caesarius and various *Erotapokriseis*. He appears, however, to have been entirely ignorant of history. Although he poses as a contemporary of the emperor Leo I, he knows nothing about the period in question apart from the fact that St. Daniel the Stylite was active at that time. Even the plague he reports — a plague that was supposedly stopped by the joint prayers of Daniel and Andrew (§§ 98-99) — seems to be apocryphal. Had he taken the trouble to consult an ordinary chronicle, he might easily have embellished his narrative with many appropriate touches. He could have mentioned the terrible fire (a fire 'such as had never been seen before')[12] that destroyed a good part of Constantinople in 465 and the rain of ashes that fell on the city. He could have alluded to the patriarch Gennadius and the translation to Constantinople of the Virgin's robe. He could have introduced several other events that caused a stir at the time, e.g. the murder of Aspar and Ardaburius, the persecution of the Arians, the declaration of Sunday as a public holiday, etc. The omission of all such widely available information shows that Nicephorus, in composing his 'historical novel', did not bother to create a plausible *mise en scène*. I cannot believe, therefore, that he possessed the antiquarian knowledge to deliberately introduce various institutions that had become extinct before his lifetime, to re-create a picture of urban life that no longer corresponded to reality or to avoid mentioning a whole string of monuments that arose after the 6th century[13]. In Rydén's view Nicephorus was a widely read and clever forger who nevertheless betrayed himself by committing a few anachronisms. In my view he was what he appears to be on the surface, namely a pretty ignorant fellow.

I. TITULATURE

Two passages have to be considered under this heading. One (§§ 205-6) has already attracted attention: it concerns the wicked χαρτουλάριος τῶν πλοΐμων, a na-

---

[12] MALAL., Bonn ed., 372; *Chron. Pasch.*, Bonn ed., I, 598.

[13] A similar judgement was expressed by N.H. Baynes in an unpublished review quoted by J. WORTLEY, *A Note on the Date of the Vita Sancti Andreae Sali*, *Byz* 39 (1969), 205 n. 2.

tive of Amastris, who is described as εἰς τῶν μεγάλων. Referring to H. Ahrweiler's monograph on the Byzantine navy[14], Rydén states that the office in question 'was not introduced until the ninth century'[15]. This, however, is by no means certain. Mme Ahrweiler is concerned to show that the office of drungarius of the fleet, which seems to be first attested in the Taktikon Uspenskij of 842/3[16] was created in the early 9th century: she suggests the reign of Michael II (820-29) or that of Theophilus (829-42). Whether she is right or not, no one will deny that an imperial navy, whatever the exact structure of its command, was in existence since about the middle of the 7th century; and since there was a navy, its affairs must have been administered by a bureau which certainly included an official in charge of the paperwork. It may be added that the seal of one Leo, chartulary of the imperial fleet, has been attributed to the 8th or 9th century[17], and there is a mention, referring to the reign of Leo V (814-20) of a χαρτουλάριος τῆς λεγομένης ἐξαρτήσεως (sic), who was certainly connected with the navy[18]. Perhaps one can go a little further. In a study of the office of chartulary, R. Guilland has observed that it had greater importance in the 8th century than in the 10th[19], so that a relatively early date would better explain the designation εἰς τῶν μεγάλων. In the 10th century the χαρτουλάριος τοῦ πλοΐμου was a fairly minor official.

The case of the chartulary being inconclusive, we may turn our attention to Andrew's master Theognostus who is described as a protospatharios, who was «later» appointed στρατηλάτης ἐν τοῖς ἀνατολικοῖς μέρεσιν (§ 2), i.e. *magister militum per Orientem*. The combination of these two titles is completely inapplicable to the 9th-10th centuries, but belongs to the period of transition from the Early to the Middle Byzantine system. The title protospatharios, setting aside the disputed passage of Theophanes, p. 243. 32 (referring to the cubicularius Narses) is securely attested at the end of the 7th century[20], but may have already existed in the 640's[21]. As for that of στρατηλάτης (except in its diminished aulic meaning) it disappears from our sources after the reign of Constans II (641-68)[22]. An author of the 9th or 10th century, unless he was an antiquarian, would not have used the expression στρατηλ. ἐν τοῖς ἀνατολικοῖς μέρεσιν; and if he meant to say that Theognostus was made supreme military commander in the East, he would have called him Domestic of the Schools and surely given him the dignity of patrician.

---

[14] *Byzance et la mer*, Paris 1966, 74.

[15] RYDÉN, *Date*, 136.

[16] N. OIKONOMIDÈS, *Les listes de préséance byzantines des IXe et Xe siècles*, Paris 1972, 53, 16.

[17] B.A. PANČENKO, *Katalog molivdovul, IRAIK* 9 (1904), 386, n° 272 (277).

[18] Ps. JOHANN. DAMASC., *Epist. ad Theophilum*, PG 95, c. 368 D.

[19] *Contribution à l'histoire administrative de l'Empire byzantin. Le chartulaire et le grand chartulaire*, RESEE 9 (1971), 406.

[20] *Liber Pontificalis*, ed. DUCHESNE, I, 373 = DÖLGER, *Regesten*, n° 259. Cf. the remarks of I. ŠEVČENKO in *ZRVI* 12 (1970), 5-6.

[21] SEBEOS, *Histoire d'Héraclius*, trans. F. MACLER, 106, where Constantine III 'nomma le fils de l'aspet, Smbat, premier spathar entre tous les spathars et candidat'. This passage appears to have passed unnoticed in discussions of the protospathariate.

[22] See Index to DE BOOR ed. of THEOPH., II, 709.

II. COINAGE

There are in the Life several passages concerning currency, and some of them, I believe, yield chronological indications. The first (§ 22) pertains to the well-known incident in the brothel: the whores rob Andrew of his garment and sell it for 1 miliarêsion, which they then divide among themselves, each whore receiving 2 λεπτά. The mention of a miliarêsion provides a *terminus post quem* of A.D. 615, when silver coinage was first issued in the Byzantine Empire on a large scale[23]. Not knowing how many whores there were in the establishment, we cannot derive any useful lesson from the division. In the same paragraph, however, we are given a more interesting piece of information, namely that Andrew would receive by way of alms 20, 30 or even more λεπτά per day. Holding these pennies (φολερά) in his hand, he would go to a hiding place where beggars congregated and played with the ὀβολοί. He would then purposely provoke the other beggars to beat him with a stick, whereupon he would scatter the φολερά and escape. It is clear that the terms λεπτά, φολερά and ὀβολοί are here used indiscriminately and that they were real coins. It remains to determine what these coins were.

Since the monetary reform of the emperor Anastasius, copper coinage was issued in denominations of 5, 10, 20 and 40 nummi, the last being what we (but not necessarily the Byzantines) call the follis. In the 6th century 1 gold solidus was theoretically equivalent to 180 folleis or 7,200 nummi, but the relation of gold to copper was not constant. In the early 10th century 1 miliarêsion was worth 24 folleis[24], so that 1 solidus = 12 miliarêsia = 288 folleis. Now fractional copper coinage continued, by and large, to be minted until the reign of Constantine V and then ceased altogether, only the follis being retained. This being so, we may enquire whether Andrew (in the author's mind, at any rate) could have collected 20, 30 or even more folleis per day. A simple calculation, using the lower rate of the 10th century, shows that in that case his daily income would have been about 1/10 of a solidus, and his yearly intake, assuming uninterrupted attendance in the streets, not far from 40 solidi, i.e. a sum equivalent to the *roga* of a guards officer. This is clearly impossible. Hence the λεπτά or obols which Andrew pocketed were not folleis, but smaller denominations of either 5 or 10 nummi pieces. Calculating on the basis of 5, we obtain a yearly income of about 10 solidi, which was the equivalent of an unqualified labourer's wages and, therefore, the right kind of sum. That also means, however, that we are dealing with a period not later than the reign of Constantine V.

Passing over the incident of the man who squandered his money on drink (§ 23) and that of the avaricious monk (§ 113), we may note the story of the magician Bigrinos who extorted 1 tremissis from a credulous woman on the pretext of giving alms to the poor (§ 130). Fractional gold (semisses and tremisses) ceased to be issued after the reign of Leo III, except as ceremonial coins, as was done in 769 when Constantine V conferred high titles on his younger sons[25], and preserved examples later

---

[23] Earlier mentions of the miliarêsion refer either to a ceremonial coin (e.g., *Nov. Iust.*, 105, 2, 1) or to the silver currency of the Persian Empire (e.g., Moschi, *Pratum*, 185, *PG* 87/3, c. 3060).

[24] *Book of the Prefect*, III. 3, ed. J. Nicole, 25.

[25] Theoph., ed. De Boor, 444.

than Leo III are of extreme rarity[26]. There is thus a prima facie case for dating the Bigrinos incident not later than the reign of Leo III, even though it could be argued that older issues continued to circulate for a long time (but hardly for two centuries) or that the name of the coin, like that of the English guinea, remained in common parlance when the coin itself had become defunct[27].

III. Monuments of Constantinople

There is no need to discuss here all the churches, monuments and quarters of Constantinople that are mentioned in the Life, since the majority of them yield no chronological indication. Two cases are, however, of importance:

a) *The Church of the Virgin at the Forum*

This church, situated in the south portico of the Forum of Constantine, appears in §§ 71-72. The Saint causes its doors to open automatically so as to admit him, and is then observed levitating in prayer in front of the ambo. As has already been said, this mention provides the only concrete argument for a late date of the Vita, since the church in question is known to have been built by Basil I[28]. Without wishing to deny the force of this evidence, I should like to offer two observations. First, we happen to be quite well informed concerning the building activity of Basil I and, if we examine the relevant passage in the *Vita Basilii*[29], we find that whereas this emperor did construct churches and chapels *de novo* in the imperial palace and in other royal residences, his effort in the city of Constantinople and its suburbs was almost exclusively directed to the repair of damaged churches and the rebuilding ἐκ βάθρων of churches that had entirely collapsed. Confining ourselves to Constantinople without the palace, we can draw up a list of 25 churches enumerated in the *Vita Basilii*, and — setting aside that of the Virgin at the Forum — not one of them was a new foundation. Since this was clearly an act of deliberate policy, we may be permitted to wonder whether St. Mary of the Forum did not likewise represent the rebuilding of an older church.

Secondly, there is the reference to the ambo, a piece of furniture that was practically *de rigueur* in churches of the Early Byzantine period, but which, to the best of my knowledge, was absent from Middle Byzantine churches, perhaps because of their smaller dimensions. No ambo has been found in any of the existing Middle Byzantine churches of Cónstantinople and none is mentioned in the detailed *ekphraseis*

---

[26] P. Grierson, *Catalogue of the Byzantine Coins in the Dumbarton Oaks Collection*, III/1, Washington D.C. 1973, 22.

[27] This is surely the explanation of the notice that during the severe winter of 927/8 Romanus I ordered that τὰ μηνιαῖα τριμίσια should be distributed to the poor in churches: Georg. Monach., Bonn ed., 909; Leon. Gramm., Bonn ed., 319. The word must have become institutionalized, since it is made clear that the distribution was made in silver, not gold: ὡς εἶναι τὰ διδόμενα... ἀργύρου ἐγκεχαραγμένου χιλιάδας δώδεκα.

[28] Theoph. Cont., Bonn ed., 339; Genes., Bonn ed., 128; Scylitz., ed. Thurn, 164-5; *Script. orig. Constant.*, ed. Preger, II, 225, 267, 288.

[29] Theoph. Cont., 322 ff.

of the Pharos, Nea and other churches of the 9th/10th centuries. It may be noted that St. Mary of the Forum, as it existed in the 10th century, was of small size[30].

b) *The Myrelaion*

The *Patria* asserts that a monastery of this name existed in the reign of Constantine V[31] but this isolated statement has been rejected by Janin who ascribed the foundation of the religious house to Romanus I[32]. Rydén follows suit and considers the mention of the Myrelaion as a *terminus post quem* for the composition of Andrew's Vita. Neither of these scholars, however, has noticed a significant detail.

The monastery of the Myrelaion (dedication unrecorded) was set up by Romanus Lecapenus in his own private mansion (ἐν τῷ οἴκῳ αὐτοῦ) and is known to have been a nunnery. It was founded before February 922, when his wife Theodora was buried there[33], so quite possibly when Romanus became emperor (920) and moved his household to the imperial palace. The archaeological researches of R. Naumann[34] have revealed that the Lecapenus mansion was built on top of a vast Early Byzantine rotunda and communicated at first storey level with its church, the present Bodrum Camii, which is itself built over a lower structure.

Though nominally transformed to religious use, the Myrelaion remained for several decades as a family establishment. This is shown not only by the successive burials of Lecapeni in it (Christopher in 932, Romanus in 948, his daughter, the empress Helena, in 961), but also by a curious story told in the Life of St. Basil the Younger with reference to the years 940-44[35]. When Romanus was still on the throne, two of his daughters remained in his house, which is described as enormous (οἶκος παμμέγιστος)[36]. One of them was robbed of a money box containing 40 lbs. of gold and, in her anger, she sent her eunuch to the City Prefect to demand a rigorous police investigation of all her household staff. Her *cubicularia*, however, begged her to follow a different course lest many innocent persons be subjected to needless ill-treatment. The eunuch was recalled, and the *cubicularia* proceeded to solicit the help of St. Basil who was living nearby. Naturally, St. Basil knew exactly where the money had been hidden — two cubits underground, next to a bed in the base-

---

[30] GENES., *loc. cit.*

[31] *Script. orig. Constant.*, II, 258.

[32] *La géographie ecclésiastique de l'empire byzantin*, I/3, Paris 1969², 351. WORTLEY, *A Note* (as in n. 13, *supra*), 204-8, rightly pointed out that the Myrelaion of Andrew the Fool was different from and earlier than Romanus's monastery. He was, however, misled by the incorrect archaeological observations of D. Talbot Rice.

[33] THEOPH. CONT., 402.

[34] *Der antike Rundbau beim Myrelaion*, «Istanbuler Mitteilungen», 16 (1966), 211 ff.

[35] For the date see CHR. G. ANGELIDI, Ὁ Βίος τοῦ ὁσίου Βασιλείου τοῦ Νέου, diss., Ioannina 1980, 89.

[36] The situation is given with great precision: ἄλλοτε πάλιν ἐν τοῖς παλατίοις τῶν Ἐλευθερίου ἀνωτέρω τῆς πόρτης τοῦ ἁγίου Στεφάνου οἶκός ἐστι παμμέγιστος, ὃν εἶναι φασί τινες Ῥωμανοῦ τοῦ βασιλέως. This passage, unknown to Janin, may be used for a more exact localization of the palace of Eleutherius. The gate of St. Stephen was probably Yenikapi, whose Byzantine name appears to be unrecorded.

ment (κατώγεον) of the house[37] — and he revealed its location on condition that the culprit remained unidentified[38]. The author of the text does not inform us that the house of Romanus was a monastery, but he makes it quite clear that it was a very grand establishment with a 'whole populace' of servants.

Now the story in Andrew's Life (§§ 80-81) is the following. A certain young thief is reprimanded by the Saint, but persists in his evil ways. Thereupon Andrew causes him to be possessed by a demon, and the thief, thus tormented, takes refuge in the church or oratory 'of the most holy Theotokos, called Myrelaion on account of her venerable image which gushes *myron* like oil'. He implores the Virgin's help, smears the miraculous oil over his whole body, and then sees the Virgin in a vision standing in front of the sanctuary doors. He is relieved of the demon and makes a solemn vow in front of the same icon to lead henceforth a virtuous life.

It is hard to imagine that a young thief could have walked off the street into the chapel of a highly exclusive nunnery, that was virtually a private residence, and proceeded to take off his clothes to anoint himself with the holy oil. The church he walked into was open to the public: hence it was not the Myrelaion of the 10th century. It was a church named after a miraculous icon, and we may imagine that long after that church had disappeared, its name persisted and was applied to the monastery of Romanus. Far from serving as a *terminus post quem* of ca 920, the mention of the Myrelaion surely takes us back to a considerably earlier period.

Rydén also asserts[39] that several other topographical names mentioned in the Vita do not appear in our sources before the middle of the 10th century: these are the Antiforum (§ 23), the Anemodoulion or Anemodourion (§ 105), the portico of Maurianus (§ 187) and the Heptascalon (§ 197). As to the Antiforum, it is true that its only mention is in the Book of Ceremonies, but it was a feature of Late Antique town planning, since a place of that name is known to have existed at Antioch, Daphne and Edessa[40]; it could not, in any case, have originated in the Middle Byzantine period. Anemodourion, as the name of the monumental weather vane of Theodosius I, is actually recorded in the middle of the 8th century[41]. The portico of Maurianus is mentioned in connection with the revival of iconoclasm by Leo V in 814[42], and since it designated one of the principal north-south streets of the capital, it was surely of much earlier date. As for the Heptascalon, I must admit that its earliest recorded occurrence is in the *Vita Basilii* with reference to that emperor's buildings[43], but I cannot attribute much importance to this fact.

---

[37] So, presumably, in the rotunda.

[38] Ed. A.N. VESELOVSKIJ, «Sbornik Otdel. Russk. Jazyka i Slov. Imp. Akad. Nauk», 46 (1889), suppl. 72-6.

[39] RYDÉN, *Date*, 136.

[40] Antioch: MALAL., 397 (suggesting it was an open space); Daphne: EVAGR., III, 28 (near public bath); Edessa: Jos. STYL., trans. WRIGHT, 18 (wrongly rendered as 'town hall'), PROC. *De aed.*, II, 7, 6. Cf. D. CLAUDE, *Die byzantinische Stadt im 6. Jahrhundert*, Munich 1969, 84.

[41] *Parastaseis* in *Script. orig. Constant.*, I, 37.

[42] THEOPH. CONT., 27.

[43] *Ibid.*, 324.

IV. THE APOCALYPSE

Byzantine apocalypses tend to be fairly simple-minded documents. True, they are made up to a large extent of *topoi* deriving from the eschatological tradition, yet each one of them reflects the fears and aspirations of the time of its composition. I know of no apocalypse that sets out to ignore the issues of the day: that, indeed, would be a negation of the prophet's primary purpose.

In the case of Andrew's revelation we are hindered by the fact that it does not contain any identifiable *vaticinia ex eventu*, apart from the rather trivial mention of several attacks on Constantinople. It has been argued at length that the first in the succession of five apocalyptic emperors foretold by Andrew is none other than Basil I[44]; and if that were so, it would follow that the text was earlier than 886, the year of Basil's death (since his reign fell short of 32 years) and probably earlier than 878 (since Basil is not known to have remitted taxes in his 12th year as the apocalypse stipulates). There is, however, no compelling reason to equate the emperor in question with Basil I. Rydén is apparently of the same opinion.

The political situation delineated at the beginning of Andrew's apocalypse clearly post-dates the collapse of Byzantine fortunes in the 30's and 40's of the 7th century. The first apocalyptic emperor will humble the Arabs (who are the only concrete enemy named in the text) and re-occupy Illyricum (called by that very name). Egypt will once again pay tax to the emperor. He will also 'tame' the 'fair-haired nations' (ξανθὰ γένη) of the West, i.e. the German barbarians who are, further down (p. 207), said to be dwelling in the general area of Rome. The author's tone, politically speaking, is one of confidence: Constantinople will indeed be attacked by many nations, but will never be captured thanks to the protection of the Theotokos. As for the Arabs, they will be defeated without any trouble. In short, the first apocalyptic ruler will reconstitute the Early Byzantine empire such as it had existed up to the reign of Heraclius. The extraordinary calamities that will befall mankind in the following reign belong to the eschatological stock in trade and do not correspond to any historical reality.

While it is true that in the late 9th and 10th centuries the Empire had no reason to be particularly fearful of the Arabs, it had other, more terrible, enemies, namely the Bulgars and the Russians. The Russians, in particular, who had the ability to strike directly at Constantinople with little or no advance warning, made a deep impression on the popular consciousness and were included in the eschatological vision, all the more readily since their very name, 'Ρώς, is linked with Gog and Magog in Ezek. 38: 2. This very connection is made in the Life of St. Basil the Younger, written in ca 956[45]. Even at the end of the 10th century, when some fifty years had

[44] In particular, by J. WORTLEY, *The Warrior-Emperor of the Andrew Salos Apocalypse*, AnBoll 88 (1970), 43-59; ID., *The Political Significance of the Andrew-Salos Apocalypse*, Byz 43 (1973), 248 ff.

[45] Ed. VESELOVSKIJ, *op. cit.*, 65. The passage is worth quoting. Basil says: Βάρβαρον ἔθνος ἐλεύσεται ἐνταῦθα λυσσωδῶς καθ' ἡμῶν, προσαγορευόμενον 'Ρὸς καὶ "Ογ καὶ Μόγ. Λέγω οὖν πρὸς αὐτόν· Κύριέ μου, κύριε, καὶ μήποτε μέλλει παραλήψεσθαι ταύτην τὴν πόλιν; Ὁ δὲ ἔφη· Ἡ μήτηρ τοῦ Κυρίου ἡμῶν Ἰησοῦ Χριστοῦ οὐκ ἐάσει ταύτην τὴν πόλιν παραληφθῆναι εἰς χεῖρας ἐχθρῶν αὐτῆς, εἰς γὰρ κλῆρον αὐτῆς δέδοται αὐτῇ παρὰ

elapsed after the attack of 941, it was believed that Constantinople was destined to be captured by the Russians[46]. Why is it, then, that Andrew's apocalypse, if it was composed only a decade after the same attack (or at any other time between the late 9th century and the mid 10th) contains no allusion whatever to the Russians? The omission did not pass unnoticed, since one medieval copyist or redactor of Andrew's Life felt obliged to insert a reference to them. I am speaking of the interpolated version represented by the manuscripts which Rydén calls C and K. At the very beginning of the apocalypse (p. 201, appar.) we find the following amplification modifying the Saint's assertion that Constantinople would never fall to an enemy: «There is a rumour afoot that the nation of the Hagarenes will get in (εἰσιέναι) and kill great throngs with their swords; and I say that the fair-haired nation will also enter (εἰσελεύσεται), the nation whose name lies in [i.e. begins with] the 17th out of the 24 letters of the alphabet [i.e. rho]. They will indeed enter and scatter on the ground the bones of the sinners, but woe to them from the two saplings (ὀρπήκων) whose swords will cut them down as the keen sickle cuts the wheat in summer time. For they will neither return home, nor will any of them be left here». In case there was any doubt concerning the identity of the fair-haired nation, another commentator added, «The 17th letter mentioned here is rho, and it designates the Rhôs, i.e. the Russians», etc.

The interpolator is not very precise in his language: in particular, the verbs εἰσιέναι, εἰσελεύσεται should be understood to mean, not 'enter within the walls of Constantinople', since neither the Arabs nor the Russians ever did so, but penetrate the immediate vicinity. He is, however, referring to a Russian attack which was opposed by two Byzantine commanders ('saplings') and led to the complete destruction of the enemy. These details do not accord with the attack of 860 nor with that of 1043, but tally quite well with that of 941. It is true that in 941 the Byzantine forces were led not by two, but by three commanders, namely the protovestiarios Theophanes who had charge of the fleet, Bardas Phokas and John Kourkouas[47], but the identity of these men was soon confused or, more probably, deliberately altered when Kourkouas had been dismissed (in 944) and Theophanes disgraced. Already in the Life of St. Basil the Younger the Byzantine commanders are represented as Phokas, Pantherios (who succeeded Kourkouas) and the enigmatic 'holy general Theodore surnamed Spongarios' who, in the view of H. Grégoire, is none other than St. Theodore Stratelates[48]. The almost complete destruction of the Russians in 941 is historically accurate, since all those captured on imperial territory were put to death and few survivors were able to return home.

It seems to me that the interpolator who found it necessary to add a reference to the Russian attack of 941 was writing not very long after that event, i.e. at a time when its omission was considered to detract from the veracity of the apocalypse. Hence, the original text was older than 941. One more detail is of significance in this connection. For the interpolator, the 'fair-haired nation' denoted the Russians,

τοῦ Θεοῦ, καὶ ἱκανῶς αὐτῆς ὑπερασπίζεται. This looks like a direct reminiscence of Andrew's apocalypse, 201-2.

[46] *Script. orig. Constant.*, II, 176.

[47] See, e.g., S. Runciman, *The Emperor Romanus Lecapenus*, Cambridge 1929, 111-2.

[48] *Byz* 13 (1938), 291 ff.

whereas in the original apocalypse, as we have seen, it stood for the Germanic barbarians in the West. The latter meaning is certainly the older of the two, and can be traced back to ca. 600 A.D., if not earlier[49]. It persists in the first and second Daniel apocalypses (9th century)[50] which are, however, of Sicilian origin. A Sicilian author would naturally equate the 'fair-haired nation' with the Lombards, but would the same association have been made by a Constantinopolitan of the 9th or 10th century? A negative indication is provided by Nicephorus's Χρονογραφικὸν σύντομον as preserved in the Arethas MS, *olim* Dresd. Da 12 (now in Moscow) of A.D. 932[51]. The entry on the first reign of Justinian II, fol. 6ʳ⁻ᵛ (corresponding to de Boor's edition of Nicephorus, 99. 22) contains the following addition: ἐπὶ τούτου εἰρήνη βαθεῖα τῇ ἐκκλησίᾳ καὶ τῇ οἰκουμένῃ γεγένηται· τούτῳ φόρους τελοῦσι Σαρακηνοί· ἔθνη τὰ ξανθὰ ἱκανῶς ἐξεπόρθησεν [-αν cod.]· μέρος πολὺ τῆς πολιτείας ἐκ τῶν Σαρακηνῶν ἀνεσώσατο, χείρας φυλάξας ἀναιμάκτους ἀπὸ χριστιανῶν. Since the reference here is to the Slavs in Macedonia, we may conclude that, from the viewpoint of Constantinople, the 'fair-haired nation' underwent a semantic evolution: first the Germans, then the Slavs, finally the Russian Vikings. Such an evolution could not have taken place overnight.

Andrew's apocalypse contains a number of other clues, some of which are very difficult to interpret. I shall not attempt to explain the reference (p. 204) to Rhiza (Rhizaion in Pontus?), Armenopetra (Petra in Lazica?), Strobilos and Karyoupolis (if that is the right reading). I am, however, struck by the prominence accorded to Thessalonica and Syllaion which, along with Rome, are destined to become the capitals of the Empire after the flooding of Constantinople (p. 211). The author evidently regarded Thessalonica as an unconquered bastion, as indicated by the words: «Thessalonica, you will vanquish your enemies, for you are the pride of the saints and have been sanctified by the Highest». Such sentiments would have made more sense in the light of the city's successful resistance to the Slavs and Avars in the 7th century than after its sack by the Arabs in 904. The case of Syllaion (Sillyon in Pamphylia) is even more curious. The author is quite emphatic: «You have been called Syllaion, but you will never be captured or taken by any of your enemies to the end of time» (p. 207 and appar.). It has been conjectured[52] that Syllaion along with part of the south-west coast of Asia Minor was temporarily in Arab hands in ca. 807 and, if that were so, we would have a clear *terminus ante quem* for the composition of the apocalypse. I shall not press this argument since the evidence is unclear; it is, however, of some significance that the one occasion when Syllaion 'hit the headlines' was when an Arab fleet (the same fleet that had been blockading Constantinople in 674-78) was completely destroyed off its coast[53].

Finally, I should like to point out that the apocalypse which, in several respects,

[49] MAURIC., *Strategicon*, XI. 3, ed. H. MIHĂESCU, 274.

[50] A. VASSILIEV, *Anecdota graeco-byzantina*, Moscow 1893, 36, 39.

[51] I am using a collation of this MS made by Oskar von Gebhardt and now in the Staatsbibliothek of Berlin-Dahlem, Nachlass Gebhardt, XXI, 25. A microfilm of it was kindly communicated to me by Prof. L.G. Westerink. For a description of the MS see L.G. WESTERINK, *Marginalia by Arethas in Moscow Greek MS 231*, *Byz 42 (1972)*, 196-244.

[52] G. HUXLEY, *On the Vita of St. Stephen the Younger*, *GRBS* 18 (1977), 102-3.

[53] THEOPH., 354.

offers the closest correspondence to Andrew's — I refer to the pseudo-Methodius (or rather Daniel) of cod. Canonicianus 19 — in clearly datable to 716/7. My reasons for this statement are set out in the Appendix.

V. VARIA

Had we possessed a proper dictionary of Byzantine Greek, we would have been in a better position to evaluate the use of certain words in Andrew's Life. Some of them appear to me unusual for a text of the 9th or 10th century, e.g. φουσκάριον (from Lat. pusca), meaning a tavern, and φουσκάριος = tavern keeper (§§ 16, 23, 26). Both of them are common in the Life of Symeon the Fool[54], and I find φου-σκιάζω ('to preserve in vinegar') in Theophanes, de Boor, 398. 30 (reproducing a source of the early 8th century), but I do not recollect encountering this term at a later date. And what would have been in the 10th century the point of saying that a φουσκάριος doing business at Constantinople was a Christian (§ 26)? I also wonder whether in the days of Constantine Porphyrogenitus anyone would have understood Andrew's obscene pun, addressed to a sodomite eunuch who had offered him some dates: Δῶρον κωλοφονίας οἱ σαλοὶ οὐκ ἐσθίουσιν (§ 57). Κολοφώνιον in the sense of a garden vegetable appears to be attested only in papyri[55].

The disputation between Epiphanius and the philosophers (§§ 46-47) is, to me, partly incomprehensible, but it does appear to have some connection with the Monothelete controversy, since one of the questions posed is whether the Father and the Son are identical as to their volitions and wills.

Then there is the story of the dissolute young man John who ends up in the underworld, in a hut full of excrement (§ 124). Above him is suspended the darkened inscription: Μονὴ αἰωνία καὶ τιμωρία βίαιος Ἰωάννου υἱοῦ Κελευστιόνου. Admittedly, this passage may be influenced by the Life of St. John the Almoner, in which the avaricious bishop Troilus sees in a dream his heavenly abode with the titulus, Μονὴ αἰωνία καὶ ἀνάπαυσις Τρωΐλου ἐπισκόπου, a titulus that is speedily removed by an angel [56]. The point of the story, however, is that it plays on an Early Christian formula of funerary epigraphy, a formula that was no longer in use in the Middle Byzantine period. Besides, would anyone in 10th-century Constantinople have been called Celeustion (or Celestinus)?

Professor Ihor Ševčenko has kindly drawn to my attention another fact that may be of importance. When Basil the Macedonian (the future emperor Basil I) first came to Constantinople as a poor man, he fell asleep outside the church of St. Diomede, whose custodian (prosmonarios) was supernaturally warned to let him in and show him the respect due to an emperor. The custodian in question was called Nikolaos Androsalites[57]. Whatever doubts we may have concerning the historicity of Basil's divinely inspired reception, Nikolaos Androsalites was a real person, since he was

---

[54] See Index to Rydén's ed. (Uppsala, 1963).

[55] See PREISIGKE, Wörterbuch der griech. Papyrusurkunden, s.v.

[56] Ed. A.-J. FESTUGIÈRE, Vie de Syméon le Fou et Vie de Jean de Chypre, Paris 1974, 379.

[57] GEORG. MONACH., 819 and 842; LEON. GRAMM., 233 and 256; GEORG. HAMART., ed. MURALT, 726 and 758-9; Slavon. Hamart., ed. ISTRIN, 505 and 523.

later promoted to synkellos, died and was buried in his own house in the quarter of Arcadianae. All the chronicles of the Logothete group give his name as Androsalites, which looks as if it had been formed from Andreas Salos, in the same way as Hagiostephanites, Hagiotheodorites, etc. If that were so, it would follow that Andrew the Fool was a well known figure by the middle of the 9th century. A possible objection is that the correspondence of Alexander of Nicaea (mid 10th century) mentions a certain Peter Androsylites[58], but I can find no obvious derivation for that form.

* * *

We may now draw together the various strands of this enquiry. Our discussion of titulature has shown that the Life of Andrew the Fool was written at a time not too far removed from the middle of the 7th century, and our discussion of coinage that it predates the middle of the 8th. The apocalypse has given us a further set of clues: it indicates a period after the loss of the eastern provinces to the Arabs, but also one in which the Arabs, though regarded as the principal enemy, did not constitute an immediate threat. We must also remember that the Life, which is full of allusions to the worship of icons, never mentions iconoclasm — a fact that suggests a date before 730. Nor is it very likely, I think, that it was written in the immediate aftermath of the siege of Constantinople in 717/18, an event that inspired acute apprehension and was followed by renewed Arab attacks, one of which involved the siege of Nicaea.

The most likely time of composition lies, I believe, in the reign of Constantine IV, after the Arab failure of 674-78, or in the first reign of Justinian II, i.e. approximately between the years 680 and 695. We tend to forget that this period provided a respite for the Empire. The Arabs were forced to sue for peace and even to pay tribute to the Romans, so that the end of their domination could be envisaged. The emperor received friendly embassies and gifts from the Chagan of the Avars and the Western kings. It was a time of hope, when «there was great tranquillity in both East and West»[59]. We have seen that the first reign of Justinian II was also regarded in the same light. The Life of Andrew the Fool, with its intensely moralistic tone, would thus be a product of the same climate as the Quinisext Council which regulated and tightened up the conduct of Christian life.

Two other general considerations appear to me to favour this re-dating of Andrew's Life. The first concerns the picture of urban life it provides, a picture that I would be tempted to describe as one of Late Antique customs in decay. With regard to this process at Constantinople, a somewhat earlier stage is represented in the Miracles of St. Artemius and a somewhat later stage in the *Parastaseis suntomoi chronikai*. The hippodrome games and factions have faded away (already in the Miracles of St. Artemius the stables of the factions are described as being abandoned)[60] and impecunious visitors to the capital park themselves in disused theatres (§ 43). But a reasonably active commercial life still goes on, and there are even Arab mer-

---

[58] J. Darrouzès, *Epistoliers byzantins du Xe siècle*, Paris 1960, 85, 91.

[59] Theoph., 356.

[60] Ed. A. Papadopoulos-Kerameus, *Varia graeca sacra*, St. Petersburg 1909, 13.

chants who cut a distinctive figure in their black clothes and brown boots (§ 45, where Ἰσραηλίτου ἐμπόρου should surely be corrected to Ἰσμαηλίτου ἐμπόρου, and § 49). The author of the Life regards these Arabs with suspicion, and in the apocalypse he looks forward to their expulsion (p. 203).What is most striking, however, is that everyday life goes on in public: taverns are frequented even by respectable people (§ 24), brothels do a brisk business, and young men of good family sit in a public bath watching prostitutes go by (§ 118). It is instructive by way of contrast to turn to the Life of St. Basil the Younger, which has often been described as offering a striking resemblance to that of Andrew the Fool. Basil, too, was something of a *salos* and he was an impecunious sponger, yet he is never shown out in the street. The only incident involving a tavern is the stock episode of the wine cask poisoned by a snake[61], which is a literary invention, since it can be traced back to the Life of Symeon the Fool[62]; for the rest, Basil spends his time indoors, and we are repeatedly told of locked gates and secluded courtyards guarded by porters.

The second consideration is of a literary nature. As Ihor Ševčenko has already observed[63], Andrew's Vita belongs to the pre-iconoclastic tradition of hagiography, the tradition of the *paterika*, of John Moschus and Leontius of Neapolis. From the 9th century onwards Lives of saints were written in a very different manner[64], the only exception being, once again, the Life of St. Basil the Younger. The resemblance between the two, is, however, by no means complete and applies largely to the lengthy visions that are introduced by way of digression. For the rest, St. Basil's Life concerns a real person, whose actions, recorded by an eyewitness, are given in a coherent temporal sequence. It may well have been influenced by the Life of Andrew, but it is not a historical fiction.

I do not claim to have resolved all the puzzles that are contained in the Life of St. Andrew Salos. Edification alone is hardly a sufficient motive for the composition of so lengthy and elaborate a text in honour of a personage who probably never existed and who certainly had no public cult. The role of Epiphanius, who plays such a prominent part in the Life, remains as obscure as ever. I believe, nevertheless, that the Life makes much better sense in the latter 7th century than it would in the middle of the 10th. It also provides, if my theory is correct, a valuable insight into popular mentality shortly before the outbreak of Iconoclasm as does also the Daniel apocalypse which it remains to discuss.

APPENDIX
A Daniel Apocalypse of 716/17 A.D.

A Daniel apocalypse that offers many points of convergence with that of An-

---

[61] Ed. S.G. Vilinskij, *Zapiski Imp. Novoross. Univ.*, 7, Odessa 1911, 313-15.

[62] Ed. Rydén, 147.

[63] *Hagiography of the Iconoclast Period* in *Iconoclasm*, ed. A. Bryer and J. Herrin, Birmingham 1977, 128.

[64] See Chr. Loparev, *Vizantijskija žitija svjatykh VIII-IX vekov*, VV 17 (1910), 15 ff.

drew the Fool has long been accessible in the careless edition of V. Istrin[65], based on cod. Bodl. Canon. 19. It has recently been re-edited with the help of a second manuscript (Fac. Medic., Montpellier, 405) by K. Berger who has appended to it a lengthy and learned commentary[66], in which he argues that the text in question was composed after Charlemagne's coronation in 800 and before the accession of Nicephorus I in 802. His reasons for so doing appear to me, however, entirely unconvincing.

The apocalypse opens with a massive invasion of Asia Minor by four Arab armies led, respectively, by Ishmael and 'the three sons of Hagar'. Ishmael makes straight for Chalcedon by following the high road of the *cursus publicus*. The second army, commanded by Ouales (i.e. Walîd) goes by way of Antioch and Cilicia to Smyrna in the Thrakesian theme and thence to Constantinople. The third, under a certain Axiaphar, invades Armenia and reaches Trebizond. The fourth, under Morphosar, marches north to Amaseia, thence to Sinope, Zaliches, Chryse Petra, Daphnousia, Chrysopolis and Damalis. The Arab armies unite and, in order to reach Constantinople, build a bridge of boats across the Bosphorus. At this juncture the Lord brings about a change of fortunes: He raises an emperor who had been considered defunct and useless, and this emperor, assisted by his two young boys (μειράκια), completely annihilates the Arabs, so that only three Arab tents are left. Then starts a glorious reign of 33 years (36 in the Oxford MS): the emperor establishes peace in the whole world, builds cities and churches. His fame spreads to the four corners of the earth and no enemy dares resist him because he has been sent by God.

When this glorious emperor and the two young boys have been laid to rest, there arises a 'ruler from the north' who causes incest and every other manner of iniquity to be perpetrated. The next ruler, equally wicked, is described either (in the Oxford MS) as a 'foul alien woman' or (in the Montpellier MS) as an alien man from the south. Constantinople sinks into the sea, only Constantine's column remaining (as also in Andrew's apocalypse), and the Empire is given to Rome. Then Dan reigns in Jerusalem, the scattered Jews are gathered, Antichrist appears, etc.

Berger has quite rightly seen that the invasion of Asia Minor is the one preceding the siege of Constantinople in 717-18, and has correctly identified the liberator emperor with Leo III. He goes on, however, to equate the wicked 'ruler from the north' with Constantine V, and the 'foul alien woman' with the Empress Irene. He also sees an allusion to Charlemagne's coronation in the transfer of the Empire to Rome. Since there is no reference to another emperor in Constantinople, he finds a *terminus ante quem* in the elevation of Nicephorus I in 802.

The impossibility of such an interpretation is at once obvious. Setting aside the fact that Leo III did not die in the 33rd year of his reign, no Byzantine author of whatever religious persuasion writing in 801 or 802 would have described Leo as a glorious liberator and God-sent ruler, his son, Constantine V, as a monster of iniquity; and the Empress Irene as a foul alien woman. Nor would a Byzantine author contemporary with the Caliph Harun ar-Rashid have imagined that the Arabs had been completely annihilated. The transition from history to eschatology should be

---

[65] *Oktrovenie Mefodija Patarskago i apokrifičeskie Videnija Daniila*, Moscow 1897, Teksty, 145-50.

[66] *Die griechische Daniel-Diegese* = *Studia post-biblica*, 27, Leiden 1976.

312

sought not where Berger fixes it[67], but at an earlier point of the story, just before the attack on Constantinople, as the following considerations demonstrate.

The invasion of Asia Minor is described in considerable detail. It is difficult to ascertain how accurately it is told because a) the text of the apocalypse, preserved as it is in two very late manuscripts, is considerably garbled, and b) our historical information on these events is sadly deficient[68]. It is certainly true that the attack on Constantinople was preceded by several raids in Asia Minor, led by the sons of the Caliph Al-Walîd. It is true that Amaseia was taken (presumably in 712). It is true that the main Arab army, under Maslama, followed the high road (by way of Amorium). A march along the shore of the Black Sea, from Sinope to Chrysopolis, is not otherwise recorded, but the place names are authentic and given in proper sequence. The Arab forces did not, however, unite on the Asiatic shore facing Constantinople, nor did they build a bridge of boats across the Bosphorus, although they may have been expected to do so: instead, they wintered in the Thrakesian theme (where they took Pergamon), crossed the Dardanelles at Abydus and advanced on Constantinople along the Thracian coast. The end of the historical section of the apocalypse lies, therefore, just before the assault on the capital, and from that point onwards everything is fantasy. A detail not noticed by Berger not only confirms this conclusion, but allows us to make another interesting observation.

In the text constituted by Berger the liberator emperor is indeed Leo III. His name starts εἰς τὸ κ´ στοιχεῖον τοῦ ἀλφαβήτου (Konon, Leo's baptismal name)[69], he is θηριώνυμος (Leo) and he arises from 'the inner land of Persia and Syria', εἰς τὴν ἔσω χώραν τῆς Περσίδος καὶ Συριακῆς ἐθνῶν (sic). Certain other details, however, do not appear to fit Leo very well. As far as we know, he did not, at that time, have two young sons: his only recorded son, Constantine, was born in 718, just before or just after the repulse of the Arabs. The statement that he had been forgotten and deemed useless, indeed believed to have died, is hardly applicable to a man who had enjoyed a very successful military career before becoming emperor. Can it be, therefore, that Leo has been rather clumsily substituted for another providential saviour? Now, if we consult the Oxford MS, we discover that the liberator's name begins εἰς τὸ η´ στοιχεῖον τοῦ ἀλφαβήτου, and that he is not called θηριώνυμος. The 8th letter of the alphabet being *theta*, the obvious candidate is Theodosius III[70], who indeed had been quite forgotten before his fortuitous elevation to the throne.

---

[67] The reference to the transfer of the Empire has, in my opinion, no connection with Charlemagne's coronation. It may be due to the well-known intention of Constans II to move his capital to Rome: THEOPH., 348, 351.

[68] See especially E.W. BROOKS, *The Arabs in Asia Minor (641-750), from Arabic Sources*, JHSt 18 (1898), 193 ff.; ID, *The Campaign of 717-718, from Arabic Sources*, ibid., 19 (1899), 19-33; R. GUILLAND, *L'expédition de Maslama contre Constantinople*, in ID., *Études byzantines*, Paris 1959, 109-33.

[69] This is presumably the origin of the Konon prophecy which was to survive for many centuries in Greek oracular books. See ISTRIN, *op. cit.*, 274, and cod. Bodl. Baroc. 170 (written in Crete in 1577), fol. 17ᵛ: Εἰς τὸν βασιλέα Κόνωνα: / Στοιχεῖον τὸ θ´ Κόνωνος λέγω / κρατήσει σὺν μείρακι τρὶς δέκα δύο / καὶ γὰρ ταπεινώσει μὲν τρεῖς βασιλείας, / αὖθις δ'ἐκ τοῦ Κόνωνος οὐδεὶς ἰσχύσει, etc.

[70] This has already been conjectured by W. BOUSSET, *Beiträge zur Geschichte der Eschatologie*, «Zeitschrift für Kirchengeschichte», 20 (1900), 288.

We know so little about Theodosius that it is impossible to verify the other details contained in the Oxford text[71]. He certainly had one son who was not an infant at the time. Did he have a second? And had he spent some time in the East before settling down at Adramytion? The Oxford MS reads, τοῦτον φυλάσσει ὁ κύριος εἰς ἕξο (sic) χώραν τῆς Περσίδος, without the addition καὶ Συριακῆς ἐθνῶν. Or is Περσίδος a corruption?

While it is difficult to explain fully all the particulars of a text that has come down to us in such poor shape, the natural conclusion is that the liberator was originally intended to be Theodosius and was, very soon thereafter, altered to fit Leo III. The date of composition is almost certainly the winter of 716-17.

---

[71] For Theodosius as ὁ πραότατος βασιλεύς, see *Epist. ad Theophilum*, *PG* 95, c. 357.

IX

ST. ANTHUSA OF MANTINEON
AND THE FAMILY OF CONSTANTINE V

Our main authority for the career of St. Anthusa of Mantineon [1] is a notice of the Synaxarion (*BHG, Auct.*, 2029h) that has come down to us in a number of slightly divergent forms. We may take as our basis the text of the codex Sirmondianus, readily available in Delehaye's edition [2]. It tells the following story.

A contemporary of the emperor Constantine Copronymus, Anthusa was born of pious parents named Strategius and Febronia. From her earliest youth she was possessed by the love of quietude and a distaste for all worldly things. In those days an ordained monk called Sisinnius had come to the region of Mantineon (τοῖς τοῦ Μαντινέου χωρίοις) and distinguished himself by his acts of piety. Placing herself under his discipline, Anthusa was bidden to enter a fiery furnace from which she emerged unharmed. The monk taught her other forms of outstanding virtue and prophesied that she would found a great monastery and receive the direction of 900 souls. She was then given the tonsure and was directed by Sisinnius to dwell on the little island of the lake adjoining the village Perkile. There she bound herself with chains and pursued a rigorous regimen. One day she paid a visit to Sisinnius and asked his leave to build a chapel of St. Anne. He offered her useful advice and foretold future developments, including the time of his own death. Some thirty nuns now joined Anthusa ; the chapel was built and Sisinnius died as indicated. Those who had formerly followed Sisinnius now flocked to Anthusa, with the result that her community expanded rapidly. She built two very big churches, one dedicated to the Theotokos, the other to the Holy Apostles. The former was reserved for the use of nuns, the latter for that of monks.

The fame of Anthusa and her strict adherence to orthodoxy reached the ears of the emperor Constantine Copronymus who despatched an emissary with the following instructions : « Proceed to that province and persuade Anthusa to adopt our views. If she consents, well and good ; if not, punish her and force her to submit to our laws, even if she is unwilling to do so. » The emissary arrived on the scene, con-

---

[1] The spelling varies : Μαντίνεον, Μαντίναιον, Μαντίνιον, Μαντίνειον.
[2] *Synax. Eccl. CP*, 848-52.

fiscated a mass of icons (both on panels and on cloths) and proceeded
to interrogate the Saint as well as her nephew who was abbot of the
men's monastery. The latter received a sound flogging, but persisted
in his confession and was released when he was about to faint. As
for Anthusa, she was stretched on the ground and whipped. Hot
coals, produced by burning her icons, were poured over her head and
feet, but, by God's grace, she remained unscratched and was exiled.

Some time thereafter the emperor came to that province at the head
of his whole army and was intending to interrogate Anthusa, but she
foiled his design by inflicting on him a temporary blindness. She
predicted to the empress, who was having a difficult pregnancy
($\delta \nu \sigma \tau o \kappa o \dot{\nu} \sigma \eta$), that she would give birth to a boy and a girl, and further
prophesied the character and future conduct of each one of them.
In recompense, the empress dedicated many $\chi \omega \varrho \iota a$ and offerings to
Anthusa's monastery, and the « tyrant » desisted from his hostile
intentions. Anthusa's fame grew as a result of this incident and many
persons came to her, some to receive her blessing, others to renounce
the worldly life, others to be healed of their diseases. Among the
visitors was a soldier who came in disguise ($\mu \varepsilon \tau a \mu \varepsilon \iota \psi a \varsigma$ $\tau \dot{o}$ $\sigma \chi \tilde{\eta} \mu a$) [3]
along with his wife and expressed willingness to make a contribution if
his wish to have a child were to be fulfilled. The Saint divined his
intention and assured him that it would be satisfied. To describe all
the miracles that had been accomplished and would be accomplished
($\pi \varrho a \chi \theta \eta \sigma \dot{o} \mu \varepsilon \nu a$) [4] by Anthusa was like counting the sand on the
seashore. Since, however, she was human, she was destined to die,
and did so on the day of the martyrdom of St. Panteleimon (27 July),
which was, indeed, her desire. She was buried in the cell in which she
had lived and went on performing miracles.

Before we proceed any further, it is worth pointing out that the
notice of the Synaxarion is a résumé of a longer Vita. The
marks of compression are visible in the abrupt introduction of
certain incidents, such as that of the fiery furnace and the flogging
of the nephew — indeed, the text does not even make it clear that
Anthusa was at the head of a double monastery. The rhetorical
flourish at the end of the notice (« If one could measure the sand on
the seashore, the drops of rain, the depth of the sea, the height of
heaven, the breadth of the earth, » etc.), borrowed though it is from
the Bible (*Sir.* 1. 2-3), is also more appropriate to an extended Vita

---

[3] The meaning of this expression is not immediately apparent. It probably
implies that the soldier was not allowed to consort with monks and nuns by the
terms of his oath and so turned up in civilian dress.

[4] Referring to posthumous miracles.

than to a short commemoration of the Synaxarion genre [5]. It may be that the shorter version edited by Delehaye from manuscript D (Paris. gr. 1587) represents an independent attempt at abbreviating the original Life, for, whereas the Sirmondianus describes the emperor's emissary by the vague expression τῶν συμφρόνων ἕνα (i.e. an iconoclast), D designates him more specifically as a μαγιστριανός [6].

Going one step further, I would suggest that the original Vita was written at a date not far removed from the Saint's demise, i.e. in the latter part of the 8th century, and ought, therefore, to be added to the meagre hagiographical production of that period [7]. My reasons for saying so are the following:

1. The author makes no attempt to excuse or explain the foundation by Anthusa of a double monastery. Yet, such establishments were condemned by the Council of 787 and altogether suppressed by the patriarch Nicephorus before 814 [8].

2. Anthusa's prediction about the « manner of life » (τὴν βιοτὴν καὶ τὴν διαγωγήν) of the children of Constantine V gives no inkling of the disastrous fate that awaited his male offspring: all of them were forcibly ordained before Christmas day 780 and mutilated on 15 August 792 [9].

3. The incident of the disguised soldier, if I understand it correctly, appears to show a direct awareness of conditions in the reign of Constantine V. Why, indeed, single out this trivial story unless there was something remarkable in a soldier's coming to a monastery and promising to make an offering?

4. The mention of a *magistrianus* (assuming it goes back to the † original) would appear anachronistic for a text written after the 8th century. Furthermore, it is a general rule that saints' Lives composed after the beginning of the 9th century fall progressively under the influence of atticism, whereas the style of Anthusa's Vita

---

[5] For a similar use of this quotation see, e.g., *Miracula S. Demetrii*, I. 3, ed. P. LEMERLE, *Les plus anciens recueils des Miracles de Saint Démétrius*, I (Paris, 1979), 75.

[6] *Synax. Eccl. CP*, 849. 54.

[7] On which see I. ŠEVČENKO, 'Hagiography of the Iconoclast Period' in *Iconoclasm*, ed. A. BRYER and J. HERRIN (Birmingham, 1977), 113-16.

[8] See P. J. ALEXANDER, *The Patriarch Nicephorus of Constantinople* (Oxford, 1958), 76-7.

[9] Theophanes, de Boor, 454. 21, 468. 11.

seems to have been distinctly colloquial : note the repeated use of
πρός instead of παρά (849. 12 : πρὸς αὐτοῦ κελευσθεῖσα εἰσελθεῖν
— 849. 18 : πρὸς τοῦ θαυματουργοῦ... οἰκεῖν ἐγκελεύεται, and
again at 851. 1, 851. 5, 852. 1) and the unclassical ἀπέστειλεν ἀπελ-
θεῖν = 'bade her go' (849. 29).

If the above remarks have any validity, it would follow that the
notice of St. Anthusa has a good pedigree and may be regarded as
a reasonably trustworthy source. Its historicity is, in any case,
partly confirmed by several *recoupements* :

1. The Synaxarion (and the Synaxarion alone) preserves a notice
of another St. Anthusa, daughter of Constantine V, who was active
in the reign of the empress Irene and died as a nun at the age of 52 [10].
It would be natural to assume that this princess was named after
the saint of Mantineon who had predicted her birth. If so, certain
chronological inferences may be drawn and I shall return to them
later.

2. When St. Peter of Atroa was in his 18th year (AD 791/2), he
was directed by the Virgin Mary to place himself under the direction
of the γέρων Paul who was living in the Phrygian mountains
called τῆς Δαγούτης. This Paul was from the Bucellarian theme
and had entered the monastery of Mantineon as a child (ἐν μονῇ ὑπὸ
τῶν ἐκεῖσε καλουμένῃ Μαντίνειον ἐκ παιδόθεν ἀποταξάμενος).
After pursuing the coenobitic life a long time (μέχρι χρόνου), he
was seconded by his abbot (unnamed) to the personal service of
certain anchorites whom he attended for a number of years (ἐπὶ χρόνους). These men were impressed by his virtue and, deeming it
inappropriate to be served by him, encouraged him to become an
anchorite himself, which he did in the Phrygian mountains [11].
Assuming, at a rough guess, that Paul was about 60 in 791/2, he
must have entered the monastery of Mantineon in the 740's.

3. The most important *recoupement* was made by P. Peeters
and concerns St. Romanus the Younger [12]. A Galatian by birth,
Romanus also joined the monastery of Mantineon as a boy (*a puero*).

---

[10] *Synax. Eccl. CP*, 613-14. The article by Ursula V. Bosch, 'Anthusa. Ein
Beitrag zum Kaisertum der Eirene', in *Byzant. Forschungen*, 1 (1966), 24-29,
is not particularly helpful.

[11] V. Laurent, *La Vie merveilleuse de Saint Pierre d'Atroa* (Bruxelles, 1956 ;
Subs. hagiogr, 29), 77-81.

[12] *Anal. Boll.*, 30 (1911), 393-427.

The establishment is described in the following terms : *Est autem Mantineon lacus, in quo medio locus est siccus, ubi aedificatum fuit monasterium sanctarum virginum ; itemque in litore huius lacus monasterium alterum aedificatum est, quod incolunt sancti patres monachi, prodigiorum patratores* [13]. At the head of the nunnery was a holy woman called Anthusa (Anysia cod.) and it was she who sent Romanus, by that time aged 40, on business to a certain region where he was captured by Arab soldiers and taken a prisoner to Baghdad. Romanus was martyred on 1 May 780 after nine years in captivity ; he was, therefore, apprehended by the Arabs in 771 and must have been born in c. 730 [14]. If we suppose that he entered the monastery in his early teens, he did so shortly before 745, i.e. at the same time as Paul.

The localization of Mantineon, which has been discussed at length by others, need not detain us long. We know from other sources that it was in the general area of Paphlagonia [15] and, more specifically, in the province of Honorias, to whose capital Claudiopolis (Bolu) it was subject [16]. The reference in the Life of St. Romanus to an island in a lake led Peeters to opt for Eftene gölü, a lake about 2 to 3 km. across, usually identified with the ancient Daphnusis [17], to the south-west of Prusias ad Hypium (Üskübü [18]). This has recently been contested by Louis Robert whose learned and complex argument I shall not attempt to summarize. In his view, the lake in question is Çağagöl near Gerede (Crateia/Flaviopolis), some distance to the east of Bolu [19]. Louis Robert is so often right that it would take a bold man to challenge him. Even so, it may be worth expressing the following reservations :

[13] *Ibid.*, 409-10.

[14] *Ibid.*, 393.

[15] SOCRATES, *Hist. eccles.*, II. 38, *P.G.*, 67, 329 ; SOZOMEN, *Hist. eccles.*, IV. 21. 1-2, ed. BIDEZ and HANSEN, 171 ; PHOTIUS, *Bibl.*, cod. 257, ed. HENRY, VIII, 15.

[16] Notice of St. Tatianus or Tation, *Synax. Eccl. CP*, 919. Cf. notice of St. Autonomus, *ibid.*, 37.

[17] Merely, it seems, on the strength of Stephanus Byzantius, Meineke, 223, who describes lake Daphnusis as being πλησίον τοῦ 'Ολύμπου τοῦ Βιθυνοῦ.

[18] Good map in W. VON DIENST, 'Von Pergamon über den Dindymos zum Pontus', in *Petermanns Mitt.*, Ergänzungsband XX, Heft 94 (1899), map II.

[19] *A travers l'Asie Mineure* (Paris, 1980), 132 ff. For all his interest in native names, Robert does not comment on the village Perkile which seems to have escaped attention from the linguistic point of view. Cf. D. DETSCHEW, *Die thrakischen Sprachreste* (Vienna, 1957), s.v. 'per' and '—κειλας'.

1. Çağagöl has no island. To this Robert replies that it was originally bigger than it is today and may well have once had an island — indeed a neighbouring village (whose exact situation is, however, unclear) is called Adaköy = 'island village'.

2. Eftene gölü, argues Robert, must have belonged to the territory of Prusias, not to that of Claudioplis. But then, how do we know that Çağagöl pertained to Claudiopolis rather than to Crateia which is much closer to it? Besides, our only evidence for linking Mantineon to Claudiopolis is a late hagiographical text which should not, perhaps, be pressed too far.

For our present purpose it is not particularly important whether Mantineon was at Eftene or Çağagöl, a question that may perhaps be settled by attentive exploration on the spot. There is, however, one detail, unnoticed by Robert, that is more pertinent, namely that Mantineon was situated on a major east-west highway as proved by the Life of St. Eudocimus. We may recall that Eudocimus, who had been invested with a military command by the emperor Theophilus, died at Charsianon and was buried there [20]. Eighteen months after his demise, his mother, who survived him, proceeded thither from Constantinople with the intention of removing his body which, in the meantime, had proved miraculous. Local opposition prevented her from accomplishing her purpose, but a priest called Joseph managed to steal the body and conveyed it to the capital. Along the way two miracles took place, the second at Mantineon, where a nun of the monastery was healed of an unspecified disease [21]. Evidently, the body was being conveyed by land, by way of Ancyra, Crateia and Claudiopolis, and if a stop was made at Mantineon, this was because it lay on the road.

We are now in a better position to understand the passage of the Synaxarion concerning the visitation of Mantineon by Constantine V. He certainly did not proceed thither $\mu\epsilon\tau\grave{\alpha}$ $\pi\alpha\nu\tau\grave{o}\varsigma$ $\tau o\tilde{v}$ $\sigma\tau\rho\alpha\tau\epsilon\acute{v}\mu\alpha\tau o\varsigma$ merely to interrogate the Saint, but must have been on campaign against the Arabs and stopped by the monastery because it happened to be on his way. If so, however, we obtain an important chronological indication, since the last campaign that Constantine is known to have personally commanded in Asia Minor was in 756 or

---

[20] On the situation of this fortress (west of Sivas) see E. HONIGMANN, 'Charsianon Kastron', in *Byzantion*, 10 (1935), 129-60.

[21] Metaphrastic Life, *BHG* 607, p. 22 ; Laudation by Constantine Acropolites, *BHG* 606, p. 217. The chronology of Eudocimus, as reconstructed by Chr. LOPAREV, *Izvest. Russk. Archeol. Inst. v Konst.*, 13 (1908), 156 ff., strikes me as fanciful.

757 [22]. This conflicts with the view of Peeters [23] that the emperor's visit took place between 771 (the date of Romanus's capture) and 775 (the date of the emperor's death), a view based on the absence of any allusion to that incident in the Life of St. Romanus. I regret to say, however, that Peeters was mistaken. The proof of the matter is provided by the notice of the princess Anthusa who, we are told, was repeatedly pressed to marry by her father (ὑπὸ τοῦ πατρὸς πολλάκις ἀναγκασθεῖσα ζευχθῆναι ἀνδρὶ οὐκ ἐπείσθη) [24], something that could not have happened if she was, at most, four years old when her father died. But if the princess Anthusa was, as I consider evident, named after Anthusa of Mantineon, and if she was born in 756-7 (or earlier), she would have been at least 18 by 775.

We may recall that Constantine V was married three times : first to the Chazar princess Irene by whom he had one son, Leo (the future Leo IV), born on 25 January 749 ; next, to Maria who seems to have died childless in c. 750-51 ; thirdly, to Eudocia who gave him five sons and at least one daughter (Anthusa). According to Lombard [25], the sons were born in the following order :

1. Christopher, born before 753, possibly, he adds, when Maria was still alive.

2. Nicephorus : date of birth unknown. Made Caesar, along with Christopher, on 2 April 769.

3. Nicetas, born in 762 or 763.

4. Anthimus, born in 767 or 768.

5. Eudocimus : date of birth unknown. Made nobilissimus on 23 April 776 by his brother, Leo IV.

The sequence is certain, confirmed as it is by the inscription in the Edirne Museum [26], but we may pause to enquire what induced Lombard to believe that Christopher was born before 753. The only evidence he offers is Theophanes, de Boor, 442, who, after describing the execution, in October 767, of the deposed patriarch Constantine II, remarks : « Did not the wretch [i.e. the emperor] have any respect for the holy font ? For two of his children by his third wife had he [the patriarch Constantine] received in his arms (δύο γὰρ τέκνα αὐτοῦ τῆς τρίτης γυναικὸς ἐν ταῖς ἀγκάλαις αὐτοῦ δεξάμενος ἦν). » This means, of course, that the patriarch Constantine had acted as godfather (ἀνά-

[22] Theophanes, de Boor, 430. Tabari refers to the same events under AH 139 (5 June 756 to 24 May 757) and AH 140 (25 May 757 to 13 May 758) : see E. W. Brooks, 'Byzantines and Arabs in the Time of the Early Abbasids', in *English Hist. Rev.*, 15 (1900), 733.

[23] *Op. cit.*, 395.

[24] *Synax. Eccl. CP*, 613. 19.

[25] *Constantin V, empereur des Romains* (Paris, 1902), 102-3.

[26] See C. Mango and I. Ševčenko in *BZ*, 65 (1972), 385 ff.

δοχος) to two of the emperor's children (sex unspecified) ; and if one
of the two was Christopher, his baptism took place during Constantine's patriarchate, i.e. between 8 August 754 and 30 August 766.
We cannot conclude from this that Christopher was necessarily born
not earlier than 754 (since the reference in Theophanes need not be
to him), but we can conclude that Lombard's date of before 753 is
due to a misunderstanding.

It may be asked whether the visit of Constantine V to Mantineon
could have taken place before 756-7. The answer, I believe, is
negative. The only other occasion that need be taken into account
when Constantine led an expedition against the Arabs was in 750
or 751, an expedition that resulted in the reduction of Theodosio-
polis and Melitene [27]. If the patriarch Nicephorus is to be trusted,
however, the occupation of Melitene coincided, more or less, with
the death of Constantine's second wife, Maria [28]. Since it is most
unlikely that the empress to whom St. Anthusa predicted the birth
of a boy and a girl was Maria, we are left with 756-7 as the only
possible date. The princess Anthusa must, therefore, have been born
in one or other of these two years, and the text of the Synaxarion
strongly suggests that she was one of twins : ἓν ἄρρεν καὶ ἓν θῆλυ
γεννῆσαι ... ἐξεῖπε, [29] which Cod. Bodl. gr. lit. 6, fol. 171ʳ renders
as δύο, ἄρρεν καὶ θύλαι (sic) ἀποτεκεῖν [30]. These twins, I would
further suggest, were the δύο τέκνα to whom the patriarch Constantine acted as godfather.

Our chronological framework is now complete and may be summarized as follows. Anthusa's double monastery was founded not
later than c. 740. The mission of the *magistrianus* probably took
place after the Council of Hieria (754). Constantine V stopped at
Mantineon in either 756 or 757, and the princess Anthusa was born
shortly thereafter. She was, therefore, the twin sister of either
Christopher or Nicephorus ; and, since she lived to the age of 52, she
must have died in either 808 or 809 [31]. It remains to suggest two
inferences of a somewhat broader nature.

[27] Theophanes, de Boor, 427. Brooks, *op. cit.*, Part II, *English Hist. Rev.*, 16
(1901), 88, note 204, argues that the siege of Melitene occurred at latest in the
autumn of 750.

[28] *Breviarium*, de Boor, 65.

[29] *Synax. Eccl. CP*, 851. 4.

[30] On this Ms see F. HALKIN, 'Un nouveau synaxaire byzantin', in *Mélanges
H. Grégoire*, II (1950), 307 ff.

[31] R. JANIN, art. '5. Anthuse', in *Dict. d'hist. et de géogr. eccl.*, III, 538, is

The first concerns the empress Eudocia. It may be too much to say that she was an iconophile, but she certainly appears in the story as the benefactress of an important monastery known for its iconophile sympathies. In other words, Constantine V was in his religious campaign as vulnerable on the « home front » as were later Leo IV with Irene and Theophilus with Theodora. The role of women in undermining iconoclasm is thereby increased.

Secondly, the foundation of Mantineon offers us a faint glimpse into religious conditions in Asia Minor at about the time when iconoclasm was promulgated as the official doctrine of the realm. The activity of Sisinnius, who had come from another province, took place before c. 740, i.e. when Arab armies were still operating not far from the area of Claudiopolis — Nicaea was under siege in 727 and Gangra captured, perhaps in 731. Elsewhere, the bewilderment of the populace found expression in iconoclastic agitation, but at Mantineon, along the military highway, it seems to have bred a more traditional form of revivalism. It is impossible to establish whether Anthusa's monastery was set up before or after the battle of Acroinon which turned the tide of Arab advance, but one cannot help being struck by the size of her following, a community of 900 being quite exceptional by Byzantine standards. Furthermore, among these 900 there were young boys drawn from a fairly wide area — Romanus, we may remember, was a Galatian. Yet, for all his anti-monasticism, Constantine V appears to have allowed this establishment to survive and become more prosperous.

The results we have achieved in this enquiry are, perhaps, rather a slim tribute to Father Halkin, whose manifold contributions to Byzantine studies can best be described in the words of the Synaxarion : to enumerate all of them would be like counting the sand on the seashore or the drops of rain.

Oxford, Exeter College

---

certainly mistaken in saying that she died « dans les dernières années du VIII⁰
siècle », since that would place her birth in 748 at the latest. As previously
suggested by me in *Journal of Theol. Studies*, N.S., 17 (1966), 486, Anthusa was
probably one of 'the emperor's daughters' (τῶν τοῦ βασιλέως θυγατέρων)
who obtained a portion of the relics of St. Euphemia on their return to Constantinople in 796. I do not know who the other daughters were. Text in F. HALKIN,
Euphémie de Chalcédoine (Bruxelles, 1965 ; *Subs. hagiogr.* 41), 103.

X

A FORGED INSCRIPTION OF THE YEAR 781

In saluting the prince of byzantinists upon his attaining the τετάρτη ἐναλλαγὴ τῶν ἀνθρωπίνων ἡλικιῶν, I should like to draw his attention to a minor, but nevertheless curious incident of Iconoclastic times, a period which Prof. Ostrogorsky has done so much to illuminate. I crave his indulgence for having to tell the story backwards.

Jérome Maurand, a Provençal priest who visited St. Sophia in 1544, claims to have seen in it a remarkable Latin inscription. The relevant passage is as follows:

„Nel muro se vedeno le arme sive excusoni di Justiniano imperattore, fatte come quelle che tiengano li gentilhomini de Lascaris [i. e. the Lascaris of Ventimiglia]. Vi se vede anchora una tabula d'oro larga uno palmo et longa doi, inclastrata al ditto muro, ove sono esculpite talle parolle in lettere antiche: christus nascitur ex virgine in eum credo tempore constantini et irenes imperatoribus (sic), o sol, itterum me videbis."[1]

We should note the mistakes in the Latin: imperatoribus (for imperatorum) and itterum; furthermore, nascitur, as we shall presently see, should have been nascetur. Maurand does not specify in which part of the building he saw this inscription.

The only scholar who, to my knowledge, has commented on Maurand's account is J. Ebersolt.[2] He states that the inscription, which he regards as a profession of faith, must have dated from the joint reign of Constantine VI and Irene (780—790); attributes the mistakes to the imperfect knowledge of Latin at that period; and notes that Latin legends continued to appear on Byzantine coins until the eleventh century. But Ebersolt did not know that the inscription in question had a long story behind it.

We may note a somewhat later reference to the same inscription by Reinhold Lubenau (1587):

---

[1] *Itinéraire de Jérome Maurand d'Antibes à Constantinople*, ed. Léon Dorez (Recueil de voyages et de documents pour servir à l'histoire de la géographie, XVII), Paris, 1901, p. 246.

[2] *Constantinople byzantine et les voyageurs du Levant*, Paris, 1918, p. 72, n. 1.

„ . . . auch sol eine grose, guldene Tafel in des turckischen Kaiser Schatz sein, darauf grichisch und lateinisch gegraben: 'Jhesus Christus sol gebohren werden von einer Magt, und ich gleube an in,' welche Tafel in S. Sophien Kirchen gefunden, wie einsmahls ein christlicher Keiser seinen Freundt in S. Sophien Kirchen hatt wollen begraben lassen und das Grab gemachet worden, hatt man einen Mann gefunden ligen und die guldene Tafel neben im, und sol die Tafel landt ihrer Jahrzahl zweitausent Jahr vor Christi Geburt gefertiget sein. Solches erzehlte mihr der Patriarch Hieremias [Jeremias II, 1572—1585], desgleichen der turckische Pfaf, welche mihr S. Sophien Kirche dieselbe zu besuchen und zu besehen erleubet, Mehemet Emir Effendi genandt".[3]

By 1587, therefore, the inscription was no longer in St. Sophia, but allegedly in the Sultan's treasury. The text was said to be both in Greek and Latin. It had been found in St. Sophia, so the story went, inside a tomb dating from 2000 B. C.

Going back in time, we pick up a reference to our inscription in Mandeville's Travels which were written shortly after 1360. I quote from the French version of the Travels:

„Dedenz leglyse de Sainte Sophie vn empereur iadis fist mectre le corps dun sien parent mort; et quant on faisoit la fosse, on trouua vn autre corps dedenz la terre, et sur ce corps vne grande plate dor fin, ou il estoient lectres escriptes en ebrieu, en grigois et en latin, qui disoient ainsi, *Ihesu Crist naistra de la Vierge Marie et ie croy en ly*. Et la date contenoit que celui estoit mis en terre deux mile ans aincois que Ihesu Crist fust nez. Et encore est la plate en la tresorie de leglise; et dit on que ce fut Hermes le sage".[4]

This is evidently the same story as that told by Lubenau, except that a third language has been added to the inscription, Hebrew. The English version of the Travels contains the same passage. In the Egerton text the inscription is given in Latin, *Jhesus Christus nascetur de virgine Maria: et ego credo in eum;* and the wise Hermes, i. e. Hermes Trismegistus, is transformed into Hermogenes.[5]

Whether Mandeville ever visited Constantinople or not, it has been established long ago that his Travels are largely a compilation from older sources. But the precise origin of the passage that concerns us has not been discovered. In his careful investigation, Bovenschen was able to trace it to Oliver Scholasticus (d. 1227), an author whom Mandeville does not appear to have used and who gives the story in a substantially different form.[6] Oliver quotes it in one of his letters as a prophecy of Christ's virgin birth:

---

[3]) *Beschreibung der Reisen des Reinhold Lubenau*, ed. W. Sahm, I/2, Königsberg i. Pr., 1914, p. 175.

[4]) *Mandeville's Travels*, ed. Malcolm Letts (The Hakluyt Society, 2 nd Ser., CI—CII), II, London, 1953, p. 237.

[5]) *Ibid.*, I, pp. 12—13 (Egerton text); II, p. 422 (Bodleian text).

[6]) „Untersuchungen über Johann von Mandeville und die Quellen seiner Reisebeschreibung," *Zeitschr. d. Gesellschaft für Erdkunde zu Berlin*, XXIII (1888), p. 216. Bovenschen is mistaken in stating that the passage in question occurs in Oliver's *Historia Damiatina*.

„Ignotus nobis per nomen proprium propheta eiusdem virginis nomen expressit. Nam in longevis Thracie muris homo quidam fodiens invenit lapideam archam. Quam cum expurgasset et apperuisset, invenit mortuum iacentem et litteras conglutinatas arche continentes hec: Christus nascetur de Maria virgine et in eum credo. Sub Constantino et Hirena imperatoribus, o sol, iterum me videbis. Si hanc prophetiam non admittitis, quia legitur in Romana historia, duorum premissorum prophetarum [i.e. Isaiah and Jeremiah] testimonium sufficit".[7]

Going a little further back, we encounter this story in the letter of Manuel I Comnenus in defence of astrology. A man, he says, was digging near the Long Walls (ἐν τῷ μακρῷ τοίχῳ), i.e. the Anastasian Walls in Thrace, and found a sarcophagus containing an enormous corpse. On the tomb was this inscription: Χριστὸς μέλλει γεννᾶσθαι ἐκ παρθένου Μαρίας καὶ πιστεύω εἰς αὐτόν· ἐπὶ δὲ Κωνσταντίνου καὶ Εἰρήνης τῶν βασιλέων πάλιν ὄψει με, Ἥλιε. In his reply to this letter, Michael Glycas objects that the prediction could not have been humanly made by a pagan "a thousand or more years" before the event; it must have been divinely inspired. The learned editors of these letters, Cumont and Boll, were not able to identify the source of this anecdote.[8]

It is with some surprise, therefore, that we find the ultimate source of the story in so obvious a text as the Chronicle of Theophanes! The details coincide with those given by Manuel; the inscription is the same except for a slight inversion (ὦ ἥλιε, πάλιν με ὄψει). The date of the inscription's discovery is given as the first year of the joint reign of Constantine VI and Irene, i.e. 780/81.[9] From Theophanes this story naturally passed into other chronicles, both Greek and Latin, such as Georgius Monachus,[10] Leo Grammaticus,[11] Cedrenus,[12] Zonaras,[13] on the one hand, Anastasius Bibliothecarius[14] and the *Historia miscella* attributed to Paulus Diaconus,[15] on the other. The last two agree between themselves and with Oliver Scholasticus almost word for word.

A link in the transmission of the story is missing. The entire tradition, both Greek and Latin, prior to Mandeville merely reports the discovery of the sarcophagus near the Long Walls and reproduces the text of the inscription. Nothing is said of St. Sophia. Mandeville, on the other hand, transposes the place of discovery to St. Sophia, says that the inscription was trilingual and, most important, asserts that the in-

---

[7]) *Epistola* 6, ed. Hoogeweg, *Die Schriften des kölner Domscholasters ... Oliverus* (Bibl. d. litterarischen Vereins in Stuttgart, CCII), Tübingen, 1894, p. 309.

[8]) *Catalogus codicum astrol. graec.*, V/1, Brussels, 1904, pp. 116—7, 128—9.

[9]) Ed. de Boor, I, p. 455. Note the scholion: οὗτος Διοσκορίδης ἦν ὁ φιλόσοφος καὶ ταῦτα προεφήτευσεν.

[10]) Ed. de Boor, II, p. 766; ed. Muralt, p. 662.

[11]) Bonn ed., p. 193.

[12]) Bonn ed., II, p. 21.

[13]) Bonn ed., III, p. 286.

[14]) Ed. de Boor, II, p. 302.

[15]) PL 95, col. 1114 A.

scription was preserved in the treasury of St. Sophia. Mandeville's immediate source remains, therefore, unidentified. And if Lubenau did indeed hear this story from the Patriarch Jeremias II, how is it that the version given by him corresponds exactly with Mandeville's and not with that found in the Greek chronicles?

Now, the important question is whether the inscription ever really existed. The only person who claims to have actually seen it is Maurand, and it is on his reliability that the case rests. Although my trust in Renaissance travellers to Constantinople is not unbounded, Maurand's account appears to me to be quite reliable in other respects. He did, for example, copy down the Latin inscription on the base of the obelisk of Theodosius II in the Hippodrome.[16] His transcription breaks off in the fourth verse — he was prevented from completing it — and it does contain a few mistakes;[17] but it is his own transcription, not one he had cribbed from another author. Yet he could have obtained all five lines of the epigram from Buondelmonti's *Liber insularum*.[18]

If Maurand did not himself see the inscription in St. Sophia, then he must have used a literary source. But the version he gives differs significantly from that given in the Latin sources known to me. Anastasius, for example (so also „Paulus Diaconus" with slight variants), has: *Christus nascetur ex Maria virgine, et credo in eum. Sub Constantino vero et Heirene imperatoribus, o sol, iterum me videbis.* If Maurand was using a text of this kind, why did he mar it with several elementary blunders? As a member of the clergy, he must have known Latin well. He was, furthermore, an antiquarian, and after his return from the East compiled a collection of the Latin inscriptions of Antibes which has won him an honorable mention in the *Corpus inscriptionum latinarum*.[19] I conclude that Maurand did see the inscription in St. Sophia which may have been bilingual; he did not attempt to copy the Greek text presumably because he did not know any Greek. The only detail which I hesitate to accept is that the panel was made of gold, for had it been of such precious material, it would have disappeard long before 1544.

But if the inscription existed, and was the one „discovered" in 781, what precisely did it mean? Its message was not explicitly directed against the Iconoclasts: the denial of the Virgin Birth was not part of the official iconoclastic programme, and even Constantine V is not accused of having held such views.[20] In the first year of her regency Irene was mostly

---

[16]) *Itinéraire*, p. 232.

[17]) *Domino* for *dominis* in the first line; *tiranis* for *tyrannis* in the second; *subditque perenny* for *subolique perenni* in the third.

[18]) G. Gerola, „Le vedute di Costantinopoli di Cristoforo Buondelmonti," *Studi bizantini e neoellenici*, III (1931), p. 274.

[19]) XII, p. 28, col. 2.

[20]) Although such an implication could be squeezed out of Constantine's famous dictum: ἡ γὰρ Μαρία αὐτὸν [sc. Christ] ἔτεχεν, ὡς ἔτεχεν ἐμὲ ἡ μήτηρ Μαρία (Theophanes, p. 415). On Constantine's views regarding Mary see Ostrogorsky, *Studien zur Geschichte des byzantinischen Bilderstreites*, Breslau, 1929, p. 29 ff.

concerned with consolidating her position and suppressing the plots of her brothers-in-law; the reversal of iconoclastic measures was to come a few years later. A token of supernatural sanction of the joint reign of Constantine and Irene would obviously have been quite helpful at this juncture. We may remember that it was in the same year (indiction 4 = 780/81) that the popular relics of St. Euphemia, which Constantine V had thrown into the sea, were miraculously „discovered" on Lemnos and brought back with great pomp to Constantinople. It is curious that in describing this incident Theophanes should use the same formula as we have found on the inscription: ἐπὶ δὲ Κωνσταντίνου καὶ Εἰρήνης τῶν εὐσεβῶν βασιλέων ... ἐπανῆλθεν [St. Euphemia] ἐν τῷ τεμένει αὐτῆς.[21]

If my interpretation is correct, we may conclude that Irene's government went to the trouble of fabricating an inscription, in Greek and Latin, and that this inscription was later placed in St. Sophia. A pagan who had died centuries before Christ had prophesied the luminous reign of Constantine and Irene. A new golden age was to begin.

ADDENDUM

As was pointed out to me by Prof. Ihor Ševčenko, our inscription occurs in three Moldavian churches of the 16th century, namely Vatra-Moldoviței (1536), Voroneț (1546), and Sucevița (ca. 1580). In all three churches there is a representation of Plato among the pagan philosophers † who are placed under the Tree of Jesse. His head is surmounted by an open sarcophagus containing a skeleton, next to which is depicted the disk of the sun. The inscription on Plato's scroll, though partly corrupted, is easily identifiable as the one we have been studying. Tte text at Vatra-Moldoviței is as follows: хŝс родитисѧ ѿ дви мр҃їа вькрѕѧ вь него 'при констанътинѣ же и еленѣ прабовѣрнї цр҃ці пкакости моѧ (sic). V. Grecu was able to trace this text to the Rumanian redaction of the Hermeneia which specifies that it had been found on Plato's tomb. In the better manuscripts of the Rumanian Hermeneia the emperors' names are correctly given as "Constantine and Irene", not as "Constantine and Helena"[22].

---

[21] Theophanes, p. 440. Note that in Georgius Monachus, ed. de Boor, II, p. 766, the inscription on the sarcophagus is given as: Χριστὸς μέλλει γεννᾶσθαι ἐκ Μαρίας τῆς παρθένου, καὶ πιστεύω εἰς αὐτόν. ἐπὶ δὲ Κωνσταντίνου καὶ Εἰρήνης τῶν εὐσεβῶν βασιλέων, ὦ ἥλιε, πάλιν με ὄψει.

[22] „Darstellungen altheidnischer Denker und Schriftsleller in der Kirchenmalerei des Morgenlandes," Acad. Roum., Bull. de la sect. hist., XI (1924), pp. 7, 12 f., 18, 52, 55, 59, Cf. I. D. Ştefănescu, L'évolution de la peinture religieuse en Bucovine et en Moldavie, Paris, 1929, pls. 33 (Vatra-Moldoviței), 43 (Voroneț); P. Henry, Les églises de la Moldavie du nord, Paris, 1930, pls. XLI, 1 (Voroneț), LXVI, 1 (Sucevița).

206

Two further instances of the use of this inscription — in Greek — were found by A. von Premerstein[23]: the first in the refectory of Lavra (1512)[24], the second in the church of the Nativity at Arbanassi (1681) in Bulgaria[25]. The text, except for misspellings, is the same in both instances: ῾Ο Χριστὸς μέλλει γεννηθῆναι ἐκ παρθένου Μαρίας, καὶ πιστεύω εἰς αὐτόν. At Lavra this text is on the scroll of the sage Διαλήδ (sic), at Arbanassi on that of Ζηαλίγης, obviously the same person.

Since our inscription is absent from the Greek text of the *Hermeneia*[26], the question arises as to how it came to the cognizance of the Athonite painter and how it later came to be included in the Rumanian *Hermeneia*. Unfortunately, no comprehensive study of the Greek textual tradition of the *Hermeneia* has yet been undertaken, so we cannot exclude the possibility that some manuscripts of this work may contain our inscription. There was, however, yet another channel of transmission, namely the various collections of "prophecies" made by pagan philosophers concerning the advent of Christ. In one such collection, contained in a 16th-century manuscript of the National Library at Athens (cod. 701), Plato is made to prophesy: ... ὁ Χριστὸς μέλλει ἐκ παρθένου Μαρίας γεννηθῆναι · καὶ πιστεύω εἰς αὐτόν. ἐπὶ δὲ εὐσεβοῦς βασιλέως πάλιν ὄψει με [ὄψιμεν cod.] ἥλιε[27]. I have not been able to find this text in any of the earlier versions of the "Prophecies"[28]; an indication, however, that it may have been included in relatively old collections of this kind is provided by a scholion on fol. 221[r] of Paris. gr. 1712 (saec. XII), the well-known manuscript of the Chronicle of Pseudo-Symeon. This, too, has been brought to my attention by Prof. Ševčenko. The scholion, which is in the hand of the principal scribe, refers to the discovery of the sarcophagus in Thrace, and reads as follows: σημ(είωσον) πε(ρὶ) τοῦ ε <ὑρε> θέντ(ος)

---

[23] „Neues zu den apokryphen Heilsprophezeiungen heidnischer Philosophen in Literatur und Kirchenkunst," *Byzant.-neugr. Jahrb.*, IX (1932), p. 366 f. On p. 343, n. 3 of the same study Premerstein notes that the story of the inscription's discovery is quoted by St. Thomas Aquinas. The relevant passage is as follows: „Invenitur etiam in historiis Romanorum quod tempore Constantini Augusti et Helenae matris eius, inventum fuit quoddam sepulcrum in quo iacebat homo auream laminam habens in pectore in qua scriptum erat: 'Christus nascetur ex virgine et ego credo in eum. O sol, sub Helenae et Constantini temporibus iterum me videbis' " (*Summa theol.*, II—II. 2. 7 ad 3). Far from being based od a source older than Theophanes, as Premerstein suggests, this account appears to be a confused version of the story as recorded by later chroniclers.

[24] G. Millet, *Monuments de l'Athos,* Paris, 1927, pl. 151, 3.

[25] A. Grabar, *La peinture religieuse en Bulgarie*, Paris, 1928, pl. LIII.

[26] *Manuel d'iconographie chrétienne*, ed .A. Papadopoulos-Kerameus, St. Petersburg, 1909, p. 82 ff.

[27] A. Delatte, *Anecdota Atheniensia*, I. Liége — Paris, 1927, p. 332.

[28] The basic discussion of these „prophecies" is by A. von Premerstein, Griechisch-heidnische Weise als Verkünder christlicher Lehre in Handschriften und Kirchenmalereien," *Festschrift der Nationalbibliothek in Wien*, Vienna, 1926, p. 647 ff. More recent studies: I. Duičev, „Константин Философ и 'Предсказанията на Мьдрит Елини'," *Зборник радова*, Визант. Инст., IV (1956), p. 148 ff.; Д. Медаковић, „Претставе античких философа и сивила у живопису Богородице Љевишке" *ibid.*, VI (1960), p. 43 ff.

εἰς τ(ὸ) μ<α>κρὸν τεῖ<χος> ἀρχ(αί)ου λαρν<α>κίου καὶ τ<οῦ> ἐν αὐτ(ῷ) κειμ<ένου> ἀνδρὸς (καὶ) ἃ <περὶ> θεολογίας ἔγρα(ψεν). Note the term θεολογία: the collections of pagan „prophecies" were usually entitled χρησμοὶ καὶ θεολογίαι ἑλλήνων φιλοσόφων.

This link between our inscription and the χρησμοί naturally leads us to make a further supposition. In view of the fact that the χρησμοί were in circulation since the latter part of the 5th century, could not the forgers of the 8th century have drawn their inspiration from an opuscule of this kind? What makes this a likely assumption is that the χρησμοί contain at least two other instances of the accidental discovery of pagan inscriptions prophesying the Incarnation of Christ. Such an inscription was allegedly found at Cyzicus during the reign of Leo I, and an identical one at Athens.[29] Another pagan inscription containing an entire Christian credo in hexameters came to light in the first year of Anastasius at Delphi in Italy (sic).[30] If Irene's advisers referred to a collection of χρησμοί for the fabrication of their text (it is characteristic of the period that they were not able to write it in hexameters), it is hardly surprising that at a later date their forgery should itself have † been included in such collections.

Dumbarton Oaks

[29] K. Buresch, *Klaros*, Leipzig, 1889, p. 111 f.; cf. Pitra, *Analecta sacra et classica specil. Solesm. parata*, V/2 (1888), p. 307.

[30] Buresch, *op. cit.*, p. 130 f.; cf. Pitra, *op. cit.*, p. 308.

XI

WHO WROTE THE CHRONICLE OF THEOPHANES?

*To the memory of George
Ostrogorsky*

In a recent article I made some comments on the Chronicle of Theophanes in the context of the bibliographic resources that might have been available in a Bithynian monastery in the early 9th century.[1] These comments were expressed on the assumption (which it did not occur to me to question) that the Chronicle was indeed the work of Theophanes Confessor and that it was written approximately between the years 811—14. A fresh perusal of the Chronicle and a few other relevant texts, all of them well known, has led me, however, to entertain some serious doubts concerning the correctness of such a belief.

The first piece of evidence to be considered is the Preface to the Chronicle (ed. de Boor, 3—4). In this short statement Theophanes (who is undoubtedly its author) tells us that the monk George, who had been Synkellos of the Patriarch Tarasios, had written a most accurate chronography from Creation to the Emperor Diocletian; and that when he had come to the end of his life and was about to depart unto the Lord „in the Orthodox faith," he entrusted to Theophanes, who was his friend, the book he had composed (presumably with a view to its publication) and gave him ἀφορμάς so as to complete it. Theophanes, aware as he was of his own inadequacy for such a great task, was unwilling to undertake it; but since George had begged him most earnestly to do so, he had no choice but to obey. Thereupon, Theophanes, too, „sought out many books" to the best of his ability and continued the work down to the reign of Michael I and the latter's son Theophylaktos. He made excerpts from ancient historians and arranged them chronologically, year by year, but did not compose anything of his own (οὐδὲν ἀφ'ἑαυτῶν συντάξαντες).

Straightforward as this Preface appears to be, it does raise a few questions.[2] In particular, what is the exact meaning of ἀφορμαί? My earlier sug-

---

[1] „The Availability of Books in the Byzantine Empire, A. D. 750—850" in *Byzantine Books and Bookmen* (Washington, D. C., 1975), 35 ff.

[2] One may wonder, for example, whether the words ἐξεδήμησεν ἐν ὀρθοδόξῳ πίστει (p. 3, 26) are merely a formula or whether they call attention to the fact that George was not an iconoclast.

10

gestion that it refers to 'incipits' (literally 'starting points') stands in need of correction: 'materials' is a more appropriate rendering.[3] If so, what was the nature and extent of these materials, and how much additional research and writing was Theophanes compelled to do? Furthermore, should we take literally his assertion that he had written nothing of his own, or should we allow (as is normally done) that the final part of the Chronicle was the Confessor's personal composition? Some biographical data may help us, if not to answer these questions, at least to place them in a proper perspective.

We do not know when George Synkellos died, but we do know that he was still writing in 810. He himself gives this date on p. 389 of his Chronicle (Bonn ed.) and on p. 4 he likewise states his intention of continuing his narrative down to the year 810. It is true that he is here guilty of an inconsistency: for after invoking divine help to demonstrate that Christ was born in A. M. 5500 and to narrate the events of the next 802 years (which, by the Alexandrian reckoning, yields 810), he goes on to give a different calculation:

Life of Christ	33 years 40 days
Subsequent period	766 years 10 months 20 days
Total	800 years,

i.e. down to the year 6300, indiction 1 (807/8). The latter date is also given on p. 10. From this one may conclude that the prefatory matter of George's Chronicle was first written in 808 and somewhat absent-mindedly revised by the author in 810. If, however, he wrote his text in sequence and assuming that the date on p. 389 is not also due to a revision, we have to allow some time for the composition of the next 345 pages of the Bonn edition. Obviously, one can think of several possible explantions, but it would be rash to conclude on this evidence that George died in 810 or 811. He could have lived on another couple of years.

As for the Chronicle of Theophanes, it is quite clear that it was completed before the latter part of 814, since on p. 502 (de Boor) Leo V is described as „pious" (εὐσεβής) and his elevation to the throne as „most legitimate" (ἐννομώτατος) — an observation that has already been made by Ostrogorsky.[4] We know that Leo took his first overt actions against icons in December

---

[3] Cf. Georgius Monachus, ed. de Boor, I, 199, with reference to Solomon's lost works on natural science that were plagiarized by the Greeks: ἀφ' ὧν οἱ τῶν Ἑλλήνων ἰατροσοφισταὶ σφετερισάμενοι καὶ τὰς ἀφορμὰς εἰληφότες, etc. Ibid., II, 456, with reference to Origen, from whom Arius τὰς ἀφορμὰς εἴληφε.

[4] Article „Theophanes", RE, 2. Reihe, V (1934), 2129. It is hardly necessary to discuss here the suggestion made by H. Grégoire in Byzantion, 11 (1936), 417, and in Bull. de la Classe des Lettres, Acad. Royale de Belgique, 5e sér., t. 22 (1936), 420 ff., namely that Theophanes is dependent on the so-called Dujčev fragment describing the Bulgarian expedition of Nikephoros I in 811. In the first place, the alleged dependence is far from conclusive. Secondly, Grégoire himself argued that the Dujčev fragment formed part of the same chronicle as the Scriptor Incertus de Leone who is, in any case, later than 820. The chronicle in question could not, therefore, have been used as a source by Theophanes. Dujčev himself in „La chronique byzantine de l'an 811", Travaux et Mémoires 1 (1965), 242 ff., while appearing to accept Grégoire's reasoning, leaves the question in suspense. Cf. also below, note 18a.

814. Furthermore, it was probably at the very beginning of 815 that Theophanes, along with other prominent abbots, was summoned to Constantinople from his monastery of Megas Agros. He was detained a little over two years in the capital, then exiled to Samothrace, where he died 23 days after his arrival, on 12 March 817.[5]

A few years ago Ihor Ševčenko and myself concluded from these data that the Chronicle must have been written entirely at Megas Agros.[6] It would also follow that the entire work, which fills 503 pages in de Boor's edition, must have been completed in about three years — not a very likely supposition if one takes into account not only the actual writing, but also the preparatory research and the complex process of chronological computation.

But there is more. In the 50th year of his life, i.e. in 810, Theophanes was afflicted with a kidney disease which left him bed-ridden for the rest of his life.[7] He was incapacitated to such an extent that when the imperial emissaries came to convey him to the capital in 815, he was unable to walk the short distance from the monastery to the seashore and had to be taken down on a cart.[8] His once portly frame wasted away and he became as thin as a skeleton.[9] We must, therefore, assume not only that the Chronicle was written in the incredibly short time span of some three years, but also by a man who was too ill to stir from his bed.

One further consideration: Theophanes was not a man of much culture.[10] This is clearly stated by Theodore the Studite[11] and is confirmed from other quarters. In those days education was more or less synonymous with service in the imperial *secreta* or in the Patriarchate, whereas the background of Theophanes appears to have been military or, at any rate, that of a rich landed squire. He devoted his adolsecence to „hunting and riding.[12]"

---

[5] So *C. Van de Vorst*, „En quelle année mourut S. Théophane le Chronographe?" *AnalBoll*, 31 (1912), 148 ff. Most scholars have followed Pargoire in dating the death of Theophanes to 818.

[6] „Some Churches and Monasteries on the Southern Shore of the Sea of Marmara," *DOP*, 27 (1973), 265.

[7] *Methodii ... Vita S. Theophanis Confessoris*, ed. *V. V. Latyšev, Mém. de l'Acad. des Sciences de Russie*, VIIIe sér., Cl. hist.-philol., XIII/4 (1918), 27, §§43—44.

[8] *Ibid.*, 29, §46. Cf. *Mango and Ševčenko, DOP*, 27 (1973), 262.

[9] [C. Van de Vorst] „Un panégyrique de S. Théophane le Chronographe par S. Théodore Studite," *AnalBoll*, 31 (1912), 22, §7. Cf. Theodore Studite, *Ep.* 140, ed *Mai, Nova Patrum Bibl.*, VIII/1, 124: νόσου δεινοπαθοῦς λίαν. *Ep.* 205, *ibid.*, 176: ἐν νόσῳ χαλεπωτάτῃ, κλινήρης ὅλος. *Ep.* II, 31, PG 99, 1204: ἐν τοιαύτῃ χαλεπωτάτῃ νόσῳ ὡς ἐνδεῶς ἔχειν καὶ τοῦ ἐπὶ κλίνης στρέφεσθαι.

[10] It is true that, according to Genesius, Bonn ed., 15, Theophanes was the author of a satirical or polemical poem in which he described the nocturnal visit of Leo V to a certain monk Antony and the emperor's deception by Theodotos Kassiteras. The story, however, is highly suspect, and even if there was some truth in it, Theophanes would have been ill advised to poke fun at the reigning emperor.

[11] „Panégyrique," 22, §8: δογματικός, καίτοι γε ἄπειρος ὢν τῆς μωρανθείσης σοφίας. The gift of discernment which Theophanes possessed was due to the purity of his heart and he was thereby able to surpass πολλοὺς τῶν γραμματίζειν καὶ φιλοσοφεῖν δοκούντων.

[12] Methodius, *Vita Theophanis*, 4, §6: κυνηγέσια καὶ ἱππάσια (sic).

12

The rank of *strator* that was conferred on him by Leo IV and the mission of supervising the fortification of Cyzicus are also indicative of a military rather than an intellectual inclination. Only when he had become a monk and retired to the island of Kalonymos did he take up the practice of calligraphy in which he had not been previously instructed (καλλιγραφίας τεχνικῆς καὶ εὐθέτου, εἰ καὶ ἀδιδάκτου) and so, by dint of much patience, was able to acquire expertise ἐπί τε τόνου καὶ γραφῆς ἀπαρόλισθα.[13] Of course, calligraphy was a specialized craft and even an educated man need not have been versed in it, although he would have been expected to have a grasp of correct accentuation and spelling. Finally, the Preface to the Chronicle (and we may remember that traditionally a preface called for 'fine' writing) is marked by a decidedly inelegant style. On a single page we may note πολλὰ παρακαλέσας (4, 5), which is colloquial; the uncouth εἰς τὰ ὑπὲρ ἡμᾶς ἐγχειρήσαντες (4, 7) in the sense of „having undertaken a task above my powers," and following closely after ὡς ὑπὲρ ἡμᾶς τὴν ἐγχείρησιν οὖσαν (4, 4); the further repetition τετάχαμεν ... κατατάττοντες (4, 15); and the ungrammatical ἡμῖν τοῖς ἀμαθέσι ... διὰ τὸν κύριον ὑπερ–εὔξηται (4, 21) instead of ἡμῶν τῶν ἀμαθῶν.

In view of the above considerations, the following hypothesis unavoidably comes to mind: Can it be that Synkellos compiled a bulky dossier on the period from Diocletian to the Emperor Nikephoros (or even Michael I) and, shortly before his death, conveyed it to Theophanes for minor editing and publication? That he intended to cover this period is explicitly stated by him, and he even specifies that he would forsake the authority of older historians when describing the events that happened in his own lifetime and would lay particular stress on the Ishmaelite apostasy and the consequent persecution of „our race" (τοῦ γένους ἡμῶν).[14] Is not the Chronicle of Theophanes this very dossier? That it is a file (and a very poorly edited one at that) rather than a finished work is apparent time and time again: the extracts, drawn from various sources, have been merely transcribed, so that the style of the Chronicle changes from one page to the next; the same persons sometimes appear under different names; cross-references are not picked up.[15] Such carelessness, however, does not in itself indicate the identity of the principal author. To test our hypothesis we have to discover more definite clues pointing to either Synkellos or Theophanes.

There are only four facts known about Synkellos and we have already mentioned three of them, namely that he was a monk, that he served as Synkellos under the Patriarch Tarasios (784—806), and that he was still writing in 810. The fourth is that he resided for a considerable time in Palestine, for he says, with reference to Rachel's tomb (between Jerusalem and Bethlehem), ταύτης ἐγὼ τὴν λάρνακα τῆς γῆς ὑπερκειμένην πολλάκις ἐκεῖσε παροδεύων ἐπὶ Βηθλεὲμ καὶ τὴν Παλαιὰν λεγομένην Λαύραν τοῦ ὁσίου Χα-

---

[13] *Ibid.*, 16, §22.
[14] Bonn ed., 10.
[15] For example, the Persian general Shahrvaraz is called both Σαρβαραζᾶς and Σάρβαρος depending on the source Theophanes happens to be using. At 355, 29 a certain John Pitzigaudes, imperial ambassador under Constantine IV, is described as ὁ πολλαχῶς λεχθεὶς πανεύφημος ἀνήρ, although he had been mentioned only once before, etc.

ρίτωνος ἑώρακα (Bonn ed., 200—01). This suggests that he was a monk in one of the Orthodox monasteries of Palestine, most probably that of St. Chariton, otherwise known as Souka.[16] He may have been a Palestinian or a Syrian, although in the 8th century the monasteries in question still attracted recruits from many parts of the Near East. The chances are that he knew some Arabic and/or Syriac. From this we may conclude that Synkellos would have shown particular interest in the events of Syria-Palestine, whereas there is nothing in the biography of Theophanes that would account for such an interest.

It is, of course, well-known that 'Theophanes' (as we shall henceforth designate the Chronicle that goes under his name) is very fully informed about the Arab world and especially events in Syria and Palestine, and is unique in this respect among Byzantine chroniclers. For the 7th and 8th centuries he relies heavily on a lost oriental source which was related to Michael the Syrian and the Syriac Chronicle of 846. We are not here concerned with the identity of this source, though we may note that it extended at least as far as 780.[17] Brooks, in his fundamental discussion of this topic,[18] has suggested that the source in question was a chronicle written in Greek by a Melkite monk in Palestine and that it reached Constantinople at the time of the dissolution of the Christian monasteries in 813. The latter date cannot, in any case, be accepted in the light of the foregoing discussion, since it does not allow sufficient time for the incorporation of the relevant material into 'Theophanes', nor need we now resort to a theory of this kind. It is much simpler to suppose that George brought this oriental chronicle along when he departed from Palestine to Constantinople, and if he did so shortly after 784 (when Tarasios was made patriarch), say at the time of the convocation of the Seventh Ecumenical Council, it is easy to understand why this source extended as far and no farther than it did. Originally, this chronicle must have been written in Syriac and it is not inconceivable that George himself could have translated it into Greek. In view, however, of

---

[16] On which see [S. Vailhé] ,,La laure de Souka ou la Vieille Laure," *Bessarione,* 3 (1897—8), 50 ff.; *id.,* ,,Répertoire alphabétique des monastères de Palestine," *Rev. de l'Orient Chrétien,* 4 (1899), 524—25; *D. J. Chitty, The Desert a City* (Oxford, 1966), 14—15. Synkellos provides other Palestinian reminiscences as well. At p. 268, with reference to the wanderings of the Israelites described in the Book of Numbers, he comments that the distance between Kadesh-barnea and the valley of Zared was less than five days, ὡς ἡμεῖς ἐπειράθημεν. At pp. 272--73, with reference to the Passover celebration at Gilgal (Joshua 5. 10—11), he adds that μέχρι νῦν new corn was harvested near Jericho at the spring equinox, which corn was used by the church of Jerusalem for the preparation of the Easter eucharist. Cf. also the reference at p. 244 to the manna from Parthia which the author had tasted.

[17] Dr. P. Speck has suggested to me that the oriental chronicle continued to 786 and contained the notice of the accession of Harun ar-Rashid on p. 461, 9.

[18] ,,The Sources of Theophanes and the Syriac Chroniclers," *BZ,* 15 (1906), 578 ff. Cf. *P. Peeters,* Πασαγνάθης — Περσογενής, *Byzantion,* 8 (1933), 405 ff.; *N. Pigulevskaja,* ,,Theophanes' Chronographia and the Syrian Chronicles," *JÖBG,* 16 (1967), 55 ff. See now also the detailed study by *A. S. Proudfoot,* ,,The Sources of Theophanes for the Heraclian Dynasty," *Byzantion,* 44 (1974), especially 405 ff. A Syriac source may also lie behind the muddled notice concerning Peter of Maiouma (Theophanes, 416—17), as argued by *P. Peeters,* ,,La Passion de S. Pierre de Capitolias," *AnalBoll,* 57 (1939), 299 ff.

the rather distinctive idiom of the 'oriental' passages, I prefer to believe that the Greek version was prepared by another hand. This problem needs further investigation, but it is not one that is directly relevant to our present purpose.

The interest in Near Eastern affairs that is apparent in 'Theophanes' is not, however, limited to the extracts from the oriental chronicle. Two other passages have to be considered. The first (p. 484) describes the disorders that took place in the Arab dominions following the death of Harun ar-Rashid (809). „For this reason," we read, „the churches in the holy city of Christ our God [Jerusalem] were devastated as well as the monasteries of the two great lavras, that of St. Chariton and St. Kyriakos and that of St. Sabas, and the other koinobia, namely those of St. Euthymios and St. Theodosios. The slaughter [resulting from] this anarchy, both among themselves [the Arabs] and against us (κατ' ἀλλήλων καὶ ἡμῶν) continued for five years." The use of ἡμῶν (which echoes τοῦ γένους ἡμῶν in Synkellos, p. 10) indicates that the author was identifying with the Christian population of Palestine. It may also be noticed that the lavra of St. Chariton is mentioned in the first place, before the μεγίστη λαύρα of St. Sabas. This is not a natural order, but it is quite understandable if the passage had been written by a former monk of St. Chariton.

The second passage concerns the same events, but is inserted under A. M. 6305 (A. D. 813), thus marking the end of the fiveyear period of troubles. Here (p. 499) we read: „General anarchy having prevailed in Syria, Egypt, Africa and all of their [the Arabs'] other dominions . . . the venerable places of the holy Anastasis, of Golgotha and the others that are in the holy city of Christ our God were profaned. And likewise the famous lavras of the desert, that of St. Chariton and that of St. Sabas, and the rest of the churches and monasteries were made desolate. And some of them [the monks] were slain in the manner of martyrs, while others reached Cyprus and from there Byzantium, and were graciously received as guests by Michael, the pious emperor, and Nikephoros, the most-holy patriarch." It may be argued, of course, that since the refugees came to Constantinople, news of their suffering could easily have reached Theophanes. Yet, it seems to me that the two passages are by the same hand; in both of them St. Chariton is mentioned before St. Sabas, and the use of ἡμῶν in the first extract points to George rather than to Theophanes.

If this argument is accepted, it would follow that George was still writing, not only in 810, but as late as 813. This possibility, contrary as it is to accepted belief, requires further justification. Now it is a matter of common knowledge that 'Theophanes' shows a pathological hatred of the emperor Nikephoros I whom he denigrates more than any previous ruler, except perhaps Constantine V. The two Triphyllios brothers, namely Niketas, Domestic of the Schools, and Sisinnios, also receive a fair share of abuse. Furthermore, it seems evident to me that whoever wrote the account of these years was actually resident in the capital at the time. This is proved by the following incident. When Nikephoros set out from Constantinople in May 811 on his ill-fated Bulgarian campaign, he raised the rates due from churches and monasteries and exacted tax arrears for an eight-year period from the households of *archons*. The unpopularity of these measures was expressed to the emperor by the patrician Theodosios Salibaras, but Nikephoros brushed him aside with the words, „If God has hardened my heart as He hardened the Pharaoh's heart, what good will come to my subjects? Do not, O Theodosios, expect from Nikephoros anything but what you see." These very words, 'Theophanes' tells us he heard from the lips of Theodosios: ταῦτα, κύριος οἶδεν, αὐτὸς ἐγὼ ξώσῃ φωνῇ ὁ συγγραφόμενος ἀκήκοα παρὰ Θεοδοσίου (490, 3). Now it should be observed that Theodosios Salibaras accompanied the emperor on campaign and was killed (or, possibly, captured) in the great débacle of 26 July 811 (491, 7).[18a] It is quite inconceivable that after setting out from Constantinople with the imperial army he should have taken a quick trip to Megas Agros to have a chat with Theophanes. Of course, it may be argued that Theophanes himself happened to come to Constantinople at this very juncture, although this is not recorded in any of his Vitae and in spite of his painful illness. Could he not, for example, have come to consult a physician? Such a possibility cannot be ruled out, but it remains to explain why Theophanes should have regarded the Emperor Nikephoros with such violent hatred.

The only obvious reason that comes to mind is that the emperor's fiscal measures would have been detrimental to Megas Agros as they were to other monasteries. It may also be conjectured that Theophanes had other, possibly private motives that are unknown to us,[19] although they were probably known at the time; if so, it was surely tactless of the Patriarch Methodios to have inserted in his panegyric of Theophanes some fulsome praise of that very emperor.[20] It is, on the other hand, much easier to explain why George would have hated the Emperor Nikephoros. First, he must have owed his appointment as Synkellos to the Empress Irene: the man who overthrew her (and the same goes for the Triphyllios brothers who played an important part in the coup) was naturally his enemy. But there is more.

[18a] The fate of Salibaras has recently been discussed by *Dujčev*, „La chronique byzantine de l'an 811," 222, who concludes that this man was not killed by the Bulgarians, and that Theophanes mentions him simply as a member of the emperor's entourage. He further points out that another Byzantine dignitary singled out in the same context, namely Peter the patrician, was taken captive by the enemy and was later liberated, as attested by the *Synax. eccles. Constant.*, ed. Delehaye, 792. Dujčev's argument is not, however, acceptable. When 'Theophanes' wrote, ἐπελθόντες οἱ βάρβαροι κατὰ τῆς Νικηφόρου σκηνῆς καὶ τῶν σὺν αὐτῷ μεγιστάνων ἀναιροῦσι τοῦτον οἰκτρῶς, ἐν οἷς ἦν καὶ Ἀέτιος πατρίκιος, καὶ Πέτρος πατρίκιος, ... καὶ Θεοδόσιος πατρίκιος ὁ Σαλιβαρᾶς, ὁ πολλὰ λυπήσας καὶ κακὰ ἐνδειξάμενος τῇ μακαρίᾳ Εἰρήνῃ, ... καὶ πολλοὶ ἄρχοντες τῶν θεμάτων σὺν ἀπείροις λαοῖς, πᾶσά τε ἡ τῶν Χριστιανῶν καλλονὴ διεφθάρη, he evidently *believed* that all these men perished at the time. He had no reason to know that Peter the patrician was taken captive and was later to be freed. If he knew that Salibaras had survived and had actually (as Dujčev assumes) conversed with him after the débacle, he would not have expressed himself as he did. Furthermore, the clause referring to the harm that Salibaras had caused to the Empress Irene implies that he was suitably punished for his misdeeds. Hence Dujčev is mistaken in suggesting that the detailed account of the Bulgarian campaign in Theophanes is based on the oral testimony of Salibaras.

[19] Cf. *Ostrogorsky*, art. „Theophanes" (as in note 4, *supra*), 2128: „Diesen Hass, der von anderen kirchlichen Schriftstellern jener Zeit keineswegs geteilt wurde ... wird man schwerlich anders erklären können als durch irgendwelche Enttäuschungen persönlicher Art, von denen jedoch die Biographen des T. schweigen."

[20] *Vita Theophanis*, 26, §41.

For in February 808, when the conspiracy of Arsaber was uncovered, the emperor punished by flogging, banishment and confiscation „not only lay dignitaries, but also holy bishops and monks and those of the Great Church, namely the Synkellos, the Sakellarios and the Chartophylax, men of high repute and worthy of respect" (pp. 483—84). Could George have been the Synkellos in question? Even if he was not, and the person referred to was a different Synkellos of the sitting Patriarch Nikephoros, we may be sure that many of George's friends and colleagues were purged on this occasion.

There are several other passages of the Chronicle that I would be inclined to attribute to George. Such is the literal quotation from the *citatorium* concerning the translation of Germanos from the see of Cyzicus to that of Constantinople (pp. 384—85), and the long speech of the Patriarch Tarasios that is given verbatim (458—60). Both of these documents probably belonged to the patriarchal archives, to which George must have had easy access. I think that George is the likely author of the personal reminiscence concerning the return of the relics of St. Euphemia in 796: τοῦτο δὲ τὸ ... θαῦμα ... σὺν τοῖς εὐσεβεστάτοις βασιλεῦσι καὶ Ταρασίῳ τῷ ἁγιωτάτῳ πατριάρχῃ ἡμεῖς τεθεάμεθα (p. 440, 7).[21] I would also attribute to George the unflattering references to Theodore the Studite and St. Platon (pp. 481, 22; 498, 20),[22] and, possibly, the account of the adornment of Tarasios's tomb by Michael I (p. 500, 10).

By now the reader may be wondering whether, in my view, any part of the Chronicle should be ascribed to Theophanes. Setting aside the personal recollection of the severe winter of 764 (p. 434, 23), which is ambiguous,[23] I would suggest that the abbot of Megas Agros had little part in the compilation of the work that has made his name immortal and which, incidentally, is not mentioned in any of his Vitae. We may imagine that in 813 George, who felt the end of his life approaching, handed over to Theophanes his bulky dossier and asked him to fill in certain gaps or verify certain chronological calculations — a task that necessitated looking up „many books."[24] But what did he understand by „many books"? Perhaps not more than five or six.

---

[21] This has already been seen by *I. Ševčenko*, „Hagiography of the Iconoclast Period" in *Iconoclasm*, ed. *A. Bryer and J. Herrin* (Birmingham, 1977), 124 n. 87.

[22] Admittedly, Theophanes and Theodore the Studite took opposite sides over the Moechian affair: „Panégyrique," 23, §10; *Ep.* II, 31, PG 99, 1204. There does not appear, however, to have been any great bitterness between the two of them. Besides, since Theophanes was Theodore's ἀνάδοχος, it would have been unseemly for him to make disparaging remarks about his spiritual son. George, on the other hand, might well have entertained a more open aversion towards the two abbots who had broken communion with the Patriarch Tarasios.

[23] In 764 Theophanes was four years old. I doubt if a child of that age would have been allowed by his anxious mother to climb, along with thirty playmates, on top of one of the icebergs that had floated down the Bosphorus. Such amusement would better fit a somewhat older boy. If, on the other hand, it is George who is reminiscing here, we would have to conclude that he, too, grew up at Constantinople, which is not impossible.

[24] We may wonder, though we cannot explain why George chose to entrust his manuscript to a relatively uncultivated man like Theophanes. The safety of a Bithynian monastery and the high connections of its abbot may have been factors that influenced his decision to do so. It may also be that Theophanes was good at sums: in the Preface to the Chronicle he appears to lay great emphasis on computation.

The sceptical reader may also require some stylistic proof of my hypothesis. The reason I have refrained from a stylistic analysis is precisely because the Chronicle is a dossier: with the exception of the final part, it is practically impossible to determine what portions were written by the author. Even the final part represents, in my opinion, an unrevised version whereas the Chronicle of Synkellos may, with some justification, be regarded as a 'final' text. How far-reaching a stylistic revision could be is made apparent by the London and Vatican versions of the *Breviarium* of Nikephoros.

If the theory put froward here meets with a measure of acceptance, it will, I believe, provide a reasonable explanation of certain difficulties that would have otherwise remained rather puzzling. We shall no longer have to suppose that a work as lengthy and as complex as the Chronicle of Theophanes was completed in three years by a man who, as far as we can tell, had neither the scholarly training nor the bibliographic resources for such a task. The unusual interest shown by 'Theophanes' in eastern affairs and, in particular, in the fate of the Melkite community under Arab domination will be accounted for. We may also gain a valuable insight into the chronological tangle that has caused so much difficulty to students of the Chronicle. Among the various hypotheses that have been proposed to explain the occasional discrepancy between the *annus mundi* and the indiction, the most convincing, it seems to me, is that of Grumel, namely that for 'Theophanes' as for Synkellos, the year started on the 25th of March.[25] Yet the difficulty remained that a true Byzantine like Theophanes would naturally have reckoned from the 1st of September. If, however, the chronology of 'Theophanes' is nothing more than the chronology of Synkellos, everything becomes clear. Synkellos used the Alexandrian era and had each year start in March not only for symbolical reasons, but also because this very system was current at that time in the ecclesiastical circles of Palestine.[26]

One last remark. The Chronicle of Synkellos combined with 'Theophanes' represents the greatest achievement of Byzantine historical scholarship and presupposes the utilization of a vast body of material, much of which would have been otherwise unknown to us. For the history of Byzantine civilization it is a matter of some importance to determine where and under what circumstances this work was carried out. If we regard Synkellos/'Theophanes' as a product of Constantinopolitan scholarship, we are thereby making a statement concerning the intellectual climate and bibliographic resources of the capital at a very crucial period, namely a few decades before the beginning of the 9th century 'renaissance.' If, on the other hand, we consider this great compilation as a combined product of Palestinian and Constantinopolitan resources — and I suggest we ought to do so — we are opening up different perspectives which may be found illuminating from ✝ other viewpoints as well.[27]

---

[25] ,,L'année du monde dans la Chronographie de Théophane," *Echos d'Orient* 33 (1934), 396 ff.

[26] Cf. *V. Grumel, La chronologie* (Paris, 1958), 95 n. 4.

[27] For some interesting observations on the intellectual activity of Melkites during this period see *A. Van Roey,* ,,La lettre apologétique d'Elie à Léon, syncelle de l'évêque chalcédonien de Harran," *Le Muséon,* 57 (1944), 1 ff.

XII

Observations on the Correspondence of Ignatius, Metropolitan of Nicaea (first half of the ninth century)

The Correspondence of Ignatius has suffered a strange fate. In January 1903 Daniel Serruys announced before the Académie des Inscriptions et Belles-Lettres his discovery of sixty-four letters of the Patriarch Ignatius of Constantinople. These were contained in a tenth-century manuscript at Vatopedi which, however, did not give their author's name; the attribution of the letters to the famous Patriarch was based on a number of personal allusions and on the fact that "Ignace se nomme lui-même dans une lettre adressée à Nicéphore, diacre et archiviste." Serruys offered a brief analysis of the new document. The letters dealing with administrative matters, he said, showed Ignatius's complete subordination to the imperial government, while the "intimate" letters revealed a mind much more mediocre and traditional than that of Photius. The French scholar also drew attention to the wealth of classical citations contained in the letters and to the monotonous use made in them of clausulae ending in a double accentual dactyl.[1]

In the same year 1903 the sixty-four letters were published by Manuel Gedeon in a collection entitled *Νέα βιβλιοθήκη ἐκκλησιαστικῶν συγγραφέων.*[2] They appeared under the title *Ἀδήλου (Θεοφάνους Νικαίας) ἐπιστολαί*, without any introductory statement except that the text had been taken from cod. Vatopedi 1035 (in fact 588) of the eleventh century.[3] At first sight it was by no means evident that the letters discovered by Serruys were the same as those published by Gedeon; they were, however, promptly equated by J. Pargoire on the basis of the first typographic sheet of Gedeon's edition which he obtained on 5 September 1903. Pargoire went one step further: he rightly saw that the author of the letters was neither the Patriarch Ignatius nor Theophanes of Nicaea (i. e. St. Theophanes Graptos), but Ignatius of Nicaea, better known as Ignatius the deacon, the biographer of the Patriarchs Nicephorus and Tarasius.[4] No further fascicules of Gedeon's *Νέα βιβλιοθήκη* were published, and even the first attracted little attention:[5] today very few copies of it are in existence. In 1911 Gedeon revived

---

[1] Comptes rendus Acad. Inscr., 1903, 38ff., 57.

[2] Vol. I, fasc. 1, Constantinople 1903, cols. 1—64.

[3] The manuscript is described by S. Eustratiades and Arcadios, Catal. of the Greek MSS in the Library of the Monastery of Vatopedi, Cambridge, Mass. 1924, 115, where it is attributed to the twelfth century (in fact, it appears to be of the tenth). It contains, in addition to the Letters that concern us, part of the commentary by Nonnus on the mythological and secular allusions in Gregory of Nazianzus, and thirty-four letters to the Patriarch Photius.

[4] Lettres inédites d'Ignace de Nicée, Echos d'Orient, 6, 1903, 375—8.

[5] It was, however, reviewed, once again by Pargoire, in Vizant. Vrem. 10, 1903, 633—4.

404

his project under a different title, namely ᾿Αρχεῖον ἐκκλησιαστικῆς ἱστορίας, of which four fascicules were published, the last on 10 July 1914. In this fourth fascicule the letters of Ignatius were reprinted (they occupy pp. 420–487), this time with a short preface. Here Gedeon explains that the transcription of the text from the manuscript as well as the annotations had been the work of the deacon Anthimos of Vatopedi, and that the original edition, i. e. that in the Νέα βιβλιο-θήκη, had been destroyed (καταστραφέντος), which explains its rarity. He further maintains his attribution of the letters to Theophanes as against Pargoire whom he quaintly calls the "papal cleric Paregorios". In the ᾿Αρχεῖον edition the call-number of the manuscript is given once again erroneously, as 388, and there are a few additional annotations to the text.

Alas, Gedeon had no better luck with the second edition of the Letters than he had had with the first. The fourth fascicule of the ᾿Αρχεῖον was never put on the market, and, as far as I know, survives today in a unique copy from Gedeon's personal collection, now preserved in the Gennadius Library. A manuscript note by one G. Arvanitidis on the last page of the book explains that the entire edition was stolen from the press before it could be distributed.

Under the above circumstances, it is hardly surprising that the Letters of Ignatius should have remained practically unknown to the scholarly world. H.-G. Beck in his compendious work on the Byzantine Church mentions their existence, but adds that he was unable to consult them.[1] Ignatius does not appear in the list of Byzantine epistolographers compiled by N. B. Tomadakis.[2] Even in specialised articles devoted specifically to Ignatius his Letters have not been utilised.[3] Exceptionally, one letter has been re-edited and discussed by G. Karlsson.[4] Fathers V. Laurent and V. Grumel[5] and, more recently, Mme W. Wolska-Conus[6] have made use of the entire collection, but their reading of it does not appear to have been very careful.

I should like to thank here Professor P. J. Alexander who first brought the Letters of Ignatius to my attention and provided me with a photostat of Gedeon's Νέα βιβλιοθήκη. For some time now I have been engaged on preparing a new edition of the Letters with translation and commentary, but since the end is not yet in sight, I should like to offer here some preliminary remarks bearing on two problems, namely the attribution of the Letters to Ignatius and the date of his occupancy of the see of Nicaea.

The first question need not detain us long. It is abundantly clear that the author of the Letters was active in the first half of the ninth century and that he was during some stage of his career metropolitan of Nicaea. Epp. 7 and 8, addressed to one Nicholas, spatharios and protonotarios, contain an urgent plea concerning the collection of the synone from the property of the Church which

---

[1] Kirche und theologische Literatur im byzant. Reich, Munich 1959, 512.

[2] Εἰσαγωγὴ εἰς τὴν βυζαντινὴν φιλολογίαν, Athens 1952, 245.

[3] E. g., E. E. Lipšic, O pokhode Rusi na Vizantiju ranee 842 goda, Istoričeskie Zapiski 26, 1948, 312ff.; G. Marenghi, Ignazio diacono e i tetrastici giambici, Emerita 25, 1957, 487–98; R. Browning, Ignace le diacre et la tragédie classique à Byzance, REG 81, 1968, 401–10.

[4] Idéologie et cérémonial dans l'épistolographie byzantine, Uppsala 1959, 126ff.

[5] See p. 406, n. 4 infra.

[6] De quibusdam Ignatiis, Travaux et mémoires 4, 1970, 329–60.

our author has been appointed to govern, and in Ep. 8 this Church is expressly designated as ἡ ἐκκλησία Νικαίας. Epp. 10 and 11 convey peremptory admonitions addressed, respectively, to the bishops of Taion and Noumerika, both of whom, as we know from the *notitiae episcopatuum*, were suffragans of the metropolitan of Nicaea. In Ep. 14, addressed to one Nicephorus, deacon and chartophylax, the author excuses himself for not having sent any offering to the fine table kept by his correspondent on the grounds that the fish of his lake (τὸ παρ' ἡμῖν λιμναῖον ὄψον) were of appalling quality. Even if he is not referring to those κακέμφατα κορδάκια which have been so fully discussed by Louis Robert[1], he surely has lake Ascanius in mind. There is further proof that our author was metropolitan of Nicaea, but the above will suffice for our purpose.

Now, as to his name. Ep. 38, addressed to the deacon Nicephorus, begins as follows:

Ἐδόκει μοι τῷ προοιμίῳ τῆς ἐπιστολῆς τῆς σῆς ὁμιλοῦντι τῷ τῆς θεολογίας ἐπωνύμῳ Γρηγορίῳ προσδιαλέγεσθαι, ἀλύοντι καὶ ἀνιωμένῳ ἐπὶ τῇ τῆς χαλάζης πληγῇ καὶ τὴν ὑφ' ἣν αὕτη αἰτίαν ἐχέθη φιλοσοφοῦντι καὶ διερευνωμένῳ τρανώτατα. ἀλλ' ἐκεῖνος μὲν πρὸς ποῖον καὶ τίνα τὸν λόγον ὑπέφερεν, εἰδότι σοι, λέγειν οὐ βούλομαι· ᾧ [δ cod. and Gedeon] δὲ σὺ νῦν ἐπέστειλας, διακόνῳ τῇ θεολόγῳ γλώσσῃ χρησάμενος, βούλομαί [corr. Gedeon: βάλλομαι cod.] σε καὶ μὴ βουλόμενον μαθεῖν. Ἰγνάτιος οὗτός ἐστιν ὁ μικρὸς εἰς εὐσέβειαν καὶ μέγας εἰς ἁμαρτίαν, οὗ καὶ τὸ εἶναι χριστιανὸν [χριστιανῷ cod.] χριστιανοὺς ἐπεβάρησεν, etc. This may be rendered roughly as follows: "It seemed to me, as I was reading the exordium of your letter, that I was conversing with Gregory Theologos who was agitated and distressed by the plague of the hailstorm, and was reflecting and enquiring most forcefully concerning the cause of its falling down. As for Gregory, I need not tell you (since you know it yourself) to what kind of person he was offering his speech; but I do wish you to know, even if you are unwilling, to whom it is that you have now addressed your letter using the instrument of your divine tongue: it is Ignatius whose piety is small while his sins are many, and whose very profession Christianity is an embarrassment to other Christians." The reference is, of course, to Gregory's Orat. XVI[2] which is entitled Εἰς τὸν πατέρα σιωπῶντα διὰ τὴν πληγὴν τῆς χαλάζης. Strictly speaking, St. Gregory was not addressing his father: in the exordium of his sermon he explains that his father was unwilling to console the people of Nazianzus, so that he, the son, was obliged to undertake this task; and he goes on to expound the causes of the calamity, namely human sins that had moved God to anger. It is surprising that Gedeon, who made many felicitous emendations in the text of the Letters, should have failed to understand that the author was here giving his own name. Furthermore, the last letter in the collection, No. 64, is entitled in the manuscript and in Gedeon's edition, Νικηφόρῳ Ἰγνατίῳ. The editor suggests the correction καὶ Ἰγνατίῳ, but it is perfectly clear that this letter is addressed to one person whom the author calls φίλος ἐμοὶ καὶ πατέρων αἰδεσιμώτατε. The addressee is the deacon Nicephorus, one of Ignatius's most frequent correspondents whom he elsewhere qualifies with the epithet πατήρ. The title of † letter 64 should therefore read Νικηφόρῳ Ἰγνατίου. The only Ignatius known to

---

[1] Sur des lettres d'un métropolite de Phrygie, Journal des savants, July-Dec. 1961, 100ff.
[2] PG 35, 933ff.

have been metropolitan of Nicaea in the first half of the ninth century is the deacon and skevophylax, the biographer of the Patriarchs Nicephorus and Tarasius. The veracity of Pargoire's identification is consequently assured.

We are on much more difficult ground in trying to determine the period when Ignatius served as metropolitan of Nicaea. Le Quien[1] placed him after Hypatius, who attended the Council of 787, and before the iconoclast Inger[2], i. e. at the very beginning of the ninth century. Vailhé, after a more attentive study of the sources, drew up the following episcopal list:

1. Hypatius in 787
2. Peter, 808– ca. 815, died 11 Sept. 826
3. Inger, 815 (?)–827
4. Ignatius under Emperor Theophilus (?), 829–842
5. St. Theophanes Graptos, 842 – 11 Oct. 845[3]

The current opinion today, however, is that Ignatius's episcopate occurred after 843, indeed after 11 October 845, the date of the death of St. Theophanes Graptos.[4] The last scholar to have studied the biography of Ignatius, Mme Wolska-Conus, believes that, having been appointed towards the end of 845, he gave up the post in 847, i. e. at the time of the death of the Patriarch Methodius or a little thereafter.[5] This is possible chronologically since Ignatius, though an old man, was alive at this time: he addressed three letters, Nos. 52, 54 and 55, to the Patriarch Methodius (843–47); but it is not at first sight very likely since Ignatius had compromised himself with the iconoclasts (to what extent it is not very clear), whereas we know that Methodius was very strict in excluding from the episcopate anyone who did not have a perfectly clean record in this respect.[6] The problem that confronts us is not merely one of chronology: it drastically affects our estimate of Ignatius's activity. If he was appointed metropolitan of Nicaea in 845, he must have been considered an iconodule in the strictest sense of the word; if before 843, his complexion changes entirely.

To begin with, it may be useful to summarise certain biographical data that are known independently of the Letters. The date of Ignatius's birth is placed

---

[1] Oriens Christianus, I, 644.

[2] I have discussed Inger in an article entitled "Eudocia Ingerina, the Normans, and the Macedonian Dynasty", Zbornik radova Vizant. Inst. 14/15, 1973, 17–27. The date 827 given by Vailhé has no absolute validity: all we know is that Inger died in or shortly after 825.

[3] S. Michel le Syncelle et les deux frères Grapti, Rev. Or. chrét. 6, 1901, 634. It may be noted that C. F. Müller, Ignatii diaconi tetrasticha iambica 54, versus in Adamum 143, Kiel 1886, 14, had already conjectured that Ignatius was made metropolitan "fortasse paulo post 830 p. Chr."

[4] This was the view of V. G. Vasil'evskij, Trudy III, Petrograd 1915, xcviii. So also V. Laurent, La Vita retractata et les miracles posthumes de S. Pierre d'Atroa, Subs. hagiogr. 31, 1958, 152 n. 3; id., Le corpus des sceaux de l'Empire byzantin, V/1, Paris 1963, 271, No. 377. In the latter work Laurent comments on our Ep. 49 (on which see below) written by Ignatius of Nicaea to his namesake Ignatius of Nicomedia in or shortly after 843, and says, "Le ton de déférence employé par l'auteur de la lettre prouve seulement qu'il devait être notablement plus jeune que le destinataire." Yet Ignatius of Nicaea must have been about seventy years old at the time! V. Grumel, too, was convinced that Ignatius occupied the see of Nicaea from 845 until 848, if not later: La 'Notitia' de Basile de Ialimbana, Rev. ét. byz. 19, 1961, 200–01.

[5] De quibusdam Ignatiis, 357–8.

[6] See V. Grumel, La politique religieuse du patriarche S. Méthode, Echos d'Orient 34, 1935, 385ff.

by Vasil'evskij ca. 770–74,[1] by Mme Wolska-Conus ca. 770–80[2] on the basis of Ignatius's own statement that he had been taught in his youth the rules of ancient prosody by Tarasius.[3] Vasil'evskij is, I believe, right in suggesting that this instruction most probably took place before Tarasius became patriarch in 784. If so, Ignatius must have been born much closer to 770 than to 780 since the study of ancient meter could hardly have preceded his secondary education (*enkyklios paideusis*) which normally extended from the age of ten/eleven to that of seventeen/eighteen.[4] We know from the Souda[5] that he held the ranks of deacon, skevophylax of the Great Church of Constantinople, and metropolitan of Nicaea; and that he was also a *grammatikos*. He could have become deacon ca. 795–800, i. e. under the administration of Tarasius whose sermons he took down stenographically. We do not know when he was promoted to the high position of skevophylax. At the very end of his life, when he wrote the *Vita Tarasii*, he was, to judge by the title of that work, a simple monk.[6] Clearly, there are many gaps to fill in the long life of Ignatius.

Turning next our attention to the Letters, we must begin by making it clear that not all of them by any means were written while Ignatius was metropolitan of Nicaea. The following can certainly be attributed to the period of his episcopate: Epp. 1, 2, 3, 4, 7, 8, 9, 10, 11, 14, 17, 18; and the following with a fair degree of probability: Epp. 6, 13 and 16. From this enumeration it appears that the episcopal letters form a block placed at the beginning of the collection. At present I am unable to date any of them on external evidence, but they do contain a number of prosopographical and other clues that may yield chronological indications.

Epp. 21–24, addressed Δημοχάρει γενικῷ λογοθέτῃ, can be approximately dated as already noted by Gedeon.[7] Theodore the Studite wrote a letter to the same personage soon after the accession of Michael II (25 Dec. 820) in which he compliments him on his virtue and learning and urges him to champion the cause of images before the new Emperor who was showing signs of true piety (βασιλεῖ τῷ ἀπαρξαμένῳ εὐσεβεῖν). Democharis had held a succession of high posts before he reached the pinnacle of his career, namely the ministry of finance (ἀρχὰς ἐξ ἀρχῶν ἀμείβουσα, εἰς τὴν κορυφαιοτάτην τῶν ἐν τέλει ἀνέδραμεν); and on one occasion he had confuted the heresiarch John, i. e. John the Grammarian.[8] Theodore also wrote a letter of condolence to the widow of Democharis.[9] There is here a slight difficulty because Theodore refers to the dead man as a strategos (ὁ θάνατος τοῦ μακαρίου στρατηγοῦ), but the description he gives of him (pious, champion of the faith, learned, wise) accords well with that of the previous letter. It may be that Democharis had been *strategos* before he became logothete or, just conceivably,

---

[1] Op. cit., xciii.

[2] Op. cit., 330.

[3] Vita Tarasii, ed. Heikel, Acta Soc. Scient. Fennicae XVII, 1889. 29.

[4] See, e. g., P. Lemerle, Le premier humanisme byzantin, Paris 1971, 100.

[5] Ed. Adler, II, 607–08.

[6] The title reads Ἰγνατίου μοναχοῦ μερικὴ ἐξήγησις, etc. Cf. Wolska-Conus, op. cit., 339 and n. 58.

[7] Νέα βιβλιοθήκη, col. 21, note.

[8] Ep. II. 82, PG 99, 1324. On the date of this letter (early in 821) see A. P. Dobroklonskij, Prep. Feodor, ispovednik i igumen Studijskij, II/1, Odessa 1914, 427.

[9] Ep. II. 110, PG 99, 1369–72.

after. Theodore also refers to his children (col. 1372 B: ἐπειδὴ καὶ τέκνα ἔχεις) whose existence is corroborated by Ignatius. If then we admit that we are dealing with one and the same Democharis, he must have died before 826, the year of Theodore's death.[1]

Ignatius's Epp. 21–24 appear to be arranged in chronological order. No. 21 is an appeal for clemency on behalf of certain *naukleroi*, natives of a small island called 'Ανδρωτή. Having been entrusted with the yearly supply of grain destined for the treasury (δημόσιος λόγος), they were apprehended in having stolen a small quantity thereof and substituted barley for wheat. The island "indecently" called Androte appears, alas, to be unknown.[2] Ignatius says that he had visited it once and deplored the hard life of its inhabitants who were obliged to fetch water and fuel from the mainland. It is not clear to me why these captains should have sought the intervention of Ignatius (was he perchance a countryman of theirs?), and what post the latter was occupying at the time. For the present, it is sufficient to note that Ep. 21 was written while Democharis was still in office.

Ep. 22 contains no concrete data except that it mentions a previous letter on the part of Ignatius. From Ep. 23, a plea on behalf of a widow, we learn that Democharis was in the process of withdrawing from his official duties. Finally, in Ep. 24 Ignatius expresses his sympathy to Democharis who had recently been relieved of his post (τῇ ἀξίας ἀποβολῇ) and consoles him with the fact that the latter had daughters and sons-in-law (ἐπὶ θυγατράσιν υἱοί σου). In the peroration he expresses the wish that he, too, may be relieved from the mire of this life so that he might be able to offer God a pure worship be it even for one day (ὡς ἂν δυνηθείημεν μιᾶς ἡμέρας χρόνον καθαρὰν αὐτῷ τὴν λατρείαν προσαγαγεῖν) and thereby purge the corruption of his soul. Since Democharis must have been dismissed in the early years of the reign of Michael II, it follows that Ignatius was at the time somehow unable to worship the Deity in a fitting manner, i. e. with icons; in other words, he was going along with the iconoclasts, even if this was contrary to his inner convictions.

Epp. 27 and 30, both addressed to Nicephorus, deacon and chartophylax, were written while the iconoclasts were in power. Ep. 33 to Joseph, abbot of the Antidion monastery,[3] is certainly prior to 846, perhaps by several years, since it refers to an ἰσάγγελος καὶ κοινὸς πατὴρ ἡμῶν, surely St. Ioannikios, as being still alive. Ep. 38, to which we have already referred, contains a clear allusion to the fact that Ignatius had at one time been drawn into the iconoclast camp (διὰ τὸ πρὸς τἀναντία παροιστρῆσαι). When he wrote Epp. 43, 44 and 46, Ignatius was confined, much against his wishes, to the monastery of Pikridion at the far end of the Golden Horn[4], and it appears from the beginning of No. 43 that this had

---

[1] Cf. Dobroklonskij, op. cit., 451–2.

[2] Νέα βιβλιοθήκη, col. 22: ὅπερ 'Ανδρωτὴν οὐκ εὐαγῶς οἱ πάλαι κεκλήκασιν. I do not understand the *double entendre*: was the island shaped like the *membrum virile*? Gedeon, a good expert on local geography, suggests that this may have been the island called Koutali of the Proconnesus archipelago, on which see the same author's Προικόννησος, Constantinople 1895, 77ff. On the other hand, one should not exclude the possibility of Androte having been an island off the Black Sea coast.

[3] On the monastery see B. Menthon, L'Olympe de Bithynie, Paris 1935, 50. Joseph was abbot at the time of the death of St. Ioannikios: Vita Ioannicii (by Sabas), ASS, Nov. II, 383A.

[4] Situated at or near modern Hasköy. See R. Janin, La géographie ecclésiastique de l'Empire byzantin, I/3, Paris 1953, 417.

happened by order of the patriarch (ὁ ἱερώτατος ἀρχιερεύς), although, unfortunately, the text is corrupt at this point. At what date did this confinement take place?

Skipping over Nos. 47 and 48 which contain little of interest, we come to No. 49, addressed to Ignatius, metropolitan of Nicomedia, which may be summarised as follows:

"Being choked by the chains of my own sins, I have strayed from the course of my salvation and am no longer able to walk a straight path; for which reason I have been placed as far as possible from the holy flock and pasture (τῆς ἱερᾶς ἀγέλης καὶ νομῆς ὡς πορρωτάτω κατῴκισμαι) and I am afraid of addressing you, a great shepherd, when I am not even a simple sheep. The monk who is bearing this letter, one of the most outstanding members of this monastery [1], is desirous of obtaining a small bishopric in your jurisdiction. If he appears worthy of it, may he receive it. I have not been bribed to make this petition."

Ignatius of Nicomedia happens to be known. He was probably appointed in 843, was certainly in office in August 844, and appears to have been deposed ca. 845 if he is the same as the Monomachos (family name) mentioned in the Life of St. Ioannikios.[2] In other words, our Ignatius was in disgrace and probably confined to the Pikridion monastery shortly after 843.[3] At the same time he remained on sufficiently good terms with some orthodox ecclesiastics, perhaps because of the ambiguity of his previous conduct. The three letters he addressed during the same period to the Patriarch Methodius (Nos. 52, 54, 55; No. 53 to Theodore, deacon and protonotarios, concerns the same matter as No. 54) are in the nature of humble supplications and do not contradict our conclusions. And if so, Ignatius had in all probability been metropolitan of Nicaea under the iconoclasts. In broad lines his career may, therefore, be reconstructed as follows: deacon ordained by Tarasius; skevophylax perhaps as late as 829;[4] metropolitan of Nicaea under Theophilus; relegated to Pikridion by Methodius in 843. By this time he was an old man, and he devoted the remaining years of his life to an apologia of his past conduct by composing the *Vita Tarasii* and, perhaps, editing his own Letters from which, we may imagine, he expunged any material that could have proved embarrassing. As he stands revealed to us, he

---

[1] Gedeon prints εἷς ὢν τῶν ἐν τῇ τιμῇ ταύτῃ προλαμπόντων, but the reading of the manuscript (p. 145) is τῶν εν τι μ̔ ταύτῃ, i. e. τῇ μονῇ.

[2] See Laurent as in p. 406, n. 4 supra. Vita Ioannicii (by Peter), ASS, Nov. II, 432 B, where the Saint, shortly before his death, advises the Patriarch Methodius to avoid the company, amongst others, of τῆς Νικομηδείας ἐπισκοπῆς ἐκπεπτωκότος Μονομάχου ἤτοι θεομάχου. Grumel, Notes pour l'"Oriens christianus', Echos d'Orient 33, 1934, 55—7, conjectured that the bishop in question was called Theophilus and that the pun was on θεόφιλος — θεομάχος. This ingenious supposition is unnecessary, since the intended joke was clearly Μονομάχος — θεομάχος. The family name Monomachos was also borne by St. Nicetas the patrician († 836). See my remarks in J. of Theol. Studies, N. S. 17, 1966, 486; D. Papachryssanthou, La Vie du patrice Nicétas, Travaux et mémoires 3, 1968, 316—7.

[3] The deserving monk he was recommending probably wished to take advantage of the wholesale change in the episcopate under Methodius. The metropolitan of Nicomedia had in the ninth century eleven suffragan bishoprics, some of them quite minor: Georgii Cyprii descriptio orbis Romani, ed. H. Gelzer, Leipzig 1890, 11.

[4] If that is the approximate date of the *Vita Nicephori* in the title of which Ignatius is styled † deacon and skevophylax. See Wolska-Conus, op. cit., 339, 348; P. J. Alexander, Secular Biography at Byzantium, Speculum 15, 1940, 204 n. 3.

does not appear to have ever been a dedicated iconoclast, and I do not believe on the available evidence that he should be equated with the Ignatius whose †poems were refuted by St. Theodore the Studite.[1] Like many, perhaps most members of the Byzantine clergy, he pursued his career regardless of the party that happened to be in control.

In offering the above reconstruction I did not take into account a somewhat obscure episode which is alluded to twice in the Letters. In Ep. 31, addressed to the monks Theophylact and Athanasius, Ignatius says of himself that he had transgressed against his first covenant with Christ by means of evil deeds, and that having later chosen the monastic life, he had defiled that also (τὴν γὰρ ἐπὶ τῇ θείᾳ μνήσει πρώτην ἠθετηκὼς εἰς Χριστὸν συνταγὴν καὶ δι᾽ ἔργων ἀσέμνων τῷ ἀντιπάλῳ προσθέμενος, εἶτα τὸν μονήρη βίον δι᾽ ἀποταγῆς τῶν κοσμικῶν φροντίδων ἑλόμενος, καὶ τῆς τῶν βεβήλων οὐκ ἀποσχόμενος ἐργασίας καὶ πράξεως, οὐχ ἥκιστα καὶ τοῦτον καταρυπώσας ἐμόλυνα). The letter concludes with the wish that the writer, who is an old man, should die before his correspondent Athanasius. The second reference occurs in Ep. 58 to Leo, protospatharios and a secretis, which may be summarised as follows:

"Supplications addressed to you find a swift response. Every inhabitant of the earth is receiving prompt relief from our common protector [who ?], but he has not extended his help to my miserable self. Yet, it is you yourselves who have dragged me away from my initial seclusion on Olympus (ἢ οὐ μέμνῃ ὅτι με τῆς ἐν ἀρχῇ μοναδικῆς ἡσυχίας αὐτοὶ κατεσπάσατε, Ὀλυμπίαθεν[2] ἀφελκύσαντες), and having done so, left me in penury instead of conferring benefits on me. Perhaps this should be so because I have committed many sins; but may you prosper."

We can only conclude from the above that at some stage in his career Ignatius voluntarily became a monk on the Bithynian Olympus. It is difficult to say whether this happened before or after his episcopate.

A more attentive study of the Letters will doubtless reveal further details of the long and devious life of Ignatius, metropolitan of Nicaea. In the meantime I can only hope that Father Richard, to whom all students of Byzantine literature are so heavily indebted, will accept this incomplete offering.

---

[1] On the other hand, I am convinced contra Wolska-Conus, op. cit., 351ff. and others, that the iconoclastic poems date from ca. 815, not from the first period of iconoclasm.

[2] This is the reading of the manuscript: Ὀλυμπόθεν would be more correct.

XIII

The Liquidation of Iconoclasm and the Patriarch Photios

If the introduction of Iconoclasm as the official doctrine of the Byzantine State is shrouded in obscurity, the same may be said of its liquidation in 843. At first sight, this appears strange, for we are reasonably well informed concerning the religious events of the period in question. The historical documentation is admittedly poor and, for the most part, about a hundred years later than the events that interest us here; on the other hand, we do possess a considerable mass of contemporary saints' Lives, not to mention other categories of evidence. And what event was worthier of celebration and description than the long-awaited Triumph of Orthodoxy? Celebrations exist in plenty; factual accounts, however, are disappointingly brief.

To be sure, the main events are well established. The Emperor Theophilos died on 20 January 842. His pious widow Theodora, acting as regent on behalf of her two-year old son Michael, set about restoring the worship of icons. She laid her plans carefully. The Iconoclastic Patriarch, the much-loathed "precursor of the Antichrist," John the Grammarian, was left in office for another year. When, at length, everything was ready, some kind of ecclesiastical assembly was convened without much publicity; and, on the first Sunday of Lent, 843, a solemn procession inaugurated the return of Orthodoxy. No active opposition on the part of the Iconoclasts is recorded. Such, in brief, are the accepted facts.[1] It is when we probe deeper that we run into difficulty.

To begin with, I should like to quote two accounts of the events of 843. They are both taken from a work conventionally called the *Synodicon vetus*, which is a compendium of all the councils, both orthodox and heretical, that took place from the time of the Apostles until the ninth century. This work has come down to us in two versions, as established by Mr. J. S. F. Parker. In the earlier version, which dates from the end of the ninth century, we find the following brief entry:

When Theophilos had blasphemously ended his life, his son Michael succeeded to the Empire together with his own mother Theodora. Fired by a godly zeal, they recalled the holy Fathers who were in banishment and,

---

1. The best discussion of these events is by J. Gouillard, "Le Synodikon de l'Orthodoxie," *TM*, 2 (1967), 119 ff.

having convened a holy local council in the residence of the Keeper of
the Imperial Inkpot (ἐν τοῖς Κανικλείου) they ejected the abominable
John from his throne and appointed St. Methodios patriarch of Constantinople. After ratifying the seven holy Ecumenical Councils, they rightly
restored the sacred icons to the reverence that had been due to them
from the beginning.[2]

We may pause to note a few points. All the credit is given to the
Emperor Michael and the Empress Theodora: in effect, this means
Theodora alone since in 843 Michael was three years old. The gathering that took place is called a σύνοδος τοπική and it assembled not in a
church, not even in one of the ceremonial halls of the Imperial Palace,
but in the private residence of a civil servant situated somewhere near
the Golden Horn.[3] The office of ἐπὶ τοῦ Κανικλείου was at that time
held by Theoktistos, Theodora's chief minister.

In the second version of the *Synodicon* we find a very different
account:

When Michael, the son of Theophilos, had succeeded to the empire
together with his mother Theodora, the orthodox faith was revealed at an
opportune moment after the abominable heresy of the iconoclasts had
dragged on for thirty years since the days of Leo the Amalekite (Leo V).
Now Manuel, who was prominent in the government, was afflicted by an
illness and all hope for him was given up. But God, who works miracles,
incited the monks of Studios to visit him ... When they approached his
bed, some of the monks put their trust in God, and fortified him, who
was nearly dead or about to die, with a promise of recovery. He, arous-
ing himself a little from the depth of his afflicted soul, asked if he could
have any such hope. Whereupon they cried out, "If you promise God to
restore the holy icons according to ancient custom, we can give you the
good tidings that you will live." When they had departed, their promise
immediately came to pass, and he arose from Hades and was delivered
from death. Perceiving himself to have unexpectedly recovered from his
illness, he brought his pious striving to bear on the Empress Theodora;
and after much conflict and discussion, the holy icons were restored. As
for the priests and bishops, some abandoned their impiety, while others
resisted the pious doctrine and were rightly ejected, among them especially the heretical Patriarch John ... In his stead was installed the pious
Methodios who exhibited on his body, like so many marks of honour,

---

2. Fabricius-Harles, *Bibliotheca graeca*, XII (Hamburg, 1809), 416, No. 147. A new edition of the *Synodicon*, begun by Mr. Parker and continued by Dr. J. M. Duffy, is due
   to appear under the auspices of the Dumbarton Oaks Byzantine Center. I am
   indebted to Mr. Duffy for communicating to me the text of the passages quoted here.
   [See now *The Synodicon Vetus*, ed. J. Duffy and J. Parker, Washington, D.C., 1979,
   132, No. 156.]

3. See R. Janin, *Constantinople byzantine*, 2nd ed. (Paris, 1964), 366.

the many wounds he had received on account of the faith and the loss of his hair caused by his fetid prison. And on an appointed day an assembly was convened and the Church regained her own beauty. And men came down from Mount Olympos, from Athos and Ida, even the congregation of Kyminas, and they proudly proclaimed the true faith. This happened on the first Sunday of Lent which is called the Sunday of Orthodoxy.[4]

This account of the *Synodicon* is copied almost verbatim from the History of Genesios[5] written at the behest of Constantine Porphyrogennetos, and it embodies that version of the events of 843 which eventually prevailed in Byzantine historiography. The legendary character of the story is all too obvious. One could even have described it as a particularly inept piece of falsification if Henri Grégoire was right in claiming that the miraculously revived Manuel had actually died on the battlefield in 838, i.e., five years before the Studite monks had raised him from the dead;[6] but of this I am not sure,[7] and Manuel's story is too tangled to be examined here. In any case, a falsification was perpetrated, and one may assume that its purpose was both to give the Studite monastery some share of the credit and to obscure the role of certain other parties who might have claimed a more direct involvement in the restoration of Orthodoxy.

When we examine the sources that are closest to the events, we come away with the impression that neither the monks nor the secular clergy covered themselves with glory at this juncture. The spirited resistance that had marked the reigns of Leo V and Michael II subsided after the death of Theodore the Studite. The doyen of the monastic corps, Ioannikios the Great, sat undisturbed on the summit of Mount

---

4. The second version of the *Synodicon* has not been published. [See now ed. cited in note 2, 196.]

5. 78-82.

6. "Etudes sur le neuvième siècle," *Byzantion*, 8 (1933), 520 ff.

7. If, as Grégoire holds, Manuel's resurrection was modelled on the healing of another patrician Manuel by Nicholas the Studite (but cf. the discreet doubts expressed on this score by P. Peeters, *AnalBoll*, 52 [1934], 146-47), and if the 'resuscitated' Manuel is merely a doublet of the historical Manuel who died in 838, it is difficult to see why this 'ghost' is made to do so many things in the reign of Michael III that he had not done earlier: he addresses the people in the Hippodrome, intervenes in the trial of the Patriarch Methodios, falls out with Theoktistos, retires to his own house, etc. Furthermore, according to Michael the Syrian, ed. Chabot, III, 113 (following Ignatios of Melitene who, in turn, had used Greek chronicles), Manuel was appointed commander-in-chief of the army after the death of Theophilos. The latter point has already been noted by Bury, *History of the Eastern Roman Empire* (London, 1912), 476. There is certainly, with respect to Manuel, some deep-seated confusion in our sources, but I can see no obvious way of removing it.

Olympos. As Bury pointed out long ago,[8] the persecution under Theophilos claimed few victims, and these were mostly foreigners: Theophanes and Theodore the Graptoi as well as Michael Synkellos were Palestinians, the painter Lazaros a Chazar.[9] The record of the secular Church was even poorer: Theophilos of Ephesus, Joseph of Salonica and Euthymios of Sardis were detained for political rather than for religious reasons.[10] The pusillanimous attitude of the bishops may conveniently be studied in the correspondence of Ignatios of Nicaea.[11]

Who, then, was responsible for restoring the images? Apart from the Empress Theodora, our sources mention Theoktistos, the *magistros* Manuel, Bardas, Petronas and the enigmatic Sergios Niketiates.[12] It is an instructive list. The primary role of Theoktistos can hardly be doubted, for not only was he the most influential member of the council of regency; the ecclesiastical assembly of 843 also took place, as we have seen, in his own house. All the others were related to the Empress: Manuel (assuming he was alive) was her uncle, Bardas and Petronas her brothers, while Sergios is described more vaguely as a relative.[13] It was, therefore, in the strictest sense an 'inside job' organized by a group of persons who had held a prominent place at the court of the Iconoclast Theophilos. Furthermore, Methodios, their candidate for patriarch, was also an insider. There is much that is unclear in his life, but there can be no doubt that after he had undergone his famous internment in a tomb—an internment, incidentally, that took place in the reign of Michael II and was caused by political considerations—he was reprieved and taken into the palace by Theophilos, allegedly on account of his learning.[14] There was certainly more to it than that.

Grégoire, who deserves the credit for having rescued Sergios Niketiates from oblivion, had an excellent intuition, although, as was often the case, he pushed it too far.[15] If we may briefly recapitulate the evidence, Sergios is mentioned as a leading figure in the restoration of Orthodoxy in the *Acta Davidis*;[16] he is also the subject of a notice in

8. *Op. cit.*, 136 ff.
9. The evidence on Lazaros has been assembled by me in *BZ*, 47 (1954), 396-97.
10. See J. Gouillard, "Une oeuvre inédite du patriarche Méthode," *BZ*, 53 (1960), 39 ff.
11. Ed. M. Gedeon, Νέα Βιβλιοθήκη ἐκκλησιαστικῶν συγγραφέων I/1 (Constantinople, 1903), 1-64. I am preparing a new edition of this correspondence.
12. The longest list (Sergios Niketiates, Theoktistos, Bardas, Petronas, in that order) is in the *Acta SS. Davidis, Symeonis et Georgii, AnalBoll*, 18 (1899), 245-46. Theophanes Cont., 148, mentions Theoktistos, Bardas and Manuel. Georgius Monachus, 811, ascribes all the credit to Theoktistos, and Genesios, as we have seen, to Manuel.
13. *Synaxarium CP*, 777/15.
14. *Vita Methodii*, PG, 100 col. 1252C. While living in the palace Methodios is said to have converted to Orthodoxy the Emperor's closest associates.
15. Grégoire, *op. cit.* (see note 6), 517 ff.
16. As in note 12 *supra*.

the Synaxarion in which it is stated that he came from Paphlagonia, was related to the Empress Theodora, and exerted himself very hard in order to bring about the restoration of the holy icons. He then led an expedition against Arab-occupied Crete where he died.[17] So far so good. We need not review Grégoire's theory that Sergios was the same as the enigmatic admiral Ibn Qatuna who carried out the Byzantine raid on Damietta in 853, and that the expedition to Crete was that of 866 rather than the earlier one of 843 (which would appear to be the more likely date). But then Grégoire went one step further. He suggested that Sergios Niketiates was the brother of the Patriarch Photios and that, on account of this compromising kinship, his services in the restoration of Orthodoxy were later suppressed. It can be shown without too much trouble that Sergios Niketiates was not the brother of Photios, although he may possibly have been his maternal uncle, as we shall see later. But even if this was not the case, Grégoire was right in thinking that Photios did have some connection with the clique that engineered the triumph of 843.

Students of the life and writings of Photios have been struck by the insistence with which he dwelt on the issue of Iconoclasm, and this at a time when all serious danger of an Iconoclastic revival appeared to have passed. We know that the condemnation of Iconoclasm was the chief dogmatic reason advanced for convoking the Council of 861. Once again, Iconoclasm was condemned, along with all the other great heresies, at the notorious Council of 867. In his Letters, in his *Amphilochia*, and, above all, in his Homilies Photios misses no opportunity of returning to this issue in terms which occasionally suggest that he regarded the suppression of Iconoclasm as almost a personal achievement. Particularly striking is a sentence in his seventeenth Homily: "For even if it is we," he says, "that have sown and first ploughed with much toil the fallow land, yet that too was not independent of imperial zeal and co-operation."[18]

The late Francis Dvornik, who devoted a study to this very question,[19] tried to show that Photios's attitude was dictated by the continued vigour of the Iconoclastic party. Iconoclasm, he says, was still rampant. But was it? We know, of course, that a few Iconoclasts remained unrepentant. Some of them are mentioned by name—Theodore Krithinos, former archbishop of Syracuse, who was condemned at the Ignatian Council of 869, a certain Paul, Theodore Gastes, Stephen Molites,

17. *Synaxarium CP*, 777-78.
18. Ed. B. Laourdas, Φωτίου ὁμιλίαι (Thessaloniki, 1959), 165; trans. C. Mango, *The Homilies of Photius* (Cambridge, Mass., 1958), 287.
19. "The Patriarch Photius and Iconoclasm," *DOP*, 7 (1953), 69 ff.

Laloudios and Leo.[20] But I see no reason to believe that these men constituted much of a threat. It also seems to me that Dvornik (to whom we all owe so much) tended to see the career of Photios too much in terms of a conflict between political parties, i.e., in terms that are perhaps more applicable to the nineteenth and twentieth centuries than to the ninth. If there was any danger of an Iconoclastic comeback, it could have come only from the top. Half a century earlier the youthful Constantine VI had threatened (so it is said) to re-introduce Iconoclasm if his marital intrigues were thwarted.[21] It is not inconceivable that the young Michael III, who was equally wilful and who, like Constantine, was saddled with a pious and meddlesome mother, may have entertained similar thoughts. Fortunately, his rebelliousness found less serious outlets.

However that may be, the attitude of Photios towards Iconoclasm was, I believe, dictated by entirely different considerations which become apparent when we examine his early life. On this score there has been much uncertainty. My own reconstruction is radically different from that proposed a few years ago by Madame H. Ahrweiler.[22] But although I cannot agree with her conclusions, I must pay tribute to the interesting and ingenious manner in which she presented her arguments; and at one point she came very close to discovering the truth as I see it.[23]

I shall begin with a passage of the *Bibliotheca*. In codices 62-67 Photios reviews in chronological order six works devoted to Byzantine history: the History of Constantine the Great by Praxagoras (lost), the *Wars* by Procopius, a History of Justinian and Justin II by Theophanes of Byzantium (lost), the History by Theophylact Simocatta, the *Breviarium* of the Patriarch Nikephoros, and, finally, a History of Michael II by Sergios the Confessor, which is lost. The last work (cod. 67) deserves particular attention if for no other reason than that it is the most recent book reviewed in the *Bibliotheca*. Photios comments on it as follows:

> I have read [a work] by Sergios the Confessor. He starts with the actions of Michael, then reverts to the lawless abominations of Kopronymos, and goes on from that point in a continuous narrative until the eighth year of the same Michael. He describes the actions [of this

---

20. See Gouillard, "Deux figures," 387 ff. Some concern to silence the iconoclasts is shown in the revised version of the Life of St. Peter of Atroa, written *ca.* 860-65: V. Laurent, *La vita retractata et les miracles posthumes de S. Pierre d'Atroa* (Brussels, 1958), 135, §86bis, and 47-49.
21. *De sanctis patriarchis Tarasio et Nicephoro*, PG, 99, col. 1852D.
22. "Sur la carrière de Photius avant son patriarcat," *BZ*, 58 (1965), 348 ff.
23. *Ibid.*, 350, note 18.

emperor] as relating both to the State and to the Church; furthermore, he gives a detailed account of his fortunes in war and of his religious views.

As regards his style, he is, more than any other [author], adorned with clarity and simplicity in the use of words of plain meaning as well as in the construction and general disposition of the discourse which consequently appears to have been written, so to speak, extemporaneously. For, indeed, his language blooms with a natural grace and does not contain any elaborate forms. This kind of style is especially appropriate for ecclesiastical history, which was, indeed, the author's intention.

There can be no doubt that this work dealt with Michael II (820-29), since Michael I reigned less than two years (2 October 811—10 July 813), while Michael III, was, as I have said, two years old at his accession and could not, therefore, be said to have held any religious views up to the age of ten (the eighth year of his reign). In order to explain Michael II's religious policy, the author inserted a retrospective excursus concerning the "abominations" of Constantine V, and then proceeded as far as Michael's eighth year, i.e., 828. Clearly, this was an anti-Iconoclastic work, and it appears to have been left unfinished since it did not extend to the Emperor's death in 829.

Who was Sergios the Confessor? Henry, the latest editor of the *Bibliotheca*, is content to say, "Le personnage est mal connu et l'oeuvre est perdue."[24] Yet there can be little doubt that he was the same person as the one commemorated by the Synaxarion in the following words:

The same day [13 May] the remembrance of our holy Father Sergios the Confessor. He was born at Constantinople of a renowned and noble family and was known as a worshipper of the holy icons. He was brought before that persecutor, the godless Emperor Theophilos; a cord was tied round his neck and he was led round the market-place like a criminal. Then he was imprisoned. After being deprived of his great wealth, he was exiled with his whole family (πανοικί), namely his wife Eirene and his children. Having suffered many sorrows and various tribulations in exile, he departed unto the Lord.[25]

All the particulars supplied by the Synaxarion are applicable to the father of the Patriarch Photios: he was called Sergios, came of a prominent family, was married to a lady called Eirene, had several children, was exiled for his faith together with his wife, and met an early death in exile. I am not, of course, the first person to have noticed this

---

24. *Bibliothèque*, I (Paris, 1959), 99, note 2.
25. *Synaxarium CP*, 682.

identity;[26] yet no-one, as far as I know, has put together all the pieces of the puzzle. To do so, we must first examine the other pieces.

The plainest part of the evidence is supplied by Photios himself. In his 'enthronistic' letter, i.e., the letter announcing his own appointment, which he addressed to the see of Antioch, he made a point of referring to his father who, "on account of correct doctrine and true faith, bade farewell to wealth and splendid office and, after undergoing every kind of suffering ... died a martyr's death in banishment;" and to his mother who was "pious and virtuous, and strove not to fall short of her husband in any of these things."[27] In another letter, a letter of consolation he wrote to his brother Tarasios on the death of the latter's daughter, Photios recalls the infinitely worse hardships that their parents had suffered, and adds: "Where is my father? Where is my mother? Did they not, after playing a short role in life—yet a role adorned by the crown of martyrdom and endurance—quickly depart from the stage?"[28] In yet another letter Photios makes this defiant statement:

> For many years every heretical council and every Iconoclastic conventicle has anathematized me, and not only me, but also my father and my uncle, men who confessed Christ and were the ornament of the episcopate. Yet, after anathematizing me, they elevated me, even against my wish, to a bishop's throne. Let, therefore, these men now who, like the others, have set the Lord's ordinances at nought and who have opened the door wide to every kind of transgression, anathematize me again so that they, too, may elevate me from earth to the heavenly kingdom, sluggish though I am.[29]

This is a highly rhetorical statement, and it has been, I think, misunderstood. For maximum effect, Photios telescopes the unjust condemnation of himself with that of his father and uncle. The uncle in question was the Patriarch Tarasios (784-806) whom Photios calls elsewhere his πατρόθειος, i.e., his paternal uncle.[30] I should like to add in passing that this description ought not to be taken literally since Tarasios could not possibly have belonged to the same generation as Photios's father. So, instead of 'uncle' we should understand 'great uncle' or, more generally, 'relative on the father's side.'[31] This, however, is a minor point;

---

26. See, e.g., F. Dvornik, The Photian Schism (Cambridge, 1948), 387.

27. PG, 102, col. 1020A; ed. I. N. Valettas, Φωτίου . ἐπιστολαί (London, 1864), 145.

28. PG, 102, col. 972-73; ed. Valettas, 459.

29. PG, 102, col. 877B-C; ed. Valettas, 501.

30. PG, 102, cols. 609B, 817B.

31. A well-known parallel is provided by Constantine Porphyrogennetos who in De admin Imp., 22/79, ed. Moravcsik-Jenkins (1967), 98, calls Theophanes Confessor (died 817) his own μητρόθειος. In fact at least four generations must have elapsed between

what I should like to stress is that Photios is here rolling into one the persecution inflicted on several members of his family: the epithet ἀρχιερέων σεμνολόγημα, 'ornament of the episcopate' refers to Tarasios; ὁμολογητὰς Χριστοῦ, 'confessors of Christ' to his father. It is either the first only or both of them that were condemned by 'icono-clastic conventicles'; Photios himself was anathematized by a different kind of heretical council, σύνοδος αἱρετική, i.e., presumably, by his Ignatian opponents in 859. Indeed, the last Iconoclastic Council took place in 837 (if it took place at all), and Photios could hardly have been old enough at the time to have merited a separate anathema. Without going into further detail, let us recapitulate the evidence that Photios provides on his own family: his father was a confessor, both he and his mother died an untimely death in exile and persecution, his father was related to that great champion of Orthodoxy, the Patriarch Tarasios. We may also gather from the addresses of Photios's Letters that he had four brothers called Tarasios, Constantine, Theodore and Sergios.[32]

This information is corroborated by other sources. At the Council of 879, which rehabilitated Photios, an official spokesman referred to "his father and mother who died in their struggle for the faith."[33] Similarly, the Life of St. Euthymios the Younger speaks of Photios as a virtuous man, "who from the very cradle had been consecrated to Christ, for whose icon he suffered confiscation and banishment in common with his father; whose life was admirable and whose death was agreeable, as God has confirmed by miracles."[34] This sentence is so constructed that the last clause, the one referring to posthumous mira-cles, could apply either to Photios or to his father; but this detail does not concern us now.

The next piece of the puzzle is a well known passage of Theophanes Continuatus which gives an account of the family of the Empress Theo-dora, wife of Theophilos, namely of her two brothers, Bardas and Petronas, and her three sisters.[35] Previous discussions of this passage have overlooked the fact that the published text, which is due to Combefis and Bekker, contains one tacit and one explicit addition. In the basic manuscript, *Vatic. gr. 167*, fol. 59ᵛ, we read the following:

Theophanes and Constantine. See *De admin. Imp., Commentary*, ed. Jenkins (1962), 80; and J. Pargoire, "Saint Théophane le Chronographe," *VizVrem*, 9 (1902), 38-39.

32. In Valettas's ed. letters 12-14, 142-43, 220, 223-24 are addressed to Tarasios; 15, 16 to Constantine; 17 to Theodore; 7-11, 85 to Sergios.

33. Mansi, XVII, col. 460B.

34. L. Petit, "Vie et office de S. Euthyme le Jeune," *ROChr*, 8 (1903), 179.

35. 174-75.

ἀδελφαὶ δὲ τρεῖς·ἥ τε εὐφήμῳ οὕτω καλουμένη ὀνόματι Καλομαρία·καὶ Σοφία·καὶ ἡ [lacuna of about 11 letters; the editors have tacitly added Εἰρήνη].[36] ἀλλ' ἡ μὲν Σοφία εἰς κοίτην ἐδίδοτο Κωνσταντίνῳ τῷ κατὰ τὸν Βαβούτζικον· ἡ δὲ Καλομαρία Ἀρσαβὴρ τῷ τηνικαῦτα μὲν πατρικίῳ ἔπειτα δὲ καὶ μαγίστρῳ·[ἡ δὲ Εἰρήνη explicitly added by the editors] τῷ Εἰρήνης τῆς μητρὸς τοῦ μετὰ ταῦτα τὸν πατριαρχικὸν θρόνον ἀντιλαβομένου Φωτίου ἀδελφῷ·μεθ' οὗ καὶ δύο τεκνώσασα παῖδας·Στέφανόν τε τὸν μάγιστρον καὶ Βάρδαν τὸν ἑαυτοῦ ἀδελφὸν καὶ μάγιστρον . τὴν συγγένειαν πρὸς τὸν πατριάρχην ἔσωζε Φώτιον· ἐξ ἀδελφοὶ γὰρ οἱ δύο μάγιστροι οὗτοι τούτου ἐτύγχανον.

A shortened paraphrase of the same passage is also found in Skylitzes[37] who, however, introduces some significant changes:

ἦσαν δὲ τῇ τοιαύτῃ βασιλίδι ἄρρενες μὲν ἀδελφοὶ δύο ἀδελφαὶ δὲ τρεῖς· Σοφία·Μαρία·καὶ Εἰρήνη·ὧν ἡ μὲν Σοφία Κωνσταντίνῳ συνήφθη τῷ Βαρβουτζίκῳ· εἰς μαγίστρους τελοῦντι· Εἰρήνη δὲ Σεργίῳ πατρικίῳ· ἀδελφῷ τυγχάνοντι Φωτίου τοῦ μετὰ ταῦτα εἰς τὸν τῆς πατριαρχίας ἀναβιβασθέντος θρόνον· καὶ ἡ Μαρία Ἀρσαβὴρ μαγίστρῳ· ἀνδρὶ γενναίῳ καὶ ἐν τοῖς τότε καιροῖς διαπρέποντι.

Let us, for the sake of argument, admit that the name of the third sister, which is left blank in Theoph. Cont. was Eirene; even so, it is clear that Skylitzes committed an error in saying that this Eirene married Sergios the brother of Photios, for, in that case, her two sons would have been Photios's nephews, not his cousins as specified in Theoph. Cont. But then we may ask (as Bury did a long time ago): Where did Skylitzes find the name of Sergios if it was not in his source? Consequently, Bury suggested adding to the text of the Continuator, after ἔπειτα δὲ καὶ μαγίστρῳ, the words <ἡ δὲ Εἰρήνη Σεργίῳ> and continuing τῷ Εἰρήνης τῆς μητρός, etc.[38] If we accept this addition, we obtain the genealogical tree No. 1. We could then go one step further and suggest that Sergios, the brother of Eirene, i.e., the uncle of Photios, may have been Sergios Niketiates;[39] but this, of course, is only speculation. Bury himself, however, later changed his mind and declared the Continuator's text to be satisfactory as it stands

---

36. The only other manuscript that contains this passage, viz. *Barber. gr, 232*, fol. 103ᵛ, has the same lacuna after Σοφία·καὶ ἡ. *Barber. gr. 232* is, however, a copy of *Vatic. gr. 167.* I am indebted to Prof. I. Ševčenko for these particulars.

37. Ed. Thurn, 98 = Cedrenus, Bonn ed., II, 161.

38. "The Relationship of the Patriarch Photius to the Empress Theodora," *EHR*, 5 (1890), 255-58.

39. The name Sergios was, in any case, very common in the family of Photios. In addition to his father and his brother, we may mention his ἀνεψιός Sergios who was held in high esteem by Romanos I: Theoph. Cont., 433-34.

Genealogical Tree: Alternative 1

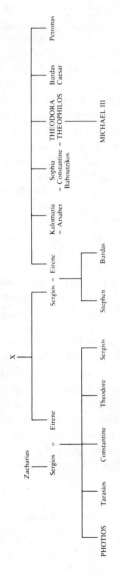

Genealogical Tree: Alternative 2

on the grounds that only two of the three sisters need have been married.[40] If so, we obtain the genealogical tree No. 2. Whichever solution we adopt, we may conclude that Photios's mother was called Eirene and that she was related by marriage to the imperial family.

The last piece of the puzzle that need concern us is the anti-Photian pamphlet contained in the Chronicle of pseudo-Symeon.[41] This venomous document begins by saying that Photios's father was the *spatharios* Sergios and that his grandfther was called Zacharias.[42] Sergios was of alien extraction, ἐθνικοῦ αἵματος, and he married a nun whom he had abducted from a convent. When the woman became pregnant, St. Michael of Synnada, who was on friendly terms with Sergios, foresaw the baleful future of the offspring and wanted to kill the mother with his staff. St. Hilarion of the monastery of Dalmatou delivered a similar prophecy. When Photios had been born, another prominent monk, the Abbot James of the monastery of Maximina, was prevailed upon to baptize him; for the parents were φιλομόναχοι, lovers of monks, and they begged all the holy men of their acquaintance to pray on behalf of Photios. Sergios even undertook the ascent of Mount Olympos to seek the blessing of the great hermit, St. Ioannikios, only to be greeted with the words: "Photios does not wish in his heart to know Thy ways, O Lord." The pamphlet goes on to relate how the young Photios excelled in pagan studies; how he sold his soul to a Jewish magician after abjuring the cross, how he became friendly with Gregory Asbestas, the deposed bishop of Syracuse, how at length the Caesar Bardas made him patriarch.

The mythical elements of the story are obvious enough, and they have recently been analysed by J. Gouillard.[43] The motif of the ravished nun, for example, is a known ingredient of the Antichrist legend. Nor need we believe the allegation that Photios sold his soul to a Jewish magician. Yet, when we examine this text, we notice several elements that clearly conflict with the purpose of the diatribe. In spite of a half-hearted attempt to blacken the character of Sergios (alien origin, irruption into a nunnery), he is made to keep impeccable company: he is a friend of St. Michael of Synnada, he consorts with St. Hilarion and

---

40. *History of the Eastern Roman Empire*, 156.
41. 668-71.
42. There is a difficulty at 668/15-17, where the printed text has οὗτος ὁ Φώτιος υἱὸς Σεργίου σπαθαρίου ἦν· οὗτινος ὁ πατὴρ Ζαχαρίας ὠνόμαστο· ὃς πάλιν ἔσχεν υἱὸν Λέοντα βασι .This suggests a lacuna, but, in fact, there is none in our only independent MS of pseudo-Symeon, viz. *Paris. gr. 1712*, fol. 250ʳ, which has βασι, i.e., presumably, βασιλέα. The same reading appears in the *Scor. V-I-4*, fol. 78ʳ, an apographon of the Parisinus. Since Zacharias could not have been the father of any emperor called Leo, one must postulate a scribal error. I am indebted for these details to Mr. A. Markopoulos who is preparing a new edition of pseudo-Symeon.
43. "Le Photius du pseudo-Syméon Magistros," *RESEE*, 9 (1971), 397-404.

the Abbot James, he pays a visit to St. Ioannikios. He and his wife are called *philomonachoi*, which was an epithet of commendation. Why should the libellist, who was writing, as is generally assumed, in the late ninth century,[44] have invented these details which redounded to the credit of Sergios, unless they were generally known to be true? Why should he have called Photios's father Sergios if that was not his name? Even the allegation of alien extraction may be true, as already noticed by Gouillard: for we are told that the Emperor Michael referred to his patriarch as *Chazaroprosopos*, 'Chazar face,' and applied to him the enigmatic epithet Marzoukas,[45] which Gouillard thinks may have been a Laz word.

We may now put together the pieces of the puzzle. The father of Photios was Sergios the Confessor, a rich dignitary, probably of foreign extraction, but whose family must have been established at Constantinople for a few generations. He married a lady called Eirene whose brother was the husband of either Kalomaria or Eirene, sisters of the Empress Theodora. Sergios was exiled, together with his whole family, by order of the Emperor Theophilos—not of Leo V or Michael II, as some scholars have assumed. This probably happened after 832/33, when Theophilos launched his persecution.[46] The harsh treatment inflicted on Sergios—surprising in the case of a man having such high connections—may well have been caused by the discovery of his historical work which was directed against the father of the reigning emperor. This hypothesis may explain the fact that the history was left unfinished. Both Sergios and Eirene died in banishment. We do not know how old Photios was at the time—perhaps in his teens. In any case, it is very unlikely that he could have entered government service before the death of his persecutor in 842. If true, this would have interesting chronological implications for other aspects of Photios's career which, however, we do not have to pursue here.

However that may be, there can be no doubt that Photios grew up under the shadow of the Iconoclastic persecution. This fact alone would account for his lifelong preoccupation with the issue of Iconoclasm. But there was, I believe, more to it than that. The glorious death of his father, his own early sufferings conferred on him an aura of martyrdom or, at any rate, of great respectability which made him later a fitting candidate for the patriarchal throne. Furthermore, he was closely identified by family ties with the very clique that had engineered the Triumph of Orthodoxy in 843. In addition to his relatives, this

---

44. See A.P. Každan, "Khronika Simeona Logofeta," *VizVrem*, 15 (1959), 134-35.
45. Pseudo-Symeon, 673-74.
46. See V. Laurent, *La Vie merveilleuse de S. Pierre d'Atroa* (Brussels, 1956), 187, §63. Cf. D. Papachryssanthou, "La Vie du patrice Nicétas," *TM*, 3 (1968), 320-21.

coterie also included Methodios and the Sicilian archbishop Gregory Asbestas. At an earlier date St. Euthymios of Sardis had belonged to the same group. Their mutual ties are well attested. When Euthymios died in 831, it was Methodios that wrote his *Vita*. This document contains a curious detail. When Euthymios was deported by the Emperor Theophilos to the little island of St. Andrew, where he was imprisoned in the same tomb-like cell as Methodios, he was interrogated concerning his acquaintances: in his reply he named only one, a female relative by marriage (κηδεστρία) of the Emperor.[47] Unfortunately, we are not given her name: it may have been one of Theodora's sisters; it could even have been the mother of Photios. The ties that linked Methodios, Gregory Asbestas and Photios are better known. The young Photios wrote a hymn that was recited at the funeral of Methodios in 847; the same Saint's *Vita* was composed by Gregory Asbestas.[48] In 858 Photios received his priestly ordination at the hands of Gregory Asbestas and throughout his life he remained this bishop's active supporter.

By comparison with Photios, his opponent Ignatios could not claim much credit in the struggle against Iconoclasm. Even his enthusiastic biographer Niketas the Paphlagonian could not adduce any significant achievements: he tells us that during the persecution Ignatios devoted himself to a strict regimen of fasting and genuflection; that he baptized a great number of children; and that he occasionally afforded hospitality to victims of the persecution.[49] In other words, he remained pretty passive; and there is evidence to suggest that most other monks did the same. There is a curious incident in the Life of one of these monks, St. Anthony the Younger. In speaking of the Triumph of Orthodoxy, his biographer does not even mention the Empress Theodora or the Patriarch Methodios; whatever credit there was is ascribed to "the gathering of our holy fathers and confessors of Christ." Even so, he is not very enthusiastic about this event which he calls "the so-called joy that had spread through the world" (τὴν γεγενημένην δῆθεν χαρὰν ἐν τῷ κόσμῳ). And he adds that when the news of this so-called joy was brought to St. Anthony, the holy man replied in a surly tone: "Indeed, Orthodoxy has been established; but after a time things will only get worse."[50] His negative response should probably be explained by the fact that Orthodoxy had been established by the wrong set of people, and he may have been prophesying the acrimonious rift that was soon to divide Methodios from the Studites.

---

47. See J. Gouillard in *BZ*, 53 (1960), 40.
48. On this *Vita* see J. Gouillard in *Byzantion*, 31 (1961), 371 ff.
49. *Vita Ignatii*, PG, 105, cols. 497D-500B.
50. F. Halkin, "Saint Antoine le Jeune et Pétronas," *AnalBoll*, 62 (1944), 211-12.

Now, I do not believe that the Patriarch Photios was as pure as snow. He had a great deal to account for, including his ordination, and he did on occasion some pretty unscrupulous things. In fighting his opponents he needed a weapon, a cause that everyone could understand: this cause was provided by the issue of Iconoclasm. He could truthfully claim for himself and his parents a glorious part in the struggle; he could and did assume the spiritual heritage of Methodios, a heritage that had been rejected by the Ignatians. This, I believe, is the main reason why he harped on Iconoclasm at every possible opportunity; why he wanted to see it condemned time and time again. To give even wider publicity to his achievements, he embarked on a programme of church decoration. In this respect, Ignatios appears to have done very little, if anything, during the eleven years of his first patriarchate (847-58). Photios seized the opportunity: he covered with iconic mosaics the Golden Hall of the palace, the palatine chapel of the Virgin of the Pharos, and had started work in St. Sophia when he was overthrown in 867. Moreover, he himself loudly proclaimed the importance of these artistic manifestations: it was as if the theme of Orthodoxy was being constantly replayed. One may recall his proud statement when the mosaic of the Virgin in the apse of St. Sophia was unveiled on 29 March 867: "If one called this day the beginning and day of Orthodoxy ... one would not be far wrong."[51]

One may wonder at this point whether this artistic zeal was due to Photios himself. The obscure figure of Gregory Asbestas naturally comes to mind. It will be remembered that the Sicilian bishop was an amateur artist who drew uncomplimentary miniatures of Ignatios in the margins of a manuscript—"for the splendid fellow was also a painter in addition to his other vices," as Niketas the Paphlagonian tells us.[52] Did Asbestas, too, take a lead in the redecoration of churches? The Sicilian Chronicle known as the Cambridge Chronicle informs us that in 844, "the archbishop Gregory introduced Orthodoxy."[53] Did he introduce it visually as well as dogmatically? In the one preserved letter of Photios addressed to Asbestas—a letter dating from the second patriarchate of Ignatios when both friends were in disgrace—the deposed patriarch urges his correspondent to go on erecting churches, "now that the abandonment and destruction of churches, instead of their former adornment, prevails in the Roman State."[54] Was he referring to conditions in Sicily under the impact of the Arab invasion or was he making a more general statement concerning the abandonment of their joint

51. Ed. Laourdas, 168; trans. Mango, 291.
52. *Vita Ignatii*, PG, 105, col. 540D.
53. A.A. Vasiliev, *Byzance et les Arabes*, I (Brussels, 1935), 345.
54. PG, 102, col. 832D; ed. Valettas, 423.

XIII

16   THE LIQUIDATION OF ICONOCLASM

artistic undertakings?

Today the quarrels of Methodios and the Studites, of Photios and Ignatios are forgotten except by a few professional Byzantinists. A somewhat wider public knows that Photios provided the definitive and most eloquent statement of the victory of icon-worship. But his artistic achievement, prompted by the circumstances that I tried to explain, is seen and admired in the apse of St. Sophia by every tourist who goes to Istanbul.

XIV

WHEN WAS MICHAEL III BORN?

THE family history of the Amorian house is notoriously obscure. It has been the subject of serious investigation in the early years of this century by Brooks, Melioranskij, and Bury who have cleared up many difficulties. Several important problems remain, however, unresolved, among them the dates of the birth and coronation of Michael III.

The *communis opinio* is that Michael was born in 839. This is based on the statement of Theophanes Continuatus that at the time of his father's death (20 January 842) Michael was in his third year (τρίτον ἔτος διανύων).[1] A different Byzantine tradition embodied in the *Vita S. Theodorae* and the *De Theophili imperatoris absolutione* asserts that Michael came to the throne at the age of five and a half, i.e. that he was born in 836.[2] Rejected by the majority of historians, the latter tradition was, nevertheless, upheld by Stein on the strength of some South Italian documents to which we shall presently return.[3] Stein's argument has been accepted by Grégoire[4] and Ostrogorsky,[5] and I, too, endorsed it on a previous occasion.[6] More recently, Dr. A. Dikigoropoulos, in a stimulating article devoted to the gold coinage of Theophilus, has argued for a compromise solution: Michael, he believes, was born in late July 838 and was crowned on September 1 of the same year.[7] Having

had occasion to review the evidence, I find that Dr. Dikigoropoulos' theory raises insuperable objections. The correct date of Michael's birth—I might as well say so at once—is almost certainly January 9/10, 840. This is not a new solution,[8] but it ought to be argued more fully than has been done in the past.

It is common knowledge that the narrative sources for the Amorian period are no earlier than the middle of the tenth century and that they are marred by confusion, ignorance, and even deliberate falsification. Our first step, therefore, should be to seek a document that is not suspect. Such a document exists: it is the monogrammatic inscription on the famous bronze doors of the southwest vestibule of St. Sophia. Here we have a piece of evidence that is strictly contemporary and "official" in the sense that it emanates directly from the imperial government. I hasten to add that I am not introducing here any hitherto unknown information. The inscription was read correctly (or nearly so) in 1885 by Canon C. G. Curtis and S. Aristarchis,[9] whose reading has been endorsed by all subsequent scholars who have had occasion to examine the doors. Now, the inscription was first engraved in 838/9 and it was emended in 840/1. Resolving the monograms, the original text was the following:

1. Κύριε βοήθει
2. Θεοφίλῳ δεσπότῃ
3. Θεοτόκε βοήθει
4. Θεοδώρᾳ αὐγούστῃ
5. Χριστὲ βοήθει
6. Ἰωάννῃ πατριάρχῃ
7. ἔτους ἀπὸ κτίσεως
8. κόσμουϛτμζ΄ ἰνδ. β΄

---

[1] Ed. Bonn, p. 148.

[2] W. Regel, *Analecta byzantino-russica* (St. Petersburg, 1891–8), pp. 11, 12, 21.

[3] *Ann. de l'Inst. de Phil. et d'Hist. Orient.*, II (1934), p. 899, note 2.

[4] In the French ed. of Vasiliev's *Byzance et les Arabes*, I (Brussels, 1935), p. 191.

[5] *Geschichte des byzantinischen Staates*, 3rd ed. (Munich, 1963), p. 182.

[6] *The Homilies of Photius* (Cambridge, Mass., 1958), p. 309, note 17.

[7] *DOP*, 18 (1964), p. 353 ff. Note that Meli-

oranskij in *Vizant. Vrem.*, VIII (1901), p. 35, dated Michael's birth to the end of 838.

[8] It has been advocated by F. Štejnman (Steinmann) in *Vizant. Vrem.*, XXI (1914), p. 22f., and, somewhat cautiously, by A. P. Každan, *ibid.*, N.S., XXI (1962), p. 96f.

[9] Ὁ ἐν Κων/πόλει Ἑλληνικὸς Φιλολ. Σύλλογος, Ἀρχαιολογικὴ Ἐπιτροπή, Suppl. to vol. XVI (1885), p. 30 and pl. III.

Subsequently, monogram No. 6 was changed to read Μιχαὴλ δεσπότη (fig. 1) while in monogram No. 8 the *annus mundi* was emended to ϛτμθ' and the indiction number to δ' (fig. 2).[10]

There cannot be the slightest doubt concerning the accuracy of the above reading.[11] The inscription was engraved on bronze plates and inlaid with silver. All the corrector could do, therefore, was to remove the silver filling from the letters he wished to erase and to rub down their outlines, but he did not succeed in obliterating them completely. In monogram No. 8, which is of particular importance to us, the original Z of the *annus mundi* is clearly visible under the Θ in the upper right-hand quarter (fig. 2). In the lower left-hand quarter the IN is original, while the little superscript Δ and the diagonal stroke that meets the right foot of the N (this is the normal sign of abbreviation) pertain to the correction. In the lower right-hand quarter the Δ is original and so is the diagonal stroke across it. This was followed by a B, still clearly visible, with a horizontal bar above it. The corrector eliminated the B and turned the Δ of ἰνδικτιῶνος into a numeral by engraving above it a horizontal bar.

The implications of the inscription are obvious. When it was first engraved, i.e. between September 1, 838 and August 31, 839, Michael had not yet been crowned and, in all probability, had not yet been born. He was, however, emperor or became emperor between September 1, 840 and August 31, 841. Indeed, the only plausible explanation for the change in the inscription is provided precisely by Michael's coronation which, we know, took place in St. Sophia. The Patriarch John the Grammarian, whose name was engraved in the first instance, remained in favour as long as Theophilus was on the throne and in office for a year after Theophilus had died: there can be no question here of a *damnatio memoriae*. If

his name was removed, this was because Theophilus had at long last begotten a son and heir: the young prince naturally took precedence over the patriarch.

The validity of this explanation is confirmed by a marginal note in the unique manuscript of Genesius, Lips. gr. 16, fol. 268ʳ: ἡ γέννησις Μιχαὴλ τοῦ υἱοῦ Θεοφίλου ἦν μ(ηνὶ) Ἰανου(αρίῳ) θ' ἐπὶ ι' ἐν ἔτει ϛτμη' ὡ(ρα̨) νυκτ(ὸς) πρ(ώτη).[12] Clearly, the scholiast had access to some very precise information, the source of which cannot now be identified. And if Michael was born in the night of January 9/10, 840, he would have just entered on his third year when Theophilus died on January 20, 842. A further confirmation is provided by Hamza of Ispahan, an author of the tenth century. The relevant passage reads as follows in Reiske's translation: *Regnabat Theophilus Michaelis in diebus Almamonis 22 annos et tres menses; deinde Michael, eius filius, cum matre in diebus Almoctaderi usque ad vigesimum octavum aetatis suae annum.*[13] Since Michael was murdered on September 23, 867, he would then have been in fact in his twenty-eighth year.

The evidence we have outlined is so weighty and consistent that we would need very serious reasons for rejecting it. What are these reasons?

At first sight, the most serious objection appears to be provided by the South Italian documents quoted by Stein. These are Numbers 21, 22, and 25 of the *Codex diplomaticus Cavensis* and are dated by its editors to 842, 843, and 845 respectively.[14] The A.D. dates are naturally not contained in the documents themselves which yield only the following indications:

No. 21: Fifth year of the Emperor Michael, September, indiction 6.

---

[10] The further inscription [Θεοφίλου καὶ] Μιχαὴλ νικητῶν, now unfortunately lost, which ran across the top of the doors must have been added when the monograms were emended.

[11] The alternative reading proposed by Dikigoropoulos, *op. cit.*, p. 355, must be rejected.

[12] Štejnman, *loc. cit.*; Dikigoropoulos, *op. cit.*, p. 354.

[13] In the Bonn ed. of De Cerimoniis, II, p. 451. I owe this reference to Prof. R. J. H. Jenkins. In the translation by J. M. E. Gottwaldt, *Hamzae Ispahanensis Annalium libri X*, II (Leipzig, 1848), p. 59, made, it would seem, from an inferior manuscript, the text is, however, rather different: *Michael, Theophili filius, cum matre, quae ad filii pubertatem usque imperavit, tempore Almotavekkeli, annos XXVIII.*

[14] *Codex diplomaticus Cavensis*, I (Naples, 1873), pp. 22, 24, 28.

No. 22: Fifth year of the Emperor Michael, April, indiction 6.

No. 25: Seventh year of the Emperor Michael, April, indiction 8.

Two questions now arise: 1. How reliable are these dates? 2. Can we be certain that these documents refer to Michael III and not to another Michael? To ascertain the chronological reliability of this material we are obliged to examine briefly the other documents of the Cava archives that are dated by the regnal years of Byzantine emperors.[15] Confining ourselves to volume I of the edition, and omitting for the time being Numbers 21, 22, and 25, we find the following:

No. 10. Editors' date 821. Indications: Second year of the Emperor Michael, April, indiction 4. The editors propose that *indictione quarta* should be corrected to *decima quarta*, but even this will not do. The month of April in the second year of Michael II (date of accession December 25, 820) would be April 822 and would correspond to indiction 15.

No. 11. Editors' date 821. Indications: Second year of the reign of Michael, October, indiction 11. The editors suggest that *undecima indictione* should be corrected to *decima quinta*, as indeed it should be if the document was drawn up in 821; but that would correspond to the first year of Michael II.

No. 103. Editors' date 892. Indications: Sixth year of the reign of Leo and Alexander, March, indiction 10. Date correct counting the regnal year from the death of Basil I (August 29, 886).

No. 126. Editors' date 910. Indications: Third year of the reign of Constantine, January, indiction 13. Date impossible since January 910

falls in the second year of Constantine VII (crowned May 15, 908) and within the lifetime of both Leo VI (d. May 11, 912) and Alexander (d. June 6, 913) who would naturally have been mentioned in the first instance as being the senior emperors.

No. 127. Editors' date 911. Indications: Fourth year of the reign of Constantine, January, indiction 14. Date impossible for the same reason as in No. 126.

No. 131. Editors' date 912. Indications: Twenty-seventh year of the reign of Alexander and Constantine, November, indiction 1. Date correct counting from the death of Basil I, although the regnal year applies only to Alexander.

No. 139. Editors' date 923. Indications (copied from a later index, the document being illegible): Fifth year of the reign of Romanus and Michael (?), February, indiction 11. In fact, February 923 corresponds to the third year of Romanus I.

No. 142. Editors' date 924. Indications: Sixteenth year of Constantine and third year of Romanus and of his son Christopher, July 1, indiction 12. In July 924 Constantine VII was in his seventeenth year (from May 15, 908), Romanus I in his fourth (from December 17, 920) and Christopher likewise in his fourth (from May 20, 921).

No. 143. Editors' date 925. Indications: Third year of Romanus, November, indiction 14. November 925 corresponds to the fifth year of Romanus I.

No. 146. Editors' date 927. Indications (taken from a later summary, the document being illegible): ninth year of Constantine Porphyrogenitus, April, indiction 15. The data are contradictory.

No. 178. Editors' date 950. Indications: Forty-second year of Constantine and fifth year of his son Romanus, July 2, indiction 8. In July 950 Constantine VII was in his forty-

[15] An attempt in this direction has already been made by Každan, *loc. cit.* (*supra*, note 8). His argumentation is, however, partly invalidated by his not knowing that Constantine VII was crowned on May 15, 908: on this date see P. Grierson and R. J. H. Jenkins in *Byzantion*, XXXII (1962), p. 133 ff.

third year and Romanus II in his sixth (from April 6, 945).[16]

No. 200. Editors' date 958. Indications: Forty-sixth year of Constantine and fourteenth of his son Romanus, November, indiction 2. Data correct counting Constantine's regnal year from the death of Alexander.

Thus, out of twelve documents we have examined, only three have correct and consistent dates. As for the rest, we do not know whether the fault lies with the editors or with the mediaeval copyists of the documents or whether the people of Salerno and Naples had only a vague idea of the regnal years of Byzantine emperors. To return to Michael III: the normal way of computing his regnal years seems to have been from the death of Theophilus on January 20, 842, as indeed was done, quite correctly, in a Neapolitan document of 866[17] and in a Neapolitan inscription, now lost, of the year 846/7.[18] Note furthermore that a document of Gaeta of October 839 is dated in the nineteenth year of Theophilus without any mention of Michael.[19]

In short, the three documents of Cava (Nos. 21, 22, 25) give no basis whatever for altering the chronology of Michael III. The indications they contain, if not mistaken, are equally inapplicable to Michael I (who reigned less than two years) and Michael II, but would fit, with only one slight correction, the reign of Michael IV (1034–1041). Whether they should be so post-dated is, however, a question that we are content to leave to specialists in South Italian diplomatics.

[16] On the date of the coronation of Romanus II, see G. Ostrogorsky and E. Stein in *Byzantion* VII (1932), p. 197; G. de Jerphanion in *Orient. christ. period.*, I (1935), p. 490 ff.

[17] *Tabularium Casinense*, I, *Codex diplomaticus Cajetanus*, I (Monte Cassino, 1887), p. 20, No. XII = B. Capasso, *Monumenta ad Neapol. ducatus hist. pert.*, I (Naples, 1881), p. 264: twenty-fourth year of Michael Porphyrogenitus, second year of Caesar Bardas, 15 January, indiction 14.

[18] Capasso, *op. cit.*, II/2 (1892), p. 224, No. 13: fifth year of Michael Porphyrogenitus, indiction 10.

[19] *Cod. dipl. Cajetan.*, I, p. 9, No. V = Capasso, *op. cit.*, I, p. 263.

The second objection, and one on which Dr. Dikigoropoulos lays great stress, is drawn from the career of Theophilus' son-in-law, Alexius Mousele. There is no need to recapitulate here the meager and conflicting information provided by Byzantine sources concerning this Armenian prince. It is enough to recall that he was married to Maria, who may have been Theophilus' eldest daughter, that he was elevated to the rank of Caesar, was entrusted with a military command in Sicily, and finally returned to Constantinople and became a monk. According to Theophanes Continuatus, Alexius gave up public office after the death of his wife Maria and the birth of Michael III.[20] Now, Dikigoropoulos supposes that Alexius left Sicily before the end of 838 and deduces from this that Michael must have been born earlier in the same year. In fact, however, we do not know when Alexius departed from Sicily. He may have arrived there, as Bury supposes, in 838 in time to break up the siege of Cefalù by the Arabs. In 839 no serious fighting is reported in Sicily. In 840 the Arabs captured a few towns in the interior of the island. Bury,[21] followed by the French edition of Vasiliev,[22] suggested that Alexius left Sicily in 839—clearly, because he thought that Michael had been born in the same year. There is nothing, however, to prevent us from supposing that Alexius departed from Sicily, say, in the early part of 840. In sum, the date of Michael's birth cannot be deduced from the career of Alexius Mousele.

Another argument advanced by Dikigoropoulos is that in most chronicles of the "Logothete family" the entry recording Michael's birth is placed after the battle of Dazimon (July 22, 838) and before the fall of Amorium (August 12, 838). Here, however, we are on very treacherous ground. For a later period, viz. for the reigns of Basil I, Leo VI, and Alexander, the Logothete's entries are in correct chronological sequence, as Prof. Jenkins has recently shown,[23] but this is far from being always the case in the

[20] P. 108.
[21] *History of the Eastern Roman Empire* (London, 1912), p. 305.
[22] *Byzance et les Arabes*, I, pp. 137, 144.
[23] *DOP*, 19 (1965), p. 91 ff.

period prior to Basil I. Examining more closely the part that concerns us, we find the following order of entries:

1. John the Grammarian appointed patriarch (January 21, 837).
2. Arab invasion of Asia Minor. Theophilus, accompanied by the domestic Manuel and a Persian contingent (under Theophobus), is defeated by the Arabs; his life is saved by Manuel (= battle of Dazimon, July 22, 838). Theophilus retires to Dorylaion. Manuel dies of wounds received and is buried in his monastery at Constantinople.
3. The Persian auxiliaries under Theophobus come under suspicion of treason and stage a revolt. Theophobus seizes Sinope. The Emperor goes to Paphlagonia and, after giving assurances to the Persians, brings Theophobus back to Constantinople. At this time (τότε δή) Michael III is born.
4. Anecdote about a horse that was stolen by the Count of Opsikion.
5. While the Emperor is at Bryas (an Asiatic suburb of Constantinople) he receives intelligence that the Caliph is on his way to besiege Amorium. Theophilus marches to Cappadocia. The Caliph detaches from his main army a force of 50,000 men which defeats the Byzantines. Theophilus barely escapes with his life (= once again, the battle of Dazimon). Siege and capture of Amorium (August 12, 838). Anecdote about Leo the Philosopher with reference to the capture of Amorium.
6. Theophilus' buildings in the Great Palace.
7. Punishment of Sts. Theophanes and Theodore, the Graptoi (July 18, 836).[23a]
8. The helmet of Justinian's equestrian statue in the Augustaion falls down and is fitted back in place.
9. Michael III crowned in St. Sophia.
10. Theophilus sets up a hospice.
11. Theophobus is executed. Death of Theophilus.[24]

It is obvious that there is considerable confusion in items 2–5. The reason for this is probably that the Logothete was using two sources which he reproduced side by side without realizing that they referred to the same set of events, viz. the war of 838: hence the duplication of the battle of Dazimon. It is also clear that the events described in item 3 could not all have happened in the three weeks that separated the battle of Dazimon from the fall of Amorium. We know that after the battle Theophilus made his way first to the plain of Chiliokomon, north of Amasia, and then to Dorylaion or, according to another source, to Nicaea. It is also reported that he had to make a hasty appearance at Constantinople in order to dispel rumors that he had been killed in battle.[25] If it is true that he went in person to Paphlagonia in order to conciliate Theophobus, this journey cannot be placed in the same brief time-span. The return of Theophobus to the capital (which, as we have seen, the Logothete connects with Michael's birth) must have taken place after the fall of Amorium. How long after, I should not like to say: the story of Theophobus is so hopelessly tangled in our sources that there is no clear way of resolving it.[26] In conclusion, the Logothete's Chronicle does not help us in determining the date of Michael's † birth.

The remaining objections to our thesis can be dealt with very briefly. The testimony of the *Vita S. Theodorae* and the *De Theophili imperatoris absolutione*,[27] which is in any case self-contradictory, should simply be dismissed. And when Photius, speaking probably in early September 867, says that

---

[23a] See J. Pargoire in *Echos d'Orient*, VI (1903), p. 187.

[24] Slavic Logothete: *Simeona Metafrasta i Logofeta Spisanie Mira*, ed. V. Sreznevskij (St.

Petersburg, 1905), p. 96 ff.; Theodosius Melitenus, ed. Tafel, p. 152 ff.; Georgius Monachus, ed. Muralt, p. 707 ff.; Leo Grammaticus, ed. Bonn, p. 221 ff. (story of the seizure of Sinope by Theophobus omitted except for initial sentence); Georgius Monachus, ed. Bonn, p. 799 ff. (birth of Michael omitted).

[25] See *Byzance et les Arabes*, I, p. 157 f.

[26] I would hesitate to adopt in their entirety Grégoire's ingenious views on Theophobus expounded in *Byzantion*, IX (1934), p. 183 ff.

[27] Since in another passage (p. 15) the *Vita S. Theodorae* asserts that Michael was killed at the age of twenty-nine: cf. Regel's comments, *ibid.*, p. xvii f.

Michael had attained the age of Christ,[28] he probably means merely that the Emperor was about thirty years old.

While we can be reasonably certain that Michael was born in January 840, the date of his coronation cannot be established with equal accuracy. I have no doubt that he was crowned in the course of the same year. For this we have, first, the testimony of Photius who states that Michael was made emperor "from the very cradle,"[29] and second, the entry in the *Annales Cavenses*, dated A.D. 840, indiction 3 (i.e., before September) which reads *Michael porfirogenitus frater ejus* (i.e., brother of Theophilus which, of course,

is wrong).[30] If the inscription on the bronze doors of St. Sophia was altered immediately after Michael's coronation, we may conjecture that this event took place towards September 840.

Historians who pass judgment on Michael's character and achievements should give thought to the dates we have attempted to establish. Michael was sixteen when he expelled his mother from the palace and not quite twenty-eight when he was murdered. It may be true to say with Bury that "Michael III reigned for a quarter of a century, but he never governed." Considering his age, however, this is hardly surprising.

---

[28] *The Homilies of Photius*, p. 309.
[29] *Ibid.*

[30] *Cod. dipl. Cavensis*, V (1878), p. 30; MGH, *Script.*, III (1839), p. 188 (omitting the indiction).

1. Monogram Number 6

2. Monogram Number 8

Istanbul, St. Sophia, Southwest Vestibule, Bronze Doors. Monogrammatic Inscriptions

EUDOCIA INGERINA, THE NORMANS, AND THE MACEDONIAN DYNASTY

Few problems of medieval history have been debated so passionately and at such inordinate length as that of the origins of the Russian state and, within that context, that of the earliest contacts between Byzantium and the Normans. For our present purpose we need remember only that the first attestation of such contacts is contained in a famous passage of the *Annales Bertiniani* which records that on May 18, 839 Lewis the Pious received at Ingelheim a Byzantine embassy which was accompanied by certain persons called Rhos; that these persons had been sent to Byzantium on a good-will mission *(amicitiae...causa)*, and that in his letter to Lewis the Emperor Theophilus had requested a safe passage for the Rhos, now homeward bound[1]. We are not here concerned with the many thorny questions that are posed by this passage, e.g. whether the Rhos had come from Kiev or from elsewhere; why their king was called *chacanus;* which were those *barbarae et nimiae feritatis gentes inmanissimae* that prevented their return to their country of origin by the same route they had followed to Constantinople[2]. The only point we should like to stress—and this can hardly be doubted—is that in 839 the Byzantine government and the Rhos were on friendly terms. The next recorded contact between the two—setting aside the alleged Russian raid on Amastris before 843 which I am unable to accept— †
was of a less friendly nature: it was the attack on Constantinople in June 860. The timing of this attack shows, incidentally, that the Russian Vikings were well informed of Byzantine military plans[3].

There appears to be yet another piece of evidence that has been surprisingly neglected in the voluminous literature devoted to *Byzantinorussica*. The person of Eudocia Ingerina, the mistress of Michael III and thereafter the wife of Basil I, needs no introduction. She is described in our

---

[1] Ed. *G. Waitz*, Script. rer. germ. (Hannover, 1883), 19 f.

[2] For a discussion of the subject see, e.g., *A.A. Vasiliev*, The Russian Attack on Constantinople in 860 (Cambridge, Mass., 1946), 6 ff.; *A. Stender-Petersen*, „Das Problem d. ältesten byzantinisch-russisch-nordischen Beziehungen," Relazioni del X Congr. Intern. di Scienze Storiche, III (Florence, 1955), 174 ff.

[3] *J. B. Bury*, A History of the Eastern Roman Empire (London, 1912), 421.

sources as Ἰγγερίνα or Ἰγγηρίνα or as ἡ τοῦ Ἴγγερος, i. e., daughter of Inger[4]. We are not the first to have noticed that the name Inger appears to be Scandinavian, equivalent to Ingvarr, i.e. Igor: both D. Obolensky[5] and the late Romilly Jenkins[6] have made this observation without, however, drawing any further inferences from it. It is true that in Greek documents Ingvarr is usually rendered by Ἴγγωρ or Ἴγγορ, but Liudprand preserves the identical form, Inger[7]. If our supposition is correct, some interesting consequences will have to be explored.

Setting aside Eudocia's father to whom we shall presently return, the name Inger occurs, as far as I know, only once in Byzantine sources: it is that of an iconoclast metropolitan of Nicaea, ca. A.D. 825. This man is known from the two Lives of St. Ioannicius, both of which tell substantially the same story. In 825 Ioannicius undertook a mission with a view to freeing the Byzantine prisoners held by the Bulgarians. After he had returned to his mountain, he was visited by Antony, abbot τῶν Ἐλαιοβώμων (modern Kurşunlu)[8], and the latter's *oikonomos* Basil. Ioannicius asked Antony to convey a message to Inger (Ἴγγερ in the Life by Sabas, Ἤγγερ in the Life by Peter): he should abandon iconoclasm because his death was approaching. Antony refused the mission knowing the bishop's stern character, but Basil agreed to perform it. Inger began by repenting, but soon he lapsed again. Fifteen days later he died suddenly while sitting on his throne[9].

The above incident is dated ca. 827 by the Bollandist Van den Gheyn[10], but this is only an approximation. Inger must have succeeded Peter who died on December 10 or 11, 826, but had been deposed earlier from the see of Nicaea[11]. The next bishop after Inger was probably Ignatius, the bio-

---

[4] The spelling varies slightly: ἡ τοῦ Ἴγγερος: Leo gramm., ed. Bonn, 230, 252, 255; Georgius monachus, ed. Bonn, 816; Theodosius Meliteus, ed. Tafel, 160, 176; Vat. gr. 153, ed. *V.M. Istrin*, Khronika Georgija Amartola, II (Petrograd, 1922), 4, 17; Theoph. Cont., ed. Bonn, 235; Genesius, ed. Bonn, 111; Cedrenus, ed. Bonn, II, 198; τοῦ Ἴγγηρος: Georgius mon., 838; τοῦ Ἴγχηρος: Zonaras, ed. Bonn, III, 414; Ἰγγερίνα: Leo gramm., 250; Vat. gr. 153, ed. *Istrin*, 11, 15; Ἰγγιρίνα: Leo gramm., 242, 249; Theod. Mel., 169, 174, 175; Ἰγγηρίνα: Georgius mon., 828, 835, 836; ps.-Symeon, ed. Bonn, 675, etc.

[5] Constantine. Porphyrogenitus, De adm. imp., Commentary, ed. *R.J.H. Jenkins* (London, 1962), 28 f.

[6] Byzantium: The Imperial Centuries (London, 1966), 159.

[7] Antapodosis, V. 15, ed. *J. Becker*[3], Script. rer. germ. (1915), 138 and 129 (table of contents of Bk. V). Cf. *V. Thomsen*, The Relations between Ancient Russia and Scandinavia (Oxford and London, 1877), 135.

[8] On this monastery see my article, „The Monastery of St. Abercius at Kurşunlu (Elegmi) in Bithynia," Dumbarton Oaks Papers, 22 (1968), 169 ff.

[9] Vita by Sabas, § 30, ASS, Nov. II/1, 360; Vita by Peter (a little more detailed), § 38, ibid., 406. The Metaphrastic Life of St. Ioannicius, PG 116,69 B, adds the further information that Inger had been a renowned ascete and was appointed for this reason to the see of Nicaea: κατ' ἐκεῖνο τοίνυν καιροῦ Ἴγγερ ἐκεῖνος ὥσπερ ἄνθεσιν ἐαρινοῖς τοῖς ἀσκητικοῖς πόνοις ἐκόμα. ἐντεῦθεν καὶ πρόεδρος τῆς τῶν Νικαέων ἐκκλησίας ἀνεδείχθη. πλὴν ἀλλὰ τὸν καρπὸν τῆς ὀρθῆς πίστεως οὐκ εἶχε, etc.

[10] ASS, Nov. II/1, 364, note 1.

[11] *J. Pargoire*, „Saints iconophiles," Échos d'Orient, 4 (1900/1), 353 f.

grapher of the Patriarchs Tarasius and Nicephorus, but we do not know when he was appointed. An attentive study of the correspondence of Ignatius, on which I am now engaged, may eventually throw some light on this problem. The reason why Inger is not designated by his Christian name in the Lives of St. Ioannicius is probably to brand him not only as a heretic but also as a barbarian.

Next we come to Eudocia Ingerina. In reconstructing her career, we must remember that our sources fall into two categories: first, the official myth of the Macedonian dynasty (Theophanes Continuatus, Genesius, the Funeral Oration by Leo VI); second, Symeon the Logothete. The Logothete shows an intimate knowledge of court gossip relating to the reign of Michael III, especially its latter part, and much of it rings true. His source cannot, however, be identified. Bury postulated a lost „Amorian Chronicle"[12], but such is the chronological inaccuracy of this part of the Logothete's account[13], that it could hardly have been based on a set of annals. More recently, A.P. Každan has argued that the Logothete had before him for the reign of Michael III a lost biography of Basil I, a biography that was highly critical of its hero, in short a *psogos*[14]. Whether this is so or not, the Logothete's source must have been close to the events of the 860'ies.

It is recorded that Michael III contracted his liaison with Eudocia in or about the year 855; that she was hated by the Empress Theodora and her chief minister Theoctistus for being impudent (δι' ἀναίδειαν); and that, to break up this association, Theodora made her son marry another Eudocia, the daughter of a certain Decapolites[15]. In 855 Michael was fifteen years old, having been born in January 840[16]. Eudocia could hardly have been much younger and may, indeed, have been slightly older than her imperial companion. Provisionally, we may place the date of her birth also ca. 840.

Our sources are extremely vague about the identity of Inger. The Logothete does not qualify him in any way, while the „Macedonian myth" merely stresses his nobility and good judgment: ἡ (Eudocia) θυγάτηρ ἐτύγχανε τοῦ παρὰ πάντων ἐπ' εὐγενείᾳ καὶ φρονήσει λαλουμένου τότε τοῦ Ἴγγερος[17]. Only in much later, derivative sources does Inger appear as a συγκλητικός[18]. Why this reticence? Eudocia was certainly a lady of good family who be-

---

[12] Eastern Roman Empire, 458 f.

[13] Cf. *R.J.H. Jenkins*, „The Chronological Accuracy of the 'Logothete'" Dumbarton Oaks Papers, 19 (1965), 95.

[14] „Khronika Simeona Logofeta," Viz. Vrem., 15 (1959), 139.

[15] Leo gramm., 229 f. I refrain from quoting the other printed versions of the Logothete's Chronicle.

[16] *C. Mango*, „When was Michael III born?" Dumbarton Oaks Papers, 21 (1967), 253 ff.

[17] Vita Basilii, 235.

[18] Ioannes Lazaropoulos, Synopsis of the miracles of St. Eugenius in *A. Papadopoulos-Kerameus*, Sbornik istočnikov po istorii Trapezundskoj Imperii, I (St. Petersburg, 1897), 79. This text was brought to my attention by Prof. N. Panayotakis.

longed to court circles. The only plausible explanation is that Inger, like his namesake, the bishop of Nicaea, was an iconoclast[19].

Scylitzes-Cedrenus[20], while repeating the above-quoted passage of the *Vita Basilii*, adds a vital piece of information: αὕτη δὲ ἦν θυγάτηρ τοῦ παρὰ πάντων ἐπὶ φρονήσει καὶ εὐγενείᾳ διαβοήτου Ἴγγερος, τοῦ γένους καταγομένου τῶν Μαρτινακίων. This has been accepted by the majority of historians, rejected by a few[21]. Yet the statement that Eudocia belonged to the family of the Martinakioi is undoubtedly correct. There are two proofs of this:

1) In or about the year 837[22] the Emperor Theophilus is said to have had recourse to an Arab prophetess who foretold him the following: a) that he would be succeeded by his son and his wife; b) that thereafter the Martinakioi would occupy the throne for a long time (μετέπειτα δὲ τοὺς Μαρτινακίους ἐπὶ πολὺ τῆς βασιλείας κατασχεῖν), whereupon Theophilus caused that same Martinakes who was a distant relative of his (τοῦτον τὸν Μαρτινάκην, καί τοί γε προσωκειωμένον αὐτῷ πως κατὰ συγγένειαν) to become a monk and to convert his house into a monastery; c) that John the Grammarian would be removed from the partiarchal throne (he had just been appointed), and that the worship of icons would be re-established, etc.[23] Evidently, these alleged prophecies are quoted because they came true, and it is only on the assumption that Eudocia Ingerina was of the Martinakes family that the text makes sense.

2) The *Menologium Basilianum*, in its notice of the Empress Theophano, first wife of Leo VI and likewise a member of the Martinakes family, says that she was the daughter of one Constantine *illustris*, who was related to three emperors (συγγενοῦς βασιλέων τριῶν)[24]. I assume this means that Constantine was related to three emperors in addition to being the father-in-law of Leo VI. If the emperors in question are Theophilus, Michael III and Basil I, the necessary link with the last must have been provided by Eudocia.

We may now assemble what little information we possess concerning the house of the Martinakioi. The earliest member of the family known to us appears to be Anastasius, an iconoclast government official who ca. 817

---

[19] This was rightly pointed out by *A. Vogt*, „La jeunesse de Léon VI le Sage," Rev. hist., 174 (1934), 24 n. 1 (pagination of offprint), who further attributed to the iconoclast leanings of the Martinakioi Theodora's hatred of Eudocia.

[20] Bonn ed., II, 198.

[21] E.g. by *E. Kurtz*, Zwei griech. Texte über die hl. Theophano, Mém. de l'Acad. Imp. de St.-Pétersbourg, 8e sér., III/2 (1898), 49.

[22] The incident is placed immediately after the elevation of John the Grammarian to the patriarchal throne, 21 April (really January), 837, and a year earlier than the construction of Sarkel on the Volga (presumably in 838). On the latter see now *H. Ahrweiler*, „Les relations entre les Byzantins et les Russes au IXe s.," Assoc. Intern. des Études Byz., Bull. d'inform. et de coordination, 5 (1971), 48. In 837, of course, Michael had not yet been born, but since we are dealing with a prophecy, no formal contradiction is involved.

[23] Theoph. Cont., 121; Genesius, 70.

[24] PG 117, 209B.

was sent to Bonita in Asia Minor and who inflicted physical punishment on St. Theodore the Studite, then serving his third exile[25]. The second member — unless he is the same as Anastasius — is the Martinakes (Christian name not given) whom Theophilus forced to become a monk, and who was evidently a person of some importance[26]. Some 45 years later we encounter the family of the Empress Theophano, herself „born of imperial blood, from among the Martinakioi of ancient splendor," viz. 1. Her father Constantine, by rank *illustris*, later promoted to patrician, married to a lady called Anna, a native of Asia Minor;[27] 2. Her uncle, the *atriklines* Michael, at whose behest the *Vita Theophanous* was composed[28].

On the basis of the above data, two scholars have attempted to reconstruct the genealogy of the Martinakioi. The first attempt, by Loparev, may be represented as follows (the dates are his)[29]:

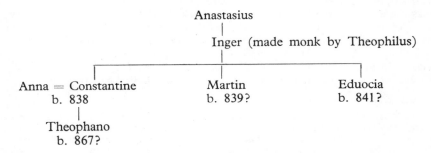

```
                        Anastasius
                            |
                Inger (made monk by Theophilus)
                            |
   ┌────────────────────────┼────────────────────────┐
Anna = Constantine       Martin                   Eduocia
   b. 838                b. 839?                   b. 841?
   |
Theophano
b. 867?
```

This tree is, however, patently incorrect since it indicates that Leo VI married his first cousin. The relationship of Eudocia to the brothers Constantine and Martin must surely have been considerably more distant. The second genealogy, that by Vogt[30], I find incomprehensible in the form in which it is printed. In fact, our evidence is too fragmentary to be reduced to a diagram. If Inger, Eudocia's father, was the person who was made a monk by Theophilus, we would have to conclude (provided the prophetic incident is correctly dated), that she was born not later than 837, i. e. that she was at least three years older than Michael III. But of this we have no proof.

---

[25] Vita A S. Theodori, PG 99, 196A, 204A (without family name); Vita B, ibid., 292 C-D (Ἀναστάσιος ὄνομα, τοῦ γένους τῶν Μαρτινακίων λεγόμενος), 293B (κατὰ πρόσωπον τοῦ Μαρτινάκι μαστίζει αὐτόν). Cf. *A. Gardner*, Theodore of Studium (London, 1905), 173; *A.P. Dobroklonskij*, Prep. Feodor ispovednik i igumen Studijskij, I (Odessa, 1913), 787 f.

[26] The Patria CP, ed. *Preger*, Script. orig. Constant., II (1907), 249, § 98 probably refers to the same person, but confuses both his dates and his identity in saying, Τὴν μονὴν τοῦ Μαρτινάκη ἀνήγειρεν Μαρτινάκης πατρίκιος ὁ θεῖος τῆς ἁγίας Θεοφανοῦς ἐν τοῖς χρόνοις Βασιλείου καὶ Μιχαήλ.

[27] *Kurtz*, Zwei griech. Texte, 2, § 2.

[28] Ibid., 21, § 30.

[29] ŽMNP, 325 (Oct. 1899), 345 f.

[30] „La jeunesse de Léon VI," 24 n. 1.

We know nothing of Eudocia's life between the years 855 and 865. Presumably she remained the Emperor's mistress. At the same time a façade of respectability was kept up, or so I suspect. It is noteworthy that while the Caesar Bardas was openly censured for his sexual behavior[31], no such accusation is made against Michael, even in the „Macedonian sources" which blacken his character in every possible way[32]. Certainly, he did not repudiate his legitimate wife, Eudocia Decapolitissa, for whom he appears to have had little use.

In 865 Basil the Macedonian was made patrician and *parakoimomenos*, a post usually occupied by a eunuch[33]. Then — we do not know the exact date — a curious matrimonial arrangement was forced on him. Now, Basil was already married to a certain Maria and had probably two children: Constantine, born ca. 859[34], and Anastasia who, if she was married to the general Christopher, could not have been born later than 856[35]. Basil, we are told, was made to divorce his wife, who was packed off to Macedonia with a large sum of money, and to marry Eudocia on condition that he treated her as his „lady" (διορισάμενος αὐτῷ κυρίαν αὐτὴν ἔχειν· ἦν γὰρ αὐτὴ τοῦ βασιλέως παλλακὴ καὶ πάνυ ἠγάπα αὐτὴν ὡς εὐπρεπῆ). As a consolation prize, Basil was given Michael's sister Thekla as a mistress (τοῦ ἔχειν αὐτὴν ἰδίως) — she had been a nun, and may have been then about forty

---

[31] *Bury*, Eastern Roman Empire, 188. Some curious information on Bardas's matrimonial affairs is contained in the Vita S. Irenes in Chrysobalanto which states that he married the sister of St. Irene and that this happened after (ὕστερον) the marriage of Michael III (ASS, July VI, 604 D). In another passage (616D), we are told that she was Bardas's *last* wife (γυναῖκα... ὑστάτην). Unfortunately, the chronology of the Vita is altogether unreliable: it tells us, e.g., that Irene, while bound for Constantinople to take part in the brideshow that was being arranged for Michael III (hence in 855), visited St. Ioannicius on Mt. Olympus (d. 846!) and that she was later appointed abbess by the Patriarch Methodius (d. 847!): ibid., 609 B-C.

[32] Cf. *Jenkins*, „Constantine VII's Portrait of Michael III," Acad. Roy. de Belgique, Bull. de la Cl. des Lettres, 5ᵉ sér., 34 (1948), 76, who offers a different explanation of this omission.

[33] It is probably for this reason that Jenkins charges Michael with homosexuality. On the office see *R. Guilland*, Recherches sur les institutions byzantines, I (Berlin-Amsterdam, 1967), 202 ff., who observes (p. 203): „Bien que la dignité de parakimomène fût la plus haute qui fut réservée aux eunuques, elle fut accordée toutefois, à un certain nombre de personnages qui ne furent pas eunuques."

[34] *Vogt*, Basile Iᵉʳ, 58 f.

[35] The question of Basil's daughters is rather complex. We know from the Book of Ceremonies, Bonn ed., 648 f., that there were four of them, viz. Anastasia, Anna, Helena and Maria. The last three were born in the purple if one may trust the 16th-century copy of an inscription on the walls of the Golden Horn: Κύριε βοήθει Λέοντος δεσπότη [sic], Ἀλεξάνδρου, Κωνσταντίνου [VII], Ἄννης, Ἑλένης, Μαρίας τῶν πορφυρογεννήτων (*A.M. Schneider*, „Mauern und Tore am Goldenen Horn zu KP," Nachrichten d. Akad. d. Wiss. in Göttingen, Phil.-Hist. Kl. 1950, 98 and fig. 3). Unless, therefore, Anastasia had died earlier (the inscription must have been put up between 906 and 912), she could not have been born in the purple. Furthermore, if the general Christopher, the victor over the Paulicians in 872, was indeed Basil's son-in-law (he is described as his γαμβρός: Leo gramm., 255), he must have been married to Anastasia, since the other three girls were all born after 867.

years old[36]. Is this extraordinary story true? We have two pieces of corroborative evidence: 1. It is repeated in substantially the same form in a source independent of the Logothete, viz. the Annals of Eutychius of Alexandria (d. 940)[37]. 2. Some time after 870 Thekla sent a man on business to Basil who asked him, „Who is your lady's lover?" (τίς ἔχει τὴν κυρίαν σου); He answered, „Neatokomites". Basil became furious, made Neatokomites a monk, and ordered Thekla to be beaten and deprived of all her property[38]. It is true that Basil had good reason to dislike Neatokomites[39]; even so, his fit of fury can best be explained, I think, if Thekla had previously occupied some place in his life.

Now we should look closely at the dates. Basil married Eudocia not earlier than 865; Bardas was „framed" and murdered by Basil in Michael's presence on April 21, 866; Basil was hastily crowned co-emperor on May 26; and Leo VI was born to Eudocia on September 1, according to the Logothete[40], or September 18 of the same year, according to Grumel[41]. This means that at the time of Basil's coronation in May, Eudocia must have been visibly pregnant.

The Logothete, of course, states explicitly that Leo was Michael's son; he implies the same of Stephen, and says that only Alexander was a legitimate son of Basil's[42]. These allegations were accepted by historians up to, and including Vogt's *Basile Ier* (1908). Bury, writing in 1912, rightly pointed out that „In the case of such an arrangement *à trois*, it is, of course, impossible for us, knowing so little as we do, to accept as proven such statements about paternity"[43]. Today, however, all historians take it for a fact that, on the contrary, Leo was Basil's son. Jenkins puts it like this: „Leo was not Michael's child because Micheal had no children, and in all probability could not have any, either by Eudocia or by anybody else. How far his homosexual tendency and his incurable alcoholism contributed to this state of affairs we need not now enquire, although contemporaries did; but the fact seems to be indisputable"[44]. This *revirement* of historians is due to an article by Adontz[45] who based himself on the then recently

---

[36] Leo gramm., 242. Theophilus was married in 821, and Thekla is described as the eldest of his five daughters. Both Brooks and Bury have argued, however, that Maria was the eldest. The evidence is clearly presented in *Bury*, Eastern Roman Empire, 465 ff.

[37] Trans. M. Canard in *Vasiliev*, Byzance et les Arabes, II/2 (Brussels, 1950), 25.

[38] Leo gramm., 256. For a textual comment on this passage see *Jenkins*, „The Chronological Accuracy," 100 n. 40.

[39] One day before Bardas's murder, Neatokomites tried to warn him of the impending danger: Leo gramm., 244.

[40] All the chronicles give Sept. 1, indiction 15, except Leo gramm., 249, who by mistake has December 1.

[41] „Notes de chronologie byzantine," Échos d'Orient, 35 (1936), 331 ff.

[42] Leo gramm., 255. Jenkins is, I think, undoubtedly right in arguing that Alexander was younger than Stephen: „The Chronological Accuracy," 98 ff. Is it perhaps significant that of all of Basil's and/or Eudocia's children, Alexander is the only one to have been buried in the same sarcophagus with his parents (De Cerimoniis, 643)?

[43] Eastern Roman Empire, 169, n. 5.

[44] The Imperial Centuries, 198 f.

[45] „La portée historique de l'oraison funèbre de Basile Ier," Byzantion, 8 (1933), 501 ff.

published Funeral Oration by Leo VI. We shall presently come back to the Oration; for the moment we need note only that it is a document of the most patent insincerity, and does not prove anything at all. Adontz, an Armenian, was simply bent on showing that the Macedonian dynasty was of Armenian origin.

If Michael's behaviour was at all rational, I can suggest only one explanation of the events of 866. In the spring of that year, say in March, he realized that Eudocia was pregnant; he wanted the child to be imperial. He could, of course, have divorced his wife and married Eudocia, which would have caused great scandal, not to speak of the reaction of his mother who by then was beginning to come out of her seclusion and who probably always retained considerable influence over him. So he hit on an ingenious plan. He would arrange a nominal marriage between Eudocia and Basil, and make the latter co-emperor[46]. This necessitated the hasty liquidation of Bardas and Basil's equally hasty coronation. Eudocia was probably crowned at a private ceremony.

But let us go on with the story to see if it bears out our theory. After recording Leo's birth, the Logothete tells us that Michael gave a big party with horse-races at the palace of St. Mamas. What was he celebrating if not the birth of his son? He naturally won the race and was praised for his skill by the patrician Basiliskianos. Thereupon, Michael ordered, in Basil's presence, that Basiliskianos should put on the imperial buskins. It was an awkward moment, and everyone hesitated. Getting angry, Michael said to Basil: „They [the buskins] suit him better than they suit you. Don't I have the authority, as I have made you emperor, to make another?" Evidently, Basil, having performed his function could now be dispensed with or, at any rate, neutralized. But what of Eudocia? She burst into tears and said, „The imperial dignity, O my lord, is a great thing and I, too, was unworthy to have been honoured with it (καὶ ἀναξίως καὶ ἡμεῖς ἐτιμήθημεν). It is not right that it should be treated with contèmpt"[47]. A very true and astute statement. The whole tragicomedy had been mounted for her benefit: which way was she to turn now?

On September 24, 867 Michael was murdered, perhaps with Eudocia's complicity. She was immediately escorted to the imperial palace „with great honour." The other Eudocia, the unfortunate Decapolitissa, was returned to her parents. And Michael was inconspicuously buried at Chrysopolis.

If Stephen was in fact born in November 867, then Eudocia must have been seven months pregnant when Michael was murdered[48]. What we know of her subsequent career is briefly the following. She bore Basil one son, Alexander, and probably three daughters who were made nuns by their father[49]. In or about 878 she had an affair with a certain Xylinites who

---

[46] For what it is worth, we have a direct confirmation of our theory in Zonaras, ed. Bonn, III, 415: ὡς ἐγκύου τῆς Εὐδοκίας οὔσης ὅτε τῷ Βασιλείῳ συνῴκιστο.

[47] Leo gramm., 249.

[48] So *Jenkins*, „The Chronological Accuracy," 99.

[49] On the daughters see supra, note 35.

was punished by being made a monk (but was later promoted to *oikonomos* of St. Sophia by Leo VI)[50]; in 879 Basil's eldest son, Constantine died; in 882 she engineered Leo's marriage to one of her own relatives, Theophano; and late in the same year or early in 883 she died, being then 43/46 years old.

★

A word about Leo's marriage. We have two versions: Leo's own statements as reported in the *Vita Euthymii*[51] and the official version of the *Vita Theophanous*. In the first Leo is made to say: „All the members of the Senate know that I married her against my will, from fear of my father and in utter distress." Indeed, history had repeated itself. Leo had a mistress, Zoe, daughter of the Armenian Zaoutzas, who was captain of the imperial bodyguard. When, after the marriage, the pious Theophano became aware of this liaison, she reported the matter to the Emperor. Whereupon Basil seized Leo by the hair, threw him to the ground and beat him with his fists. This is the unofficial and, I suspect, the true version.

The *Vita Theophanous*, commissioned by the lady's uncle, tells quite a different story[52]. The customary bride show was arranged for Leo; beautiful maidens were collected from the provinces and, at Eudocia's instigation, from Constantinople as well. Among the latter was Theophano, daughter of Constantine Martinakios. Now, believe it or not, Eudocia had never heard of her. But when she came to inspect the maidens, she was immediately attracted by Theophano; she questioned her and found out that the latter was of „imperial blood," whereupon, she took her straight to Basil, who confirmed the selection by placing a ring on Theophano's finger. Poor Leo does not seem to have been consulted.

The next year (883), after Eudocia's death, Leo appears to have plotted against Basil's life. This was betrayed by Santabarenus, and many conspirators were arrested. Among the suspects was the Byzantine commander-in-chief on the Arab front. Leo was placed under arrest and, as Jenkins has shown, remained in gaol for three years: Basil even wanted to have him blinded[53]. While he was out of the way, another plot on Basil's life was hatched by John Kourkouas and sixty-six noblemen. This, too, was betrayed — on March 25, 886. On July 20, Leo was released — perhaps because it was clear that he was not implicated in the second plot. Leo even went out in public procession with Basil, and the people shouted „Glory be to God!" To which Basil replied: „Are you praising God on account of my son? You will suffer many misfortunes and painful days on his account"[54].

---

[50] Leo gramm., 257.

[51] VII. 5 ff., ed. *de Boor*, 20 f.; ed. *P. Karlin-Hayter* (Brussels, 1970), 38 ff.

[52] Ed. *Kurtz*, 5 f., §§ 8—10.

[53] „The Chronological Accuracy," 101 ff.

[54] Leo gramm., 260 f.

On August 21, Basil fell victim to a plot which left him with fatal wounds[55]. The practical arrangements were probably in the hands of Stylianus Zaoutzas, the father of Leo's mistress, but Leo must have been aware of what was going on.

The first act of the new reign was to collect the remains of Michael III at Chrysopolis and convey them with full imperial honors to the church of the H. Apostles. Leo even forced his brothers to accompany the procession[56]. Such were the relations between Leo and Basil.

Finally, we come to the Funeral Oration, delivered when Leo was twenty-two, i. e. in 888. He tells us that Basil was the most splendid man that ever lived and that he was descended from the royal house of Armenia; that Eudocia was the most beautiful, aristocratic and virtuous woman that ever lived; Michael could have married her, but Divine Providence had predestined her for another; that Basil and Eudocia attained to the imperial dignity against their wishes and without doing any violence; and that then Michael departed from life by God's „inscrutable judgment", etc[57]. Now, this is the document, redolent of filial affection, on which Adontz based the legitimacy of Leo VI. We may imagine that the young man was pretty embarrassed at having to tell such a string of lies and half-truths. Why did he do so? The answer is clear: he had gone too far in dissociating himself from his predecessor, in suggesting to all and sundry that he was not Basil's son. The interests of state and dynasty had to be safeguarded, and it was probably Stylianus Zaoutzas himself, Basil's murderer, who suggested the speech.

★

We may now attempt to draw some conclusions. We have encountered two men called Inger, the first being a metropolitan of Nicaea ca. 825, while the second was Eudocia's father, somehow related[58] to the Martinakioi, an iconoclast family that claimed a distant kinship with the Amorian dynasty. The name Martinakes („little Martin") points to a western or a Balkan[59]

---

[55] *Vogt*, „La jeunesse," 38 ff. As pointed out by Jenkins, „The Chronological Accuracy," 103 n. 57, Basil's murder is explicitly recorded by Tabari: *Vasiliev, Byzanze et les Arabes*, II/2, 10.

[56] Leo gramm., 262 f.

[57] *A. Vogt* and *I. Hausherr*, Oraison funèbre de Basile Ier, Orient. Christ., 36/1 (No. 77), 1932, 44, 52, 54, 56. On close reading certain passages of the Oration yield interesting insights, e.g. the statement on p. 56, οὐ βιασάμενοι οὐδὲ ἄρπαγμα τὴν ἀρχὴν ποιησάμενοι, ἀλλ' ἄκοντες ἐπὶ τοῦτο καταστάντες. If our explanation of the events is correct, Basil may well have been in two minds about accepting the crown on Michael's terms in 866.

[58] The statement of Scylitzes, quoted by us *supra*, p. 20 (θυγάτηρ . . . Ἴγγερος, τοῦ γένους καταγομένου τῶν Μαρτινακίων) suggests it was Inger rather than, say, his wife, who belonged to the clan of the Martinakioi. Since, however, we are dealing with a derivative and uncritically edited text, it may be unwise to lay too much stress on the masculine form of καταγομένου.

[59] On the occurrence of the name Martin in the Balkans cf., e. g., *E. Follieri* and *I. Dujčev*, „Un' acolutia inedita per i martiri di Bulgaria dell' anno 813"' Byzantion, 33 (1963), 84, verse 211.

origin. If it is granted that Inger is a nordic name (and I can find no other explanation of it)[60], we would have to assume that at least one Scandinavian or north German family reached Constantinople by the end of the eighth century at the latest, converted to Christianity and married into Byzantine gentry. This is several decades earlier than any previously postulated contacts between the Northmen and Byzantium. It may also throw some light on the embassy of 839: the Rhos who came to Constantinople perhaps the previous year may have been well received because they found a fellow-countryman at the court of Theophilus.

It would be tempting to imagine Eudocia Ingerina as a Scandinavian beauty and to attribute to her influence the atmosphere of jollity and drunkenness (so different from normal Byzantine *mores*) that prevailed at the court of Michael III. That, however, may be too fanciful an interpretation. If we are right in believing that Eudocia was of partly Scandinavian orgin, it would follow in any case that there was some nordic blood in the veins of the „Macedonian" dynasty. As for the paternity of Leo VI, we shall never, of course, know the truth beyond any reasonable doubt: but the evidence as we have it gives stronger support to Michael's claim than it does to Basil's.

---

[60] For a partial list of names ending in — ερ see *Dornseiff* and *B. Hansen*, Rückläufiges Wörterbuch d. griech. Eigennamen (Berlin, 1957), 122. They are mostly Latin (e. g. Κέλερ, Νίγερ, Πούλχερ), Germanic (ʻΡάδιγερ, ʻΡεκίμερ, ʻΡιγίμερ, etc.) Turcic (ʼΙλιγερ) and Semitic. On Κούβερ, Γούβερ, Γούμερ see. *I. Dujčev*, „Nai-ranni vrŭzki meždu Pŭrvobŭlgari i Slavjani," Bŭlg. Akad. na Naukite, Izv. na Arkheol. Inst., 19 (1955), 333. A few names beginning in Ing-, such as Ινγας, Ινγασις, Ινγαμις occur in southern Asia Minor (*L. Zgusta*, Kleinasiatische Personennamen, Prague, 1964, № 472 ff.), but I do not believe that they are relevant to our problem.

THE LEGEND OF LEO THE WISE

In the chaotic mass of Byzantine oracular literature an important place is occupied by a collection of prophecies which bear the name of the Emperor Leo the Wise (886—912). The extent of this collection is not easily definable, since the „authorship" of many items varies from one manuscript to another: the same text may be attributed to the Emperor Leo, to Methodius of Patara, to the prophet Daniel, to a certain monk Leontius, or to any one of several other popular seers. Excluding such doubtful items,[1] the main body of Leonine oracles falls into two groups: 1) a collection of usually sixteen iambic poems, couched in erudite Greek, each oracle being accompanied by a symbolical picture (figs. 1—16),[2] and 2) a group of longer poems in popular Greek, part of which are clearly datable to the thirteenth century.[3]

It is not my intention to present here a full discussion of the difficult problems of dating and exegesis that are raised by these oracles. No such discussion should be attempted, in any case, until the manuscript tradition of the oracles has been thoroughly explored. That in itself is no small undertaking, since there exist, as we shall see, scores of pertinent manuscripts, scattered all over Europe and the Near East, in addition to early translations both into Latin and into Slavic languages. Furthermore, the Leonine oracles, like all prophetic literature of a popular kind, do not present a stable text. As time went on, they were altered and interpolated in various ways to fit the expectations and hopes of each particular period. Consequently, a search for the *Urtext* appears to be almost futile: the most that can be attempted is to establish different recensions and distinguish between strata of interpolations. The purpose of this paper is, however, a different one, namely to trace the stages by which the rather colourless emperor of the Macedonian dynasty became a seer of such enduring fame. The development of the „Leo

---

[1] For example, the curious poem that has recently been interpreted as a satirical song referring to the empress Theophano, wife of Romanus II and Nicephorus Phocas. See G. Morgan, „A Byzantine Satirical Song?" BZ 47 (1954), 292—97. This poem is found in three mss: in one it is anonymous, in the second it is ascribed to Leo the Wise, in the third to the prophet Daniel.

[2] Most easily accessible in PG 107, 1129 sq. Older editions listed below, pp. 80 sq.

[3] Published by E. Legrand, *Les oracles de Léon le Sage*, Paris, 1875 (Collection de monuments pour servir à l'étude de la langue néo-hellénique, n.s., no. 5). The historical introduction by Ch. Gidel (pp. 7—16) is of little value. It is reprinted in Gidel's *Nouvelles études sur la littérature grecque moderne*, Paris, 1878, 303—12.

Legend" cannot, in my opinion, be entirely separated from the problem of the Oracles, and may therefore provide a useful introduction to the study of the latter.

To begin with, however, a few observations about the Oracles may not be out of place. The illustrated series is certainly the more ancient of the two. The course of events described therein is roughly as follows. There will reign a succession of five emperors: the first, a wily and boastful man of canine aspect, whose progeny (?) will be destroyed by a serpent; the second, a flying serpent of foul oriental stock, who will cause disturbance in the City, and will be blinded by two crows (fig. 1); the third is represented by two symbols, an eagle bearing a cross (fig. 2) who will seize power from the south, and a unicorn (fig. 3) who will be bold and warlike, but will fall unexpectedly on wet ground; the fourth (figs. 4 and 5), an old man bearing a scythe and a rose, will erect pagan temples, and will live (reign ?) nine years; the fifth and last, represented by a bull (fig. 6), will be virtuous and have a happy end. He will be followed by a bear rearing young cubs (fig. 7), presumably an emperor of another line hoping to set up his own dynasty, whose reign will mark the division of the Empire. Constantinople will be the scene of bloodshed and civil war, in the course of which all sinners will be destroyed (fig. 8). An old man, represented by the cunning fox (fig. 9), will profit from the confusion and seize power. The next two oracles (nos. X—XI and figs. 10—11) are in prose and appear to be an interpolation. Constantinople will fall when the twentieth letter (? K=20) is acclaimed along its walls. He (the wicked king?) will have fingers like scythes,[4] and will blaspheme against the Lord. There follows a diatribe against a wicked patriarch whose name is John ('Ἰῶ) (?).[5] He is an instigator of murders, and will have his long beard cut off. At this point the anointed is revealed, whose name is Menahem (καὶ ἀποκαλυφθήσεται ὁ ἠλειμμένος ἐπώνυμος Μεναχείμ).[6] The remaining oracles (nos. XII—XVI and figs. 12—16) are devoted to the appearance and consecration of the liberator-king, a gentle man endowed with the gift

---

[4] ὃς ἔχει τοὺς δακτύλους αὐτοῦ δρεπανωτούς, ὅ ἐστι δρέπανον τῆς ἐρημώσεως, καὶ ἐν τῷ ὑψίστῳ βλασφημία. This is an old motif associated with the Antichrist. Cf. Apocalypsis Esdrae, ed. Tischendorf (Apocalypses apocryphae, Leipzig, 1866), 29₆: οἱ δάκτυλοι αὐτοῦ ὡς δρέπανα. Same detail in Cod. Laud. gr. 27: ἔστι δὲ δρεπανοδάκτυλος (V. Istrin, Откровение Мефодия Патарского и апокрифические видения Даниила, I, Moscow, 1897, 214).

[5] It seems that the text is disturbed at this point, since the name 'Ἰῶ or John is usually given to the liberator-king. See Istrin, op. cit., II, 291—92; Eulogios Kourilas, Τὰ χρυσόβουλλα τῶν ἡγεμόνων τῆς Μολδοβλαχίας καὶ τὸ σύμβολον 'Ἰῶ ἢ 'Ἰωάννης, Εἰς μνήμην Σπ. Λάμπρου, Athens, 1935, 245—54.

[6] This passage appears to be derived from a Jewish source of the second or third centruy A. D. The word ἠλειμμένος (for χριστός) is associated with Aquila's translation of the O.T. (so in Ps. 2. 2, Dan. 9. 26 and elsewhere). Cf. Philastrius Brixiensis, De haer., cxlii, PL 12, 1276; F. Field's preface to Hexapla (Oxford, 1875), I, xix. On the messianic name Menahem („comforter") see W. Bousset, Die Religion des Judentums im späthellenistischen Zeitalter, 3rd ed., Tübingen, 1926, 227; H. Gressmann, Der Messias, Göttingen, 1929, 458 sq.; J. Klausner, The Messianic Idea in Israel, transl. W. F. Stinespring, New York, 1955, 463—64.

of foreknowledge, who had been concealed, either dead or asleep, in the western part of Constantinople.[7] The City of Seven Hills will reign once more.

In Lambeck's edition, reproduced by Migne, Leo's Oracles are followed by an anonymous *Paraphrasis* which is concerned only with the advent of the liberator-king. The latter is identified by various personal characteristics, and appears from an island to which he had been banished. He is revealed at the end of the Ismaelite empire,[8] and lives in the western part of Constantinople, near the Sigma. Since his exploits appear to be directed chiefly against the Turks, it may be surmised that the *Paraphrasis* was composed in the fourteenth or early fifteenth century.[9]

Thus the Leonine Oracles are concerned not with the end of the world, but with the fate of the Byzantine Empire and especially of its capital. The advent of the righteous king who had been asleep is, of course, a widespread motif in medieval messianic tradition. The most pertinent parallel is provided by the "Visions" of Daniel which describe the appearance of the aged king, named John, in the "right-hand part" of Constantinople. He will be escorted to St. Sophia by four angels and crowned there, after which he will vanquish the Ismaelites.[10] The rest of the eschatological story, which is told in the Revelations of Methodius, the Visions of Daniel, the Life of St. Andrew the Fool and other texts, is, however, absent from the Leonine Oracles. The liberator-king, after his prescribed reign of thirty-two years, does not go to Jerusalem to lay down his crown on Golgotha or the Mount of Olives. Nothing is said of the wicked queen who profanes the holy sanctuaries. Constantinople is not submerged by the sea. There is no Antichrist,

---

[7] This led to the formation of the famous legend about the „emperor turned into marble" (ὁ μαρμαρωμένος βασιλιᾶς) who lies concealed in a cave near the Golden Gate. See N. Politês, Παραδόσεις, Athens, 1904, I, 22; II, 658—74; N. Beês in BNJ 13 (1937), 244 γ΄— 244 λς΄.

[8] Col. 1141: καὶ δεδώκασι τὴν στρωμνὴν αὐτοῦ ἐν ταῖς νήσοις, πλέοντος καὶ ἁλιεύοντος ἑβδοματικῷ ἑβδόμα (sic) χρόνῳ, εἰς τὸ τέλος τῶν Ἰσμαηλιτῶν ἀποκαλυφθήσεται. The Lat. translation (by one D. Moufflet) is most unsatisfactory: „sedemque habere coegerint in insulis, ubi navigationem piscatoriamque artem exercet per totam hebdomadam, tandem ex Ismaelitis revelabitur." J. Döllinger („Der Weissagungsglaube und das Prophetentum in der christlichen Zeit" in *Kleinere Schriften*, ed. F. H. Reusch, Stuttgart, 1890, 475) expresses surprise that the liberator of the Byzantine Empire should be a Moslem. Veselovskij („Опыты по истории развития христианской легенды, "ЖМНП, 179 [1875], 59—60) believes that the liberator comes from the country of the Ismaelites, but that he himself is a Greek. It seems clear, however, that τέλος means „end" and not „country". Cf. Pseudo-Methodius in Istrin, *op. cit.*, I, Texts, 35: καὶ ἐν τῷ καιρῷ ἐκείνῳ ἤτοι ἐν τῷ ἑβδοματικῷ ἑβδόμῳ χρόνῳ, ἡνίκα πληροῦται ὁ ἀριθμὸς τοῦ χρόνου τῆς δυναστείας αὐτῶν, etc. ἑβδοματικῷ ἑβδόμῳ χρόνῳ echoes Dan. 9. 24—25.

[9] Veselovskij (*op. cit.*, 60—61) is, I believe, mistaken in dating the *Paraphrasis* from the time of the Latin Empire of Constantinople. The enemy whom the liberator conquers is the Turk (see col. 1144 B: καὶ ἐξελεύσεται κατὰ τῶν Ἰσμαηλιτῶν καὶ κρατήσει αὐτούς, and our previous note), whereas the one reference to the Latins (col. 1145C: φέρων τε τὸν πόλεμον καὶ τῶν ξανθῶν τὰς μηχανάς) is rather obscure.

[10] Istrin, *op. cit.*, I, Texts, 137.

62

no Gog and Magog, no Last Judgment. Even the fall of Constantinople is mentioned only in Oracle X which, as we have seen, is probably an interpolation. Thus it is possible (although I do not wish to insist on this point) that the original version of the Oracles did not foretell the capture of Constantinople. The belief that Constantinople would never fall is occasionally expressed, for example in the Life of St. Andrew the Fool which dates from the ninth or tenth century.[11] Even in the twelfth century, Tzetzes entertained the hope that Constantinople would be constantly enlarged and glorified under God's protection, and this in spite of the explicit oracle, οὐαί σοι Ἑπτάλοφε, ὅτι οὐ χιλιάσεις, which Tzetzes was able to interpret in a favourable sense by means of curious grammatical acrobatics[12]. A contrary conviction, that Constantinople was ultimately destined to fall, was, however, current at the same time, and continued to be present even after the date set for the downfall, 1026, had passed without incident.[13]

It is not easy to date the illustrated series of Leonine Oracles on the basis of their content, but there are two factors which prove conclusively that they are as old as the twelfth century, and possibly earlier. In the first place, the *Vaticinia Pontificum*, known under the name of Joachim of Flora, contain fifteen oracles which are a literal, though incomplete translation of the Leonine collection.[14] The Latin translation originated not later than the last quarter of the thirteenth century, and was accompanied, as can be seen, for example, from an important manuscript at Monreale of the late thirteenth or early fourteenth century, by illustrations very similar to those in the Greek original.[15] This shows, incidentally, that the curious pictures that are found in the Greek manuscripts (reproduced here after Lambeck's † edition) are not merely a degenerate product of the last phase of Byzantine book-illumination, as Kondakov had thought,[16] but are copied from originals of the Comnenian period, if not earlier. The existence of such illustrated books of oracles is attested in the early ninth century.[17]

The second proof of the antiquity of the Leonine Oracles is that several passages from them are quoted by Nicetas Choniates. The most extensive

---

[11] PG 111, 853B.

[12] *Joannis Tzetzae epistolae*, ed. Pressel, Tübingen, 1851, 53—54; *Chiliades*, ed. Kiessling, Leipzig, 1826, hist. 276, 278, pp. 347—49.

[13] According to the horoscope of Vettius Valens, Constantinople was destined to last 696 years after its foundation (Cedrenus, I, 497; Zonaras, III, 14—15; Glycas, 463; *Catal. codd. astrol. graec.*, V/1, 118—19, 131-32). Cf. Ch. Diehl, „De quelques croyances byzantines sur la fin de Constantinople", BZ 30 (1929-30), 192—96; Lathoud, „La consécration et la dédicace de Constantinople," *Echos d'Orient* 24 (1925), 191.

[14] See H. Grundmann, „Die Papstprophetien des Mittelalters," *Archiv für Kulturgeschichte*, XIX-1 (1928), 77—138.

[15] A. Daneu Lattanzi, „I 'Vaticinia Pontificum' ed un codice monrealese del sec. XIII—XIV," *Atti della R. Accad. di Scienze Lettere e Arti di Palermo*, Ser. 4, vol. III, pt. 2, fasc. 4 (1944), 757—92 and pls. I—VI.

[16] Having examined two mss of the Oracles, Marc. Cl. VII cod. 3 and Palermo I. E. 8, Kondakov expressed the following verdict: „Toutes ces illustrations n'ont aucune signification artistique ou intellectuelle; elles ne font que terminer en fait l'histoire des miniatures byzantines, cette histoire qui en réalité était finie depuis longtemps déjà." (*Histoire de l'art byzantin considéré principalement par les miniatures*, II, Paris, 1891, 177—78).

[17] Theophanes Cont., 36; slightly different accounts in Pseudo-Symeon, 610—11 nd Cedrenus, II, 63.

excerpt is taken from Oracle VI which alludes to the happy reign of the „bull-like emperor." Nicetas tells us that Isaac II Angelus (1185—95) considered this oracle to refer to himself and was never tired of repeating it.[18] Two more quotations are given in connection with the last illness of John II Comnenus (April 1143). That emperor was encamped in Cilicia, close to a mountain known as the Crows' Nests, when he accidentally wounded himself with a poisoned arrow. The infection spread rapidly, especially as John refused the advice of his physicians to have his arm amputated. Shortly after Easter (April 4), there was a torrential rain, and the emperor's bed had to be moved to a dry spot. This reminded him of the oracle, „Thou shalt fall unexpectedly in a wet place" (τόποις δ'ἐν ὑγροῖς καὶ παρ' ἐλπίδα πέσῃς), while those members of his suite who took interest in foretelling the imperial succession believed that another ancient prediction (τὸ παλαίφατον τοῦτο λόγιον) which proclaimed, „Alas, thou shalt fall prey to terrible crows" (ὢ πῶς γενήσῃ βρῶμα δεινῶν κοράκων), had come to pass. This they connected both with the name of the neighbouring mountain and with the hot iron with which the emperor's wound had been cauterised.[19] The predictions quoted here are derived from the Leonine Oracles III and I respectively.

We are further told that Alexius II (born September 10, 1169) received his name on account of a prophecy which foretold that the Comnenian line would last as long as the word AIMA (A = Alexius I; I = John II; M = Manuel I; A = Alexius II).[20] The word αἷμα is the title of the first and seventh Leonine oracles, and, as Lambeck has pointed out, it is echoed by the last line of the second oracle, „Having the unit (i. e. the letter α) as his beginning and his end" (ἀρχὴν ἔχων τε τὴν μονάδα καὶ τέλος). Nicetas also thinks that Manuel's reign of thirtyeight years was meant by the ancient prophecy (τὸ παλαιότατον ἐκεῖνο λόγιον), „The last part of thy name shall conquer thee" (ἀλλ' ὑστάτη σε κερδανεῖ λαβὴ λόγου), since the last syllable of Manuel's name (ηλ) denoted the figure 38.[21] The prophecy in question comes from the third Leonine oracle.

Nicetas quotes another oracle with reference to Andronicus I which, he says, was found in books and often repeated by word of mouth:

αἴφνης δ'ἀναστὰς ἐκ τόπου πλήρους πότου
ἀνὴρ πελιδνός, ἀγέρωχος τὸν τρόπον,
στυγνός, πολιός, ποικίλος χαμαιλέων,
ἐπεισπεσεῖται καὶ θερίσει καλάμην.
πλὴν ἀλλὰ καὐτὸς συνθερισθεὶς τῷ χρόνῳ
ἐσύστερον τίσειεν ἀθλίας δίκας
ὧνπερ κακῶς ἔπραξεν ἐν βίῳ τάλας·
ὁ γὰρ φέρων μάχαιραν οὐ φύγῃ ξίφος.

„A livid man, arrogant of manner, sullen, grey-haired, a changeful chameleon, having suddenly arisen from a place full of wine, will burst in and mow down

---

[18] 464—65. The quotation in Nicetas differs somewhat from the printed text of the Oracles; the verse order is also not the same.

[19] Nicetas, 55.

[20] Ibid., 220.

[21] Ibid., 289.

64

the corn; but he, too, will be cut down in time, and will later pay miserable penalties for the evil deeds which, wretched man that he was, he had committed in his life. For he who bears a dagger will not escape the sword." The „place full of wine" refers, according to Nicetas, to Oenaeon on the Black Sea to which Andronicus had been relegated.[22] These prophetic verses are not to be found in the Leonine Oracles as they are preserved today, but they call to mind the fourth and fifth oracles which speak of an old man bearing a scythe and a rose, who will cut down the grass and live (reign ?) nine years (τρὶς τρεῖς δὲ ζήσας ἐν βίῳ κύκλους γέρων | ἤχθη [ἴθι?] πρὸς ᾅδην, δύο λιπὼν ἐν μέσῳ). It may be recalled that Isaac Angelus, who himself expected to reign thirty-two years,[23] used to say that a reign of nine years had been originally allotted to Andronicus, but that the latter's misdeeds had reduced this span to three years, the remainder having accrued to himself.[24] The oracles in question (nos. IV and V) are immediately followed by the one concerning the „bull-like" emperor which, as we have seen, Isaac thought to refer to himself. The illustrations of Oracles IV and V (figs. 4 and 5) also call to mind the portrait of himself which Andronicus set up outside the church of the Forty Martyrs in Constantinople. He was represented on it not in imperial costume, but as a peasant in a dark cloak that parted at the bottom and white boots reaching up to the knees. In his hand he held a stout scythe or reaping-hook (δρέπανον), the curve of which enclosed the bust of a youth shown down to his throat and shoulders (ἀγαλματίαν μειρακίσκον ἕως φάρυγγος καὶ ὤμων προφαινόμενον). By this image, says Nicetas, Andronicus made clear that he had murdered the young successor to the throne (Alexius II).[25] I am unable to explain the real meaning of this singular portrait which does not appear to have been discussed by scholars of imperial iconography. It seems evident, however, that the oracular pictures, deformed as they are through a long process of copying, have a connection with the portrait of Andronicus.

The above references in Nicetas indicate that the oracles we are discussing had a wide circulation throughout the twelfth century. They were then considered to be „ancient", and were thought to apply to the Comnenian emperors, roughly as follows:

John II	:	Oracles I and III
Manuel I	:	Oracle III
Andronicus I	:	Oracles IV and V
Isaac II	:	Oracle VI.

Although the sequence is more or less chronological, the correspondence between emperors and oracles is a hit-or-miss affair. Let us consider, for example, John II and Manuel I. The latter is represented by the warlike unicorn, which is appropriate enough. But the unicorn falls on wet ground,

---

[22] *Ibid.*, 462—63.
[23] *Ibid.*, 549. This is the usual length of the reign assigned to the liberator-king. Cf. Istrin, *op. cit.*, II, 264, 270, etc.
[24] Nicetas, 567—68.
[25] *Ibid.*, 432.

and this, as we have seen, was applied to the death of John II. On the other hand, John was also the victim of „terrible crows" which, in the Oracles, is the fate of the flying serpent. The serpent, however, that foul oriental monster who causes grievous upheaval in the City, could hardly have been meant as a symbol of the well-loved John II. It would have been more applicable to Andronicus I whose reign was, in fact, foreshadowed by the appearance of a comet shaped like a tortuous serpent.[26] Had the Oracles been composed *ex post facto* concerning the Comnenian dynasty, they would have made less contradictory references to historical persons. I conclude, therefore, that the Oracles were already in existence by the beginning of the twelfth century (though perhaps not exactly in the same form or sequence in which they are now preserved), and that various passages from them, taken out of context, were made to fit *tant bien que mal* the successive monarchs of the Comnenian house.[27] Consequently, I cannot agree with the view of Bousset[28] that the illustrated Leonine Oracles were composed around 1180. It is possible, however, that they were collected and re-edited during this period. By the middle of the thirteenth century the collection had assumed a form quite similar to that of our editions, as shown by the Latin text of the *Vaticinia Pontificum.*[29]

Prophecies of this kind were known in the fourteenth century to Nicephorus Gregoras who writes as follows concerning the death of Andronicus II: „There had been for a long time in the emperor's possession a book of unknown authorship which contained cryptic writings and dim indications of the future emperors by means of pictures. Therein the judgment and prudence of this emperor were denoted by the figure of a fox as well as other tokens, and the manner of his death by a chair set up in a place of this kind [referring to the latrine in which the emperor died] and two youths, dressed in black and with heads uncovered, standing by. The black dress of the youths, their bare heads and the fact that there were two of them indicated that the emperor had worn black [i. e. monastic] garb and had been deprived of the imperial crown over a period of two years."[30] Nicephorus' desription does not fit

---

[26] *Ibid.*, 326—27.

[27] Other prophecies of this kind were also in circulation during the Comnenian period. We are told, for example, that the predictions ἐν ἀκεσωδύνοις πεσεῖται and ἀγκῆρι καυθεὶς πεσεῖται, written τοῖς πονήσασι τὰς περὶ τῶν βασιλέων αἰνιγματώδεις γραφάς, were applied to the death of Alexius I (Zonaras, III, 759—60).

[28] „Beiträge zur Geschichte der Eschatologie," *Ztschr. f. Kirchengesch.*, 20 (1900), 281 sq. He states that the first ten oracles refer to the Comnenian emperors, whose names are indicated by the acrostich AIMA. The line οὐαί σοι, πόλις ἑπτάλοφε, ὅταν τὸ εἰκοστὸν στοιχεῖον εὐφημίζεται εἰς τὰ τείχη σου (Oracle X) as well as κῶ καὶ κῶ ἡ τοῦ πτωχοῦ ἐπικράτησις (Oracle XI) refer, according to him, to the downfall of the Comneni. The empty throne (fig. 10) and the onslaught of Islam (supposedly indicated by the crescent in fig. 11) are followed by the appearance of the liberator-king who is patterned after messianic tradition and the Alexander legend. Bousset's hypothesis is accepted by Grundmann, *op. cit.*, 87.

[29] On the mss and editions of the *Vaticinia* see, in addition to Grundmann's study quoted in note 14, *id., Studien über Joachim von Floris*, Leipzig, 1927, 196 sq.; Francesco Russo, *Bibliografia Gioachimita*, Florence, 1954, 41 sq.

[30] I, 463.

66

exactly the illustrations of the Leonine Oracles, but it does bear an analogy to figs. 9 and 10. In connection with the death of Michael VIII (1282), the same author makes some general observations about oracles which are not without interest for our enquiry. He states that he had not found, either in historical or other writings, any mention of the author of any particular oracle. It was often reported that a given prophecy had been fulfilled in such and such a manner, „but who it was that first pronounced each one of these is a matter that no one knows or can explain, unless one wishes to tell a lie."[31] This may indicate that the Leonine collection, which was certainly well-known by the middle of the fourteenth century, was considered anonymous by Nicephorus Gregoras. „It should also be considered," he adds, „that some persons, wishing to make jest of those who indulge in such matters, compose new verses in imitation of the oracles and secretly disseminate them among the people, so as to confuse with their lies the veracity of the former [i. e. of the genuine oracles]; for many persons were apprehended in having done this in our time."[32]

* * *

The second set of oracles, published by Legrand after three manuscripts (Par. gr. 929, 970 and 426), is a heterogeneous medley that need not detain us too long. Legrand's edition is misleading because it combines without any distinction the original text with an interpretation couched in a similar language and meter; the two may be easily separated, however, on the basis of two of the Paris manuscripts used by Legrand (970 and 426) as well as of the Serbian version of these oracles which usully goes under the name of Stephen Lazarević,[33] all of which preserve the uninterpolated text.

The first of these oracles speaks of a warlike tumult in Hungary, and of an old fox who had gone there with Serbian soldiers and German shields, but who fell and rotted there.[34] The interpreter adds that the uproar was raised by the Hungarians, Zechi, Alans, Vlachs and Cumans, and that the old fox represented the Turks. A man named Dionysius will arise in Serbia and invade Bithynia with a great army of man-eaters, to wit the nations which Alexander imprisoned in the north (lines 26—36). The original text goes on to speak of an old woman who leaps over a moat, and of Mary who brings flour from the mill to make sour-sweet cakes for the mountain goats; the loaf is, however, seized and cut up by greedy rulers. This is followed (lines 120—124) by an unmistakable reference to John III Vatatzes, repre-

---

[31] *Ibid.*, I, 150—51.

[32] *Ibid.*, I, 152.

[33] Published by Dj. Daničić in *Starine* 4 (1872), 81—85. See also *id.* in *Glasnik* 11 (1859), 168—69; Dj. Polívka in *Starine* 24 (1891), 154—55; Istrin, *op. cit.*, II, 323—24.

[34] The third line of this oracle, καὶ πτερὸν ἀποτινάζουν (крнла потресѣютъ in the Serbian version), is considered by R. Jakobson as a possible model for *Slovo o Polku Igoreve*, v. 76, въсплескала лебедиными крылы на синѣмь море (Univ. Libre de Bruxelles, *Ann. de l'Inst. d'Hist. Orient. et Slaves*, VIII [1945—47], 305—06). This could only be so if the oracle were not later than the middle of the 12th century, which appears to be unlikely.

sented by a bramble with a scarlet rose and an Armenian thorn. This bramble
from across the sea spreads to Scutari:

> Καὶ ἡ βάτος ἀπὸ πέρα
> ἥπλωσεν κ' ἔπιασεν τόπον
> τὸ λεγόμενον Σκουτάριν
> ἔχων ῥόδον λασκαράτον
> μὲ τ' ἀρμένικον ἀκάνθιν.

These verses are duly explained by the commentator who, strangely enough,
appears to think that the „Armenian thorn" refers to the Latins (lines 132—
133).[35] It may be noted that the commentator does not display much historical knowledge: he informs us, for example, that the Crusaders took Constantinople in 1202 (A. M. 6610), held it sixty-two years (lines 142—145),
and were driven out by Theodore Lascaris (lines 154—157). He inveighs
against Michael VIII Palaeologus (lines 160 sq.), the union of the Churches
and the *azyma*.[36] The Latins (we now revert to the original text) take courage
(line 180). A red thistle spreads from beyond the sea, and occupies a place
called the Vineyard. This is the king of Germany who encamps at Rufinianae
(?), a suburb of Constantinople.[37] He has come to assist the „fair-haired
nation of Rome," i. e. the Latins.[38] There follows a big battle between
different nations; what its outcome is we are not told by the oracle which
ends on an enigmatic note. A falcon comes to survey the scene, and watches
it on Sunday, Monday, Tuesday and Wednesday.

For the purpose of this study there is no need to pursue any further
the analysis of the oracles published by Legrand. We have dwelt only on
the first of them, which is the longest and most interesting. The date of
its composition appears to coincide with the Latin Kingdom of Constantinople; I am unable, however, to explain the references to Hungary or to
the king of Germany, who could hardly be Frederick II, since the latter
entertained friendly relations with the Nicene Empire. Possibly we may
have here a confused reminiscence of Frederick Barbarossa whose approach
to the Byzantine capital caused great panic. As for the commentary, it cannot
be earlier than the end of the thirteenth century.

---

[35] The Klontzas ms (Marc. gr. Cl. VII cod. 22, f. 82r) explains this line by saying
that Vatatzes was assisted by the king of Armenia. Marc. gr. Cl. IV cod. 38, fol. 16v says
that the daughter of Theodore Lascaris was born of an Armenian mother. The daughter
in question was Irene who married John Vatatzes, but her mother was Anna Comnena,
Theodore's first wife, not his second wife, the Armenian Phillippa. Cf. Heisenberg in
BZ 14 (1905), 176.

[36] It is hard to understand why Gidel in his preface to Legrand's ed. (p. 14) should
state that the author of the oracle was favourably disposed towards Union and may have
been a Benedictine monk.

[37] Lines 204—05: σκηνωρεῖ ἐν τῷ ἀμπέλι | εἰς τῆς ρουφιάνας τὸ λέγουν.
For the erroneuos form 'Ρουφιαναί, found in late Byzantine texts, cf. J. Pargoire
„Rufinianes," BZ 8 (1899), 454, 457.

[38] The „fair-haired nation" refers to Westerners in oracular literature down to
the 16th century; from that time onwards it usually applies to the Russians. See Istrin, *op.
cit.*, II, 273—74; M. Lascaris, Τὸ 'Ανατολικὸν Ζήτημα, I-2 Athens, n. d., 231—36.

68

* ⋆ *

It may have been apparent from the foregoing analysis that the Oracles of Leo the Wise have little connection with the emperor Leo VI. We have no evidence to show that the real Leo wrote any prophecies or, for that matter, that he dabbled in the occult beyond the normal interest in such pursuits shared by all his contemporaries. True, it has been proved that the epithet *Sophos* was applied to Leo in his lifetime,[39] but he must have earned it on account of his erudition and literary works, such as his sententious sermons and hymns,[40] and not on account of his supposed mantic gifts.[41] The Emperor's official pronouncements on magic and divination are very severe. In the 65th novella he criticizes older legislation which admitted a distinction between pernicious and beneficial magic. Persons convicted of magic, be it for averting disease or damage to their crops, are to suffer the ultimate penalty.[42] In the *Tactica* the use of astrology is likewise condemned. Professional astronomers, we are told, consult Ptolemy, the „Chaldaean Observations", Aratus and John Lydus; whereupon follows this remark: „The information on horoscopes, however, which is scattered in the aforesaid works, being as it is rejected by God's Church, is repugnant to our majesty."[43]

We need not, of course, assume that Leo himself adhered too strictly to the letter of his pronouncements. We are told, for example, that following an eclipse of the moon (March 20, 908),[44] he ordered the metropolitan Pantaleon of Synada to cast a horoscope. As the bishop was on his way to report his findings to the emperor, the all-powerful chamberlain Samonas asked him, „On whom will the misfortune fall?" „On you," replied the bishop, „but if you get over the 13th of June, you will suffer no harm from that time onward." To the emperor Pantaleon declared that the eclipse foreboded danger for the second man of the Empire (since the moon is second in importance among celestial bodies), and Leo, with evident relief, took that to refer to his brother Alexander. Shortly thereafter, however, Samonas was betrayed as the author of a libellous letter against the emperor and sent to a monastery.[45]

---

[39] Cf. H. Grégoire in *Byzantion* 5 (1929), 399—400; Honigmann, *ibid.* 9 (1934), 206 n. 5; V. Laurent in *Echos d'Orient* 34 (1935), 461.

[40] Cf. C. A. Spulber, *Les Novelles de Léon le Sage*, Cernauţi, 1934, 42; F. Dölger, *Byzanz und die Europäische Staatenwelt*, Speyer am Rhein, 1953, 200, n. 13.

[41] As supposed by Lebeau, *Histoire du Bas-Empire*, XIII, Paris, 1832, 392; H. Monnier, *Les Novelles de Léon le Sage*, Bordeaux, 1923, 211—14; S. Runciman, *History of the First Bulgarian Empire*, London, 1930, 148, n. 1, and others.

[42] *Les Novelles de Léon le Sage*, ed. P. Noailles and A. Dain, Paris, 1944, 236 sq.; Monnier, op. cit., 54, 200; Spulber, *op. cit.*, 248—49. This decree overrules the law of Constantine which declared beneficial magic to be legal. *Cod. Theod.*, IX. 16. 3; *Cod. Just.*, IX. 18. 4. Cf. *Basil.* LX. 39. 25; Harmen., VI. 10. 4.

[43] PG 107, 1092.

[44] For the date see R.J.H. Jenkins, „The 'Flight' of Samonas," *Speculum* 23 (1948), 234 and n. 99.

[45] Theoph. Cont., 376; Leo Gramm., 284; Theodosius Melitenus, ed. Tafel, 198—99; Cedrenus, II, 272.

It was perfectly normal to consult a diviner regarding disturbing natural phenomena. Had not Constantine himself, the Equal of the Apostles, decreed that if the palace or any public building was struck by lightning, the old custom of consulting the haruspices should be followed, *et diligentissime scribtura collecta ad nostram scientiam referatur?*[46] Leo himself was well versed in astronomy, and accurately predicted to Symeon, king of Bulgaria, the solar eclipse of June 7, 894. But when Symeon, in his correspondence with Leo Choirosphactes, challenged the Emperor to foretell on the strength of his science the fate of the Byzantine prisoners held by the Bulgarians, he was either being jocular or betraying his native superstition.[47]

We may now briefly consider the two instances of prediction that are attributed to Leo. The first was addressed to Constantine Ducas after the latter's escape from Bagdad. Standing in front of the mosaic of Christ in the Chrysotriclinos, Leo admonished Constantine in these words: „Be not deceived by the rumour that a Constantine shall reign over the Romans. I swear to thee by the all-seeing Justice and by Our Lord's icon that the kingship is not thine because thou art named Constantine, but that it has been divinely granted from of old to my dearest son, as I have been informed by many holy men. If then thou attemptest to put him to death, thy head will be carried in through this door without thy body."[48] This, add the chroniclers, was precisely what came to pass after Constantine's unsuccessful attempt to seize the imperial palace by night.

The second alleged prophecy was delivered by Leo on his deathbed. On seeing his brother Alexander, whom he heartily disliked, approaching him, he uttered these obscure words: „Behold the evil year of thirteen months" (ἰδὲ ὁ κακὸς καιρὸς μετὰ δεκατρεῖς μῆνας).[49] The chroniclers are pleased to point out that Alexander died thirteen months later. The coincidence may be remarkable, but Leo was not in fact prophesying. He was merely quoting a proverb, which is still current today in the form ἀνάποδος χρόνος δεκατρεῖς μῆνες, and is applied to persons of a perverse or evil character, presumably because the embolic year of thirteen months, prior to the introduction of the Julian calendar, was thought to be unlucky.[50]

Neither of the above instances is sufficient to establish Leo as a prophet. We have, on the other hand, a contemporary source to show that he was capable of brushing aside a prediction about the length of his own life. Certain persons, probably friends of Stylianus Zaoutzes (the passage is unfortunately mutilated), had started the rumour that Leo would live thirty three years: instead of punishing them, he merely made fun of their unfounded pro-

---

[46] *Cod. Theod.*, XVI. 10, 1.

[47] G. Kolias, *Léon Choerosphactès*, Athens, 1939, 77—79 (text), 33—35 (commentary).

[48] Theoph. Cont., 373; Cedrenus, II, 269, *et al.*

[49] Theoph. Cont., 377; Pseudo-Symeon, 715; Leo Gramm., 285; Cedrenus, II, 274, *et al.* The Latin translators, misunderstanding the Byzantine use of μετά + acc., give the meaningless rendering „En malus temporis articulus post tredecim menses."

[50] See S.P. Kyriakidês in Γέρας ᾿Αντωνίου Κεραμοπούλλου, Athens, 1953, 556-57.

gnostications.[51] Contrast this with the superstitious credulity of Heraclius, of Manuel I, Andronicus I, Isaac II or Alexius III.[52]

Setting aside the accusation of paganism made against Leo „the philosopher" by his pupil Constantine, which refers to Leo, the iconoclast archbishop of Thessalonica, and not to the emperor,[53] we must conclude, pending further evidence, that Leo VI was neither a prophet nor a magician. Our historical sources for the reign of Leo VI are admittedly very meagre; even so, it is surely significant that there is no mention of Leo's occult interests in any of the earlier chronicles, such as Theophanes Continuatus, the various adaptations of Symeon Logothete (Leo Grammaticus, Theodosius Melitenus, Georgius Hamartolus Continuatus, etc.), Cedrenus (except for one manuscript), not even in such popular compilations as those of Manasses, Glycas and Joel. The *Patria* of Constantinople, compiled *ca.* 995, has nothing to say of Leo's wonderful predictions, for all its interest in *mirabilia*. It appears that the concept of Leo as an astrologer did not develop until the twelfth century. In one manuscript of Cedrenus (cod. C = Coislin 136, saec. XII) we read: „This emperor applied himself to studies, and especially to the astronomical science of horoscopes."[54] According to Zonaras, Leo was prompted to contract his fourth marriage to Zoe Carbonopsina not only by his desire to have an heir, but also by certain prophecies which assured him of this. „For he was," adds Zonaras, „a lover of multifarious learning, including even the occult kind that divines the future by means of incantations, and he devoted himself to the motion of the stars, and studied the science of horoscopes that is derived therefrom, and found that he would have a son to succeed him in the kingship."[55] This is repeated in the fourteenth century chronicle of Ephraem who is wholly dependent on Zonaras.[56] A similar statement is also made by Nicephorus Gregoras in his *logos* concerning the sainted empress Theophano, except that the emperor's atsrological speculations are connected not with his fourth but with his second liaison, with Zoe, daughter of Zaoutzes. According to this document, Leo turned to the study of oracles and astrology when he perceived that Theophano was unable to bear him a son. „For from the time of his youth he had devoted much study to astronomical learning and to writings on horoscopes; whence he had derived considerable foreknowledge of the future concerning himself and his successors. He learned from that source that a son would be born

[51] *Vita Euthymii*, ed. De Boor, Berlin, 1888, 19₂₋₇; ed. P. Karlin—Hayter, *Byzantion* 25-27 (1957), 43.

[52] On the superstitions of the Comnenian emperors see L. Oeconomos, *La vie religieuse de l'Empire byzantin au temps des Comnènes et des Anges*, Paris, 1918, 65 sq.

[53] As shown by Kolias, *Léon Choerosphactès*, 67—68. Constantine's accusation and the apology of the same Constantine for having assailed his master are printed by Matranga, *Anecdota graeca*, II, Rome, 1850, 555—59; reprinted in PG 107, lxii-lxiv and 660—64 among the works of Leo VI. These works are erroneously referred to Leo VI by Matranga, *op. cit.*, I, *Praefatio*, 25 sq.; Hergenröther, *Photius*, II, 669 sq.; N. Popov, Имйерайор Лев VI Мудрый, Moscow, 1892, 15, and others.

[54] Cedrenus, II, 274, apparatus.

[55] III, 445. Cf. Short Chronicle in Sakkelion, Πατμιακὴ βιβλιοθήκη, Athens, 1890, 302.

[56] 115, vv. 2632 sq.

to him to succeed him in the kingship, and likewise that his son would have a son, and that son would have another, and so for a long time. This he considered to be a divine doctrine, like some inescapable destiny. For this reason even while his wife [Theophano] was living he had secret relations with a fair maiden of noble stock."[57] It is, of course, well known that Leo's successive marriages were dictated by his desire to have a male heir, and it is quite conceivable that he should have turned in his anxiety to consulting prophets and clairvoyants. We have seen from his speech to Constantine Ducas that the succession of his son had been predicted by „holy men"; indeed it is possible that the name Constantine, like that of Alexius II,[58] was chosen on account of some such prophecy. From this it was only one step to assert that Leo had himself divined the future thanks to his profound studies.

I am indebted to Mr John Parker for pointing out to me a twelfth-century document which, if it refers to Leo VI, would indicate that the prophetic fame of the Macedonian emperor was by no means well established at that time. In an encomiastic speech addressed to Manuel I by Euthymius Malakes, bishop of Neopatras, the emperor's *sophia* is favourably compared to that of another emperor who was called *sophos*. „One of the emperors," says Euthymius, „is known as *sophos*, and has inherited this name. As for me, I am not exactly aware of his wisdom: for I have not encountered any writing of this sage, nor have I heard of any achievement (τρόπαιον) of this man. If, however, he was in fact wise, that was due to excessive study and certainly to lengthy practice; for it is said that he spent almost more time being instructed by teachers than wearing the diadem in the palace."[59] This characterization applies very well to Leo VI, although it is surprising that the learned bishop should not have been acquainted with Leo's literary works.

Even if Leo was not highly regarded by some intellectuals of the twelfth century, his prophetic fame was by 1200 a matter of common knowledge among the populace. This we learn from the Russian pilgrim Antony who was in Constantinople in May 1200. In his very detailed description of St. Sophia, he mentions an image of the „emperor Kyr Leon o Sophos" (царь Корлѣи о софосъ) which had a precious stone in its head and illuminated the church at night.[60] „This same Kyr Leon," adds Antony, „took the writing which was in the tomb of the holy prophet Daniel [at Babylon, add some manuscripts], and copied it learnedly, [setting down] who was to be emperor

[57] Hergenröther, *Monumenta graeca ad Photium ejusque historiam pertinentia*, Regensburg, 1869, 81—82; Ed. Kurtz, *Zwei griech. Texte über die hl. Theophano, Mém. de l'Acad. Imp. des Sciences de St. Pétersbourg*, VIIIe sér., vol. III, no. 2 (1898), 42.

[58] Nicetas Choniates, 220.

[59] K. G. Mpones, Εὐθυμίου τοῦ Μαλάκη τὰ σῳζόμενα, II, Athens, 1949, 48₂₅₋₃₁. In his notes on this passage (*ibid.*, 84) Mpones appears to think that Manuel is being compared to Solomon, but this is surely impossible.

[60] In all probability, this was not the mosaic in the lunette over the imperial door, as has often been claimed (Kondakov, *Византийские церкви и йамяшники Кэнсшаншинойоля*, Odessa, 1886, 115, 124; T. Whittemore, *The Mosaics of St. Sophia at Istambul, Preliminary Report on the First Year's Work*, Oxford, 1933, 18, and others). Antony implies that Leo's image was in the nave, next to a door leading out of the church. See Chr. Loparev's edition of Antony, *Православный Палесшинский Сборник* XVII-3 (1899), lxxxiii.

in Tsargrad as long as Tsargrad stands."[61] This is a very significant passage.
It proves that certain oracles of Leo the Wise were already current by 1200;
it also shows that these oracles, like much mediaeval eschatological literature,
purported to be derived from the prophet Daniel. A similar prophetic document is mentioned in the Chronicle of Salımbene de Adam in connection
with the siege of Constantinople by the Crusaders in 1203: „Deinde Basilo-
graphya,[62] id est regalis scriptura cuiusdam prophete Danielis Achivi, qui
de imperatorum Constantinopolitanorum successionibus enigmata scripsit,
producitur in medio. Ubi cum legeretur, quod natio flava cesarie ventura
esset urbis excidio urbemque gravi expugnatura prelio, tamen ad ultimum —
quod in ipsos decidat! — peritura, hoc facto confisi Achivi repente irruunt
in Latinos."[63] Leo's journey to Babylon is probably to be connected with
a Russian legend that has survived in a number of recensions of the late
fifteenth or sixteenth century. This legend tells how the Byzantine emperor
Leo, renamed Basıl „in holy baptism," sent three emissaries to Babylon to
obtain a „sign" (знамеı ие) from the tomb of Ananias, Azarias and Misael.
Undetected by the huge serpent which was coiled round the walls of Babylon,
the emissaries entered Nebuchadnezzar's palace and took two crowns as
well as other regalia which they brought back to Leo and his wife Alexandra.[64]
In some versions of the legend the insignia of kingship are passed on to
prince Vladimir at Kiev. It is possible that there existed a Byzantine source
of this tale and that it came to Russia by way of a south Slavic translation.[65]
We may add at the risk of spoiling Antony's story that Leo had no need to go
to Babylon to find Daniel's grave, since the prophet's body was preserved
at Constantinople near the gate of St. Romanus.[66] It was encased in a marble
sarcophagus supported by lions and adorned with sleeping angels in the
form of infants.[67]

The next link of our enquiry concerns the execution of Alexius Murtzuph-
lus by the Crusaders at the end of 1204. As is well known, the unfortunate
Alexius was thrown down from the top of Theodosius' column in the Forum
Tauri. The story is told by Byzantine sources without any marvellous embel-

[61] Loparev's ed., 7—8, 53—54, 74; Mme B. de Khitrowo, *Itinéraires russes en Orient*, Geneva, 1889, 91. After the words „copied it," one ms adds, „and kept it at his house. After his death, many years later, it was brought by some people to Tsargrad and translated by philosophers into the Greek tongue."

[62] βασιλογραφεῖον. Cf. Du Cange, *Gloss. med. graec.*, Append., col. 36, s.v.

[63] MGH, *Scriptores*, XXXII, 23—24. On the *natio flava*, see above, n. 38.

[64] Perhaps a corruption of Alexander, Leo's brother and co-emperor.

[65] See A. Veselovskij, „Отрывки византийского эпоса в русском," *Славянский Сборник* 3 (1876), 122 sq. and esp. 157; I. N. Ždanov, „Повести о Вавилоне и 'Сказа-ние о князех Владимирских'," ЖМНП, Aug. 1891, 262 sq.; Sept. 1891, 51. M. O. Skripil' („Сказание о Вавилоне граде," Акад. Наук СССР, *Труды Отд. Древне-русской Литер.* 9 [1953], 119—44) argues against the Byzantine origin of the Babylon legend.

[66] Antony of Novgorod, ed. Loparev, 27; *Script. orig. Constant.*, ed. Preger, II, 245; Stephen of Novgorod, ed. M.N. Speranskij, *Из старинной Новгородской литера-туры XIV века*, Leningrad, 1934, 57; anonymous Russian pilgrim, *ibid.*, 135. Cf. J. Ebersolt, *Sanctuaires de Byzance*, Paris, 1921, 108—09.

[67] *Manuelis Philae carmina*, ed. E. Miller, I, Paris, 1855, 51, no. cviii.

lishments.[68] The western conquerors were, however, informed of the prophetic nature of the reliefs on the column. Villehardouin relates that among
the sculptured figures there was one in the form of an emperor who was
falling down.[69] Robert de Clari mentions both the columns of Theodosius
and of Arcadius, and says that „par dehors ches columbes si estoient pour-
traites et escrites par prophetie toutes les aventures et toutes les conquestes
qui sont avenues en Constantinoble, ne qui avenir i devoient." Among these
sculptures were represented ships making an assault upon the city, and
an inscription saying „que de vers Occident venroient une gent haut tondue
a costeles de fer, qui Constantinoble conquerroient."[70] More or less the same
is reported by Gunther of Paris who says that the sculptures which represented
ships and ladders were „Sibylle vaticinia", and that the Greeks, on seeing
the ladders erected on the Venetian ships, mutilated some of the reliefs
with stones and hammers, hoping to bring bad luck on the invaders.[71] In
the fourteenth-century Chronicle of Morea (which by mistake places the
column in front of St. Sophia) the authorship of the prophetic inscription
on the column is acribed to Leo the Wise. I quote from the French version
of the Chronicle:

„Adonc vint j. sages homs grex anciens de la cité, qui leur dist et conta
comment au temps de Lion le philosophe, quant il fu empereor de Constantinople, par son grant sens si ordonna et fist moult de chosez, lezquelles avin-
drent, et aucunes sont a avenir a la cité; et entre lez autres choses, si fist
faire j. pillier moult grant qui est encores devant l'ecglise de Saint Sophie;
et la drecha hert, et y escript lettres entaillies, lezquelles devisent et dient
ainxi: De cy sera desroupez li faulx empereor de Constantinople.

„Et quant li marquis et li autre baron oÿrent et virent les lettres ainxi
entaillies, si s'accorderent tout, et dirent que, puis que ceste prophesie estoit
escripte en cel pillier, car il estoit raison que elle fust ores acomplie par cestui
faulx empereor qui ainsi faussement avoit moudri son seignor. Et lors firent
monter cellui Morchufle sus le pillier, et puis le desrouperrent aval; et morut
en tel maniere."[72]

This is probably the earliest evidence for the belief, often found thereafter, that Leo's predictions were inscribed or represented on certain monuments of Constantinople. The tenth-century *Patria* has much to say about
such prophetic representations foretelling τὰ ἔσχατα τῆς πόλεως, but it does
not mention Leo's name in this connection.

---

[68] Nicetas Choniates, 804—05; Acropolites, 11.

[69] Ch. 308, ed. Edmond Faral, II, Paris, 1939, 116.

[70] Ch. 92, ed. Philippe Lauer, Paris, 1924, 89; cf. ch. 109, p. 104. See also English
trans. by Edgar Holmes McNeal (*The Conquest of Constantinople*, New York, 1936), 111
and n. 117. Ships full of armed soldiers were in fact represented on the Column of Arcadius. See E. H. Freshfield, „Notes on a Vellum Album, etc.", *Archaeologia* 72 (1932),
pls. XV, XVI, XVIII, XIX, XXI, XXII.

[71] Ch. 21, ed. Riant, *Exuviae sacrae Constantinopolitanae*, I, Geneva, 1877, 112.

[72] *Chronique de Morée*, ed. J. Longnon. Paris, 1911, 18, §§ 58—59; same account
in Greek version, Τὸ Χρονικὸν τοῦ Μορέως, ed. P. Kolonaros, Athens, 1940, 38—39,
vv. 875 sq. Leo's name is absent from the Aragonese version (*Chronique de Morée*, ed. A.
Morel-Fatio, Geneva, 1885, 14, § 51).

In the fourteenth and fifteenth centuries the „Leo legend" becomes a common folklore motif. In a magical manuscript at Bologna (Bibl. Univ. 3632, fol. 285^v) of the fifteenth century Leo the Wise is pictured along with famous physicians and diviners.[73] In the *Beautiful Tale of the Ass, the Wolf and the Fox* (late fifteenth century?) the cunning fox describes herself in these terms: „I am an astronomer, a diviner and a pupil of Leo the Wise."[74] More interesting for our enquiry are the popular tales picked up by Russian pilgrims at Constantinople, in particular by the anonymous pilgrim (1390),[75] Alexander (ca. 1395) and the monk Zosima (1419—1422). From their accounts of the curiosities of Constantinople it appears that Leo the Wise had assumed the place previously occupied by Apollonius of Tyana. The following marvels were ascribed to him:

i) The Serpent Column in the Hippodrome. It was Leo who enclosed snake's venom in this column. Anyone bitten by a snake within the city had only to touch this column in order to be healed.[76]

ii) The Egyptian Obelisk in the Hippodrome. The anonymous pilgrim tells us that on (?) this pillar there were sixteen statues, eight in bronze and eight in stone. Each one held a broom which appeared to be made of wax. During Leo's reign these statues swept the streets in the night and remained idle in the day.[77]

iii) A palace hall in which the sun, moon and stars revolved as in the heavens.[78]

iv) A stone toad which stood in front of the *Apolikaptia* (?) monastery (variants: *Apolikanti, Apokalipsia*),[79] not far from that of Christ Pantocrator. This toad walked through the streets by night and consumed all the refuse[80]. The same story, except that the toad is replaced by a marble tortoise, is given in the seventeenth-century chronicle by pseudo-Dorotheus of Monembasia who adds that this tortoise (some said there were two tortoises) was

---

[73] *Catal. codd. astrol. graec.*, IV (1903), 43; Sp. Lambros, Νέος Ἑλληνομνήμων 15 (1921), 37.

[74] W. Wagner, *Carmina graeca medii aevi*, Leipzig, 1874, 127, vv. 103—04, and 139, vv. 507—08. On this work see Krumbacher, *Gesch. d. byz. Lit.*², 880—83.

[75] On the date, see my study in BZ 45 (1952), 380—85. The text of the anonymous pilgrim has come down to us in two divergent recensions, the *Беседа* (ed. N. L. Majkov, *Сборник Отд. Русск. Яз. и Слов. Имп. Акад. Наук* 51, no. 4, 1890) and the *Сказание* (ed. M. N. Speranskij, *op. cit.*, 83—140). The *Беседа* contains more information on Leo the Wise than the *Сказание*.

[76] Alexander in *Полное Собрание Русских Летописей*, IV (1848), 358=Khitrowo, *Itin. russes en Orient*, 164. Cf. Zosima, ed. Loparev, *Прав. Палест. Сборник* VIII-3 (1889), 5 = *Itin. russes*, 203.

[77] *Беседа*, 25—26 = *Itin. russes*, 237—38. Cf. *Сказание*, 134.

[78] *Беседа*, 26 = *Itin. russes*, 238. This calls to mind the famous throne-room of Chosroes (Nicephorus, ed, De Boor, 16; Georgius Monachus, ed. De Boor, II, 671—72; Cedrenus, I, 721—22, etc.). Cf. also *Callimaque et Chrysorrhoé*, ed. M. Pichard, Paris, 1956, 16—17, vv. 423 sq. On astral ceilings in general see K. Lehmann, „The Dome of Heaven," *Art Bulletin*, 27 (1945), 1—27.

[79] This monastery has not been identified. Cf. Janin, *La géographie ecclésiastique de l'Empire byzantin*, I-3, Paris, 1953, 46.

[80] Zosima, ed. Loparev, 7 = *Itin, russes*, 204. Cf. H. Carnoy and J. Nicolaidès, *Folklore de Constantinople*, Paris, 1894, 13.

preserved in the sultan's stable.[81] The monument in question was probably the one called Χελώνη which gave its name to a church of St. Procopius, and which Janin places on the third hill.[81a]

v) The tomb of the prophet Daniel. The stone angels at the head and foot of the sarcophagus were made by Leo the Wise.[82] This recalls Antony's statement quoted above.

vi) Constantine's bath in the Great Palace. Leo the Wise conveyed water into a big stone trough in which the poor could wash themselves without charge. The water flowed out of a wooden barrel held together by seven nails and iron hoops. Next to it was a lantern which burned day and night. Facing this was a statue in the form of a sentinel holding a bow and arrow. This bath was in use three hundred years after Leo's death, but when the Latins began collecting an entrance fee, the statue discharged its arrow which split the barrel, so that the water stopped flowing. The lamp, too, was extinguished. The Latins broke off the statue's head.[83]

vii) The „True Judges." This was a pair of statues, probably imperial, since they were made of porphyry. According to Zosima, they were close to the Peribleptos monastery.[84] They passed judgment on financial disputes and false accusations. To establish the fair price of any item, a sum of money was placed in the statue's hand which would close when it held the correct amount and drop the excess. Or the litigants would place their hands in the statue's mouth, and it would bite off the hand of the guilty party. These statues had been mutilated by the Crusaders: one was broken in two pieces, the other had its arms and legs broken off and its nose was missing.[85] Pero Tafur (1437/38) was shown in the middle of the Hippodrome a statue of gilded brass called „the Just" of which the same story was told; „but," he comments, „I would place more faith in anything found in the Evangelists."[86] Dorotheus of Monembasia tells us that only half of one hand was left in his time and was kept in the sultan's stable. On one occasion this hand, called δικαιοκρίτης, fixed at one gold piece the price of a horse valued at over one hundred, and the horse died that same night.[87] Similar legends were attached to the chain on the withered cypress tree that stands in the

---

[81] Βιβλίον ἱστορικόν, Venice, 1750, 363. On this work see below, p. 81.

[81a] Constantinople byzantine, Paris, 1950, 102—03, 308.

[82] Беседа, 20 = Itin. russes, 232.

[83] Беседа, 23 = Itin. russes, 235-36; cf. Сказание, 133—34. A similar tale, except that the fountain gushed with wine and was destroyed by the Turks, in Carnoy and Nicolaidès, op. cit., 12—13 (without indication of source). The statue of an archer and a torch that could not be extinguished also apper in the legends concerning Virgil and Gerbert. See D. Comparetti, Virgilio nel medio evo, Florence, 1946, II, 25, 82—83, 90—91.

[84] Ed. Loparev, 7 = Itin. russes, 204.

[85] Беседа, 26—27 = Itin. russes, 238; Сказание, 134.

[86] Travels and Adventures, trans. Malcolm Letts, London, 1926, 143.

[87] Βιβλίον ἱστορικόν, 363. The story of the „hand of righteousness" was still current in Greece at the end of the 19th century. See N. Politês, Παραδόσεις, I, 19—20; II, 651—55. Politês connects this legend with the pair of bronze hands at the Modion of Constantinople (Script. orig. Constant., ed. Preger, I, 28; Anna Comnena, XII. 6. 8), but he is probably mistaken in this.

courtyard of the church of St. Andrew in Krisei (Kodja Mustafa Pasha Mesdjidi).[88]

viii) The most interesting of these marvels was a series of imperial and patriarchal portraits in the monastery of St. George of Mangana. The existence of these paintings is well-documented and cannot be doubted. The fullest account of them is given in the anonymous pilgrim's *Skazanie*, although there is unfortunately some confusion in the text. The paintings were in the narthex (*pritvor*)[89] of the church, on the right hand side as one went out. The imperial series included eighty rulers, of whom seventy-seven were represented and three were still to come. The last emperor was to be Manuel, the son of John V. There were one hundred (one hundred and thirty?) patriarchs, of whom three (six?) were still to come. The *Beseda* gives an abridged account of these paintings, but preserves the name of the last patriarch, John or Jonas, which is absent from the *Skazanie*.[90]

We have other references to these prophetic paintings. In the early fifteenth century Macarius of Ancyra in an unpublished canonical work referred to the portraits of the patriarchs in the Mangana church, among whom was represented one Neophytus, labelled ὑποψήφιος („candidate"). This Neophytus occupied the patriarchal throne for a short time in 1154,. but was never consecrated.[91] It would appear, therefore, that the patriarchal series was in existence by the middle of the twelfth century (it could hardly have been older than the reign of Constantine IX who built the Mangana church), and that the portrait of each new incumbent was added to it. This is of interest for the study of Byzantine iconography. We know that in the pre-Iconoclastic period the portraits of the patriarchs of Constantinople were preserved in the episcopal palace and placed in churches.[92] In 1200 Antony of Novgorod was shown the portraits of all the patriarchs and emperors of Constantinople in the galleries of St. Sophia.[93] The existence of such comprehensive series of patriarchal portraits both in St. Sophia and in the Mangana church may throw some light on the representations of the Constantinopolitan patriarchs in the church of St. Sophia at Ochrid.

Leonardus Chiensis, writing immediately after the fall of Constantinople in 1453, speaks of the Mangana portraits in these terms:

„Tabula illa, quam Leoni Sapienti ascribunt, apud monasterium Sancti Georgii de Mangana contstructa, vetusto tempore in Constantinopoli

---

[88] A. Van Millingen, *Byzantine Churches in Constantinople*, London, 1912, 107—08; Carnoy and Nicolaidès, *op. cit.*, 112—14.

[89] *Притвор* usually means a narthex, which may be on the west, north or south side of a church. Cf. E. Golubinskij, *Исторiя Русской Церкви* , I-2, 2nd ed., Moscow, 1904, 69—70.

[90] *Сказание*, 132—33; *Беседа*, 18 = *Itin, russes*, 230. Cf. my remarks in BZ 45 (1952), 384—85.

[91] V. Laurent, „La forme de la consécration épiscopale selon le métropolite d'Ancyre Macaire," *Orient. Christ. Per.*, 13 (1947), 554—55. The text is contained in cod. Par. gr. 1379, f. 29r.

[92] John of Ephesus, *Eccles. Hist.*, II. 27; cf. I. 36; III. 16. J. Kollwitz, „Zur Frühgeschichte der Bilderverehrung," *Röm. Quart.* 48 (1953), 17—18; A. Grabar, *L'iconoclasme byzantin. Dossier archéologique*, Paris, 1957, 213—14.

[93] Ed. Loparev, 23 = *Itin. russes*, 101.

occultata mysterioso jam signo detecta, jacturam demonstrat. Haec, Pater beatissime, cellulis distincta quadratis, imperatorum ordinem successionemque ponebat, finiendum tamen in hoc ultimo Constantino. Ita quoque patriarcharum alia in longum tracta tabula ordinem praescribebat. Nam ille spiritu prophetico illustratus tot cellulas figurandorum imperatorum tabulae inscripsit, quot a primo Constantino Magno, Constantinopolis conditore, usque ad ultimam captivitatem futuri erant. In dies itaque cellulae illae repletae, unam modo et ultimam, in qua hic, sub quo urbs periit, collocandus erat, si coronatus fuisset, vacuam praetendunt."[94]

Chalcocondyles also refers to a similar catalogue of emperors and patriarchs. Unfortunately, his text appears to be corrupt or incomplete at this point, so that the following translation is not altogether certain:

„I marvel," he says, „that some persons do not consider the Sibylline oracles to be true, since the enumeration (γραφήν) of emperors in Byzantium, [made], as they say, by the emperor Leo the Wise ... [lacuna] ... The enumeration ended with this emperor [John VIII?] and with the patriarch who died at Florence in Italy.[95] For that list (πίναξ) contained neither the emperor Constantine, since he was killed by barbarians and did not die in the imperial dignity, nor Gregory who departed to Italy.[96] Spaces were incised in this book (βιβλίῳ) for the emperors after him [Leo VI?] down to the death of this emperor [John VIII?], and to those who attained to the episcopate of the City, be they many or few, down to [the death of] this patriarch [Joseph II?]. It is said that there are many works of this emperor [Leo VI] that deserve admiration, since he had experience of stars and spirits and was conversant with their power, and especially two or three that are worthy of mention."[97]

When the long-awaited collapse occurred in 1453 in the reign of a Constantine, the Oracles of Leo the Wise received — or so it was thought — a striking confirmation. „This", says a Russian author concerning the fall of Constantinople. „was God's dispensation because of our sins, and so that everything that had been foretold concerning this city at the time of Constantine the emperor, and Leo the most-wise, and Methodius bishop of Patara might be fulfilled."[98] Had not Leo in fact predicted: „Woe to thee, City of seven hills, when the twentieth letter [K=20] is acclaimed along thy walls"?[99] True, no angel came down from heaven to hand a sword to the unknown liberator who was expected to be standing in front of Constantine's

---

[94] PG 159, 926D—927A.

[95] Joseph II who died at Florence in 1439.

[96] Gregory III who went to Rome on 1452 and died there in 1459.

[97] Ed. E. Darkó, II, Budapest, 1927, 169 = Bonn ed., 405—06.

[98] Хронограф редакции 1512 года, Полное Собрание Русских Летописей, XXII-1 (1911), 450. Cf. Степенная Книга, ПСРЛ, XXI-2 (1913), 501.

[99] PG 107, 1136C. That the letter K was in fact interpreted as the initial of Constantine XI is shown by a Russian translation of this prophecy (late 15th century): „Горе тебе, Седмохолмии граде, егда како Константин славославится на здех твоих; тогда приближися падение и погубление силных твоих, иже в неправде судящих". (М. N. Speranskij, „Повести и сказания о взятии Царьграда Турками," Акад. Наук СССР, Труды Отд. Древнерусской Литер. 10 [1954], 150 n. 1).

column when the Turks broke into the city.[100] This only meant, however, that the predestined deliverance would occur at some later date which the attentive study of the Oracles wuld reveal. In the *Chronicon maius* of Phrantzes we find this passage:

„Furthermore, the most-wise Leo, emperor of the Romans, himself made a horoscope (θεμάτιον) and found that the powerful and mighty domination of the Agarenes was to abide for [the length of] a thrice-numbered circle (τρισαρίθμου κύκλου)[101], i.e. three hundred years, but he has made no mention of the perturbation (συστροφή) [of their empire for a period] of fifty-six years.[102] Also, according to the prophecies of holy men, the fair-haired nation together with the avengers (?) will put all of Ismael to flight."[103]

*　*　*

It was in the two centuries after the fall of Constantinople that Leo's Oracles attained their greatest popularity both in the East and in the West. The number of manuscript copies produced during this period is truly staggering. The most splendid of these is now at Oxford (Barocc. gr. 170), a slender volume embellished with twenty-four full-page illustrations.[104] It was written in 1577 by Francesco Barozzi[105] on the island of Crete, and dedicated by him to Giacomo Foscarini, the Venetian admiral whose proud name can still be read on the Rialto bridge. From Barozzi's preface we learn that Foscarini had given him in 1576 a damaged copy of the Oracles which he wished to be translated into Latin and interpreted. Pursuant to this request, Barozzi produced an emended text based on the collation of several other manuscripts. He mentions the tradition that the oracles and the accompanying illustrations had been copied, though often carelessly, from a marble column

---

[100] Ducas, 289—90; Chalcocondyles, ed. Darkó, II, 160—61 = Bonn ed., 396—97.

[101] Cf. Oracle XIV, PG 107, 1140A: κρυβέντος εἰς γῆν τρισαναρίθμους κύκλους.

[102] This refers to the horoscope of Stephen of Alexandria, according to which the Ismaelite empire would prosper for 309 years and remain in a state of confusion for another 56, so that the total length of its rule would be 365 years (Phrantzes, 315, Bonn ed). On Stephen's horoscope, cf. Constantine Poprphyrogenitus, *De adm. imp.*, ch. 16.

[103] Bonn ed., 316: τὸ ξανθὸν γένος ἅμα μετὰ τῶν πρακτόρων ὅλον Ἰσμαὴλ τροπώσουσι. This is borrowed from the well-known inscription on Constantine's tomb as expounded by Gennadius Scholarius. Banduri, *Imperium Orientale*, Paris, 1711, I, lib. VII, 185: τὸ δὲ ξανθὸν γένος μετὰ τῶν προκτόρων (προκτητόρων, i.e. „previous owners" corr. Banduri] ὅλον Ἰσμαὴλ τροπώσουν. This oracle was first published in the Chronicle of Pseudo-Dorotheus in 1631 and again by Matt. Cigala (Kigalas), Νέα σύνοψις διαφόρων ἱστοριῶν, Venice, 1637 (inaccessible to me). See also Banduri, *op. cit.*, II 871—72; Leo Allatius, *De Georgiis diatriba* (along with Georgius Acropolites), Paris, 1651, 404.

[104] Henry O. Coxe, *Catalogi codd. mss. bibl. Bodl. pars prima*, Oxford, 1853, 285; N. Beês in BNJ 13 (1937), 215—16; B. Laourdas, Κρητικὰ παλαιογραφικά, Κρητικὰ Χρονικά 2 (1948), 539—40.

[105] On Barozzi see Girolamo Tiraboschi, *Storia della letteratura italiana*, VII-2, Venice, 1796, 489; M. Vogel and V. Gardthausen, *Die griech. Schreiber des Mittelalters und der Renaissance*, Leipzig, 1909, 422.

on which Leo the Wise had carved them.[106] In his dedication to the Venetian admiral, he proudly claims that his work which reveals all the secrets of the future down to the end of world will prove an *immortale iuvamentum* to the entire human race. The lengthy commentary which Barozzi mentions in his preface does not appear to have survived.

Among other manuscripts, mention should be made of Marc. Cl. VII cod. 22, written in 1590 by the Cretan George Klontzas and profusely illustrated by him;[107] a fragment, written between 1584 and 1595, formerly in the Uvarov collection;[108] Berlin, Staatliche Bibl. 297 (sixteenth century);[109] Palermo, Bibl. Naz., I. E. 8 (sixteenth century)[110] and its doublet, Marc. Cl. VII cod. 3;[111] Marc. Cl. IV cod. 34 (sixteenth century),[112] Cl. IV cod. 38 (sixteenth century),[113] Cl. XI cod. 32 (sixteenth century);[114] Turin, B. V. 27 (fifteenth century?);[115] Paris, Suppl. gr. 82 (A. D. 1617);[116] Oxford, Barocc. 145 (fifteenth and sixtenth century);[117] Laud. 27 (fifteenth or sixteenth century);[118] Laud. 93 (sixteenth century);[119] Milan, Ambros. 723 (R 115 suppl.) of the sixteenth century;[120] London, B. M. Add. 28828 (fourteenth century?);[121] Jerusalem, Taphou 121 (A. D. 1667, written in Moscow);[122] Taphou 422 (early sixteenth century);[123] Metochion 501 (A. D. 1698);[124] Sinai 1864 (seventeenth century);[125] Copenhagen 2147 (fifteenth or sixteenth cen-

---

[106] Fol. 2v: „In corrigendis vero, ordinéque disponendis tum carminibus ipsis, tum figuris non parvum sudoris, atque vigilię impendi, quandoquidem cum propter eorum incuriam, qui primum carmina, et figuras ab ipsa marmorea columna mendose, confuseque, transtulerunt, in qua (ut communis omnium extat opinio) sapientissimus ille Imperator ea exculpere fecerat: tum propter ignorantiam eorum, qui posterius in multis exemplaribus ea perperam scripsere, ita mutila, ac depravata legebantur, ut nemo hactenus quid boni ex eis potuerit dicere."

[107] Lambros, Νέος Ἑλληνομνήμων 3 (1906), 240 sq.; 4 (1907), 20 sq., 238 sq., 404 sq.; 6 (1909), 215, 223 sq.; 11 (1914), 439; 12 (1915), 41 sq.; 13 (1916), 477; Beês, *op. cit.*, 216; Moravcsik, *Byzantinoturcica*, I, 145.

[108] G. Destunis, „Рукописный греческий лицевой сборник пророчений," *Древности, Труды Имй. Моск. Археол. Общ.* 14 (1890), 29—72.

[109] Beês, *op. cit.*, 219 sq.

[110] A. Daneu Lattanzi, „Il codice degli oracoli di Leone della Bibl. Nazionale di Palermo," *Atti dello VII Congr. Intern. di Studi Biz.*, I (1953), 35 sq.

[111] Lambros, Νέος Ἑλληνομνήμων, 19 (1925), 110—13.

[112] *Ibid.*, 98 sq.

[113] *Ibid.*, 107—10.

[114] *Ibid.*, 113—16. On ff. 2r—3r this ms contains versified oracles by one Arsenius Marcellus, patriarchal protonotary, with curious coloured pictures.

[115] *Ibid.*, 116—24.

[116] Omont, *Invent. sommaire des mss. gr. de la B. N.*, III, 1888, 214.

[117] Coxe, *op. cit.*, 247—51.

[118] *Ibid.*, 508—10.

[119] *Ibid.*, 582.

[120] Martini and Bassi, *Catal. codd. gr. bibl. Ambros.*, II, Milan, 1906, 835.

[121] M. Richard, *Inventaire des mss grecs du British Museum*, I Paris, 1952, 52.

[122] Papadopoulos-Kerameus, Ἱεροσολυμιτικὴ Βιβλιοθήκη, I, 202; cf. Addenda, III, 326.

[123] *Ibid.*, II, 541.

[124] *Ibid.*, V, 59.

[125] V. Beneševič, *Catal. codd. mss. gr. qui in monast. S. Catharinae in monte Sina asservantur*, III-1, St. Petersburg, 1917, 243.

tury);[126] Mount Athos, Iviron 181 (sixteenth century);[127] Gregoriou 31 (sixteenth century);[128] Xeropotamou 248 (seventeenth century);[129] Vat. gr. 695 (fourteenth or fifteenth century);[130] Vienna, Suppl. gr. 172 (sixteenth century),[131] and many more.

The abundance of manuscripts, especially of the sixteenth century, indicates that Leo's Oracles were greatly in demand not only in the Turkish dominated East,[132] but likewise in the West where the Turkish menace was causing serious concern. „Je voudrois bien," wrote Montaigne, „avoir reconu de mes yeux ces deus merveilles: du livre de Joachim, abbé calabrois, qui predisoit tous les papes futurs, leurs noms et formes; et celuy de Leon l'emperur, qui predisoit les emperurs et patriarches de graece."[133] The relevance of the Leonine Oracles (especially the illustrated series) for the events of that period was established by a very natural change of interpretation: instead of referring to Byzantine emperors, each oracle with its accompanying picture referred to a Turkish sultan. As time went on, this interpretation naturally had to be revised to include each latest sultan. Great expectations were aroused towards the end of the sixteenth century, thus coinciding with similar speculations in the East, where the year 1592 marked the beginning of the eleventh Moslem century.[134] The specific application of the Leonine Oracles to the events of this period appears in the Palermo manuscript and its twin Marc. gr. cl. VII cod 3, the Klontzas monuscript in the Marciana, the printed edition of the Oracles by De Bry brothers (on which see below, p. 80), and in other versions. In the Palermo codex and Marc. gr. cl. VII cod. 3, both written in the reign of Selim II (1566—74), the following sultans are mentioned:

Mehmed II: Lambeck's Oracle III and fig. 3

Beyazid II: Lambeck's Oracle VI and fig. 6

Selim I: Lambeck's Oracle VII and fig. 7

Suleyman I: Lambeck's Oracles IV and V, figs. 4 and 5

Selim II: Lambeck's Oracle XII, vv. 4—6 and fig. 11.

---

[126] Ch. Graux, *Notices sommaires des mss grecs de . . . Copenhague*, Paris 1879, 77—79.

[127] Beês, *op. cit.*, 218—19.

[128] Lambros, *Catal. of the Gr. Mss on Mt Athos*, I, Cambridge, 1895, 48—49.

[129] *Ibid.*, 218.

[130] Devreesse, *Codd. Vatic. graeci*, III, Rome, 1950, 171.

[131] H. Hunger, *Katalog der griech. Handschriften der Oesterreich. Nationalbibl. Suppl. graec.*, Vienna, 1957, 105 sq.

[132] On the abundance of prophetic literature, including Leo's Oracles, in the 16th century Greek libraries of Constantinople, see R. Foerster, *De antiquitatibus et libris mss Constantinopolitanis commentatio*, Rostock, 1877, 19, 24, 25.

[133] *Les Essais de Michel de Montaigne*, I, xi, éd. municipale, vol. I, Bordeaux, 1906, 50—51. This passage was written after 1588, and may have been inspired by Vigenère's French translation of Chalcocondyles, published in 1577. See *ibid.*, vol. IV (*Les sources des Essais* par Pierre Villey,) Bordeaux, 1920, p. 22.

[134] J. von Hammer, *Gesch. d. Osmanischen Reiches*, 2nd ed., II, Pesth, 1834, 572: „Mit der Tag- und Nachtgleiche des 1592. Jahres nach Christi Geburt begann das zweite Jahrtausend der Hidschret unter den grössten Erwartungen, weil nach dem historischen Aberglauben des Morgenlandes der Beginn jedes Jahrhunderts, und so viel mehr jedes Jahrtausends die Epoche der Erscheinung eines grossen Mannes, dessen Geist sein Jahrhundert beherrscht."

The same interpretation, though amplified, appears in the edition of the De Bry brothers (reproducing the 1596 Brescia edition which is inaccessible to me). Here the first oracle (fig. 1) is made to refer to the destruction of the Byzantine Empire by the Crusaders; the second (fig. 2) to Baldwin of Flanders; then follow the sultans from Mehmed II to Suleyman I inclusive as in the Palermo codex. The verse *Falcifer, trimestre tibi spatium praescribo* in Oracle VI of the edition (corresponding to Lambeck's Oracle IV, v. 3: δρεπανηφόρε, τετράμηνόν σοι γράφω) is interpreted to mean that three more sultans will reign after Suleyman I, and thereafter will come the end of the Ottoman Empire. This is represented by Oracle XIV of the edition which is not found in any Greek manuscript and is an obvious fabrication. In a pastoral Renaissance setting a shepherd is rescuing a sheep from the jaws of a wolf. This is explained by the legend: *En lupum qui ovem cupiebat devorare, pastor occidet et hominem inveniet. Sic perdet qui occupavit.* The sultan referred to is Mehmed III (1595—1603) reigning at that time. He is to be the last sultan since he bears the same name as Mehmed the Conqueror (*sic perdet qui occupavit*). In the Uvarov fragment, written between 1584 and 1595, the division of the Turkish Empire (μελισμός = Lambeck's no. VII) is placed in the reign of Murad III. Slightly earlier is the versified oracle found in the Berlin and other manuscripts, and which may be rendered as follows:

„There is a column in Constantinople, and it stands in a place called Xerolophus. It is a piece of carved white marble, most beautiful, and it has all the oracles that were made there by the son of Basil the Macedonian, Leo the most-wise, the great emperor. For he says that five kings descended from Hagar will, by the dispensation of God, our Master and Lord, rule this city — I mean Constantinople — and dominate it with great might. He has these kings carved on the column, and in their hands they hold bared swords; and in the midst of the five rulers stands an upright snake, most savage of aspect. And of the fifth he says that he will forthwith come to an end, and a Christian emperor will once more rule this city," etc.[135] This text is followed by a picture of the Xerolophus column. On its shaft is an upright serpent reminiscent of fig. 1 and five turbaned kings holding drawn swords. The fifth sultan after the capture of Constantinople was Selim II (1566—1574).

The Klontzas manuscript (Marc. gr. Cl. VII, cod. 22), like the Uvarov fragment, places the division of the Ottoman Empire in the reign of Murad III. Klontzas' interpretation of the Oracles is as follows:

Mehmed II: Bear with three cubs, similar to fig. 7, labelled ἡ πρώτη ἄρκτος ((f. 89r).

Beyazid II: Lambeck's Oracle I and fig. 1 (ff. 98r, 100v, 112r).

Selim I: Oracles II and III and figs. 2 and 3 (ff. 112v, 118r, 118v, 119r).

Suleyman I: Oracle IV and fig. 4 (f. 120r).

Selim II: Oracle VI and fig. 6 (f. 129r). On f. 140r is a fantastic picture of Selim, bull-headed, shaking hands with death. Behind him can be seen

---

[135] Beês, *op. cit.*, 242—44α' and fig. 10; slightly different text in Istrin, *op. cit.*, II, 324.

jhe Xerolophus column with turbaned Turks and an upright snake on it, tust as in the Berlin manuscript. In the foreground is an open coffin containing a skeleton with a crown on its head.

Murad III: Oracle VII (μελισμός) and fig. 7 (ff. 145v—146r).

The intense interest in Leo's Oracles in the sixteenth and seventeenth centuries prompted their repeated appearance in print. The following early editions are known to me:

1. *Vaticinium Severi, et Leonis Imperatorum, in quo videtur finis Turcarum in praesenti eorum Imperatore, una cum alijs nonnulis in hac re Vaticiniis*, Brescia, 1596 (inaccessible to me). Latin and Italian only. Presumably based on Marc. gr. Cl. VII cod. 3. [136] Oracle XIV is fictitious (see above, p. 79). At the end are added a „Vaticinium Maumectanorum" and a „Vaticinium Maumectis prophetae saracenorum et turcarum".

2. *Acta Mechmeti I Saracenorum principis . . . vaticinia Severi et Leonis in Oriente Impp. cum quibusdam aliorum aliis, interitum regni Turcici sub Mechmete hoc III praedicentia . . . per Io. Theodorum et Io. Israeiem de Bry fratres*, 1597. Latin only. Apparently similar in all respects to Brescia edition.

3. First edition of Greek text with emendations by Jan Rutgers, *Variarum lectionum libri sex*, Leyden, 1618, 467—84. Figures not reproduced. Text based on a manuscript brought from Constantinople by George Dousa.[137] In his preface (p. 467) Rutgers notes: „Nam Versiones quae ex Italia prodierunt, tales sunt, ut, quod vulgo dicitur, neque coelum, neque terram tangant. Iconas studio omisimus, quod eae saepius jam recusae sunt."

4. *Imperatoris Leonis, cognomine Sapientis Oracula*, edited by Peter Lambeck (Lambecius) along with Georgius Codinus, Paris, 1655, 233—94. Greek text based on Rutgers' edition with variants from a manuscript at Amsterdam. Followed by an anonymous *Paraphrasis* taken from the same Amsterdam manuscript. Lambeck's edition reprinted in Venice Byzantine Corpus and by Migne, PG 107, 1121—68.

5. *Tableaux prophetiques des empereurs Severe et Leon, avec leurs epigrammes predisans la ruyne de la monarchie des Turcs . . . par Artus Thomas, sieur d'Embry Parisien*. Appended to *Histoire generale des Turcs, contenant l'Histoire de Chalcondyle, trad. par Blaise de Vigenaire . . . continuée jusques en l'an M. DC. XII par Thomas Artus; et en cette Edition, par le Sieur de Mezeray, jusques en l'annee 1661*, vol. II, Paris, 1662, 67—116. Latin text based on De Bry edition with French translation and commentary incorporating data from a manuscript with coloured illustrations (p. 76: „car ie tiens que les couleurs servent beaucoup a l'intelligence des Propheties"). In his introduction Artus cautions Christians against putting much faith in these oracles, especially as it is difficult to distinguish those that are by Leo from those that are by Severus. The former was indeed a good Christian and may have been granted a revelation from above, whereas the latter was a pagan and must have made use of astrology. The Turks, on the other hand, ought to

---

[136] Cf. Daneu Lattanzi, „Il codice degli Oracoli," 36.
[137] Cf. H. Omont, „Martin Crusius, Georges Dousa et Théodose Zygomalas," *Revue des ét. grecques* 10 (1897), 70.

pay attention to these prophecies and change their religion (pp. 73—75). At the end (pp. 110—11) is appended an oracle in Turkish.

6. *Allusioni d'alcune predizioni tolte de Leone e Severo, Imperadori di Constantinopoli, cadente con il suo imperio della setta Maomettana, e risorgente alla nostra Santa Fede Cattolica*, Verona, 1716 (inaccessible to me).

7. A. Loberdos, Βίβλος χρονικὴ περιέχουσα τὴν ἱστορίαν τῆς Βυζαντίδος, vol. IV, Venice, 1767 (inaccessible to me).

We may also mention here the edition of an oracle (actually, a garbled condensation of the illustrated series) by Du Cange,[138] and the numerous quotations from a *Paraphrasis*, ascribed to a certain Rhuzanus, in Meursius' well-known lexicon.[139]

Meanwhile, the memory of the wonderful monuments contrived by Leo the Wise was still lingering among the Greeks. We have spoken of the Chronicle by pseudo-Dorotheus of Monembasia, first published in 1631.[140] In addition to the stories of the marble tortoise and the porphyry hand, this compilation ascribes to Leo a somewhat improper amatory adventure which recurs in the Virgilian legend. Leo, we are told, was in love with a noblewoman and sought to visit her at night. She let down a basket from her window, and after Leo had climbed into it, she hauled it up half way and left the emperor perched in that undignified position until morning to the amusement of the populace. Thereupon all fires were extinguished in the city. When the emperor's help was solicited in this matter, he directed that the woman should be placed in the market square and the fire extracted from her private parts where she had hidden it. In this way the woman's shame was greater than the emperor's.[141] This anecdote, as applied to Virgil, had a wide currency in the Renaissance through such popular books as *Les faits merveilleux de Virgille*,[142] and it was often represented on prints.[143] It is likely, therefore, that pseudo-Dorotheus borrowed it from the Virgilian repertory, although similar stories are also found in earlier eastern sources, e. g. in the Greek Life of Leo, bishop of Catania.[144]

Dorotheus' stories about Leo the Wise passed to Russia, where they circulated in the form of a short opuscule, of which three manuscript copies

---

[138] Notes to Zonaras, II, Paris, 1687, 124—25.

[139] *Glossarium graeco-barbarum*, 2nd ed., Leyden, 1614, See index of unpublished authors under Rhuzanus. On Rhuzanus cf. Lambros, Νέος Ἑλληνομνήμων 19 (1925), 117.

[140] See E. Legrand, *Bibliographie hellénique ou description raisonnée des ouvrages publiés par des Grecs au XVIIe s.*, I, Paris, 1894, 290 sq.; K. N. Sathas, Νεοελληνικὴ φιλολογία, Athens, 1868, 223.

[141] 1750 ed., p. 364. Cf. F. Liebrecht, „Neugriechische Sagen," *Zeitschr. f. deutsche Philologie* 2 (1870), 181—83; *id.*, *Zur Volkskunde*, Heilbronn, 1879, 86—87.

[142] Comparetti, *op. cit.*, II, 108 sq., 153 sq.

[143] See, for example, Arthur M. Hind, *Early Italian Engraving*, II, London, 1938, pls. 45, 46 (Florentine, *ca.* 1460—70); Le C. d'I*** [Jules Gay], *Iconographie des estampes à sujets galants*, Geneva, 1868, 11, 585, 733 (16th century).

[144] *Acta Sanctorum*, Feb., vol. III, 228 (Latin trans.). The Greek text is unpublished; *Bibl hagiogr.gr.*, no. 981.

of the seventeenth and eighteenth centuries have been preserved.[145] This opuscule is made up of five episodes, viz. the three already mentioned plus two which in Dorotheus' Chronicle are placed in the reign of Michael III and concern another Leo, to wit Leo the Mathematician, iconoclast archbishop of Thessalonica (cf. below, pp. 89 sq). These additional stories concern the golden plane tree, singing birds, roaring lions and organs that had been ostensibly made by Leo the Mathematician for the emperor Theophilus and were melted down by Michael III,[146] and the wonderful mirror (in reality a system of fire-signals from the Anatolian frontier to Constantinople) which made known all the invasions of the Empire by foreigners, and which was likewise destroyed by Michael because the news of a Saracen incursion interrupted one of his debauches.[147]

It is interesting to note that the same cycle of legends was still, with a few variations, current at Conastantinople in the seventeenth century. This we learn from the French traveller Du Mont who visited the city in 1690.[148] He was told there that the Serpent Column in the Hippodrome had been set up as a talisman against snakes by „Leon Lisaurien" (sic). This emperor's fame had even spread among the Turks. „Les Turcs", writes Du Mont, „parlent beaucoup de la force merveilleuse de cet Empereur, et même on garde encore aujourd'hui au Chateau du grand Caire, dix Boucliers qui sont traversés d'un pieu qu'on dit qu'il lança dessus; le pieu y est encore attaché et les tient tous cousus les uns avec les autres." The Greeks, a most superstitious people, had further stories about the emperor Leo. „Ils disent", continues Du Mont, „qu'il avoit fait par art magique deux Tortües, d'une grandeur et grosseur surprenante, qui tiroient un chariot dans lequel il se faisoit porter, mangeoient et beuvoient, quoi quelles ne fussent point naturelles. Ces Tortües sont encore dit-on dans le Jardin du grand Seigneur; mais elles sont immobiles depuis sa mort. Il avoit encore bâti un arbre avec

---

[145] Ju. A. Javorskij, „Византийские сказания о Льве Премудром", *Изв. Отд. Русск. Яз. и Слов. Имп. Акад. Наук*, XIV-2 (1909), 55—84.

[146] Dorotheus, 1750 ed., 342. Cf. Theoph. Cont., 173, 257; Cedrenus, II, 160, and other chroniclers.

[147] Dorotheus, 343. The import of the messages received from the Anatolian frontier was interpreted by means of two clocks. Each hour on their dial represented a different message. See *De Cerimoniis*, 492—93 (Bonn ed.); Theoph. Cont., 197—98; Pseudo-Symeon, 681, and other chronicles. The tradition concerning a huge mirror in the palace is reported by Buondelmonti in 1422 („ibiquem alto et supra mare erat speculum immensurabilis magnitudinis, circumspectum a longe nimis"), Bonn ed. (along with Nicephorus Bryennius), 180; ed. Gerola, *St. biz. e neoell.* 3 (1931), 272. Cf. Greek version of Buondelmonti, ed. Legrand (*Description des îles de l'Archipel par Christophe Buondelmonti*, Paris, 1897, 85): κάτοπτρον ἦν μεγέθους τινὸς ἐξαισίου λίαν πόρρωθεν ὁρώμενον. A magic mirror of this sort is also said to have existed at St. Sophia, Kiev: A. Veselovskij, „Мелкие заметки к былинам," ЖМНП, Nov. 1885, 188—89. On the mirror and plane tree see N. G. Polites, Βυζαντιναὶ παραδόσεις, Λαογραφία 6 (1917-18), 347—59; J. Psichari, „L'arbre chantant," *Mélanges offerts à Emile Chatelein*, Paris, 1910, 628—38; Comparetti, *op. cit.*, II, 79 sq.; etc.

[148] Cf. J. Ebersolt, *Constantinople byzantine et les voyageurs du Levant*, Paris, 1918, 167

ses branches, et ses feuilles qui sembloit naturel, et il y avoit mis cent oiseaux machinaux de diferente espece, qui chantoient tous chacun en leur maniere pour peu qu'il fit de vent, et par leurs ramages naturels, rendoient une melodie charmante, voila les contes ordinaires, dont ils vous endorment quand vous les voulés écoûter."[149]

* * *

We have mentioned on several occasions the penetration of the Leonine Oracles into Russia. If Istrin's supposition is correct, this occurred by way of a south Slavic translation.[150] The oracles that enjoyed a certain popularity in Russia were those published by Legrand and especially the inscription of Constantine's tomb which in Russian sources is often ascribed to Leo the Wise. The latter is referred to in the epilogue to Nestor Iskander's *Tale* concerning Tsargrad:

„Understand, O wretched man, that just as all the predictions of Methodius of Patara and of Leo the most-wise and the signs concerning this city have been fulfilled, so the ultimate ones will not pass by, but will be similarly fulfilled. For it is written: 'The fair-haired nation (русии же род) together with the past founders (с прежде создательными = μετὰ τῶν προκτητόρων) will vanquish all of Ismael and take the City of Seven Hills with its former possessions (с прежде законными его = μετὰ τῶν προνομίων), and will reign there."[151]

It is not certain whether this epilogue, which in some manuscripts is followed by Daniel's vision, is part of the original text or an addition of slightly later date.[152] Already in the Chronicle of 1512 the translation русии род becomes руский род,[153] which explains the popularity of this oracle, often found in Russian miscellanies.[154]

---

[149] *Nouveau voyage du Levant*, La Haye, 1694, 173—74.

[150] *Op. cit.*, II, 322. On the Serbian translations of the Oracles see above n. 33 and Šafarik, *Gesch. der südslawischen Literatur*, III, Prague, 1865, 223.

[151] Archimandrit Leonid, *Повесть о Царьграде* (Памятники древней письменности и искусства, no. 62) St. Petersburg, 1886, 40; M Branun and A. M. Schneider, *Bericht über die Eroberung Konstantinopels*, Göttingen, 1940, 33; *Хронограф редакции 1512 г.*, 460; *Никон. Лет.*, ПСРЛ, XII (1901), 97, and other Russian chronicles. Cf. I. I. Sreznevskij, „Повесть о Цареграде," *Ученые Записки II Отд. Имп. Акад. Наук* 1 (1854), Append., 132—35.

[152] See N. A. Smirnov, „Значение „Повести" Н. Искандера о взятии Турками Константинополя," *Виз. Врем.* 7 (1953), 70; M. N. Speranskij, „Повести и сказания о взятии Царьграда Турками," Акад. Наук СССР, *Труды Отд. Древнерусской Лит.* 10 (1954), 149—50. On the textual problems of the *Tale* see also B. Unbegaun, „Les relations vieux-russes de la prise de Constantinople," *Rev. des ét. slaves* 9 (1929), 13 sq.

[153] Cf. M. Laskaris, Τὸ Ἀνατολικὸν Ζήτημα, I-2, 231—33.

[154] Cf. Sreznevskij, *op. cit.*, 134—35. There exist several Russian versions of this prophecy. One foretells the liberation of Constantinople in 1653. A translation after the printed version in Dorotheus was made by the monk Arsenij Suchanov. Another translation was made in 1651 by Gabriel metropolitan of Nazareth. See S. Belokurov, *Арсений*

The role of Byzantine prophetic literature in the development of the theory of „Moscow the Third Rome," in which the Leonine Oracles play a modest part,[155] has often been told and so need not concern us here. I should like, however, to draw attention to the *Book of Oracles* (Χρησμολόγιον) by Paisius Ligarides, an eminently curious work that has never been published.

The Book of Oracles, contained on Cod. Hieros. Taphou 160,[156] was written in 1656. It was translated into Russian and appears to have had a considerable circulation. I have given elsewhere a short biography of Paisius Ligarides;[157] for the present it will be sufficient to recall that in 1656 Paisius, though holding the rank of metropolitan of Gaza, was residing in Wallachia. He went to Russia in 1662, took a prominent part in the trial of the Patriarch Nikon, and gained considerable influence over the Czar Alexis Michajlovič. He never left Russia again, and died at Kiev in 1678.

Two copies of the *Book of Oracles* were made in 1657 for Macarius, Patriarch of Antioch. In the description of the latter's travels by Paul of Aleppo we find this curious passage:

„We obtained moreover, from the aforesaid Metropolitan of Gaza, another book in Greek, the contents of which he had gathered from every country and from many authors. He had named it the Χρησμός, or Book of Oracles; and it was perfectly unique, there being no other copy of it whatever in existence. Its contents were, Prophecies from the Prophets, predictions of the Wise Men, and denunciations of the Saints, in the matters foretold them concerning the events in the East brought about by the children of Hagar, and concerning Constantinople, and their capture of that city; things of very great curiosity, as regarding the past; and likewise their prophecies of the prepared and predestined dispositions of the future. Of this book I had two copies taken by the same writer [a certain Baba Yani of Chios who had an innate propensity for wine]; but it was after encountering great difficulty in persuading the proprietor to give it us to copy; for he, that is, the Metropolitan of Gaza, was altogether unwilling, until we gained his consent by several presents, and shamed him into the liberality of allowing us to do so. Every person looking into this precious book is wrapt

Суханов, *Чтения в Имп. Общ. Ист. и Древн. Росс. при Моск. Унив.*, 1891 pt. 1, 247; 1894 pt. 2, lxii-lxxv, 221—24. This prophecy is mentioned by Juraj Križanić in his *Exposition of Historical Prophecies* (written in 1674), *Чтения*, 1891 pt. 2, 44—45. There is also a Georgian version of this same prophecy translated by Brosset in Le Beau's *Histoire du Bas-Empire*, XXI, Paris, 1836, 330—31.

[155] See M. D'jakonov, *Власть Московских государей*, St. Petersburg, 1889, 62—64; Hildegard Schaeder, *Moskau das dritte Rom*, Darmstadt, 1957, 40 sq.; D. Strémooukhoff, „Moscow the Third Rome: Sources of the Doctrine," *Speculum* 28 (1953), 89.

[156] Papadopoulos-Kerameus, Ἱεροσολυμιτικὴ βιβλιοθήκη I, 255—57; III, 327—28. This ms does not apper to be an autograph, as stated by Papadopoulos-Kerameus; but it could well be one of the two copies made by Baba Yani of Chios. Another copy (18th century), Cod. Metoch. 23 (*Ibid.*, IV, 36).

[157] *The Homilies of Photius* (Dumbarton Oaks Studies III), Cambridge, Mass., 1958, 12—15.

in wonder at its prophecies, sayings, and other contents. Afterwards, the said prelate sent us a letter from this country, informing us, that when he was in the country of the Majars, they had plundered him, and taken everything he had; and among other things, that they had robbed him of this very book . . . He sent to intreat us that we would get him a copy of it written, to supply his loss; and to God be all glory, always and for ever, in all circumstances, Amen!"[158]

The *Book of Oracles* is a bulky work which occupies 271 folios of manuscript. It consists of two parts: oracles already fulfilled, from Adam to the fall of Constantinople, and oracles whose fulfilment was yet to come. The work is dedicated to the Czar Alexis whom Paisius hails as the future liberator of the Greek people. Several considerations indicated that the end of the Turkish Empire was at hand. For example, Constantinople had been founded by a Constantine and lost by a Constantine; similarly Mehmed conquered it, and a sultan whose name began with M would lose it (Mehmed IV, 1648—87).[159] A Turkish oracle proclaimed that two hundred years after the fall of Constantinople the Ottomans would be driven out by the Christians. The two hundred years had passed, and now Alexis was showing himself victorious on all fronts: he had taken Smolensk (1654), had vanquished the Poles and the Tartars, and had terrified the Black Sea with his ships. Indeed, had not the name Alexis been chosen by Providence to indicate that the Czar would be the „Protector" of the Greek nation?

Paisius devotes considerable space to the Leonine Oracles, especially those in demotic Greek, which he attributes to the monk Leontius. Part of these oracles concern the dissolution of the Byzantine Empire, from the First Crusade to the fall of Constantinople (ff. 156r sq.), while another part foretell the ultimate liberation of Constantinople (ff. 264v sq). In each instance Paisius gives the appropriate passage of the oracles in a version differing very widely from Legrand's edition, quotes the explanation of the

---

[158] *The Travels of Macarius, Patriarch of Antioch*, trans. F. C. Belfour, II, London, 1834, 344.

[159] Cf. Robt. Walsh, *Narrative of a Journey from Constantinople to England*, 2nd ed., London, 1838, 42—43: „Constantinople was taken and lost at different times by persons who bore the same name. The Latins, under a Baldwin, obtained possession of it, and under a Baldwin they were again driven out of it. The city was rebuilt, and made the seat of the Greek empire by a Constantine, the son of Helena, and in the patriarchate of a Gregory; it was taken, and the empire of the Greeks destroyed, under a Constantine, the son of Helena, and in the patriarchate of a Gregory; the Turks obtained possession of it under a Mahomet, and they are firmly persuaded that they will lose it under a Mahomet — and that. Mahomet the present reigning sultan [Mahmud II, 1808—39]; and, to complete this chain of names, when the Greek insurrection broke out, a Constantine was the heir apparent to the Russian throne, and a Gregory was the patriarch of Constantinople. They hanged at the time one of these ominous persons, and the other has since abdicated the crown. Still they are persuaded that events will happen as they are decreed, and the fatal combination of Mahomet, Gregory and Constantine, will yet destroy their power in Europe."

anonymous scholiast, and often adds another explanation, either his own or drawn from some other source. Here is a sample of his interpretation. The obscure verse καὶ τὸ κούει πλεονάζει (Legrand, v. 24; in other versions this appears as καὶ τὸ κούη κούη κράζουν: see Legrand, p. 105) is connected with the arrival of the First Crusade before Constantinople and a clash that occurred between the Crusaders and the Greeks. So Paisius explains: „And since, among all the rest, the French especially distinguished themselves, who in their tongue say γουΐ γουΐ for 'yes', Leontius wrote κούΐ κούΐ κράζει, or, as others have it, καὶ τὸ κούΐ πλεονάζει" (f. 157r).

Paisius is not always so silly, and at times makes a serious effort to find the correct interpretation. For the lines:

Τὸ ψωμὶ θορῶ καὶ κόπτουν
ὅλον εἰς ὀκτὼ κομμάτια
οἱ δυνάσται πλεονέκται
καὶ βιάζουνται ἀλλήλους, etc.

(cf. Legrand, vv. 107 sq.), two explanations are given: this refers either to the division of Constantinople between the Venetians, Genoese, Pisans, French and other westerners after the capture of the city, or to the division of the Turkish Empire into eight units in the reign of Beyazid II (to wit, between the sultan, his six sons and his brother Djem). Paisius says that he would have accepted the second explanation, but for the next lines of the oracle (ἦλθε βάτος ἀπὸ πέρα, etc.: cf. Legrand, vv. 120 sq.) which clearly refer to John Ducas Vatatzes, so that the first explanation is to be preferred.

The same set of oracles hints at the reconquest of Constantinople by Michael Palaeologus, his attempt to unite the Churches, the Council of Florence, the defeat of Beyazid I by Tamerlane and the fall of Constantinople. There follows the interpretation of the inscription on Constantine's tomb by Gennadius Scholarius which closes the section on oracles already fulfilled.

The cycle of Leonine oracles is also used to describe the eventual liberation of Constantinople and the advent of King John. Paisius quotes here the *Paraphrasis* (f. 263r: περὶ τοῦ θρυλλουμένου πτωχοῦ καὶ ἐκλεκτοῦ βασιλέως, etc. = PG 107, 1141) and a conflation of Oracles XIII and XIV (f. 264r: κήρυξ τε φανεὶς τρὶς ἀνακράξει μέγα, etc. = PG 107, 1137B; cf. Legrand, p. 46). The liberation of Constantinople will result from an alliance between the Christian powers, as indicated by „Leontius" (τὸ ἀκούσασιν ὁ λέων, etc. = Legrand, vv. 261 sq). The lion of this prophecy is Spain; the pard is Poland; the basilisk is Muscovy; the fox is Venice; the wolf is France. The same is indicated by this oracle of Leo the Wise which was found on the Column of Constantine (f. 265r):

τὰ πλήθη καὶ τὰ φῦλα
συνοδεῖ τῶν ἑσπερίων
καὶ ξηρᾶς διὰ θαλάσσης
ἕνα [τὸν] πόλεμον συνάψουν
καὶ τὸν Ἰσμαὴλ τροπώσουν.

The advent of King John is described by the „archon Leontius" (f. 266v: τὸ πρωῒ ὁ κληρονόμος / ἔρχεται, βαστᾷ σκαμνίον, etc.; cf. Lengrad, p. 43), by Leo the Wise (f. 267r: κήρυξ βοήσει τρὶς ἀναφωνήσας μέγα: cf. above; and περιφράσσεται τ' ἀμπέλι, etc. = Legrand, p. 44), by a distich which Paisius found in an old book (ὅταν ὁ τλήμων, ὁ πένης, etc. = Legrand, p. 46) and by the verses which the „angel-bearer" (ἀγγελοφόρος) is going to address to Constantinople (f. 268r: χάρηθι (sic) παντάλαινα Βαβυλὼν νέα = Legrand, p. 43). The resurrection of Constantinople is also foretold in the poem by Leo the Wise inscribed under a capital of the golden gate of St. Sophia (sic) which was thrown down by an earthquake and was read after the Turkish conquest (f. 268v: inc. Βύζαντος αὐλή, ἑστία Κωνσταντίνου = Lambecius, Comment. de bibl. Caes. Vindob., VI, 1780, 93 sq).

After John's reign follows the usual story about the emperor who lays down his crown in Jerusalem, his four sons and the Wicked Queen. Finally, the precursor of the Antichrist appears in the guise of a wolf (f. 269v: ἔρχεται ἀπέκει ὁ λύκος, etc. = Legrand, p. 46) preceding the bear who is the Antichrist (ἔρχεται ἀπέκει ἡ ἄρκτος, etc. = Legrand, p. 47). The latter's name is Βενέδικτος according to the Cabbalists, or Λατεῖνος according to Hippolytus,[160] both of which add up to 666 (f. 270r).

* * *

In western Europe the Oracles of Leo the Wise fell into almost complete oblivion by the eighteenth century, while in the East they continued to nourish the hopes of liberation from the Turkish yoke. Down to our own days, prophetic literature promising the reconstitution of the Byzantine Empire with the help of Russia (or occasionally of Germany) has been assiduously read by the Greek public, especially when political events seemed to foreshadow the attainment of the national goal, as in the time of Peter the Great, Catherine II and during the Greek Revolution[161]. The most popular of these prophetic texts was known as *Agathangelos*, and purported to have been written at Messina in 1279, published at Milan in 1555, and translated from the Italian into Greek by the archimandrite Theocletus Polyeides in 1751. In actual fact, Polyeides was the author or rather the fabricator of this text. In 1767 one Nikolaos Zertzoules, head of the Academy of Jassy and translator of Newton into Greek, wrote a *Brief Interpretation of the Oracles of Leo the Wise concerning the Resurrection of Constantinople.*[162] In fact, he missed by a year the „devastation of Constantinople" which, according to the famous monk Dionysius of Fourna, was to occur in 1766, to be followed by the innundation of England in 1767, and the Second Coming in 1773.[163]

---

[160] *De Antichristo*, 50.

[161] See discussion of this subject by Eugenios Kourilas, Θεόκλητος ὁ Πολυείδης, Θρακικά 5 (1934), 69—162; Beês, *op. cit.*, 244κη'—244λς'.

[162] Sathas, Νεοελληνικὴ φιλολογία, 500; Beês, *op. cit.*, 244λβ'; Kourilas, *op. cit.*, 106.

[163] D. Sarros, Παλαιογραφικὸς ἔρανος, Ὁ ἐν Κων/πόλει ῾Ελληνικὸς Φιλολογικὸς Σύλλογος 33 (1914), 83.

Among this welter of false predictions voices were sometimes raised to protest against the fatalistic awaiting of the millennium. As early as 1618 Matthew of Myra wrote:

ἐλπίζομεν καὶ εἰς τὰ ξανθὰ γένη νὰ μᾶς γλυτώσουν,
νἀλθοῦν ἀπὸ τὸν Μόσχοβον, νὰ μᾶς ἐλευθερώσουν.
Ἐλπίζομεν εἰς τοὺς χρησμούς, 'ς ταῖς ψευδοπροφητείαις,
καὶ τὸν καιρόν μας χάνομεν 'ς ταῖς ματαιολογίαις.[164]

Or witness the disappointment of Athanasius Hypselantes after the treaty of Küçük Kaynarci (1774):

„If then, in the time appointed by the oracles, after so many and so great victories of the Muscovites over the Ottomans, in such an opportune moment, we, the Romaioi, have not been liberated, it is indeed difficult that the resurrection of the Romaic Empire should occur in the future, seeing that no oracle of any other prophet remains concerning this; and not only difficult, but almost impossible, on account of the persistence of our evil ways, our lack of mercy, our vengefulness towards one another, and our customary invectiveness."[165]

The same sentiments are echoed by the prolific Constantine Daponte who notes that according to the oracles the Byzantine Empire was to arise again 320 years after its fall (1773); but since this did not occur, „neither the Romaioi nor the Russians are ever going to reign in Constantinople till the end of the world."[166]

Leo's predictions, however, were not forgotten. Indeed, among the earliest books printed at Athens after Greece became an independent state, was a collection of oracles, including those of Leo, edited by Petros Stefanitzes, a veteran of Missolonghi and friend of Lord Byron.[167]

* * *

In the foregoing pages I have attempted to bring together whatever material is available to me at present concerning Leo the Wise as a legendary figure. It need hardly be said that this material is far from being exhaustive and leaves many problems in the dark. There is one question, however, that we should try to answer: why did Leo VI become a prophet, an astrologer and a magician? It may be argued that Leo's elevation to prophetic status is not an isolated case, but part of a more general phenomenon. Apocryphal literature often hides under the authoritative names not only of

---

[164] Legrand, *Bibl. grecque vulgaire*, II, Paris, 1881, 314.

[165] Ἀθανασίου Κομνηνοῦ Ὑψηλάντου, Τὰ μετὰ τὴν Ἅλωσιν, Constantinople, 1870, 534.

[166] Ἱστορικὸς κατάλογος (1784) in Sathas, Μεσαιωνικὴ βιβλιοθήκη, III, Venice, 1872, 119—20.

[167] Συλλογὴ διαφόρων προρρήσεων... ἐκδ. παρὰ τοῦ ἰατροῦ Π. Δ. Στεφανίτζη Λευκαδίου, Athens, 1838. Described by Beês, *op. cit.*, 217—18. I have not had access to this edition.

recognized prophets and ancient sages, but also of emperors and patriarchs. We have already mentioned the supposed inscription on Constantine's tomb which was allegedly expounded by the Patriarch Gennadius Scholarius. Prophecies were also ascribed to the Patriarch Tarasius, to Constantine the Great and to „Chosroes king of the Persians." The earliest editions of the Leonine Oracles bear on their titlepage the name of Septimius Severus.[168] Books of divination, in particular a *Brontologion*, were attributed for no obvious reason to the Emperor Heraclius.[169] In the case of Leo VI, the surname *Sophos* and his reputation for learning may have been sufficient ground for imputing prophecies to him; I believe, however, that this was aided, if not caused, by the confusion of two homonyms, the Emperor Leo and the philosopher or Mathematician Leo, iconoclast archbishop of Thessalonica. In fact, this confusion has lasted down to our own day, being further complicated by the intrusion of a third homonym, Leo Choerosphactes.[170]

Leo the Mathematician was one of the most prominent figures in the intellectual revival under the Emperor Theophilus. An attempt has recently been made to present him as a practical scientist indifferent to religious controversies,[171] but this appears to be a somewhat anachronistic characterization. I see no reason to doubt that Leo was a student of astrology, not only as a science but also as a method of divination. The chronicles mention several prophecies made by Leo and tell how he applied the principle of astral sympathy to produce a plentiful harvest at Thessalonica.[172] Leo's addiction to astrology is further attested by an epigram under his name in the Palatine Anthology.[173] We have already mentioned the accusation of paganism made against Leo by his pupil Constantine. In spite of his iconoclastic leanings, Leo the Mathematician became a legendary sage and was credited, as we have said, with the construction of the wonderful clocks regulating the fire-telegraph system, as well as of the golden plane tree and other mechanical contrivances in the palace. Note that these marvels are ascribed to Leo only in popular and relatively late chronicles.[174] The Emperor Manuel Comnenus (if the document in question is genuine) quoted the story of Leo's averting famine at Thessalonica as an instance of the useful application of astrology, but he was reprimanded by Michael Glycas for using the example of an impious iconoclast.[175]

---

[168] This attribution may be due to Suidas, s. v. Ξηρόλοφος.

[169] See M. A. Andreeva, „ Политический и общественный элемент византийско-славянских гадательных книг", BSL 3 (1931), 435 sq.

[170] On the confusion between the literary works of the three Leos, see G. Kolias, *Léon Choerosphactès*, 66—67.

[171] E. E. Lipšic, „Византийский ученый Лев Математик", Виз. Врем. 2 (1949), 106—49.

[172] Theoph. Cont., 189, 191, 197, 232; Pseudo-Symeon, 677; Cont. of Georg. Monachus, 829 (Bonn ed.); Cedrenus, II, 170, 173; Genesius, 104—05; Glycas, 541.

[173] IX, 201 = PG 107, 664.

[174] Pseudo-Symeon, 681; Manasses, 205; Glycas, 543. In the other sources the author of these marvels is not named.

[175] *Corpus codd. astrol. greac.*, V-1 (1904), 116, 136—37.

Greek astrological and other apocryphal manuscripts contain a great number of opuscules under the name of Leo who is sometimes styled „the wise," at other times „the philosopher" or „the emperor." One that is frequently found is entitled περὶ βασιλείας [or βασιλέων] καὶ ἀρχόντων,[176] and may be a genuine work by Leo the Mathematician. Besides this, we find *Scholia on the Observation of the Ascendant* (σχόλια εἰς τὴν ὡριμαίαν),[177] a *Seleno-dromion*,[178] a treatise on divination with the Gospels and Psalter sometimes attributed to the prophet Chaleth,[179] a work on sickness,[180] a *Seismologion* sometimes ascribed to Hermes Trismegistus,[181] an opuscule *On the Solar Eclipse in the Regal Triangle*,[182] a short piece on the letters of the alphabet,[183] an alphabetical dream-book,[184] a *Physiognomicon*,[185] a text on astragalomancy,[186] an *Orneosophicon*,[187] a collection of questions and answers on biblical subjects that is even found in a Turkish version,[188] and perhaps others as well.

In scanning the titles of these opuscules it becomes apparent that the Names of Leo the Philosopher, Leo the Wise and Leo the Emperor are interchangeable, and that the last appears only in relatively late manuscripts (Marc. gr. 335, saec. XV; Berol. 314, saec. XVII; Athen. 1275 and 1350, saec. XIX; Petrop. Musaei Palaeogr., saec. XVII). Thus we have here a clear illustration of how Leo the philosopher, i. e. probably the archbishop, was transformed into the emperor.

---

[176] *Ibid.*, II (1900), 22, 52; IV (1903), 14, 92—93; V-4 (1940), 86—87; VII (1908), 36; VIII-1 (1929), 41—42, 63, 81.

[177] *Ibid.*, I (1898), 66.

[178] *Ibid.*, III (1901), 4; cf. IV (1903), 40.

[179] *Ibid.*, IV (1903), 74; VII (1908), 33; VIII-3 (1912), 4; VIII-4 (1921), 20; IX-2 (1953), 49; XI-1 (1932), 111. Published by M. Speranskij, „Leon's des Weisen Weissagungen nach dem Evangelium und Psalter," *Archiv f. slavische Philologie* 25 (1903), 239—49; cf. *id.*, Из истории отреченных книг. I. Гадания по Псалтири (Памятники древней письменности и искусства, 129), 1899, 152.

[180] *Corp. codd. astrol. graec.*, V-4 (1940), 8; IX-2 (1953), 108; XII (1936), 6.

[181] *Ibid.*, VII (1908), 65, 167 sq.; IX-2 (1953), 80; X (1924), 24, 132—35.

[182] *Ibid.*, VII (1908), 150—51. Also published by F. C. Hertlein in *Hermes* 8 (1874), 173—76.

[183] *Corp. codd. astrol. graec.*, XII (1936), 6.

[184] *Ibid.*, 24.

[185] *Ibid.*

[186] *Ibid.*, 26—27, 146 sq.

[187] Revilla, *Catálogo de los códices griegos de la Bibl. de el Escorial*, I, Madrid, 1936, 171. This work is actually by Demetrius Pepagomenus, ed. R. Hercher, *Cl. Aeliani de animalium natura*, II, Leipzig, 1866, 335 sq.

[188] N. F. Krasnosel'cev „Addenda к изданию A. Васильева 'Anecdota graeco-byzantina'," *Леш. Исш.-Фил. Общ. при Имп. Новоросс. Унив., Визанш. Ошд.* 4 (1899), 123 sq. The editor (*ibid.*, 105—06) suggests that this opuscule is the work of Leo the Mathematician.

Leo the Mathematician possessed all the characteristics that we have been studying in this paper: he was a prophet, he was credited as early as the twelfth century with the construction of mechanical marvels, and he was the author or supposed author of astrological works, one of which concerned the reigns of emperors. It does not seem, therefore, too far-fetched to suggest that the legendary figure of Leo the Wise arose through a confusion with his less illustrious homonym, a confusion that could easily have resulted † from a careless reading of popular chronicles.

Dumbarton Oaks
Harvard University.

Fig. 2. Oracle II, MS Laud. Gr. 27, f. 75ᵛ
Photo Bodleian Library

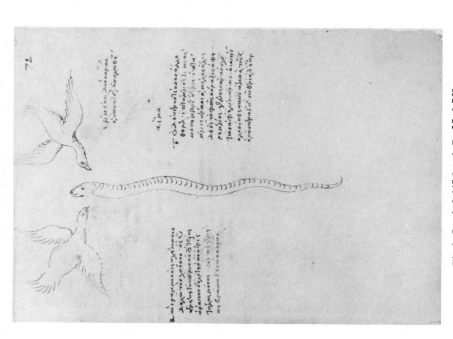

Fig. 1. Oracle I, MS Laud. Gr. 27, f. 75ʳ
Photo Bodleian Library

Fig.4. Oracle IV (V), MS Laud. Gr. 27, f. 77ʳ
Photo Bodleian Library

Fig.3. Oracle III, MS Laud. Gr. 27, f. 76ʳ
Photo Bodleian Library

Fig. 6. Oracle VI, MS Laud. Gr. 27, f. 77v
Photo Bodleian Library

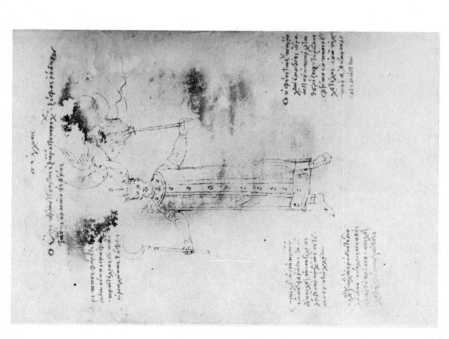

Fig. 5. Oracle V (IV), MS Laud. Gr. 27, f. 76v
Photo Bodleian Library

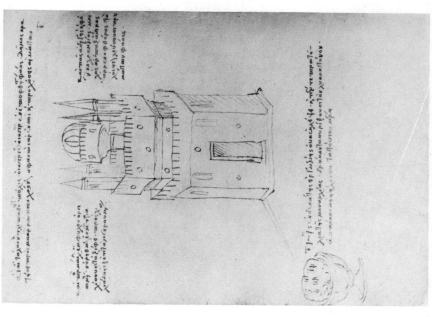

Fig. 8. Oracle VIII, MS Laud. Gr. 27, f. 78v
Photo Bodleian Library

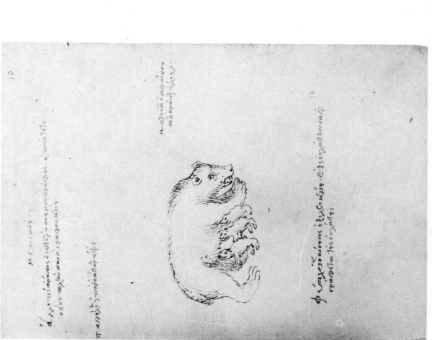

Fig. 7. Oracle VII, MS Laud. Gr. 27, f. 78r
Photo Bodleian Library

Fig. 10. Oracle X, MS Laud. Gr. 27, f. 79v
Photo Bodleian Library

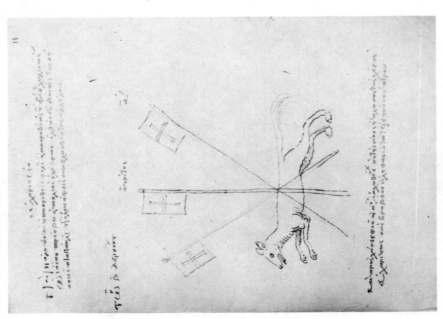

Fig. 9. Oracle IX, MS Laud. Gr. 27, f. 79r
Photo Bodleian Library

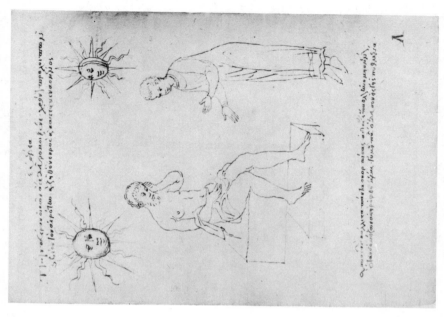

Fig. 12. Oracle XII, MS Laud. Gr. 27, f. 80v
Photo Bodleian Library

Fig. 11. Oracle XI, MS Laud. Gr. 27, f. 80r
Photo Bodleian Library

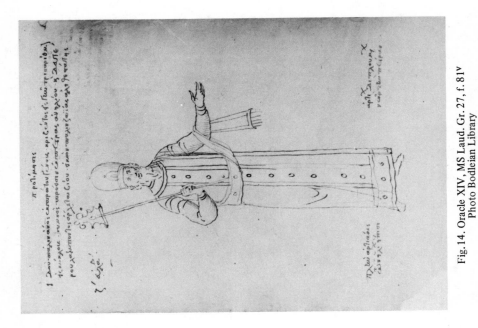

Fig. 14. Oracle XIV, MS Laud. Gr. 27, f. 81v
Photo Bodleian Library

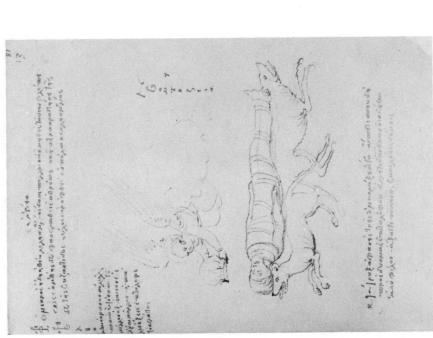

Fig. 13. Oracle XIII, MS Laud. Gr. 27, f. 81r
Photo Bodleian Library

Fig. 16. Oracle XVI, MS Laud. Gr. 27, f. 82ᵛ
Photo Bodleian Library

Fig. 15. Oracle XV, MS Laud. Gr. 27, f. 82ʳ
Photo Bodleian Library

XVII

CHYPRE
CARREFOUR DU MONDE BYZANTIN

It is a commonplace to say that Cyprus, by virtue of its geographical position, has always been a crossroads, a melting pot, a meeting place of east and west, to quote some of the clichés that invariably appear in popular books and tourist brochures. Like all commonplaces, this one is true only in part or, to put it in another way, it is truer of some periods than of others. For the importance of Cyprus — and I take it that the term "carrefour" denotes in our discussion not simply a crossroads, but an important crossroads — always depended on outside factors. When the island lay on a vital line of communication, whether commercial or military, it automatically acquired great significance; but there were long periods, as the medieval history of Cyprus clearly shows, when this was not the case.

We should begin, therefore, by inquiring which were the major routes that passed through Cyprus. At once we may make an obvious observation, namely that contacts between the island and the nearest mainland coast, that of southern Asia Minor, were not of great significance for the simple reason that the mountainous Cilician coast was itself a somewhat peripheral area. Had it been otherwise, the port of Kyrenia would have emerged as an important centre, but it did not do so until it was discovered by British tourists. It is equally clear that the main contacts of the island were with the Syrian coast and, to a lesser extent, with Egypt. An examination of the available evidence for the Early Byzantine period (which I shall not detail here) shows that relations with Syria and Palestine were extremely close, that Cypriot sailors went regularly to Alexandria, and that there was also commercial intercourse with Italy. Contacts with Constantinople appear to have been rarer and mostly confined to administrative business. It is also abundantly clear that there were many Syrians and other Orientals living on the island as evidenced, *inter alia*, by the prevalence there of the

Monophysite heresy[1]. It is more difficult to document for this period the role of Cyprus in international trade, but it appears *a priori* likely that it was used as a regular stopping place on the major route extending from Syria to Italy and farther west.

This situation was radically altered by the advent of the Muslims. For several decades in the 7th century Cyprus acquired a new military significance, first as a base of Byzantine operations for the relief of Egypt, then, after the fall of Alexandria, as the object of Arab expansion in the direction of Constantinople, the stages being Cyprus, Rhodes Cos, Chios and Cyzicus[2]. Obscure as these events are, it is reasonably clear that Cyprus was under Muslim domination far about thirty years. The treaty of 688, whereby the tax revenues of Cyprus as well as those of Armenia and Georgia were divided in equal parts between the two powers, represented a major concession by the Arabs. But whereas the Caucasus continued to be an area of conflict, in Cyprus the condominium was seldom disturbed and actually persisted for three centuries. Surprisingly, many historians have failed to grasp the significance of this state of affairs and have claimed that Cyprus remained a bone of contention between Byzantines and Arabs, that now one side, now the other had the upper hand. Yet the evidence, meagre as it is, indicates that during the period 688 - 965 neither the Byzantines nor the Arabs found it worth their while to make a determined effort so as to occupy and hold the island. Granted that for the Arabs, after they had settled down to their routine of overland raids into Asia Minor, possession of Cyprus was no longer vital, the reverse was surely the case for Byzantium: for if they managed to re-occupy the island, they would have been admirably placed both to harass the Emirate of Tarsus from the rear and to make descents on the Syrian coast. And yet, except for a brief and barely noticed attempt in the reign of Basil I, except for the ill-fated expedition of Himerios in 910 (which did not involve a systematic occupation of Cyprus), Byzantium did no such thing. I am unable to give a satisfactory explanation of this failure or this omission. Vasiliev and his Belgian editors have suggested that the local population was not eager to be absorbed into the Empire[3], which, if true, may have been a

1. Much of the relevant evidence has been assembled by M. Sacopoulo, *La Théotokos à la mandorle de Lythrankomi*, Paris, 1975, 79 ff.

2. This has been well brought out by A. Papageorgiou, Les premières incursions arabes à Chypre et leurs conséquences, 'Αφιέρωμα εἰς Κ. Σπυριδάκιν, Nicosia, 1964, 152 ff.

3. *Byzance et les Arabes*, II/1, *La dynastie macédonienne*, Brussels, 1968, 63 - 64. Nicholas

contributing factor[4]. But whatever was the main cause, the conclusion can hardly be avoided that during the period in question Cyprus was not considered to be a place of much importance.

Professor Lemerle has already drawn attention to the fact that the re-integration of Cyprus into the Empire (965) is treated very casually in our sources, which suggests that this operation did not require any great effort and did not attract much attention[5]. What is also significant is that we hear practically nothing of Cyprus, now under undisputed Byzantine rule, until the end of the 11th century. It is surely no coincidence that the same period has left hardly any monuments on the island. Only with the revolt of Rhapsomates in 1092 does Cyprus emerge into the light of history. When, a few years later, the Latin Kingdom of Jerusalem was established, the island immediately assumed a position of primary importance which it retained until its conquest by Richard Lion Heart. It is with the period 1092 - 1191 that I should like to concern myself with particular regard to internal conditions and contacts with other areas.

In the 8th/9th centuries the population of Cyprus may be estimated with reasonable accuracy at about 60,000 - 75,000[6], and I see no reason

Mystikos, in writing to the Caliph al-Muqtadir (*Letters,* ed. Jenkins - Westerink, 1. 133) says that the Cypriots did not regard the Arabs as enemies, but this is a diplomatic statement that cannot be used as evidence of their real attitude.

4. I cannot follow A.I. Dikigoropoulos, The Political Status of Cyprus, A. D. 648 - 965, *Report of the Department of Antiquities, Cyprus, 1940 - 48*, Nicosia, 1958, 107 ff., who believes that the stumbling block to an *enosis* with the Empire was iconoclasm.

5. Séance de clôture de la section médiévale, Πρακτικὰ τοῦ Πρώτου Διεθνοῦς Κυπρολογικοῦ Συνεδρίου, II, Nicosia, 1972, 153 - 154. It would be interesting in this connection to consider what role the occupation of Cyprus played in the planning of the Cilician and Syrian campaigns of Nikephoros Phokas. My impression is that this role was very slight and that no tactical support was provided from Cyprus.

6. This figure is based on the amount of the tax collected by the Arabs (i.e. half of the total tax), viz. either 7,000 or 7,200 dinars. It is considered "ridiculously small" by G. Hill, *History of Cyprus*, I, Cambridge, 1940, 257, yet there is every reason to accept it since we are told that it was increased by 1,000 dinars by the Caliph 'Abd al-Malik and lowered again to the original amount by al-Mansûr (754 - 775) who refused to enrich himself by oppressing the Cypriots: Balâdhuri, trans. P. K. Hitti, *The Origins of the Islamic State*, I, New York, 1916, 238. The Moslem practice at the time was to impose a poll-tax of 1 dinar on every adult male (*ibid.,* 173, 190 - 191). If the proportion of adult males was one quarter to one fifth of the total population, our estimates of the latter would be in the magnitude 57,600 - 72,000. This is not at all an unreasonable figure: in the second half of the 18th century the population of the island was about 85,000. See Sir R. Storrs and B. J. O'Brien, *The Handbook of*

to believe that it had changed appreciably by the 11th. That this population was largely Greek-speaking I have no doubt, although I find
it hard to imagine that three hundred years of cohabitation with the
Arabs had left no permanent trace[7]. How cautious we ought to be on
this score may be illustrated by the following example. In 1090 a certain
abbot George founded the monastery (which still exists today) of St.
John Chrysostom at Koutsovendi, not far from Nicosia, and a few years
later it was added to by the governor of the island Eumathios Philokales[8]. There is no obvious reason for supposing that either George
or Philokales was anything but a Greek. What is more, St. Neophytos
the Enkleist spent there the early part of his monastic career, from 1152
until 1158[9]. Neophytos was, by Byzantine standards, an unusually
chatty author, and he does provide some information concerning his
residence at St. Chrysostomos. Again, not a hint that he was living in
a non-Greek or partly non-Greek community. Yet, we have clear evidence that at the very same time and, indeed, very soon after its foundation this monastery was subject to the Maronite patriarch of Lebanon,
who appointed the abbot, and that some at least of the monks were
reading the Scriptures in Arabic[10]. As to the military personnel that
was brought to Cyprus during the last century of Byzantine rule, a
good proportion of it was of Armenian stock[11]. There was also a contingent of the so-called Tourkopouloi.

Cyprus, London, (1930), 42, and, more fully, Th. Papadopoullos, *Social and Historical Data on Population* (*1570 - 1881*), Nicosia, 1965, 44 ff.

7. Oriental names were not unknown in medieval Cyprus. Among other examples we may quote that of cod. S. Sabae 23 which was bought (in the 13th century?) for a church at Kition by one John τοῦ παπᾶ Βραχίμη and his wife Gouzire: J. Darrouzès, Autres manuscrits originaires de Chypre, *REB*, 15 (1957), 146. Cf. also *infra*, note 14. According to Machairas, ed. Dawkins, § 158, the languages spoken in Cyprus before the Latin conquest were Greek and Syrian (i.e. Arabic).

8. C. Mango and E.J.W. Hawkins, *DOP*, 18 (1964), 334 ff.

9. See C. Mango and E.J.W. Hawkins, The Hermitage of St. Neophytos, *DOP*, 20 (1966), 123.

10. This is attested by marginal notes dated 1120/21, 1140/41, 1153 and 1238/9 contained in cod. Vat. Syr. 118 and in the famous Rabula Gospels (Laurent. Plut. I. 56). The first, third and fourth are translated by J. Leroy, *Les manuscrits syriaques à peintures*, Paris, 1964, 235, 146 notes 1 and 2; for the second see Assemani, *Bibl. apost. Vatic. codd. mss. catal.*, 1/3, Rome, 1759, 114 - 115, and Leroy's note, *op. cit.*, 235 note 2. It is difficult to imagine that the monastery of St. John of Kusbandù in the island of Cyprus was different from that of Koutsovendi. Cf. also C.P. Kyrris, Military Co-lonies in Cyprus in the Byzantine Period, *BSl*, 31 (1970), 177 - 178.

11. See Kyrris, *op. cit.*, 159 ff. The defenders of Cyprus in 1191 were Greeks and

It would appear from what little data we have that the ruling class of Cyprus was not of native origin. This certainly applies to the office of governor *(dux)* which, after the revolt of Rhapsomates, was filled by persons of the highest standing appointed directly from Constantinople. Such were Eumathios Philokales (whom we have mentioned), Constantine Katakalon, Leo Nikerites, Constantine Kamytzes, Alexios Doukas, Andronikos Synadenos, Elpidios Vrachamios[12]. Among them only Leo Nikerites, a professional soldier and administrator, may not have belonged to a prominent family[13]. Concerning the lower echelons of the administration we have too little information to draw any conclusions[14]. What is significant, however, is that the top posts in the Church were also occupied by aristocratic appointees from the capital. Such was the archbishop Nicholas Mouzalon (ca. 1110) to whom we owe the most detailed picture of Cyprus at the time[15]. Two examples of provincial prelates are even more instructive. About 1180 the bishop of Tamasos (which was certainly no great centre) was Niketas Hagiostephanites[16],

Armenians according to Benedict of Peterborough: C.D. Cobham, *Excerpta Cypria*, Cambridge, 1908, 7, 9. Cf. also W. von Oldenburg (1211), *ibid.*, 13.

12. Partial list in D.A. Zakythinos, Περὶ τῆς διοικητικῆς διαιρέσεως. . . ἐν τῷ βυζαντινῷ, κράτει, *EEBΣ*, 17 (1941), 268 - 270. On Nikerites see Lampros, *N. Ἑλλ.*, 5 (1908), 485 and N. Banescu, *Les duchés byzantins de Paristrion (Paradounavon) et de Bulgarie*, Bucharest, 1946, 93 - 95. On Synadenos see Lampros, *op. cit.*, 8 (1911), 147, and H. Ahrweiler, *Byzance et la mer*, Paris, 1966, 220. On Alexios Doukas (Bryennios), probably the grandson of Anna Comnena, see D. I. Polemis, *The Doukai*, London, 1968, No. 80. It is impossible at present to arrange the above governors in strict chronological order.

13. He is the only person of that name listed by A. P. Každan, *Social'nyj sostav gospodstvujuščego klassa Vizantii XI - XII vv.*, Moscow, 1974, 219.

14. Among officials holding the rank of *magistros* we may mention Epiphanios Paschalis (a westerner?) who, some time before 1091, set up the monastery of the Virgin τῆς Ἀλύπου: Darrouzès, Autres manuscrits, 141; and Nikephoros Ischyrios who in 1106 founded the monastery of Asinou and who, most definitely, should not be identified with Nikephoros Katakalon. It may be noted that Ischyrios had a daughter called Gephyra (if the extant 14th century copy of the inscription may be trusted). Modern scholars have classicized this to Zephyra (e.g. M. Sacopoulo, *Asinou en 1106,* Brussels, 1966, 10 - 11), but it seems more likely to me that Gephyra conceals a Semitic name, perhaps Ghufaira, as suggested to me by Dr. Albert Hourani. Incidentally, the inscription in question refers to Gephyra's death on 17 December 1106, not in 1099 as scholars have interpreted it.

15. See S.I. Doanidou, Ἡ παραίτησις Νικολάου τοῦ Μουζάλωνος ἐκ τῆς ἀρχιεπισκοπῆς Κύπρου, Ἑλληνικά, 7 (1934), 109 ff. Cf. F. Dölger, *BZ*, 35 (1935), 8 ff.; Hill, *History of Cyprus*, I, 303 - 304.

16. Typikon of Machairas monastery in Κυπριακὰ τυπικά, ed. I.P. Tsiknopoullos, Nicosia, 1969, p. 15, § 16.

i.e. a member of a family which at that time had attained to the rank
of *sebastos*[17]. The bishop of Paphos from 1166 onwards was Basil Kinnamos whose family name will be familiar to all readers of *Digenes Akrites*[18].

The impression that Cyprus was governed on a colonial basis is confirmed by several converging indications. The testimony of the artistic
monuments is, I believe, particularly instructive. During the reign of
Alexios I and, more particularly, after the revolt of Rhapsomates, we
find that a high style, which had no local antecedents, was suddenly
brought to Cyprus. In architecture it is embodied in the so-called "église
à trompes d'angle", which, in the 11th century, was the most "progressive"
type of church, surely originating in Constantinople, but today known
to us largely from examples in Greece[19]. In painting the new style first
confronts us in the chapel of the Holy Trinity built by Eumathios Philokales in the Chrysostomos monastery, and is taken up, almost immediately, in the monastery of Asinou (1106)[20]. Throughout the 12th
century painting in Cyprus follows the latest fashions of Constantinople[21],
culminating in the decoration of Lagoudera (1192), surely the work
of a metropolitan artist who was trapped by the Latin conquest; after
which this high art disappears as suddenly as it had come. The majority
of the relevant monuments are monastic, i.e. they were put up by
prominent persons, no doubt in accordance with the contemporary
institution of the *charistikê*. Orthodox architecture and painting continued
in Cyprus after the conquest and the monasteries remained sufficiently
prosperous to be able to afford expensive commissions; yet, as far as
we can tell[22], the sophisticated Comnenian style, i.e. the style of the
Byzantine ruling class, was quickly abandoned[23], which is equivalent

17. Každan, *op. cit.*, 114, 151.

18. See Mango and Hawkins, The Hermitage of St. Neophytos, 124, 205.

19. See my remarks in *DOP*, 27 (1973), 130 - 32, and, more fully, in Les monuments
de l'architecture du XIe siècle et leur signification historique et sociale, *TM*, 6 (1976),
358 ff.

20. By a pupil of the Chrysostomos Master according to D. Winfield, Hagios Chrysostomos, Trikomo, Asinou, Πρακτικὰ τοῦ Πρώτου Διεθνοῦς Κυπρολογικοῦ Συνεδρίου,
II, 1972, 285 ff.

21. See A.H.S. Megaw, Byzantine Architecture and Decoration in Cyprus, *DOP*,
28 (1974), 85 ff.

22. Unfortunately, only one decoration, that of Moutoullas (1280), is securely
dated in the 13th century. For further attributions see A. Papageorgiou, Ἰδιάζουσαι
βυζαντιναὶ τοιχογραφίαι τοῦ 13ου αἰῶνος ἐν Κύπρῳ, Πρακτικὰ τοῦ Πρώτου Διεθνοῦς
Κυπρολογικοῦ Συνεδρίου, II, 201 ff.

23. The contrast between pre- and post-conquest painting is most dramatically

to saying that it was an importation that did not grow roots in local soil.

Another pertinent indication is provided by the mass flight of the ruling class after the Latin occupation. Of this we are informed by St. Neophytos who, in ca. 1196, wrote a short account of the "calamities" of Cyprus for the benefit of a prominent émigré who had fled to Constantinople "together with all his people" and had been honoured by the emperor with the title of sebastos[24]. His "people" were presumably his retainers, perhaps a contingent of troops that owed allegiance to him. In the same opuscule Neophytos tells us that the rich men "with great haste sailed away in secret to foreign lands and to the Queen of Cities"[25]. To the list of the fugitives we may with some confidence add the bishop of Paphos, Basil Kinnamos. We know that he was still in office in 1190[26]. Two years later the emperor Isaac II protested to the Genoese authorities on the grounds that a Lombard ship, bound for Constantinople, had been attacked in the neighbourhood of Rhodes by Genoese and Pisan pirates. Among the passengers was the bishop of Paphos whom the pirates held prisoner[27]. Of course, not all members of the ruling class were able to leave, and some stayed behind after doing homage to the conqueror. In the list of noble Cypriot families of the 16th century we may still discern a few names going back to the Comnenian aristocracy[28].

How did the Byzantine administrators look upon the Cypriot people? It is interesting to note that Skylitzes refers to them as τὸ ἔθνος τῶν Κυπρίων[29], and we know that the term ethnos was normally applied to foreigners and barbarians, not to "one of us". According to Muzalon, the ordinary people were subjected to the most appalling fiscal extortion. This statement may be qualified to make allowance for rhetorical

seen in the Enkleistra of Neophytos. Cf. Mango and Hawkins, The Hermitage of St. Neophytos, 198 ff.

24. Cobham, Excerpta Cypria, 10.

25. Ibid., 11.

26. See V. Laurent in REB, 7 (1949), 54 f. Basil's successor, Bakchos, is first attested in 1194.

27. Miklosich and Müller, Acta, III, 38; Dölger, Regesten, No. 1612 (Nov. 1192).

28. E. de Lusignan, Description de toute l'isle de Cypre, Paris, 1580, 82ᵛ - 83ᵛ, e.g. Bisasces ou Philocaliens (Philokales), Cappadoce (Kappadokes), Contestephe (Kontostephanos). Note that the Laskaris and Palaiologos families were late arrivals in Cyprus: ibid., 82ʳ. A branch of the Kinnamos family may also have stayed on: see J. Darrouzès in REB, 8 (1950), 184, No. 107 (Paris. gr. 1152).

29. Ed. Thurn, 429 = Cedrenus, Bonn ed., II, 549 - 550.

exaggeration, but it cannot be brushed aside since it is confirmed from other quarters. Already in the 9th century the Byzantine representative in Cyprus had to be reprimanded by the patriarch Photios for oppressing the people[30]. The revolt of Theophilos Erotikos in 1042/3 is expressly associated with high taxation[31]. But we can go even further: at the time of the condominium the total tax yield of Cyprus was a little less than 15,000 gold pieces; in 1191 the island is said to have paid to the emperor 700 lbs. of gold per annum, i.e. 50,400 nomismata at the old rate of 72 to the lb[32]. This figure (assuming it is correct) may have included commercial duties and the yield of the crown estates[33] in addition to personal taxes; even so, it bears eloquent testimony to the success of the Byzantine tax collectors[34].

A few further touches may be added from the *Hodoiporikon* of Constantine Manasses who visited the island in 1161/2. That he should have found it a cultural desert need not surprise us. When he describes Cyprus as evil-smelling and depressing (τὴν κάκοσμον πικρίαν) and compares it to a prison from which escape is nearly impossible (because of the prevalence of piracy), we may feel that he was not being very polite to his host, the governor Alexios Doukas, unless the latter, too, shared the same feelings. Rather more distressing, however, is the following humorous incident that Manasses relates (he, at any rate, thought it was humorous): when once he attended church, he found himself standing next to a Cypriot, "more senseless than all other Cypriots" (πάντας δὲ νικῶν ἀφροσύνῃ Κυπρίους), who was reeking of wine and garlic. Manasses, who was about to faint from the unbearable stench, told the man to move away. This produced no result, so Manasses repeated his request. Still no reply. Then, losing his patience, the Constantinopolitan scholar struck the man in the face and so was delivered of the offender[35]. The unfortunate Cypriot, who may not even

---

30. *Φωτίου ἐπιστολαί*, ed. I. N. Valettas, London, 1864, 527, No. 213.

31. Skylitzes, ed. Thurn, 429 = Cedrenus, Bonn ed., II, 549.

32. Arnold of Lübeck, *Chron. Slavorum*, *MGH*, Script. XXI, 178. Cf. A. Andréadès, Le montant du budget de l'Empire byzantin, *REG*, 34 (1921), 36 - 37.

33. For the imperial orchards at Nicosia see Tsiknopoullos, Κυπριακὰ τυπικά, p. 16, § 22. For the *kourator* of Cyprus see Psellos, *Scripta minora*, ed. Kurtz - Drexl, II, 110, and Konstantopoulos, Βυζαντιακὰ μολυβδόβουλλα, 50.

34. One is reminded of the condition of the island prior to 1878 when "the sole object of the Government. . . appears to have been the extraction of money from the inhabitants": Storrs and O'Brien, *Handbook of Cyprus*, 32.

35. K. Horna, Das Hodoiporikon des Konstantin Manasses, *BZ*, 13 (1904), 337

have understood the words addressed to him, knew better than to hit back. The distinguished visitor was, after all, the governor's guest.

Cyprus must have been at the time a predominantly rural area. The evidence on this score is very scanty and not entirely concordant. While some Arab sources speak of flourishing towns and an active trade [36], the two Greek saints' Lives that are concerned with the island in the 9th and 10th centuries, those of St. Constantine the Jew and St. Demetrianos, evoke a setting that was entirely rustic [37]. I should imagine that there were a few sizable agglomerations and that these tended to expand in the course of the 12th century as a result of commercial relations with Syria-Palestine, the installation of a Venetian colony in 1147, traffic with the Armenian kingdom of Cilicia and the growing pilgrim business [38]. The presence of an important Jewish settlement [39] is a pointer in the same direction. It is doubtful, however, if these agglomerations merited as yet the name of cities since they were either very poorly protected or entirely unprotected by fortifications. The circumstances of the revolt of Rhapsomates make it quite plain that neither Nicosia (which by this time appears to have become the capital) nor Limassol could be defended against a small expeditionary force: safety could be found only in the mountains [40]. The defensive works undertaken soon thereafter by Alexios I were, in all likelihood, confined to the three castles of the northern range, namely St. Hilarion, Buffavento and Kantara.

v. 98 (lack of culture), 342 v. 8 (evil-smelling), 344, v. 89 ff. (Cypriot smelling of garlic), 346 v. 153 ff. (Cyprus compared to a prison).

36. Thus Mukaddasi, *Description of Syria*, trans. G. Le Strange, London, 1892, 82, speaks of "populous cities" and adds that Cyprus "offers the Muslims many advantages in their trade thither, by reason of the great quantities of merchandise, stuffs and goods, which are produced there. The island is in the power of whichever nation is overlord in these seas." Mukaddasi's work was completed in 985, i.e. twenty years after the Byzantine reconquest of the island. One may wonder whether the author regarded this occupation as a temporary phenomenon. He may not, however, have been well informed on Cyprus. On the Arab evidence see N. Oikonomakis, Ἡ ἐν Κύπρῳ ἀραβοκρατία κατὰ τὰς ἀραβικὰς πηγάς, *Πρακτικὰ τοῦ Πρώτου Διεθνοῦς Κυπρολογικοῦ Συνεδρίου*, II, 193 ff.

37. ASS, Nov. IV, 636, 637; H. Grégoire, S. Démétrianos, évêque de Chytri, *BZ*, 16 (1907), 204 ff.

38. One should take, however, account of the disastrous draught and famine of 1176 - 79, as a result of which, according to St. Neophytos, the country became deserted and there was massive emigration. See Tsiknopoullos, *Κυπριακὰ τυπικά*, p. 13, § 11 and p. 107.

39. Benjamin of Tudela, ed. M.N. Adler, London, 1907, 14 - 15 (before 1167).

40. Anna Comnena, ed. B. Leib, II, 162 - 164.

Possession of the island was now predicated on these castles as well as on the pre-existing ones of Kyrenia and Paphos [41]. The story of the Latin conquest shows, once again, that none of the 'cities' could be held against an enemy [42]. The castle of Nicosia (or what passed for such) was so weak that in 1192 the Templars were unable to defend it against an insurgent mob [43]. In 1211 Famagusta was still "but slightly fortified" [44]. Archaeological exploration has brought ample evidence of the destruction and abandonment of Cypriot towns in the 7th century, but no evidence, as far as I am aware, has been found of any urban development during the Byzantine period [45]. One may hope that this important question will receive further attention when normal conditions return to the unfortunate island. It would be particularly interesting to gain some knowledge of the Byzantine origins of Nicosia and Famagusta [46].

In evaluating the relations of Cyprus with the outside world during this period I shall confine myself to two pieces of evidence. The first stems from the study of the Greek manuscripts that were either written on the island or passed through it. Father Darrouzès, who has carried out this laborious task, concludes as follows: "Le fait capital. . . c'est que le pays avec lequel Chypre a eu le plus de relations après le Xe siècle est la Palestine. Le mouvement de livres que représente le nombre de manuscrits chypriotes à Jérusalem est dû aux relations entre monastères orthodoxes. . . Chypre a été une étape pour des manuscrits errants et ces volumes venaient d'Orient, plutôt que du Nord, c'est-à-dire By-

41. For Kyrenia castle see A.H.S. Megaw in *JHS*, 72 (1952), 116 - 117. The date of the Byzantine castle at Paphos (Saranda Kolonnes) remains unclear: see Megaw in *DOP*, 26 (1972), 322 ff.

42. See especially the account by Richard of London (Geoffrey Vinsauf), *Itinerarium peregrinorum*, ed. W. Stubbs, Rolls Series, 38a, 182 ff.

43. L. de Mas Latrie, *Histoire de l'île de Chypre*, I, Paris, 1861, 33.

44. Oldenburg in Cobham, *Excerpta Cypria*, 14.

45. On the other hand, it is recorded that in 653/4 Muawiya caused a city to be built in Cyprus for the Arab garrison which he stationed on the island. This was subsequently destroyed and no trace has been found of it. In view of the Umayyad preference for flat inland sites, one may wonder whether this city might have been Nicosia. This view gains some support from the statement of Lusignan, *Description*, 31^v, that "Anciennement y auoit [at Nicosia] vn Temple de Mahomet, edifié du temps que les Sarrasins occuperent ceste Isle, par l'espace de quinze ans, viuant l'Empereur Charlemaigne." Cf. Hill, *History of Cyprus*, I, 285.

46. Megaw in *DOP*, 28 (1974), 80, points to a few Constantinopolitan reminiscences in the nomenclature of Nicosia: there were churches of St. Sophia and the Hodegetria, and the main street was called Mesê. An even more telling case in provided by the monastery of St. George of Mangana.

zance"[47]. The second piece of evidence is provided by the career and writings of St. Neophytos the Enkleist, an individual of middling social status. The Saint left the island only once when, as a young man, he tried to find a suitable monastic retreat in Palestine. His search, which lasted six months (1158), proved ineffectual and so he returned to Cyprus. His next thought was to seek salvation on Mount Latros near Miletus, but divine Providence did not allow him to go any farther than Paphos[48]. Such was the extent of his geographical horizons. Though he spent the rest of his life confined to his cave, he did maintain some outside contacts. These included the south coast of Asia Minor: a person brought him from Attaleia a flask of *myrhon* emitted by the relics of St. Andronikos, and he found this to be very efficacious[49]. But Neophytos was much better informed of events in Syria-Palestine. He relates at length the dreadful story of a Georgian monk of St. Sabas who was deceived by the devil in the year 1184[50]; he knew in detail the consequences of the capture of Jerusalem by Saladin[51] and the damage caused at Antioch by the earthquake of 1170[52]. We may also remember that the founder of the important Machairas monastery was a Palestinian monk[53].

As shown by the above examples, Cyprus was restored during the last century of Byzantine rule to its normal place in the Near East. It was once more a crossroads, but not, properly speaking, a 'carrefour du monde byzantin.' For the main route running through it now led to lands that were no longer Byzantine, but Frankish, Moslem and Armenian; and it was the continued importance of the same route that assured the much greater prosperity of the island under the Lusignans and the Venetians.

47. *REB*, 15 (1957), 132 - 133.
48. Mango and Hawkins, The Hermitage of St. Neophytos, 123.
49. H. Delehaye, Saints de Chypre, *AnalBoll*, 26 (1907), 180.
50. *Ibid.*, 162 ff.
51. *Ibid.*, 172 f.
52. *Ibid.*, 212.
53. This man, also called Neophytos, came from the region of the Jordan which he abandoned because of Saracen raids: Tsiknopoullos, Κυπριακὰ τυπικά, p. 11, § 7.

XVIII

THE PHANARIOTS AND THE BYZANTINE TRADITION

Two conflicting judgments have often been expressed concerning the Phanariots. The first is that they were a thoroughly iniquitous lot who lived by intrigue and base adulation, who were indifferent to the real interests of their compatriots and who cynically exploited the Rumanian principalities that they were appointed to govern; who, furthermore, constituted a sinister cabal that exerted a profound influence on the affairs of the Ottoman Empire and entirely controlled the Greek Church. This unfavourable judgment is stated most fully in a book entitled *Essai sur les Fanariotes*, published in 1824 by one Mark Philip Zallony, a Roman Catholic Greek who knew the Phanariots well and who was afraid that they might assume control of the independent Greek state that was then in the process of being born.[1] It is in a purely derogatory sense that the epithet 'Byzantine' has often been applied to the Phanariots.

The other judgment is that the Phanariots, in spite of certain unavoidable vices that were due to the corruption prevailing in the Ottoman Empire, were animated by the purest patriotism; that they made a great contribution towards civilising their Rumanian subjects; above all – and this is the point I should like to stress – that they worked in the fields of politics, education and literature for the regeneration of the Greek people and of *ellinismos*. Needless to say, this second judgment has been voiced by the majority of Greek historians.[2] Other, more balanced views have been expressed concerning the Phanariots,[3] but the two I have mentioned are those most frequently encountered.

We may begin with a brief historical sketch. In speaking of the Phanariots we do not mean all the Greek inhabitants of a particular quarter of Istanbul; we mean more specifically a Greek oligarchy that resided largely in the Phanar (whither the Ecumenical Patriarchate moved in 1600) and that owed their privileged position, in one way or another, to service in the Ottoman administration. The first Phanariot in this restricted sense is considered to have been Panayotis Nikousios (1613–73), son of a petty tradesman, who rose to the position of Grand Interpreter to the Porte and who contributed to the conquest of Candia by the Turks in 1669.[4] Panayotis did not, however, establish a dynasty since his only son wasted all his money on alchemy.[5] The privilege of founding a dynasty was reserved for Panayotis's successor, Alexandros Mavrokordatos, who, in spite of many vicissitudes, served as Grand Interpreter for nearly forty years (1673–1709) and who is chiefly remembered for his leading role in the conclusion of the treaty of Karlowitz in 1699.[6] Until 1821 the highly influential post of Grand Interpreter remained a prerogative of the Phanariot Greeks who also succeeded in securing for themselves another, not inconsiderable position, that of Interpreter to the Navy. The latter's chief function was to serve as intermediary between the Turkish Grand Admiral and the islanders of the Aegean.

A much greater prize was, however, awaiting the Phanariots. The two Rumanian principalities of Wallachia and Moldavia had long been tributary to the Turks, but enjoyed a considerable measure of independence under the rule of local princes. The latter, we may note in passing, allowed their country to become deeply infiltrated by Greek interests, ecclesiastic, cultural and economic. This situation continued until the beginning of the eighteenth century when, in the context of the war between Peter the Great of Russia and Charles XII of Sweden, the two *hospodars*, Brîncoveanu and Cantemir, aligned themselves with forces hostile to Turkey. The Porte now decided to have these provinces governed by men it could more effectively control, and began choosing the incumbents among the Phanariots. The first Greek prince of Moldavia was Nikolaos Mavrokordatos, Alexandros' son, appointed in 1709 and, once again, in 1711; the same man was transferred in 1715 to the governorship of the richer province of Wallachia. The Phanariot administration of the two principalities continued until the outbreak of the Greek Revolution in 1821 and, during

this period, Moldavia experienced 36 changes of princes and
Wallachia 38. Allowing for periods of foreign occupation, the
average length of rule was 2.5 years. All the *hospodars* of the
two principalities were recruited from among eleven families.[7]

The results of the Phanariot administration of Rumania
were, by most accounts, disastrous.[8] 'It is impossible,' writes
R. W. Seton-Watson, 'to conceive a more disheartening task
than that of recording in detail the history of these hundred
years in Wallachia and Moldavia, and the western reader
would only read it with impatience and under protest.'[9] The
Greeks themselves freely admitted the wickedness of their own
régime. The Phanariot historian, Athanasios Komninos
Ypsilantis, exclaims:

> What harmful innovations have occurred in these unhappy
> lands . . . on account of the Greeks! I pass over in silence all
> the things I know . . . and in particular the innovations
> introduced by the *hospodar* Nikolaos [Mavrokordatos] and
> his son, the *hospodar* Konstantinos: they form a shameful
> story. This only I say that the Greeks have destroyed the old
> privileges of these two principalities that were beneficial to
> their inhabitants, and they will surely see at God's tribunal
> Who it is that they have sinned against.[10]

Another contemporary Greek, Konstantinos (Kaisarios)
Dapontes, looks back to the days of Brîncoveanu, the last native
prince of Wallachia, as to a golden age. 'Wallachia,' he says,
'was like a rose-garden and most populous; there were then
700,000 families living there, and now there are scarcely
70,000.'[11]

There is no need for our purpose to give a more detailed
historical account of the Phanariots, nor would I be competent
to do so. I should like, however, to touch on some factual matters
that are relevant to our discussion.

In the first place, it has to be made clear that the Phanariots
were in no way descended from a medieval Byzantine aristocracy. Broadly speaking, the noble Byzantine families (or, at
any rate, families that bore the illustrious old names) disappeared at Constantinople towards the end of the sixteenth
century.[12] In the course of the seventeenth there arose a new
élite of provincial origin, and it is from among its ranks that the

44

Phanariots eventually emerged.[13] The claim to aristocratic Byzantine ancestry is a myth that the Phanariots themselves strove to propagate and that later became enshrined in a book called *Le livre d'or de la noblesse phanariote* by E. R. Rangavis.[14] Fortunately, this myth was bolstered not by any deliberate falsification, such as was perpetrated in the late seventeenth century by the 'iatrosophist' Ioannis Molyvdos 'Comnenus',[15] but only by vague references to unspecified 'Byzantine authors' and to documents preserved in family archives which, needless to say, have never been produced. It is not necessary to demonstrate that, e.g., the Aristarkhis family had no good claim to be descended from the Emperor John I Tzimiskes, that the Mourouzis family had no demonstrable kinship with the Comnenes of Trebizond, that the Rangavis family had nothing to do with the Emperor Michael I Rhangabes or the Ypsilantis family with the eleventh-century patriarch John Xiphilinus, that the Neroulos family could not reasonably claim the fifth-century Egyptian poet Nonnus among its ancestors. The truth is rather more prosaic. It will be enough to consider here the eleven families that attained so-called princely status. The Mavrokordatos' came from Chios, first appearing at Constantinople in the early seventeenth century: their lineage can only be traced back to the sixteenth.[16] The Ghika family was Albanian and also emigrated to Constantinople in the early part of the seventeenth century, soon rising to high honours thanks to the protection of a fellow-Albanian, the Grand Vizier Mehmet Köprülü.[17] The Ypsilantis and Mourouzis families, which were intermarried and may have been partly of Laz extraction, came from Trebizond, where they seem to have been engaged in petty shipping and farming; they migrated to Constantinople about 1665 and attained a measure of prominence only in the first half of the eighteenth century.[18] The Racovitza (Racoviţă) and Callimachi families were both Rumanian, the first of noble ancestry, while the second was descended from a Moldavian peasant called Calmăşul who climbed the hierarchical ladder at Constantinople, hellenised his name to Kallimakhis, and was made *hospodar* of Moldavia in 1758.[19] The Soutsos family was certainly established at Constantinople in the second half of the sixteenth century; according to another tradition (perhaps malicious), its ancestor was a certain

Diamantakis Drakos of Epirus, the son of a milkman (*sütcü* in Turkish) who lived in the seventeenth century.[20] The Rosetti or Rossetti family was clearly of Italian origin, but was already settled at Constantinople in the seventeenth century.[21] The Karatzas (Karadja) family bore a common Turkish name meaning 'black' or 'swarthy': it seems to have come from Caramania in Asia Minor and was resident at Constantinople in the second half of the sixteenth century. There exist, however, other accounts of its origin.[22] The Mavroyenis family, which fancifully claimed kinship with the Morosinis of Venice, came from Paros and Mykonos and reached Constantinople only after 1750.[23] The Khantzeris (Handjeris or Handjerlis) were also latecomers: the oldest member of the family to have attained a position of prominence was, rather exceptionally, a cleric – Samuil, who became Patriarch of Constantinople in 1763.[24]

In short, the leading Phanariot families were a hodgepodge of enterprising Greeks, Rumanians, Albanians and Levantine Italians. Most, if not all of them originated outside Constantinople, and they attained high position in the course of the seventeenth and eighteenth centuries. They cannot, therefore, be regarded as having a more direct pipeline to the Byzantine tradition than other contemporary Greeks living within the Ottoman Empire.

The second question I should like to raise concerns the financial resources of the Phanariots. Naturally, it is not easy to obtain any precise information on this matter since they took good care to cover their tracks. Broadly speaking, however, it may be said that their resources, which were considerable, were due, in the first instance, not to trade in the normal sense of the word, but to various lucrative positions that they managed to obtain within the Turkish system.[25] Thus, the Mavrokordatos fortune was founded by Alexandros' father-in-law, a certain Scarlato or Scarlati who, from being a poor man, made himself a millionaire by holding the government office of *beylikçi* which enabled him to fix customs duties.[26] When, after the Turkish failure at Vienna, Mavrokordatos was imprisoned and fined 300 purses, he was able, though with some difficulty, to produce the greater part of this enormous sum within a year.[27] By way of comparison, the annual tribute of Wallachia to the Porte was at that time 280 purses.[28] He could hardly have made himself so rich on his salary as dragoman which he found insufficient even for his expenses while he was accompanying the Grand Vizier on campaign, and had to supplement by claiming the revenues of the metropolis of Adrianople.[29] Of course, as dragoman he had access to some fringe benefits like the yearly retainer of 4000 *livres* he drew from the French Embassy and the very substantial bribe he is said to have received from Austria as a reward for the Treaty of Karlowitz.[30]

Manuil Ypsilantis, the first member of that family to have attained prominence, was in the early years of the eighteenth century chief purveyor of furs to the Grand Vizier, an office he inherited from his brother-in-law. He accompanied his Turkish master on the Morean expedition of 1715 and came back a very rich man.[31] After a long and devious career which brought him into politics, he was impaled by order of the government (1737) and his fortune confiscated: it amounted to the staggering sum of 1800 purses, including the estate of his brother and that of his nephew which were seized at the same time.[32]

These two examples may show how Phanariot families rose to the surface. Once, however, the Danubian principalities were opened to their ambition, opportunities for enrichment were vastly increased. That, of course, depended on personal initiative. A few of the Greek *hospodars* proved to be honest, such as Konstantinos Mavrokordatos (1711–69) who, although he had ruled Wallachia six times and Moldavia four times, was obliged to sell his ancestral house at Constantinople and to pawn his grandfather's library to an English merchant.[33] The majority of *hospodars*, however, did very well for themselves. Zallony, who is admittedly a biased observer, says that after a reign of only two years a *hospodar* might have amassed 10,000,000 francs.[34] Ioannis Karatzas, who ruled Wallachia from 1812 to 1818, did even better: he got away with 90,000,000 piastres which he deposited in foreign banks.[35] The intense rivalry for the *hospodar*'s office shows all too clearly what benefits were involved. Furthermore, these were not confined to the *hospodar*'s person, but also extended to a large circle of relatives and clients on whom he conferred offices and patents of nobility in Rumania.[36] According to the same Zallony, a Greek *boyar* could count on anything between 100,000 and 1,000,000 francs as the illicit reward of his service. Among the most coveted posts were those of *Grand Postelnik* or Chief Minister who was able to sell various dignities to the local nobility, of *Spathar*, i.e., chief of militia, of *Ağa*, i.e., chief of the municipal police of Bucharest, of *Comisso*, i.e., the prince's equerry, of *Caminar* which involved no duties but was rewarded with a cut from the tax on wine, of *Armash* who inspected the Gypsies and the collection of gold from the rivers.[37] Furthermore, if he was an enterprising man, the Phanariot could combine his Rumanian profits with some lucrative concession obtained from his Turkish protectors, as did, e.g., in the mid-eighteenth century, the notorious Stavrakoğlu who, while holding the title of *Spathar* and acting as agent (*kapıkâhyası*) for the *hospodar* Constantine Racovitza, also won for himself the monopoly of selling tobacco at Constantinople.[38]

After serving his term in Rumania, the successful Phanariot could afford to build for himself a town house in the Phanar and a country villa on the Bosphorus, if he did not have them already.[39] Apart from this, he seldom purchased any landed property. He spent a great deal on imported furniture, rich clothing, crockery and jewellery for his wife.[40] The rest of his capital he loaned at interest as unobtrusively as possible so as not to excite the suspicion of the authorities.[41] The Church, as we shall see presently, was a frequent recipient of such loans.

It should be apparent from the above that the Phanariots, as a class, had carved out for themselves a very comfortable niche in the existing Ottoman system. The game they played was not without its dangers – witness the number of *hospodars* and dragomans who served prison sentences or were beheaded – but it was obviously worth the candle. Furthermore, the Phanariots had nothing to gain by changing a system that they had learnt so well to manipulate. If anything, they might have wished to extend the same form of exploitation to other provinces of the Ottoman Empire, and they are said to have had designs of this kind on Serbia, the Peloponnese and Cyprus.[42] There was a profound contrast between the Phanariot class and that of the Greek merchants that rose to prominence and riches in the eighteenth century. In the perspective of history we may realise that the Greek merchant, too, did well out of the Ottoman Empire, but this is not a view he held at the time. What he knew all too well was that his efforts were constantly thwarted by Ottoman officialdom the arbitrary impositions of which he could escape only by flying the Russian or the British flag. The Phanariot, therefore, was a man who fed on the existing system, while the merchant fed himself by circumventing it. The former tended to be a reactionary, the latter a liberal.

The third question I should like to raise concerns the intimate relationship between the Phanariots and the Church. In this respect the Phanariots merely continued an existing tradition: already in the sixteenth century influential Greek *arkhons*, like Mikhail Kantakouzinos, were able to appoint and depose patriarchs, and, before the advent of the Phanariots proper, Rumanian princes often had a controlling voice in the affairs of the Greek Church. The influence exercised by the Phanariots on the Church of Constantinople cannot be exactly defined. In terms of recognised institutions, it was limited to the existence of certain appointments called *offikia* that were open to laymen and entitled their holders to a seat on the Synod. These posts, like that of Grand Logothete, Grand Skevophylax, Grand Chartophylax, etc., were usually occupied since the end of the seventeenth century either by Phanariots or their protégés.[43] It may be worth noticing that the Phanariots themselves very seldom took holy orders: I can mention only two patriarchs of the eighteenth century, Ioannikios Karatzas and Samuil Khantzeris, who belonged to prominent Phanariot families.[44] What appears on paper is, however, only the tip of the iceberg: the real hold of the Phanariots on the Church was political and financial. Political, because the Phanariots enjoyed the confidence of the Turkish authorities; financial, because the Church was chronically in debt[45] and was obliged to use the Phanariots as its bankers. We should remember that all important ecclesiastical offices were sold for ready cash: that of Patriarch cost at the beginning of the eighteenth century 3,000 florins, i.e., $16\frac{1}{2}$ purses, but this soon went up to 80 purses or even more.[46] Since the nominees seldom had so much money at their disposal, they had to borrow it at about 10 per cent interest. It is said that the Phanariots regularly invested their assets in subsidising the appointment of patriarchs and metropolitans, which enabled them, of course, to pick their own candidates and keep them in a state of lasting subservience.[47]

While it is true that the Phanariots constantly interfered in the affairs of the Church, often in a most unceremonious manner, it is equally true that they remained steadfastly faithful to the Church and identified themselves with its interests as they interpreted them. Their benefactions, which were not perhaps commensurate with their wealth, were directed almost entirely to the Church: gifts of money, of real estate, of plate, of vestments, even of wax for candles. When they subsidised education, it was education under ecclesiastical auspices.[48] Many Greek *hospodars* founded monasteries in Rumania which they usually assigned to the Holy Sepulchre, Mount Sinai or Mount Athos: there can be no doubt that this represented a form of investment.[49] The involvement of the Phanariots was not limited to the Church of Constantinople. The Church of Rumania was, of course, entirely in their pocket since all senior ecclesiastical appointments were at the *hospodar*'s pleasure; furthermore, they showed an active interest in the affairs of the other Eastern Patriarchates, especially that of Jerusalem which was, incidentally, a major landholder in Rumania. Panayotis Nikousios, Alexandros and Nikolaos Mavrokordatos laboured ceaselessly to defend the Holy Sepulchre and other places of pilgrimage in Palestine against the encroachments of Roman Catholics. The great volume of correspondence between leading Phanariots and the Patriarchs of Jerusalem[50] offers sufficient evidence of this concern, which also had obvious financial implications.[51]

I have attempted by way of introduction to discuss certain characteristics of the Phanariots that must have conditioned their behaviour as a class. I should now like to turn to their literary culture in order to find out whether they represented a definite way of thinking, a tradition, and whether this could be called a Byzantine tradition. In speaking of Phanariot literature, I am including under this heading not only the writings of bona fide Phanariots, which are not very numerous, but also those produced in their milieu, whether in Constantinople or Rumania. I shall begin with a few general remarks.

At the risk of making a sweeping generalisation, I would venture to say that Greek literature after the fall of Constantinople splits up into two main streams. The first, which may be

50

labelled Franco-Greek (in the demotic acceptation of *Frangos*), is largely the literature of the Greek islands: it includes the so-called Rhodian and Cypriot love songs, the chronicle of Makhairas, the Cretan plays of the seventeenth century and the *Erotokritos*. Most of these works have some literary merit; with the possible exception of Makhairas, they are all dependent, however loosely, on western prototypes and are not explainable in terms of Byzantine antecedents. In so far as post-conquest Greek literature has attracted the attention of western scholars, this attention has been confined almost entirely to the Franco-Greek stream.

The other main stream, which is quite copious but entirely devoid of literary merit, represents the writings of Greeks living under Ottoman domination. Their content is largely theological, but there are also chronicles, collections of letters, laudations, epigrams, poems commemorating memorable events and school textbooks. This stream perpetuates the literary genres of medieval Byzantium, exhibits the same range of interests, the same stock of assumed knowledge, the same rhetoric, the same linguistic dichotomy, the same lack of any poetic feeling as does Byzantine literature. The writings of the Phanariots belong to this second tradition, of which they form the historical termination.

Furthermore, it seems to me that the literary culture of the Phanariots has been greatly exaggerated. It is difficult to understand today the admiration that has been lavished on a work so essentially mediocre as the *Peri kathikonton* (*Concerning Obligations*), acknowledged to be the masterpiece of Nikolaos Mavrokordatos.[52] Yet Nikolaos was unquestionably one of the most cultivated Phanariots. As for Konstantinos Dapontes, the distinguished alumnus of the academies of Bucharest and Jassy and 'the most productive Greek author of the eighteenth century',[53] his tedious verbiage will defeat the patience of the most determined reader. The literary world of the Phanar, the 'world of tchelebi Yorgakis', as George Seferis has aptly called it,[54] will remain forever enshrined in the *New Erotokritos* of Dionysios Photeinos, purged, as the author informs us, of its barbarous and nearly incomprehensible Cretan dialect, and rendered into the 'mellifluous speech of educated Greeks'.[55]

We may now examine a few specimens of Phanariot writing

so as to show both their mentality and something of their content. The first document that claims our attention is the collected letters of Alexandros Mavrokordatos. These are mostly in high rhetorical style and were actually used in the Greek schools as models of epistolography along with the letters of Libanius and Synesius and the *Peri epistolikon typon* of Theophilos Korydalefs.[56] I shall single out from them a few topics of interest.

First, there is Alexandros' attitude towards his Turkish masters. He states repeatedly that he has served them faithfully:

> We conform to the prescription of the Gospel, 'Render unto Caesar the things which are Caesar's'; it is not the custom of us Christians to confuse what is temporary and corruptible with what is divine and eternal.[57]

The trouble stems from the fact that the Turks are extremely contemptuous towards Christians. To make matters worse, the Sultan is constantly changing his ministers. 'I have succeeded by dint of great exertion,' he says, 'to win one vizier's favour; but now he has fallen and another has taken his place, and then another. Each time I have to start afresh.'

In matters of ethics Alexandros counsels prudence or, as we would say, dissimulation. One of his correspondents had been ordered to audit government expenditure over the previous ten years and was afraid of exposing influential embezzlers. 'You should have excused yourself,' says Alexandros, 'on the pretext of being incapable of the task. Now, however, that you are under orders, you ought to engage as many collaborators as possible so as to spread the responsibility.'[58] Another correspondent had been cruelly treated by the authorities and was seeking Alexandros' advice. 'Be patient,' he says, 'and prudent. Whatever punishment is inflicted on you, be it the confiscation of your property or even imprisonment, call it a great blessing so all can hear you.'[59]

With regard to contact with the West, Alexandros has this to say:

> It often leads to the corruption of the ancestral customs that adorn our nation. I have often deplored the fact that Greeks who have gone abroad have not only acquired disgusting and spurious manners, but have also polluted their minds with

alien doctrines and have drawn thousands of simple souls into the same abominations. Would that they had suffered shipwreck upon their departure. [60]

Finally, with regard to language, Alexandros distinguishes between two idioms, the Hellenic, i.e., ancient Greek which is used for display, and the vulgar used for serious communications. In writing from Belgrade to Dositheos, Patriarch of Jerusalem, he says, 'Forgive me if I have erred in describing these matters in Hellenic as if I was playing a game, whereas I should have been serious and used the vulgar dialect.'[61] On the other hand, he is greatly incensed when his sons, whom he had left at home in the care of a schoolmaster, wrote him in the vulgar tongue.

> When will you cease, O beloved ones, chattering in the dialect of the marketplace? Two or even three months have gone by, and you have not sent me a single letter wrought in Attic, such as would be an exemplar of your diligence and would serve to console me on this dreadful expedition. Has your course of rhetoric come to no good end? Is this the result of your studies that you do not hesitate to speak barbarously to your father whom you know to prize the charms of rhetoric and artful elegance more than nectar and ambrosia?[62]

Alexander was not in the end disappointed: his dutiful son Nikolaos reduced him to tears of joy by sending him a letter conceived in such convoluted Hellenic, that he even had to be gently reprimanded for using expressions that were too contrived.[63] Here is the father's delighted reaction:

> Let those who disparage the present time for its unproductiveness and poverty keep silent. Nature has not been reduced to such sterility. Nay, God has given an Athens to Hellas, and to Athens He has given a Libanius.[64]

Anyone who is acquainted with Byzantine epistolography will immediately recognise a familiar strain in these letters. For the educated, Libanius still rules the Muses. But what do we find when we step down one rung on the ladder of sophistication? It is, even more emphatically, Byzantium. Here is the list of recommended reading compiled by Konstantinos Dapontes for the benefit of the Princess Eleni Mavrokordatou:

Let me tell you those books that I find to be full of sweetness. Here they are: The *Oktoikhos* of John Damascene, the *oikoi* in honour of the Virgin [i.e., the Acathist Hymn] – and add to them those in honour of St. John the Baptist as being of equal grace; the seven prayers to the Virgin contained in the missal ·(*synopsis*); the Exposition of the Liturgy by Nicholas Cabasilas; the Chapters of the deacon Agapetus addressed to Justinian, the ornament of the ages; the book by Stephen on the Making of Gold; not to mention your Constantine [i.e., Dapontes himself] who is like honey unto the heart.[65]

An instructive list considering it was drawn up in the middle of the eighteenth century.

What little there is of Phanariot historiography is also revealing. Alexandros Mavrokordatos wrote a vast historical work divided into three parts, called *Iudaica*, *Romaica* and *Mysica*, of which only the first has been published.[66] In the Preface the author tells us that Greeks were ignorant of history because so many of their books had been destroyed; furthermore, being enslaved, very few of them went abroad, and those who did so sought commercial gain rather than instruction. The author, who had had the opportunity of travelling in the West and knew many languages, proposed, therefore, to offer to his compatriots the fruits of his wide reading. If, on the strength of this promise, we expect to find in the *Iudaica* any reflection of Renaissance scholarship, we are quickly disappointed. On the first page the author informs us that history is divided into six periods: 1 and 2 from Creation to Abraham, 3 and 4 from Abraham to the Incarnation, 5 and 6 from the Incarnation to the Second Coming. This is to be followed by a seventh period, which is that of 'endless repose in the eternal mansions.' The *Iudaica* covers periods 1 to 4 and is based on the authority of the Old Testament. When we lay down the heavy tome, we do so with the realisation that things had not changed much since the days of Zonaras and Manasses: Moses, the greatest of historians, the seven aeons of universal history corresponding to the seven days of the week are still with us.

The book that tells us most about the activities of the Phanariots (not without bias and considerable inaccuracy) is undoubtedly the historical work of the physician Athanasios

54

Komninos Ypsilantis, commonly known as *Ta meta tin Alosin*, i.e., *Events after the Conquest*. The published part, consisting of Books VIII, IX, X and extracts of Book XII, is only a small section of a vast ecclesiastical history in twelve books that starts with Julius Caesar and goes down to 1789.[67] The skeleton of the work is provided by the succession of the Patriarchs of Constantinople starting with the apostle Andrew: it is they who occupy the centre of the stage, while the affairs of the four other apostolic sees, of Byzantine emperors and Turkish sultans are dealt with marginally. In other words, we have before us a work that stands in direct succession to Socrates and Sozomen, Theodoret and Nicephorus Callistus; and its avowed purpose was to propagate Orthodoxy and confound the heretics.[68]

In reading works of Phanariot literature, such as those of Konstantinos Dapontes, who served as secretary to the *hospodars* Konstantinos and Ioannis Mavrokordatos, and the History of Athanasios Ypsilantis, one cannot help noticing again and again the extent of their geographical horizon. To be sure, Western Europe was not entirely ignored, but the part of the world that especially interested the Phanariots extended from Moscow in the north to Alexandria in the south. It was the world not of *ellinismos*, but of Orthodoxy, and its centre was naturally Constantinople which, to quote the expression of Iakovos Argeios, the tutor of Nikolaos Mavrokordatos, 'presides today not only over Europe, but also over Asia and Africa'[69] – as, in fact, it did thanks to the existence of the Ottoman Empire. When the notorious Stravrakoğlu, whom I have already mentioned, built his palatial residence on the Bosphorus, he decorated his own room with views of Wallachia and Moldavia, and his wife's room with views of Constantinople and Moscow[70] – not, I might add, with a view of the Parthenon. Dapontes' *Catalogue of Distinguished Men* (1700–84) deals with the following categories of people in this order: patriarchs of Constantinople, Alexandria, Antioch and Jerusalem; Orthodox bishops, priests and monks; Czars of Russia; Phanariot *hospodars* and interpreters; other *arkhons* of Constantinople, tradesmen and finally teachers.[71]

That the dream of recreating the Byzantine Empire was very much alive in Phanariot circles may be taken for granted. The same Konstantinos Dapontes saw in 1738, when he was at

Bucharest, a vision of the double-headed eagle wearing the imperial crown, as well as of Constantine and Helena.[72] The Oracles of Leo the Wise had spoken of a mysterious ox that would bellow when the awaited emperor John appeared to liberate Constantinople: now the emblem of Moldavia was an ox-head and all the *hospodars*, on their accession, assumed the ceremonial name of John.[73] The most influential Greek oracular work of the eighteenth century, the so-called Book of Agathangelos, was dedicated to Grigorios Ghika, *hospodar* of Wallachia.[74] As envisaged at the time, the restoration of the Byzantine Empire was to come about not by internal revolution, but by a providential intervention either of the Russian Czar or the German Emperor (or both combined), and it was widely believed that this was to happen 320 years after the Fall, i.e., in 1773. This very nearly came to pass. The Russo-Turkish war that broke out in 1768 resulted, however, not in the liberation of Constantinople, but in the Treaty of Küçük Kaynarca which, favourable as it was to Greek interests, aroused profound disappointment. I quote the reaction of Konstantinos Dapontes:

The time appointed by the oracles for the restoration was 320 years after the Conquest, and it so happened that this time coincided with the six years' war when [the Russians] approached the City, surrounded it and were on the point of taking it, but did not take it. For this reason the Russians will no longer be able to capture it no matter what means they use or what forces they bring down to the Crimea . . . For if God, constrained by our sins – may He forgive me for daring to say so – prevented that which was affirmed by the oracles from happening at the appointed time; if, I say, He saw fit that the utterances of so many astronomers, scholars and saints should prove vain in preference to giving the Empire to men unworthy not only of this Empire but of life itself, how is it possible henceforth that the resurrection of the Romaic Empire should happen when no assurance or oracle concerning this has remained? This being so, neither the Greeks nor the Russians will reign in the City unto the end of the world. May merciful God take pity on us and grant us the Heavenly Kingdom, and never mind about the earthly one.[75]

56

The disappointment of these deeply felt messianic hopes came about at a time when French rationalism was beginning to exert some impact upon the better educated Greeks – first upon the mercantile Greek diaspora and, a little later, upon the rising Greek bourgeoisie resident in the Ottoman Empire. In spite of ecclesiastical opposition, several attempts were made to introduce the 'new learning' into the curriculum of Greek schools in the place of the Aristotelianism of Theophilos Korydalefs that had held sway since the beginning of the seventeenth century.[76] French novels, often of the worst kind, were avidly read at Constantinople, and even a few Phanariots took up the cause of Enlightenment by translating more serious French works into Greek. Rallou, daughter of the *hospodar* Alexandros Soutsos, is said to have translated the Marquise de Lambert's *Avis d'une mère à sa fille*, Aikaterini Soutsos rendered into Greek Mably's *Entretiens de Phocion*, Konstantinos Manos is credited with a translation of Barthélemy's *Voyage du jeune Anacharsis*, etc.[77] All of this was harmless enough. When, however, the French Revolution broke out, when French agents began disseminating subversive proclamations in Ottoman territory, when, in particular, Napoleon landed in Egypt (1798) and so attacked directly the world of Islam, some stand had to be taken. The Church of Constantinople reacted violently by hurling its anathemas at French godlessness and affirming that the Sultan's Empire had been set up by God's decree. These and similar views were expressed in a number of pamphlets of which the most notorious is the *Patriki didaskalia* (*Paternal Doctrine*) published at the Patriarchal Press of Constantinople in that same year 1798 under the name of Anthimos, Patriarch of Jerusalem.[78] The circumstances surrounding the publication of this and other reactionary tracts are, unfortunately, very obscure. It is likely enough that the Phanariots had a hand in them, although I have no conclusive proof of this. I should like, however, to draw attention to a statement made by Zallony, namely, that in the course of a conversation he had in 1818 with the metropolitans of Nicomedia, Derkoi, Sophia and Thessaloniki he was informed by them that the Phanariots imposed the following conditions on the clergy: to keep alive an undying hatred of the Roman Catholic Church; to forbid all marriages between Orthodox and Roman Catholics; to insist on the observance of 195 fast days per year; to promote the pilgrimage to Jerusalem; finally – and this is the important point – to declare that the concept of political liberty had been inspired by the devil, whereas the Sultan's Empire existed by God's grace.[79]

Western godlessness, egalitarianism and antiquarianism triumphed in the end, but not without having produced a strange Phanariot hybrid in the proclamations of Rigas Velestinlis. This famous revolutionary who, we may remember, made his career entirely within the Phanariot framework, traced in 1796 his blueprint for regenerated Greece. The well-known map he printed in that year includes, in fact, the entire Balkan peninsula as well as western Asia Minor, while its lower left-hand corner is occupied by an inset plan of Constantinople which was evidently meant to be the capital.[80] Rigas elaborated his rather fuzzy ideas in the Revolutionary Manifesto of 1797 which is addressed to

> The People descended from the ancient Hellenes who inhabit Rumeli, Asia Minor, the Mediterranean islands, Vlakhobogdania, and all those who groan under the unbearable tyranny of the most foul Ottoman despotism or who have been forced to depart to foreign kingdoms so as to escape this heavy yoke, all, I say, Christian and Turk alike without any distinction of religion.[81]

The ornamental detail and phraseology of this manifesto are admittedly of Western inspiration: Rigas speaks of Hellenes, not of Romaioi, although he has no clear conception of who these Hellenes may be; he lays down the design of the revolutionary flag which, by way of compromise, was to represent the club of Hercules surmounted by three crosses; he wants the soldiers to wear classical helmets and heroic costume, i.e., black jerkins, white shirts and red hose. If we make allowance for all this romantic claptrap, what emerges is not a Hellenic democracy, but, in fact, a somewhat dechristianised Byzantine democracy.[82]

The people of Vlakhobogdania were not, of course, greatly stirred by the appeal to join the new Hellenic Commonwealth, as Alexandros Ypsilantis was to discover in 1821. The story of his failure does not need retelling. One might be tempted to call it a farce had it not ended in tragedy, when the Turks, justifiably

58

alarmed by the turn of events, carried out an indiscriminate massacre of the leading Phanariots in Constantinople and even hanged for good measure the unfortunate Patriarch Grigorios V who was a fanatical opponent of the Revolution. This marks the end of the Phanariots as a significant element in history. Many of them settled in Greece. Some remained in Turkey and even succeeded in regaining influential posts in the Ottoman administration, like Spyridon Mavroyenis (1816–1902) who was chief physician to Abdul Hamid, like his son Alexandros (d. 1929) who served as Turkish ambassador to Washington. Some Phanariots stayed in Rumania. A few emigrated to Western Europe.

R. W. Seton Watson writes:

> The Greek Revolution of 1821 is inaugurated in Moldavia and Wallachia by the son of a former hospodar, but ends like one of those dissolving views that are thrown upon the screen. For a moment it is Greek, then the outlines fade and waver and vanish, and suddenly in the twinkling of an eye the Greek is gone and has been replaced at every point by the Roumanian . . . There is no other example of the leaders of a national revolt so completely misconceiving the nature of their own problem as to address themselves in the first instance to a people which was not only alien in blood, but indifferent and even hostile to all their aims and outlooks.[83]

In this 'misconception' lies the paradox of the Phanariots. It would be injudicious to pass a general judgment on an aristocracy that was constantly divided and whose members, especially at the end of the eighteenth century, championed the conflicting interests of Russia, Austria and France while remaining Ottoman civil servants. I do not believe that there ever existed a Phanariot master-plan for a settlement of the Eastern question. I am aware that some Phanariots became infected with liberal ideas, and that a few of them even won the crowns of 'ethno-martyrdom'. But if we are to draw a conclusion, it is that the Phanariots, not by virtue of their descent, but by virtue of their position in the Ottoman Empire, the sources of their wealth, and their close identification with the Church, represented a

Byzantine tradition that was basically anti-national.[84] Those of them that espoused the 'new ideas' simply superimposed them, as did Rigas Velestinlis, upon their innate Byzantinism without realizing that the two were mutually exclusive. For all of their political finesse, they did not perceive that their world had ceased to exist. Those Phanariots and Patriarchs who implacably opposed French philosophy and revolution had perhaps a clearer understanding of what was about to happen.

NOTES TO CHAPTER 2

This paper was read at a symposium entitled 'After the Fall of Constantinople', held at Dumbarton Oaks, Washington, D.C., in May 1968. It is presented here without any substantial alterations, i.e., as a sketch and nothing more. 'La question phanariote', wrote Émile Legrand in 1888, 'est beaucoup plus compliquée qu'elle ne le paraît de prime abord; elle n'est pas de celles que l'on tranche au pied levé; elle demande au contraire à être mûrie par une longue étude, et nous abandonnons volontiers à d'autres le soin de la résoudre.' *Bibliothèque grecque vulgaire*, IV, p. v. Legrand's wish has not, unfortunately, been realised. Much has been written about the Phanariots, mostly in a polemical or sentimental vein, but we still lack a comprehensive study based on the enormous mass of available source-material, Greek, Rumanian and Turkish. Hence the danger of passing general judgments as I have had to do.

Among books that are readily accessible, N. Iorga's *Byzance après Byzance* (Bucharest, 1935, 1971) remains very useful in spite of the opacity of its style. J.-C. Filitti, *Rôle diplomatique des Phanariotes de 1700 à 1821* (Paris, 1901) deserves mention, although it is hardly relevant to the subject of our discussion. Manuel Gedeon and Émile Legrand have both in their voluminous works made notable contributions. By contrast, A. A. Pallis, *The Phanariots: A Greek Aristocracy under Turkish Rule* (London, 1951) is decidedly superficial. Nor does Sir Steven Runciman, *The Great Church in Captivity* (Cambridge, 1968) Chapter 10, offer any new insights. I particularly regret not having been able to attend the symposium 'L'époque phanariote' held at Thessaloniki in October 1970, the programme of which is given in *Balkan Studies*, XI (1970) 318–23. Its proceedings have not yet been published. †

1. I quote from the first French edition (Marseille, 1824). There is a second French edition under the title *Traité sur les princes de la Valachie et de la Moldavie* (Paris, 1830); an English translation in Charles Swan, *Journal of a Voyage up the Mediterranean* (London, 1826) II, p. 271 ff.; and a Greek translation, *Pragmateia peri ton igemonon tis Moldovlakhias* (Athens, 1855).

2. Among the earliest apologies we may quote Jacovaky Rizo Neroulos (himself a Phanariot), *Cours de littérature grecque* (2nd ed.; Geneva–Paris, 1828) p. 33 ff. See also Skarlatos Byzantios (a protégé of the Kallimakhis family), *I Kônstantinoupolis*, I (Athens, 1851) p. 574, indignantly refuting the

60

'slanderer Tzalonis'; E. I. Stamatiadis, *Viographiai ton ellinon megalon diermineon tou Othomanikou kratous* (Athens, 1865) pp. 14 f., 24. K. Paparri-gopoulos, *Istoria tou ellinikou ethnous* (4th ed.; Athens, 1903) v, p. 570 ff., considers the chief achievement of the Phanariots to have been the hellen-isation of Roumania which would have been complete had their government been allowed to last another fifty years! Among more recent apologies see K. Amantos, 'Oi Ellines eis tin Roumanian pro tou 1821', *Praktika Akadimias Athinon*, xix (1944) 416, 429 ff.; Archimandrite H. Konstantinidis, *To ekpolitistikon ergon ton Phanarioton* (Istanbul, 1949) p. 11.

3. Already by Ch. Pertusier, *La Valachie, la Moldavie et de l'influence politique des Grecs du Fanal* (Paris, 1822). The re-appraisal of the Phanariots in this century owes much to N. Iorga. See, for example, his *Roumains et Grecs au cours des siècles* (Bucharest, 1921) p. 48 ff. Th. H. Papadopoullos, *Studies and Documents relating to the History of the Greek Church and People under Turkish Domination* (Brussels, 1952) p. 49 ff., is critical of the Phanariots for the unexpected reason that they undermined the jurisdiction of the Church.

4. On Panayotis see K. Dapontes, *Istorikos katalogos* in Sathas, *Mesaioniki Vivliothiki*, iii (Venice, 1872) pp. 165–6, who says that he was the son of a furrier of obscure family; Athanasios Komninos Ypsilantis, *Ta meta tin Alosin* (Constantinople, 1870) p. 161 ff.; I. Sakkelion, 'Panayotaki tou Mamona . . . dialexis meta tinos Vanli [sic] efendi', *Deltion Istorikis kai Ethnologikis Etaireias*, iii (1890) 240 ff.; Stamatiadis, *Viographiai . . .*, 29 ff.

5. Ypsilantis, *Ta meta tin Alosin*, p. 165; Stamatiadis, *Viographiai . . .*, p. 29 ff.

6. On his career see especially A. Stourdza, *L'Europe orientale et le rôle historique des Maurocordato (1660–1830)* (Paris, 1913) p. 30 ff.; K. Amantos, 'Alexandros Mavrokordatos o ex aporriton', *Ellinika*, v (1932) 335 ff.; and N. Camariano, *Alexandre Mavrocordato, le Grand Drogman. Son activité diplo-matique 1673–1709* (Thessaloniki, 1970).

7. For a chronological list of the hospodars see, for example, C. C. Giurescu (ed.), *Istoria României în date* (Bucharest, 1971) p. 455 ff.

8. This judgment is already expressed in the *History of Moldavia* by Nicholas Costin issued in 1729 under the *hospodar* Grigorios Ghika and im-mediately translated into Greek (Paris, Bibl. Nat., Suppl. gr. 6). See C. B. Hase, 'Notice d'un manuscrit . . . contenant une Histoire inédite de la Moldavie', *Notices et extraits des manuscrits de la Bibliothèque du Roi*, xi/2 (1827) 282. Cf. E. Habesci, *The Present State of the Ottoman Empire* (London, 1784) p. 198 f.; W. Wilkinson, *An Account of the Principalities of Wallachia and Moldavia* (London, 1820) pp. 44 f., 95; M. Kogalnitchan, *Histoire de la Valachie, de la Moldavie et des Valaques transdanubiens* (Berlin, 1837) i, p. 371 ff., etc. For an indictment of the Phanariot regime backed by economic statistics see N. A. Mokhov, *Moldavija epokhi feodalizma* (Kishinev, 1964) p. 359 ff.

9. R. W. Seton-Watson, *A History of the Roumanians* (Cambridge, 1934) p. 127.

10. Ypsilantis, *Ta meta tin Alosin*, p. 263. Ypsilantis was admittedly very hostile to the entire Mavrokordatos family. Legrand goes so far as to suggest

that he was paid by the Turks to write his History, but this I find most unlikely: Legrand, *Ephémérides daces*, II (Paris, 1881) p. xii f.

11. K. Dapontes *Istorikos katalogos, loc. cit.*, p. 160. He adds: 'The Turks, too, did not gobble up then as much as they do now, or rather, to tell the truth, they [the native princes] did not give them as much to eat as we are giving them.'

12. Cf. A. Vakalopoulos, *Istoria tou neou Ellinismou*, II/I (Thessaloniki, 1964), p. 354 ff. It is interesting to observe that a board of trustees set up by the Patriarch Ioasaph in 1564 comprised the following laymen: Antonios Kantakouzinos of Galata, the *arkhon* Mozalos [i.e., Mouzalon] son of Gabras, Konstantinos Palaiologos, and Karatzas of Caramania: M. Gedeon, *Khronika tou patriarkhikou oikou kai naou* (Constantinople, 1884) p. 137 f.

13. La Croix, *La Turquie chrétienne* (Paris, 1695) p. 6 f., who served at Constantinople in the 1670s, gives the following list of 19 noble Greek families: Juliani, Rosetti, Diplomatachi [Diplovatatzi?], Mauro Cordati, Chrisosculi, Vlasti, Cariofili, Ramniti, Mamenadi, Cupraghioti, Musselimi, Succii, Veneli, Cinchidi, Contaradii, Mauradii, Ramateni, Francidi, Frangopoli. Cf. J. Aymon, *Monumens authentiques de la religion des Grecs* (The Hague, 1708) p. 479. Note that of the above families only three (the Rosetti, Mavrokordatos and Soutsos) emerged in the top rank of Phanariot aristocracy. La Croix (p. 4 f.), makes the further observation that the true Byzantine aristocracy was extinct save for the families of 'Cantacuzene, Paleologue, Assanii et Rali', which, however, 'auroient même beaucoup de peine à prouver leur Généalogie'; and that their representatives had sunk to the level of menial artisans.

14. E. R. Rangavis, *Le livre d'or de la noblesse phanariote* (1st ed.; Athens, 1892). I am quoting from the 2nd edition (Athens, 1904).

15. See O. Cicanci and P. Cernovodeanu, 'Contribution à la connaissance de la biographie et de l'oeuvre de Jean (Hierothée) Comnène', *Balkan Studies*, XII (1971), 146 f.

16. See E. Legrand, *Généalogie des Maurocordato de Constantinople* (Paris, 1900).

17. The 'founder' of the family was George Ghika, prince of Moldavia (1658–9) and thereafter of Wallachia (1659–60). Cf. E. Kourilas, 'Grigorios o Argyrokastritis', *Theologia*, XI (1933) 219 ff.; Rangavis, *Livre d'or*, p. 85 ff.; C[arra], *Histoire de la Moldavie et de la Valachie* (Jassy[?], 1777) p. 87 ff.

18. See the exhaustive study by S. Skopeteas, 'Oi Ypsilantai', *Arkheion Pontou*, XX (1955) 150 ff. S. Ioannidis, *Istoria kai statistiki Trapezountos* (Constantinople, 1870) p. 136 ff., claims that these two families reached Constantinople after 1697.

19. For a contemporary account of the rise of the first Kallimakhis see Dapontes, *Istorikos katalogos*, p. 174 ff. Cf. Ypsilantis, *Ta meta tin Alosin*, p. 350.

20. There exists a list of manuscripts belonging to the *arkhon* Ioannis Soutsos (ca. 1570): R. Foerster, *De antiquitatibus et libris manuscriptis Constantinopolitanis commentatio* (Rostock, 1877) p. 19. See also note 13 *supra*. For the Drakos tradition see Ypsilantis in Hurmuzaki, *Documente privitoare la*

istoria Românilor, XIII, ed. A. Papadopoulos-Kerameus (1909), p. 189; S. Byzantios, *I Konstantinoupolis*, p. 114, n. 1. The Soutsos and Drakos families appear to have been intermarried: an Alexandros Drakos Soutsos is recorded as Grand Khartophylax (1741–60).

21. See note 13 *supra*. Antonios Rosetti, prince of Moldavia (1675–8), is said to have been the son of the Constantinopolitan nobleman Laskaris Rossetos, Great Logothete of the Patriarchate, and of Bella, grand-daughter of Mikhail Kantakouzinos. Dapontes, *Khronographos* in Sathas, *Mesaion. Vivl.*, III, 17. Rangavis, *Livre d'or*, p. 183 ff., derives the family from Genoa. I do not know whether they were related to the Rossettis of Coron: Moustoxydis, *Ellinomnimon*, I (1843) pp. 157, 295.

22. See note 12 *supra*. Rangavis, *Livre d'or*, p. 75 ff., says that the family came from Epirus, while Skopeteas, 'Oi Ypsilantai', 150, claims it for Trebizond. Given the commonness of the name, more than one family may be involved.

23. The notorious Nikolaos Mavroyenis (b. 1738), Dragoman of the Fleet, then *hospodar* of Wallachia (1786–90), was the son of Petros Mavroyenis, Austrian vice-consul at Mykonos. An exorbitant laudation of Nikolaos by Manolaki Persianos is reprinted by Legrand, *Bibl. grecque vulgaire*, VII (1895) p. 365 ff. The same personage figures prominently in Thomas Hope's *Anastasius, or Memoirs of a Greek*, where this 'individual of the Tergiumanic genus' is described as belonging to the 'most distinguished family in the island of Paros' (2nd ed.; London, 1820) I, p. 38 ff. See also Th. Blancard, *Les Mavroyéni: histoire d'Orient de 1700 à nos jours*, 2 vols. (Paris, 1909).

24. On Samuil see Germanos, metropolitan of Sardis, in *Orthodoxia*, XI (1936) 300 ff.; Papadopoullos, *Studies and Documents*, p. 387 ff. He was a rich man and, presumably, a native of Constantinople. I have not been able to ascertain the origin of the family whose name is probably derived from Turkish *hançer* = dagger.

25. The notion that the Phanariots were 'merchants on a grand scale' (A. J. Toynbee, *A Study of History*, II (London, 1934) p. 224) is, I believe, incorrect. There may have been a few exceptions like Adamakis Mourouzis who is described as a rich merchant from Trebizond. He married the grand-daughter of Panayotis Nikousios. Having been accused of embezzlement, he barely saved his life by paying 50,000 scudi. Stamatiadis, *Viographiai*, p. 56 (who erroneously calls him Asimakis).

26. Legrand, *Généalogie des Maurocordato*, p. 48. See also the Venetian document of 1631 quoted by A. Stourdza, *L'Europe orientale*, p. 354: '. . . un greco nominato Scarlato, il quale da modesta fortuna salì a grande richesse nell'amministrazione dei dazii, in modo da lasciare, morendo, un milion d'oro in contanti oltre molti beni stabili'. Cantemir is, as often, quite wrong in stating that Skarlatos made himself rich by holding the office of '*Sorguj*, or purveyor to the court for sheep and oxen'. *History of the Ottoman Empire*, trans. Tindal (London, 1734) p. 356 n. 12. This is repeated by Zallony, *Essai*, p. 22, and by others.

27. P. G. Zerlentis, 'Ioannou tou Karyophyllou ephimerides', *Deltion Istorikis kai Ethnologikis Etaireias*, III (1889) 305 ff.; Dapontes, *Khronographos*, p. 31; id., *Istorikos katalogos*, p. 167 f. 1 purse = 500 piastres.

28. Ypsilantis, *Ta meta tin Alosin*, p. 233; thereafter increased to 400 purses (*ibid.*, p. 234).

29. Dapontes, *Khronographos*, p. 33; id., *Istorikos katalogos*, p. 168. Cf. Th. Livadas, *Alex. Mavrokordatou ... epistolai 100* (Trieste, 1879) p. xciv f., and letter 73, p. 125 ff. addressed to Neophytos, metropolitan of Philippo-polis, who wished to borrow money from Mavrokordatos. The letter may be summarised as follows: 'I have no landed property, no ships, no workshops. I live by lending capital at interest. My salary does not cover half of my expenses. Many of my creditors have failed me. You may have my friend-ship, but not my money.'

30. Stourdza, *L'Europe orientale*, p. 63 n. 1; Seton-Watson, *History of the Roumanians*, p. 93. A sidelight on Alexandros' parsimony and, incidentally, on the degree of influence he enjoyed is provided by the following incident. Having married his daughter Roxandra to the prince Matthaios, son of Grigorios Ghika, he subsequently felt obliged to have his son-in-law banished to Cyprus because the latter was a drunkard and 'was dissipating his [Alexandros'] daughter's fortune' (Dapontes, *Khronographos*, p. 61).

31. Skopeteas, 'Oi Ypsilantai', 221.

32. Ypsilantis, *Ta meta tin Alosin*, p. 342, who puts the blame for this on Konstantinos Mavrokordatos.

33. *Ibid.*, p. 375. It is amusing to note that the historian, instead of commending Konstantinos for his honesty, accuses him of bad management.

34. Zallony, *Essai*, p. 64. Wilkinson, who was British Consul at Bucharest and, therefore, reliably informed, puts the private income of the Prince of Wallachia at about 2,000,000 piastres (*An Account of the Principalities*, p. 68). At that time (1818) 30 piastres equalled £1. He makes it clear, however, that the Prince had almost unlimited opportunity of manipulating the system to his advantage.

35. Seton-Watson, *History of the Roumanians*, p. 193. Cf. Wilkinson, *An Account*, pp. 122, 206 ff.

36. Nikolaos Mavrokordatos, who did not trust his compatriots, forms an exception in this respect. In the instructions to his son Konstantinos which he composed in 1727, he says: 'You should have a small retinue and few Phanariots' (Legrand, *Ephémérides daces*, 1, p. 341). He himself gave an important post to only one Greek. Konstantinos, contrary to his father's advice, appointed many Greeks (Ypsilantis, *Ta meta tin Alosin*, p. 340).

37. These offices are described by Wilkinson, *An Account*, p. 51 ff.; Pertusier, *La Valachie*, p. 55 ff.

38. Legrand, *Recueil de poèmes historiques en grec vulgaire* (Paris, 1877) p. 191 ff.

39. Thus Alexandros Ypsilantis owned a house at Kuruçeşme (on the Bosphorus) worth 500 purses or more, 'since he lifted (*esikose*) much wealth from Wallachia, more than anyone does these days' (Dapontes, *Istorikos katalogos*, p. 172). Many interesting details on the residences of the Phanariots at Arnautköy may be found in Gennadios, metropolitan of Heliopolis, *Istoria tou Megalou Revmatos* (Istanbul, 1949), p. 157 ff.

40. Carra, *Histoire de la Moldavie*, p. 206, remarks: 'Ce qu'il y a de singulier chez ces despotes de Moldavie et de Valachie, c'est que toutes leurs

64

richesses, argent, bijoux, hardes & ameublemens sont toujours dans des malles ou coffres de voyage, comme s'ils devoient partir à chaque instant; & dans le fait, ils n'ont pas tort, car ils ont sans cesse à craindre d'être déposés par force ou enlevés ou assassinés ....'

41. Cf. *supra*, note 29. We may also quote the case of the Grand Dragoman Alexandros Ghika who was put to death in 1741. His sequestered property, worth more than 700 purses, consisted of a house at the Phanar and another at Kuruçeşme, bonds to the amount of 380 purses, and 20 purses in cash (Dapontes, *Istorikos katalogos*, p. 172 f.). On financial loans there is much interesting material in N. M. Vaporis, *Some Aspects of the History of the Ecumenical Patriarchate of Constantinople in the Seventeenth and Eighteenth Centuries* (New York, 1969).

42. Zallony, *Essai*, p. 207.

43. See La Croix, *La Turquie chrétienne*, p. 191 ff.; Gedeon, *Khronika tou patriarkhikou oikou*, p. 191 ff.; Papadopoullos, *Studies and Documents*, p. 60 ff.

44. Both of these Patriarchs represented the extreme right wing, and were responsible for suspending the teaching activity of Evgenios Voulgaris whom they considered to be too 'modern'. See Patriarch Konstantios I, *Viographia kai syngraphai ai elassones* (Constantinople, 1866) p. 358 f.; Gedeon, *Khronika tis Patriarkhikis Akadimias* (Constantinople, 1883) p. 163.

45. The amount of the debt naturally varied greatly. In 1641, when it was paid off by Basil Lupu, prince of Moldavia, it amounted to 300 purses: Ypsilantis, *Ta meta tin Alosin*, p. 145. La Croix, *La Turquie chrétienne*, p. 144 ff. (referring to ca. 1670) estimates the annual income of the Patriarchate at less than 40,000 *écus*, whereas the debt stood above 400,000 *écus*. On the eve of the Greek Revolutionary War it was more than 3000 purses: Papadopoullos, *Studies and Documents*, 132.

46. Ypsilantis, *Ta meta tin Alosin*, p. 296. This lamentable practice was started by Symeon of Trebizond who, in 1465, bought the patriarchal office for 500 florins, a sum that was gradually increased by his successors. See V. Laurent, 'Les premiers patriarches de Constantinople sous domination turque', *Revue des études byzantines*, XXVI (1968) 233 ff. On the institution of the *peşkeş* (fee paid to the Ottoman Treasury for the appointment of an Orthodox bishop) see, for example, J. Kabrda, *Le Système fiscal de l'Église orthodoxe dans l'Empire ottoman* (Brno, 1969) p. 59 ff.

47. Zallony, *Essai*, p. 157 f.

48. On Phanariot piety and benefactions to the Church see M. Gedeon, 'Phanariotika ypomnimata', *Ekklisiastiki alitheia*, III (1883) 325 ff., 372 ff.; id., *Khronika tis Patriarkhikis akadimias* (Constantinople, 1883) pp. 107, 150, 230 ff., 234 f.

49. In Moldavia in 1803 about 20 per cent of the land was in the possession of monasteries (Mokhov, *Moldavija*, p. 377). Wilkinson, *An Account*, p. 70, remarks: 'Some of the monasteries are now the richest establishments in the country. The greater number are in the gift of the reigning princes, who let them out for a space of time to the highest bidders.'

50. Collected by Legrand, *Bibl. grecque vulgaire*, IV (1888), and VII (1895); Hurmuzaki, *Documente*, XIV/2 (1917).

51. In addition to foreign pilgrims, the Greeks, too, perhaps in imitation

of the Moslems, took up the custom of going to Jerusalem in pilgrimage. They could then style themselves *hacı*, after 'pouring 4,000 or 5,000 piastres down the throats of the *Agiotaphitai*', to quote the expression of Korais, *Bekkariou peri adikimaton kai poinon* (2nd ed.; Paris, 1823), p. lviii, n. 1.

52. Published at Bucharest in 1719. This work owes more to the Bible and the Church Fathers than to the Greek and Latin classics. The only 'modern' reference it contains (p. 109) is to Christopher Columbus who is commended for having caused the Gospel to be preached in the New World.

53. B. Knös, *L'histoire de la littérature néo-grecque* (Uppsala, 1962) p. 489.

54. Seferis, *Erotokritos* (Athens, 1946).

55. First published at Vienna in 1818. I have used a two-volume edition (Smyrna, 1863).

56. On this textbook, first published in 1625, see H. Rabe, 'Aus Rhetoren-Handschriften', *Rheinisches Museum*, LXIV (1909) 288 f.; C. Tsourkas, *Les débuts de l'enseignement philosophique et de la libre pensée dans les Balkans. La vie et l'oeuvre de Théophile Corydalée* (Thessaloniki, 1967) p. 98 f.

57. Ed. Livadas, No. 85, p. 145 f. Alexandros expresses similar views in his *Phrontismata* (Vienna, 1805), quoted by Amantos in *Ellinika*, V (1932) 339. Nikolaos Mavrokordatos is also critical of those who challenge the authority of the Sultan (*Peri Kathikonton*, p. 110). Cf. likewise his letter to Khrysanthos, Patriarch of Jerusalem, in Hurmuzaki, *Documente*, XIV/2, No. DCCLXIV.

58. Ed. Livadas, No. 59, p. 95 f.

59. *Ibid.*, No. 60, p. 96 f.

60. *Ibid.*, No. 77, p. 130 f.

61. *Ibid.*, No. 87, p. 146 ff.

62. *Ibid.*, No. 14, p. 20.

63. *Ibid.*, No. 15, p. 22; No. 18, p. 23 ff.

64. *Ibid.*, No. 20, p. 27 f.

65. Dapontes, *Kathreptis gynaikon* (Leipzig, 1766) II, p. 396. Agapetus was used as a textbook at the Academy of Bucharest (Legrand, *Bibl. grecque vulgaire*, VII, 80). The *peri khrysopoiias* is a work on alchemy attributed to Stephen of Alexandria (seventh century). The Preface to the *Mirror* constitutes an interesting cultural document. It may be summarised as follows: It would have been an admirable thing if we strove to understand the text of the Old Testament as did Sts. John Chrysostom, Gregory and Basil. But, alas, we have completely forgotten our noble ancestral language, that of the Hellenes (meaning the language of the Bible!), and so must depend on translations into vulgar Greek. Which is why I have retold in simple language various stories from the Old Testament and have added to them, for the sake of amusement, a few more recent stories.

66. A. Mavrokordatos, *Istoria iera itoi ta Ioudaika* (Bucharest, 1716).

67. Books VIII–X are those published by G. Aphthonidis (Constantinople, 1870). Extracts translated into French by Ph.A. Dethier, *Monum. Hung. hist.*, XXI/2 (1875?) 435–512. Parts of Book XII ed. A. Papadopoulos-Kerameus in Hurmuzaki, *Documente*, XIII (1909) 159–92; addenda to the Aphthonidis ed., *ibid.*, 513–31.

68. Aphthonidis ed., p. xvi.

69. Alexandros Mavrokordatos, *Ta Ioudaika*, Preface.

66

70. Legrand, *Recueil de poèmes historiques*, p. 202.

71. Sathas, *Mesaioniki vivliothiki*, III p. 71 ff.

72. Dapontes, *Kathreptis gynaikon*, II p. 400 f.

73. See E. Kourilas, 'Ta khrysovoulla ton igemonon tis Moldovlakhias kai to symvolon Io i Ioannis', *Eis mnimin S. Lamprou* (Athens, 1935) 245 ff.

74. E. Kourilas, 'Theoklitos o Polyeidis', *Thrakika*, v (1934) 142.

75. Dapontes, *Istorikos Katalogos*, p. 119 f. Similar passage in verse in his *Geographiki istoria* (Legrand, *Ephémérides daces*, III, p. lxv ff.). Cf. also the sentiments of Ypsilantis, *Ta meta tin Alosin*, p. 534.

76. In Rumania the reorganisation of the curriculum dates from the rule of Alexandros Ypsilantis (1776). See D. V. Economidès, 'Les écoles grecques en Roumanie jusqu'à 1821', *L'hellénisme contemporain*, Ser. 2, IV (1950) 248 ff. At the Patriarchal school of Istanbul the 'new learning' was excluded until the early nineteenth century (Gedeon, *Khronika tis Patriarkhikis Akadimias*, p. 245 ff.). It is interesting to observe in this connection that the poet Georgios Soutsos in his play called *The Catechumen or the Cosmogonical Theatre* (Venice, 1805) could still maintain that, although Newton's system had some merit, that of Moses remained 'the most perfect and the most divine of all others, old and new'. So much for the spread of Enlightenment.

77. See M. Gedeon, 'Peri tis Phanariotikis Koinonias', *O en Konstantin-oupolei Ellinikos Philologikos Syllogos*, XXI (1892) 65 ff. The same works were being translated into Greek and published by others. Mably, rendered into Greek by I. Kaskambas, appeared at St. Petersburg in 1813; *Anacharsis* was published in Vienna (1819) in the version of G. Sakellarios and Rigas.

78. See the thorough investigation by R. Clogg, 'The "Dhidhaskalia Patriki" (1798): An Orthodox Reaction to French Revolutionary Propaganda', *Middle Eastern Studies*, v (1969) 87 ff.

79. Zallony, *Essai*, p. 133 ff.

80. Cf. G. Laïos, 'Oi khartes tou Riga', *Deltion Istorikis kai Ethnologikis Etaireias*, XIV (1960) 231 ff. Rigas was not alone in imagining a Greece that would stretch to the Danube. The same solution was advocated for practical reasons by D. Dufour de Pradt, *De la Grèce dans ses rapports avec l'Europe* (Paris, 1822) p. 75, who, however, did not believe that the population of the Balkan peninsula was descended from the ancient Hellenes. Rumelia and Bulgaria, he thought, were inhabited almost entirely by Turks.

81. Rigas, *Vasiki Vivliothiki*, x, ed. L. I. Vranousis (Athens, 1953), p. 371.

82. I refrain from reproducing here the immense bibliography on Rigas. The Byzantine component of his thought is well brought out by D. Zakythinos, 'O Rigas kai to orama tou oikoumenikou kratous tis Anatolis' in *I Alosis tis Konstantinoupoleos kai i Tourkokratia* (Athens, 1954) pp. 127–35.

83. Seton-Watson, *A History of the Roumanians*, p. 192.

84. G. Finlay, *History of Greece*, ed. Tozer, v, p. 245, is, I believe, essentially right in saying: 'This Greek official aristocracy [the Phanariots] . . . was quite as anti-national in its policy as the ecclesiastical hierarchy established by Mohammed II.'

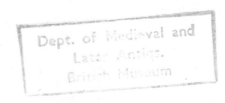

ADDENDA ET CORRIGENDA

STUDY II

P.9   N.G. Wilson, Scholars of Byzantium (London, 1983),24, points
       out that Apollonius Dyscolus was not used as a school textbook.
       I should have named Dionysius Thrax in his place. The floruit of
       Choeroboscus has lately been dated between the middle of the 8th
       century and the beginning of the 9th: W. Bühler and Chr. Theodor-
       ides, Byzant. Zeitschrift 69 (1976), 397–401.

STUDY III

P.52   Prayer rugs: The term epeuchion also appears in Const.Porphyr.,
       De Cerim., Bonn ed.,465 and in the inventory of the monastery
       of Theotokos Koteine, ed.S. Eustratiades, Hellênika,3 (1930),332.

P.56   Pagan philosophers: M.D. Taylor,'A Historiated Tree of Jesse,'
       Dumbarton Oaks Papers, 34/35 (1980/81),125 ff.,has argued that
       the enlarged iconography of the Tree of Jesse including pagan
       philosophers, as it appears in Byzantine and post-Byzantine church
       decorations, is traceable to a western model, possibly created at
       Orvieto in c. 1262-64. This reinforces my contention that the icon-
       ography in question has nothing to do with a 'Hellenic survival'.

STUDY IVa

P.256 J. Grosdidier de Matons informs me that the enigmatic term pina
       probably denotes the wrapping or casing of a candle rather than
       its wick.

STUDY V

P.57   Statue of Constantine/Helios: I am now inclined to believe that this
       was a statue of Constantine wearing the radiate crown of the Sun
       god and not a re-used statue of a pagan divinity.

P.58   Palace of Lausus: I owe the following corrections to Michael
       Vickers: The Cnidian Athena must have been made of green stone
       rather than emerald; Lysippus (4th century BC) must, of course,
       be dissociated from Bupalus (6th century BC): the former was
       probably responsible for the Eros, the latter for the Samian Hera.

P.75   Serpent Column: For the history of this monument after the Tur-
       kish conquest see V.L. Ménage in Anatolian Studies,14 (1964),
       169-73.

2

STUDY VI

P.695 ff. See now the important study by J.-M. Sansterre, Les moines grecs et orientaux à Rome aux époques byzantine et carolingienne, 2 vols.=Acad. Royale de Belgique, Mém. de la Cl. des Lettres, Coll. in-8°, 2ᵉ sér., T. LXVI/1 (1983).

P.698 Our knowledge of the biography of Maximus Confessor has been completely altered by the publication of an early Syriac Life by S. Brock in Analecta Bollandiana, 91 (1973), 314 ff. For a survey of subsequent discussion see J.-M. Sansterre in Byzantion, 51 (1981), 653 ff.

P.703 ff. To the literary production of the Oriental colony in Rome one should probably add the Miracles of St. Anastasius the Persian wrought in Rome, which have come down to us in both Greek,ed. H. Usener, Acta M. Anastasii Persae (Bonn, 1894),14 ff. and in Latin, Analecta Bollandiana, 11 (1892),233 ff.

P.716 ff. Greek minuscule: I need hardly say that my suggestions were meant as a 'trial balloon'. Pending the study of the latest manuscript discoveries in the monastery of St. Catherine on Mt Sinai the entire problem of the origin of the Greek minuscule may be left in abeyance.

STUDY VII

Pp.33-34 Paris. gr. 1115 has been meticulously described by J.A. Munitiz in Scriptorium, 36 (1982),51 ff. The author's views concerning the colophon strike me, however, as unconvincing.

P.34 Hypatius of Ephesus: J. Gouillard in Rev. des études byz., 19 (1961), 63 ff. has shown that this author was known to Theodore the Studite.

P.36 For a revised opinion on Theophanes see Study XI.

P.37 The Bibliotheca of Photius: See now W.T. Treadgold, The Nature of the Bibliotheca of Photius (Washington D.C., 1980), whose main conclusions I do not share, and N.G. Wilson, Scholars of Byzantium, 93 ff.

STUDY IX

P.403 Magistrianos: I was mistaken in stating that this title does not occur after the 8th century. I find it in the Life of St. Basil the Younger, ed. S.G. Vilinskij, Zapiski Imp. Novoross. Univ., 7 (1911), 285.8.

STUDY X

My omission to point out that the Greek inscription embodies the well-known Early Christian formula XMΓ has been noted by A. Frolow in Byzantinoslavica, 26 (1965), 399. On the pagan philosophers see Addendum to Study III.

STUDY XI

I remain unmoved by the criticism of my thesis by I.S. Čičurov in Vizant. Vremennik, 42 (1981), 78 ff.

STUDY XII

P.405 Letter 64 is probably by Nicephorus, Ignatius being the addressee.

P.409 Vita Nicephori: Strong arguments for dating this text (or, at any rate, its Epilogue) after 842 have been put forward by I. Ševčenko, 'Hagiography of the Iconoclast Period' in Ideology, Letters and Culture in the Byzantine World (Variorum Reprints, 1982), V 17 and notes 91,92.

P.410 The identification of Ignatius the deacon with the iconoclastic poet of the same name now appears likely to me.

STUDY XIV

P.256 On Alexius Mousele see W.T. Treadgold in Greek, Roman and Byzantine Studies, 16 (1975), 329 ff.

P.257 On the chronology of Symeon Logothete see W.T. Treadgold in Dumbarton Oaks Papers, 33 (1979), 171 ff.

STUDY XV

P.17 The Russian raid on Amastris: The problem ought to be reconsidered in the light of the new arguments adduced by I. Ševčenko 'Hagiography of the Iconoclastic Period,' 11 ff. for the attribution of the Life of St. George of Amastris, including the posthumous miracles, to Ignatius the deacon. For a different opinion see A. Markopoulos in Jahrb. d. Österr. Byzantinistik, 28 (1979), 75 ff.

STUDY XVI

My article appeared simultaneously with B. Knös, 'Les Oracles de Léon le Sage,' Aphierôma stê mnêmê tou Manolê Triantaphyllidê (Thessaloniki, 1960), 155 ff. (based on the previously unexploited MS Va4a of the Royal Library, Stockholm; otherwise disappointing). Further contributions by A.D. Kominis in Epetêris Hetaireias Byzant. Spoudôn, 30 (1960/61), 398 ff.; C.J.G. Turner in Hellênika, 21 (1968), 40 ff.; Ph.K. Bouboulidis in Epet. Hetair. Byzant. Spoudôn, 38 (1971), 207 ff.; A. Markopoulos in Mnêmôn, 5, (1975), 35 ff.; T.A. Sklavenitis in Mnêmôn, 7 (1978), 46. Of greater importance is A. Pertusi, 'Le profezie sulla presa di Costantinopoli (1204) nel cronista Veneziano Marco (c.1292),' Studi Veneziani, NS 3 (1979), 13 ff. The text edited by R. Maisano, L'Apocalisse apocrifa di Leone di Costantinopoli (Naples, 1975), is a Daniel apocalypse that has no connection with Leo the Wise.

The illustrations of the Oxford manuscripts of Leo's Oracles (Laud. gr. 27, Canon gr. 126, Barocci 145 and Barocci 170) have been reproduced by I. Hutter, Corpus der byzant.Miniaturen- handschriften, 2/II (Stuttgart, 1978); those of Marc. cl. VII, 22 by A.D. Paliouras, Ho zôgraphos Geôrgios Klontzas (Athens, 1977).

In this reprint the illustrations are reproduced not from Lambeck's edition (as stated on p.62), but from Laud. grec. 27.

STUDY XVIII

So much has been published on the Phanariots in the past ten years, mainly by Romanian and Greek scholars, that I despair of giving a comprehensive bibliography. For a sampling of re- cent research see Symposium L'Epoque phanariote, Institute for Balkan Studies, No.145 (Thessaloniki, 1974).

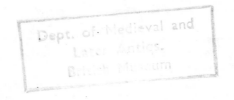

INDEX

Please note that the transliteration of Greek names
and terms is not uniform in all the studies.